Internet Banking:
Problem and Future Outlook

Internet Banking: Problem and Future Outlook

Anju Gautam

RANDOM

RANDOM PUBLICATIONS

NEW DELHI (INDIA)

Internet Banking: Problem and Future Outlook

ISBN 978-93-5111-806-0

Published in 2016 in India by

RANDOM PUBLICATIONS

4376-A/4B, Gali Murari Lal, Ansari Road
New Delhi-110 002
Phone : +9111-43580356, 011-23289044, 011-43142548
e-mail: sales@randompublications.com,
info@randompublications.com, randomexports@gmail.com

Reprinted 2026

Type Setting by : Friends Media, Delhi-110089

Preface

Indian banking sector has made rapid strides in reforming and aligning itself to the new competitive business environment. Indian banking industry is in the midst of an IT evolution. Technological infrastructure has become an indispensable part of the reforms process ins the banking system, with the gradual development of sophisticated instruments and innovations in market practices. Internet is a vast network of individual computers and computer networks connected to and communicate with each other using the same communication protocol — TCP/IP (Transmission Control Protocol/ Internet Protocol).

When two or more computers are connected a network is created; connecting two or more networks create 'internet-work' or Internet. The Internet, as commonly understood, is the largest example of such a system. Internet is often and aptly described as 'Information Superhighway', a means to reach innumerable potential destinations. The present book deals with the vital issues related to information technology like e-banking in India - problems and prospects, e-delivery channels in banks a fresh outlook, internet banking in India future outlook, future outlook of ATMs in India

– Author

Contents

1

Internet Banking

Internet is a vast network of individual computers and computer networks connected to and communicate with each other using the same communication protocol — TCP/IP (Transmission Control Protocol/ Internet Protocol). When two or more computers are connected a network is created; connecting two or more networks create 'internet-work' or Internet. The Internet, as commonly understood, is the largest example of such a system. Internet is often and aptly described as 'Information Superhighway', a means to reach innumerable potential destinations.

The destination can be any one of the connected networks and host computers. Internet has evolved to its present state out of a US Department of Defence project ARPANet (Advanced Research Project Administration Network), developed in the late- 1960s and early -1970s as an experiment in wide area networking. A major perceived advantage of ARPANet was that the network would continue to operate even if a segment of it is lost or destroyed since its operation did not depend on operation of any single computer.

Though originally designed as a defence network, over the years it was used predominantly in areas of scientific research and communication. By the 1980s, it moved out of Pentagon's control and more independent networks from US and outside got connected to it. In 1986, the US National Science Foundation (NSF) established a national network based on ARPA protocol using commercial telephone lines for connectivity. The NSFNet was accessible by a much larger scientific community, commercial networks and general users and the number of host computers grew rapidly. Eventually, NSFNet became the framework of today's Internet. ARPANet was officially decommissioned in 1990. It has become possible for innumerable computers operating on different platforms to communicate with each other over Internet because they adopt the same communication protocol, viz, TCP/IP.

The latter, which stands for 'Transmission Control Protocol/ Internet Protocol', is a set of rules which define how computers communicate with each other. In order to access Internet one must have an account in a host computer, set up by any one of the ISPs (Internet Service Providers). The accounts can be SLIP (Serial Line Internet Protocol) or PPP (Point to Point Protocol) account. These accounts allow creating temporary TCP/IP sessions with the host, thereby allowing the computer to join the Internet and directly establish communication with any other computer in the Internet. Through this type of connection, the client computer does not merely act as a remote terminal of the host, but can run whatever programmes are available on the web.

It can also run several programmes simultaneously, subject to limitations of speed and memory of the client computer and modem. TCP/IP protocol uses a unique addressing scheme through which each computer on the network is identified. TCP/ IP protocol is insecure because data packets flowing through TCP/ IP networks are not normally encrypted. Thus, any one who interrupts communication between two machines will have a clear view of the data, passwords and the like.

This has been addressed through Secured Socket Layer(SSL), a Transport Layer Security (TLS) system which involves an encrypted session between the client browser and the web server. FTP or File Transfer Protocol is a mechanism for transferring files between computers on the Internet. It is possible to transfer a file to and from a computer (ftp site) without having an account in that machine. Any organization intending to make available to public its documents would normally set up a ftp site from which any one can access the documents for download. Certain ftp sites are available to validated users with an account ID and password.

E-MAIL

The most common and basic use of Internet is the exchange of e-mail (electronic mail). It is an extremely powerful and revolutionary result of Internet, which has facilitated almost instantaneous communication with people in any part of the globe. With enhancements like attachment of documents, audio, video and voice mail, this segment of Internet is fast expanding as the most used communication medium for the whole world. Many websites offer e-mail as a free facility to individuals. Many corporates have interfaced their private networks with Internet in order to make their e mail accessible from outside their corporate network.

WORLD WIDE WEB (WWW)

Internet encompasses any electronic communication between computers using TCP/IP protocol, such as e-mail, file transfers etc. WWW is a segment of Internet, which uses Hyper Text Markup Language (HTML) to link together files containing text, rich text, sound, graphics, video etc. and offers a very convenient means of navigating through the net. It uses hypertext transfer protocol (HTTP) for communication between computers. Web documents can contain links to other related documents and so on, in a tree like structure.

The person browsing one document can access any other linked page. The web documents and the web browsers which are the application programmes to access them, are designed to be platform independent. Thus any web document can be accessed irrespective of the platform of the computer accessing the document and that of the host computer. The programmeming capabilities and platform independence of Java and Java applets have further enriched the web.

The 'point and click' method of browsing is extremely simple for any lay user of the net. In fact, the introduction of web since early 1990 has made Internet an extremely popular medium and its use in business has been enhanced dramatically. The next in the HTML genre is the Extensible Markup Language (XML), which allows automated two-way information flow between data stores and browser screens. XML documents provide both the raw content of data and the data structure and is projected by its proponents as taking the web technology beyond the limits of HTML.

WIRELESS APPLICATION PROTOCOL (WAP)

WAP is the latest industry standard which provides wireless access to Internet through handheld devices like a cellular telephone. This is an open standard promoted by WAP forum and has been adopted by world's all major handset manufacturers. WAP is supplemented by Wireless Application Environment (WAE), which provides industry wise standard for developing applications and services for wireless communication networks.

This is based on WWW technology and provides for application for small screens, with interactive capabilities and adequate security. Wireless Transaction Protocol (WTP), which is the equivalent of TCP, sets the communication rules and Wireless Transport Layer Security (WTLS) provides the required security by encrypting all the session data. WAP is set to revolutionize the commercial use of net.

SECURITY

One of the biggest attractions of Internet as an electronic medium is its openness and freedom. It is a public domain and there is no restriction on who can use it as long as one adheres to its technical parameters. This has also given rise to concerns over the security of data and information transfer and privacy. These concerns are common to any network including closed user group networks. But over the Internet, the dimensions of risk are larger while the control measures are relatively fewer.

It will be sufficient to say here that the key components of such concern are:

- Authentication, *viz.*, assurance of identity of the person in a deal,
- Authorization, *viz.*, a party doing a transaction is authorized to do so,
- The privacy or confidentiality of data, information relating to any deal,

- Data integrity, *viz.*, assurance that the data has not been altered and
- Non repudiation, *viz.*, a party to the deal can not deny that it originated the communication or data.

THE INTERNET AND THE WORLD WIDE WEB

Prior to the Internet, World Wide Web and its associated technologies, the impact of technology for the purposes of business transactions had been peripheral. The Internet and the World Wide Web have fundamentally changed commerce. Commerce's basic mode of communication, written and verbal communication between a business and its customer or business and its suppliers or partners, remained unchanged since Adam Smith's first observations on economic markets. Electronic communication, in the form of digital mainframe computers and microcomputers (personal computers) connected to the Internet, has radically transformed commercial activity for customers and businesses alike. The transformation has been so fundamental that new terms such as 'e-Commerce', 'e-Business', 'e-Markets' and the 'new e-Economy' are freely used to describe the modern phenomenon of Internet-based commercial activity. e-Commerce may be described as the sharing of product and service information, developing and maintaining human commercial relationships, and transacting business over the Internet and the World Wide Web. Technologies such as telephony have influenced business activity in the past, but their influence has not been revolutionary. Such technologies have not fundamentally changed how businesses organize themselves and how they interact with their customers, suppliers or partners. In contrast, the Internet and the World Wide Web have revolutionized business activity.

- Provides an introductory description of the current IT, Internet and World Wide Web technology underpinning e-Commerce;
- Comments on its implications for business and e-Commerce;
- Explores potential future developments in Internet and World Wide Web technology that will affect e-Commerce.

This introductory reading on e-Commerce technology should enable you to describe Internet and World Wide Web technology to enable e-Commerce. Critically, the reading should enable you to state and understand the main elements of an e-Commerce system architecture and assess e-Commerce security technology for confidentiality and payments.

Memex

The Internet's evolution has encompassed over fifty years of technological and conceptual development. The original concept of the Internet is attributed to Vannevar Bush. He worked in a team of engineers during World War II in the United States. His experience of working in an expert team of scientists led him to think about the problem of processing and sharing information among the team. His solution was the invention of a machine called Memex (MEMory EXtension). He envisaged that Memex would work like the human brain, which finds information by association. His ideas provided the conceptual framework for subsequent work on developing the technology of the Internet and World Wide Web.

ARPAnet

The Internet began in 1969 as a communications medium project of the US Department of Defence, and its associated academic and research agencies. It needed a network of computers to enable collaborative work among the different agencies. In its original form, the Internet consisted of a decentralized digital network that connected defence, research and academic mainframe computers. This network was called the ARPAnet after the agency that led the project, the department's Advanced Research Projects Agency (ARPA). The purpose of the ARPAnet was to connect various government and related computers, and in the event of disaster or war to preserve the integrity of information passing between these important government agencies. ARPAnet was privatized in 1990, and as it was gradually released to the public domain it began to be transformed into the Internet that we know today.

The World Wide Web

Around the same time, Tim Berners-Lee, a research scientist working at the European CERN physics lab in Switzerland, conceived the World Wide Web and released it to the public domain in 1991. The problem that Tim Berners-Lee faced was how to share research knowledge among scientists who used different brands of computers and associated software at CERN. He developed the method of hypertext link for connecting information stored on different computers. In his words, his motive for inventing the Web was: 'I realised that if everyone had the same information as me, my life would be easier. The original idea for linking electronic documents was Ted Nelson's. He coined the term 'hypertext' in the early 1960s. Marc Andreessen developed the first graphical browser for the Internet. It enabled people seeking information on the Internet to find it quickly and efficiently.

A major effect of the Internet and the Web over the 1990s was to enable executives and business strategists to develop new ways of doing business electronically. These new electronic approaches are termed e-Commerce 'business models'. Business models that combine the use of the Internet and Web technologies with fundamental business transformation are referred to as 'e-Business'.

The term e-Business is used to describe a business that shares its production or service information with customers and business suppliers or partners, fosters the development of customer relationships electronically, and enables business to be transacted from personal computers or other electronic devices, such as mobile phones or personal digital assistants (PDAs). One of the most successful e-Commerce business models is the US company Dell Computers. It has a $14 million per day Internet-based revenue stream, or a quarter of its total revenue. Though a survey by NOP in 1999 revealed that only 15 per cent of the companies surveyed used the Internet for making online sales, Gartner Research predict that 97.5 million US users will adopt e-billing and online account management by 2005.

INTERNET AND WORLD WIDE WEB TECHNOLOGIES

The microcomputer or Personal Computer (PC) forms the basis of e-Commerce. The Internet would not have the wide reach that it has into peoples' homes in the absence of the PC. Most office PCs are linked to a computer network and PCs at home are connected to the Internet via modems or dedicated data transfer cables.

Local area Networks and Wide area Networks

PCs on local area networks (LANs) and wide area networks (WANs) are connected to the Internet. LANs and WANs are digital computer networks that connect PCs to enable sharing of information between separate computers. LANs are limited to a geographical area such as an office, whereas WANs connect computers over a wider geographical area. The computers on a LAN or WAN share information in the form of addressed packets of data. The capacity of a single computer is increased by connecting it to a LAN or WAN, as it can share computer programs and information. A computer that is linked to a network can download and use computer programs and share storage and printing facilities, and take advantage of network capabilities for sending and receiving data and information.

Client-server Architecture

A computer on a LAN or WAN that provides resources like application programs or printer connections is known as a 'server'. A server provides other computers known as 'clients' on the LAN or WAN with software and other resources. This set-up is called client-server computing architecture. A server that is linked to the Internet is called a 'host computer'. A server computer is capable of running server software, which needs to be compatible with the network operating system.

The client and server are independent and perform specialized tasks to process information and run computer applications. If you use Microsoft Word on your computer, the client, it is probable that a server will have provided the Microsoft Word software for you to use. The client-server architecture is the basis of the Internet too.

The Internet and Protocols

The Internet is the sum total connection of LANs, WANs and stand-alone computers around the world. The term 'Internet' is short for 'inter-networking' or an interconnected set of networks. It is the global network of computers, whether the computer is on a LAN in an office, or a WAN in an industry extranet, or an independent computer in a private home. An Internet-connected computer is known as an Internet host computer. The Internet is also known as the 'Net', the 'Information superhighway' or 'Cyberspace'.

The set of rules for moving information over the Internet is called a 'protocol'. The transmission control protocol (TCP) is used for sending large amounts of information between host computers on the Internet. Vinton Cerf wrote the basic ideas for TCP on the back of an envelope over lunch, and in 1983 the core protocols of the Internet transmission control protocol/Internet protocol (TCP/IP) became the standard protocol for transmitting information over the Internet.

Intranet

An intranet consists of networked internal connection of computers owned by an organization and makes use of Web technology. An intranet may be mounted on a LAN or a WAN. An intranet makes use of Internet technology such as TCP/IP, HTML, Java and HTTP to make it interoperable and to provide it with Web capability. The basic elements of an intranet are a computer network, a computer designated as a server containing server software and the Internet protocols TCP/IP.

An intranet offers several benefits to an organization: improved sharing and communication of information, open standards and cross-platform collaboration. For example, a car manufacturing company may connect its information systems on purchasing with its accounting information systems to form an intranet for sharing and processing information between two departments in the company.

An intranet is a company's own internal information transfer system that offers: e-mail, communication among different computers, connection to remote offices, a Web browser interface and special-interest news groups. For e-Commerce, an intranet is used to provide a corporate image and unified 'experience' for a customer that combines product information, ordering and customer care.

Extranet

An extranet is used for business-to-business (B2B) e-Commerce. It is the networked connection of computers of two or more companies. It is a private communication system to support trade and is used for communication and transactions between business partners, suppliers or special customers. For example, a car manufacturing company may connect its computers with its various suppliers of components for the cars it makes. Another example is the airline industry's OneWorld network, which enables customers to transfer seamlessly between airlines to reach their destinations.

Design principles

Intranets and extranets share the same design principles formulated for the Internet. The Internet design principles are:

Interoperability. There are varying operating systems that control computer functions on the many different computers on the Internet. Normally a given operating system cannot communicate with a different one. A standard to enable varying operating systems to communicate with each other was introduced by the US Department of Defence, which originally financed the Internet. Interoperability means that independent implementations of Internet protocols can work seamlessly.

Consequently, operating system developers such as Microsoft or Apple incorporate software into their operating systems that enables them to operate with other computers over the Internet. Internet-compatible systems use the TCP/IP common protocol for communication. Interoperability for e-Commerce means that companies and customers do not have to purchase and upgrade software from the same vendors. Their computers will be able to communicate over the Internet because of the standard protocols.

Layering. The Internet can be regarded as a series of layers of software. The structure of the Internet is layered. It is a five-layer system consisting of: interconnect level (National Access Points, NAPs), national backbone providers, regional Internet providers, local Internet service providers, and the business and consumer market. The bottom layers of software, interconnect and network, are concerned with operating the computer hardware. The higher layers, business and consumer market, come closer to the needs of the person using the Internet. The most relevant layer is the layer that processes the information required by the Internet user; this is called the 'application' layer. These different hardware and application layers need to communicate with each other and they do so by using well defined interfaces. The Internet layering standard has resulted in increased reliability of Internet software and it is invisible to the Internet user.

Simplicity. The layering has resulted in simplicity of software design. Each layer is concerned only with its own functionality, making its design simpler. For example, the layer concerned with physical devices like mouse operations are hidden from the higher layers that process information. This kind of simplicity has contributed to increased software reliability too.

Uniform naming and addressing. Each Internet host computer has an Internet Protocol (IP) address that uniquely identifies it on the Internet from the millions of other computers also on the Internet. The IP address is expressed in a uniform format or 'dotted quad'. An example is: '17.10.2.3'. As the dotted quad is not meaningful to humans the domain name system (DNS) is used to provide a symbolic name for the dotted quad. An example is: 'sol.brunel.ac.uk'. The DNS is capable of translating the symbolic name into the required IP address to enable Internet operations.

End-to-end protocols. The Internet does not process information. It enables the transfer of 'packets' of information between computers. This is called end-to-end protocol. The Internet enables the transfer of information or 'content' of the packet. The transmitting or receiving computers, known as the 'end' system, do the actual processing of information.

The combined use of the Internet, intranets and extranets by companies has resulted in the term 'virtual organization' or 'networked organization'. The virtual organization is to be contrasted with the physical organization; the latter is restricted by geographical, physical space. Companies can combine computer-networking technology with information technology (IT) and information systems (IS) to develop a network of computers that can capture, process and share information and knowledge in virtual or cyberspace, where time and space are defined differently from physical time and space. Amazon.com may be classed as a virtual organization. Virtual organizations tend to be flatter because access to information and knowledge is potentially open to all employees who have access to a PC.

THE WORLD WIDE WEB

The World Wide Web, also known as the 'Web' or 'WWW', consists of pages of information depicted as text, graphics, sound, or video clips. A Web page may contain Java applets - Java programs that are downloaded from the server and run on the local computer. The Web consists of over a million Web servers, and an untold number of Web browsers. What distinguishes the Web from other computer media is its ability to link Web pages dynamically; this is known as hypertext links or simply links. The Web combines computer network technology with hypertext to provide a 'global information system'. One Web page can be linked to another by a hypertext link and the user merely has to click on the link to display related information. A link appears as highlighted on the Web page. It is this hypertext linking capability of the Web that makes it a powerful source of information. The Web is a client-server architecture system, and a Web user can access the Web servers with a Web browser such as Netscape or Microsoft Explorer.

Hypertext

A document on the Web is composed using hypertext technology. Hypertext is an electronic document system that can be read non-sequentially and interactively. The reader does not have to read it like a book, she/he can click on hyperlinks of related information. The Apollo space programme to record its documentation used a hypertext system. e-Commerce Web sites are built using hypertext documents, and other hypermedia.

Hypertext Transfer Protocol

The Web differs from the Internet by the protocol it uses to transfer information between computers. The Web uses the hypertext transfer protocol (HTTP) to connect and transfer hypertext documents stored on Web servers, also known as Web sites. All the computers on the Internet that use the HTTP protocol compose the Web.

The Web browser

A Web browser is a graphical interface for searching, accessing and viewing hypertext and multimedia files on the Web. The first browser, called Mosaic, was invented by the US company Netscape Communications, founded in 1994 by Marc Andreessen. He set himself the problem of transferring sound and pictures over the Web. His solution was the first graphical Web browser. It allowed basic functions such as retrieving and displaying hypertext files. The growth of the Internet and the Web is largely because of the invention of the graphical browser which makes it easier for people to search and view information. Two popular browsers are Netscape Communicator and Internet Explorer. They are more sophisticated than the original Mosaic browser and enable e-mail messaging, HTML authoring, and extensions such as scripting, plug-in and multimedia.

INTERNET SEARCH ENGINES

The Internet is unarguably the most voluminous information store in the world. Finding information on the Internet requires complex computer algorithms. These algorithms form the backbone of Internet search engines designed to help people find the information they want. Organizations need search engines to find information about customers or business competitors or partners. Search engines are computer programs that locate specific Web pages, files or multimedia items stored on the Internet. Search engines such as Google or Autonomy use different algorithms or techniques to search for Web pages.

UNIFORM RESOURCE LOCATOR

The uniform resource locator (URL) is the address of a particular Web site on the Internet. It consists of domain names and a pathway that locates a particular host computer that is connected to the Internet. An example URL is www.yahoo.com or www.dell.com. A URL consists of the protocol that is to be used to make the Internet connection (the WWW in the examples), the name of the host computer ('Yahoo' or 'Dell') and the domain (.com). In the case of commercial companies, the name of the host computer connected to the Internet is usually the registered name of the company.

HYPERTEXT MARK-UP LANGUAGE

Hypertext mark-up language (HTML) is used to author information on a Web page. HTML documents are text files that are interpreted by a Web browser. The browser reads the HTML file and interprets the HTML instructions. The browser has to do this interpretation each time a hypertext file is loaded.

A Web page can be divided into 'frames' or sub-pages. Each frame is used to display separate but relevant information designed by the Web author. Multimedia can be facilitated by extensions to HTML or by 'plug-ins' or add-on programs that make the Web client more versatile to deal with additional media types. An example of extension is Secure HTTP that enables sophisticated encryption and decryption algorithms for sensitive e-Commerce data like payments for transactions.

It takes time to learn to write HTML code. Authoring tools are available for automatically converting documents in Microsoft Word to HTML files, ready to load on to a Web server. Hot Dog Pro, Adobe PageMill and Microsoft FrontPage are examples. A Web site consists of one or more Web pages linked together by hyperlinks. The contents of a Web site are known as 'content'. HTML is not capable of processing or interacting with Internet users. To process data captured through a Web form JavaScript is required.

MULTIMEDIA

Multimedia is a tool capable of providing the transfer of sound and images like pictures over the Internet. Multimedia applications require lots of memory and bandwidth - the physical capacity of data cables to carry and transfer data. For example, one minute of music requires 5 MB of data. The transfer of sound and images in real time requires special software which is added to TCP/IP and HTTP protocols. On the client end, a player is required to interpret the data and render it into sound or images. Multimedia Internet Mail Extensions or MIME is an Internet standard for multimedia Internet e-mail. MIME enables e-mail to be cast as types consisting of HTML, text, images or video. Example MIME types are: image/jpeg, video/ mpeg or application/pdf.

JAVA, APPLETS, JAVASCRIPT AND INTERACTIVITY

The Internet is popular because it is interactive. Interactivity means that the Internet user (or client) can actively request information from and provide information to the server. Such interactivity is important for e-Commerce applications. CGI script and JavaScript provide interactivity on the Internet.

Java is a programming language originally intended for programming consumer electronic devices like microwave ovens, dishwashers or electronic clocks. As there are many manufacturers of these products, Java's developer, Sun Microsystems, designed Java to be ubiquitous, meaning that it should be operable on any manufacturer's device. Virtual Java machines that are independent of PC operating systems interpret Java, a feature that makes it ideal for Internet programming. Java programs created for the Internet are called applets. Java applets are embedded in HTML documents.

An applet is a Java programme that is executed on the client machine. It is loaded by the Web browser and restricted to prevent security breaches. The applet is executed on a Java virtual machine in the browser.

JavaScript, originally called LiveScript, was developed independently of Java by Netscape to provide interactivity. It is used to process data captured via forms on the Internet and to create interactive Web sites, and both the server and the client side use it. JavaScript is embedded in HTML and is interpreted by a browser. Web pages that contain JavaScript can be transferred around the Internet, because JavaScript is platform-independent or interpreted. ActiveX is a competitor of JavaScript. Scripts can be used in e-Commerce to validate service or product order form entries.

Common Gateway Interface

CGI programs are text files that consist of line or programming code similar to JavaScript; such programs are called CGI script. Pear is an example of CGI programming. CGI is used to create interactive Web sites that pass information from a Web browser to a server using a form, very useful for organizational needs. A form is a document that is created to interact with a user, take data from the user and send it to the server for processing, usually via a database.

INTERNET BANKING ENVIRONMENT

On August 8, 2001, the FFIEC agencies (agencies) issued guidance entitled *Authentication in an Electronic Banking Environment*. The 2001 Guidance focused on risk management controls necessary to authenticate the identity of retail and commercial customers accessing Internet-based financial services. Since 2001, there have been significant legal and technological changes with respect to the protection of customer information; increasing incidents of fraud, including identity theft; and the introduction of improved authentication technologies. This updated guidance replaces the 2001 Guidance and specifically addresses why financial institutions regulated by the agencies should conduct risk-based assessments, evaluate customer awareness programmes, and develop security measures to reliably authenticate customers remotely accessing their Internet-based financial services.

This guidance applies to both retail and commercial customers and does not endorse any particular technology. Financial institutions should use this guidance when evaluating and implementing authentication systems and practices whether they are provided internally or by a service provider. Although this guidance is focused on the risks and risk management techniques associated with the Internet delivery channel, the principles are applicable to all forms of electronic banking activities.

KEY POINTS

The agencies consider single-factor authentication, as the only control mechanism, to be inadequate for high-risk transactions involving access to customer information or the movement of funds to other parties. Financial institutions offering Internet-based products and services to their customers should use effective methods to authenticate the identity of customers using those products and services.

The authentication techniques employed by the financial institution should be appropriate to the risks associated with those products and services. Account fraud and identity theft are frequently the result of single-factor (*e.g.*, ID/ password) authentication exploitation. Where risk assessments indicate that the use of single-factor authentication is inadequate, financial institutions should implement multifactor authentication, layered security, or other controls reasonably calculated to mitigate those risks.

Information Security Booklet, December 2002, financial institutions should periodically:

- Ensure that their information security programme:
  - Identifies and assesses the risks associated with Internet-based products and services,
  - Identifies risk mitigation actions, including appropriate authentication strength, and
  - Measures and evaluates customer awareness efforts;
- Adjust, as appropriate, their information security programme in light of any relevant changes in technology, the sensitivity of its customer information, and internal or external threats to information; and
- Implement appropriate risk mitigation strategies.

BACKGROUND

Financial institutions engaging in any form of Internet banking should have effective and reliable methods to authenticate customers. An effective authentication system is necessary for compliance with requirements to safeguard customer information, to prevent money laundering and terrorist financing, to reduce fraud, to inhibit identity theft, and to promote the legal enforceability of their electronic agreements and transactions. The risks of doing business with unauthorized or incorrectly identified persons in an Internet banking environment can result in financial loss and reputation damage through fraud, disclosure of customer information, corruption of data, or unenforceable agreements. There are a variety of technologies and methodologies financial institutions can use to authenticate customers. These methods include the use of customer passwords, personal identification numbers (PINs), digital certificates using a public key infrastructure (PKI), physical devices such as smart cards, one-time passwords (OTPs), USB plug-ins or other types of "tokens", transaction profile scripts, biometric identification, and others. The level of risk protection afforded by each of these techniques varies. The selection and use of authentication technologies and methods should depend upon the results of the financial institution's risk assessment process.

Existing authentication methodologies involve three basic "factors":

1. Something the user *knows* (*e.g.*, password, PIN);
2. Something the user *has* (*e.g.*, ATM card, smart card); and
3. Something the user *is* (*e.g.*, biometric characteristic, such as a fingerprint).

Authentication methods that depend on more than one factor are more difficult to compromise than single-factor methods. Accordingly, properly designed and implemented multifactor authentication methods are more reliable and stronger fraud deterrents. For example, the use of a logon ID/password is single-factor authentication (*i.e.*, something the user knows); whereas, an ATM transaction requires multifactor authentication: something the user possesses (*i.e.*, the card) combined with something the user knows (*i.e.*, PIN). A multifactor authentication methodology may also include "out–of–band" controls for risk mitigation.

The success of a particular authentication method depends on more than the technology. It also depends on appropriate policies, procedures, and controls. An effective authentication method should have customer acceptance, reliable performance, scalability to accommodate growth, and interoperability with existing systems and future plans.

RISK ASSESSMENT

The implementation of appropriate authentication methodologies should start with an assessment of the risk posed by the institution's Internet banking systems. The risk should be evaluated in light of the type of customer (*e.g.*, retail or commercial); the customer transactional capabilities (*e.g.*, bill payment, wire transfer, loan origination); the sensitivity of customer information being communicated to both the institution and the customer; the ease of using the communication method; and the volume of transactions. Prior agency guidance has elaborated on this risk-based and "layered" approach to information security.

An effective authentication programme should be implemented to ensure that controls and authentication tools are appropriate for all of the financial institution's Internet-based products and services. Authentication processes should be designed to maximize interoperability and should be consistent with the financial institution's overall strategy for Internet banking and electronic commerce customer services. The level of authentication used by a financial institution in a particular application should be appropriate to the level of risk in that application. A comprehensive approach to authentication requires development of, and adherence to, the institution's information security standards, integration of authentication processes within the overall information security framework, risk assessments within lines of businesses supporting selection of authentication tools, and central authority for oversight and risk monitoring. This authentication process should be consistent with and support the financial institution's overall security and risk management programmes.

The method of authentication used in a specific Internet application should be appropriate and reasonable, from a business perspective, in light of the reasonably foreseeable risks in that application. Because the standards for implementing a commercially reasonable system may change over time as technology and other procedures develop, financial institutions and technology service providers should develop an ongoing process to review authentication technology and ensure appropriate changes are implemented.

The agencies consider single-factor authentication, as the only control mechanism, to be inadequate for high-risk transactions involving access to customer information or the movement of funds to other parties. Single-factor authentication tools, including passwords and PINs, have been widely used for a variety of Internet banking and electronic commerce activities, including account enquiry, bill payment, and account aggregation. However, financial institutions should assess the adequacy of such authentication techniques in light of new or changing risks such as phishing, pharming, malware, and the evolving sophistication of compromise techniques. Where risk assessments indicate that the use of single-factor authentication is inadequate, financial institutions should implement multifactor authentication, layered security, or other controls reasonably calculated to mitigate those risks.

The risk assessment process should:

- Identify all transactions and levels of access associated with Internet-based customer products and services;
- Identify and assess the risk mitigation techniques, including authentication methodologies, employed for each transaction type and level of access; and
- Include the ability to gauge the effectiveness of risk mitigation techniques for current and changing risk factors for each transaction type and level of access.

ACCOUNT ORIGINATION AND CUSTOMER VERIFICATION

With the growth in electronic banking and commerce, financial institutions should use reliable methods of originating new customer accounts online.

Moreover, customer identity verification during account origination is required by section 326 of the USA PATRIOT Act and is important in reducing the risk of identity theft, fraudulent account applications, and unenforceable account agreements or transactions. Potentially significant risks arise when a financial institution accepts new customers through the Internet or other electronic channels because of the absence of the physical cues that financial institutions traditionally use to identify persons.One method to verify a customer's identity is a physical presentation of a proof of identity credential such as a driver's license. Similarly, to establish the validity of a business and the authority of persons to perform transactions on its behalf, financial institutions typically review articles of incorporation, business credit reports, board resolutions identifying officers and authorized signers, and other business credentials. However, in an Internet banking environment, reliance on these traditional forms of paper-based verification decreases substantially. Accordingly, financial institutions need to use reliable alternative methods.

MONITORING AND REPORTING

Monitoring systems can determine if unauthorized access to computer systems and customer accounts has occurred. A sound authentication system should include audit features that can assist in the detection of fraud, money laundering, compromised passwords, or other unauthorized activities. The activation and maintenance of audit logs can help institutions to identify unauthorized activities, detect intrusions, reconstruct events, and promote employee and user accountability. In addition, financial institutions should report suspicious activities to appropriate regulatory and law enforcement agencies as required by the Bank Secrecy Act. Financial institutions should rely on multiple layers of control to prevent fraud and safeguard customer information. Much of this control is not based directly upon authentication. For example, a financial institution can analyse the activities of its customers to identify suspicious patterns. Financial institutions also can rely on other control methods, such as establishing transaction dollar limits that require manual intervention to exceed a preset limit.

Adequate reporting mechanisms are needed to promptly inform security administrators when users are no longer authorized to access a particular system and to permit the timely removal or suspension of user account access. Furthermore, if critical systems or processes are outsourced to third parties, management should ensure that the appropriate logging and monitoring procedures are in place and that suspected unauthorized activities are communicated to the institution in a timely manner. An independent party (*e.g.*, internal or external auditor) should review activity reports documenting the security administrators' actions to provide the necessary checks and balances for managing system security.

CUSTOMER AWARENESS

Financial institutions have made, and should continue to make, efforts to educate their customers. Because customer awareness is a key defence against fraud and identity theft, financial institutions should evaluate their consumer education efforts to determine if additional steps are necessary. Management should implement a customer awareness programme and periodically evaluate its effectiveness. Methods to evaluate a programme's effectiveness include tracking the number of customers who report fraudulent attempts to obtain their authentication credentials (*e.g.*, ID/password), the number of clicks on information security links on Web sites, the number of statement stuffers or other direct mail communications, the dollar amount of losses relating to identity theft, etc.

CONCLUSION

Financial institutions offering Internet-based products and services should have reliable and secure methods to authenticate their customers. The level of authentication used by the financial institution should be appropriate to the risks associated with those products and services. Financial institutions should conduct a risk assessment to identify the types and levels of risk associated with their Internet banking applications. Where risk assessments indicate that the use of single-factor authentication is inadequate, financial institutions should implement multifactor authentication, layered security, or other controls reasonably calculated to mitigate those risks. The agencies consider single-factor authentication, as the only control mechanism, to be inadequate in the case of high-risk transactions involving access to customer information or the movement of funds to other parties.

INFORMATION SEARCH ON THE WEB

In the e-retail literature, much is made of the *similarities* between the new electronic ways (clicks) to sell goods to consumers and the traditional ways (bricks). One can talk about e-stores, e-shop fronts, e-shoppers, e-malls and so on. We highlight some of the *differences* between clicks and bricks. These differences arise from the totally different technologies which are used in a clicks store compared with a bricks store, and the totally different approach used by e-shoppers to find goods and services, to compare prices and to generally browse around. The essential concept is *search* - the process by which e-shoppers find information about products and services.

THE BACKGROUND TO SEARCHING THE INTERNET AND THE WEB

The Internet is a worldwide network of servers and machines, originally set up (as the ARPAnet) to facilitate information exchange between US government contractors and university researchers (Wolinsky, 1999). From the earliest days of the Internet, a major activity has been *searching* for information. As the Internet grew, a variety of tools were set up to help users perform searching to find the required information.

Nowadays, the focus of activity is the World Wide Web, which uses Internet technology with an improved user interface, making huge amounts of information available to the end-user, often a home computer user. Much of this information is about products and services for mass distribution provided by e-retailers.

The interface employed by most users is a graphical Web browser, typically Microsoft Internet Explorer or Netscape Navigator. In practice much of the information is textual in nature, with graphical layout (such as the use of lists) to provide structure and additional graphics to provide other information and 'decoration'. Although much has been made of the idea of e-malls, where a group of e-shops congregate together like a conventional shopping mall, the typical user experience involves focusing on a specific website often linked to one company's offerings.

SURVEYS ON WHAT PEOPLE DO AND WHERE PEOPLE 'GO' ON THE WEB

A computer scientist would say that what e-shoppers actually do is to use a Web browser to examine data from the Web rendered into graphical images. A typical user would say something rather different - the experience is that you explore a virtual world and that at any moment you are at one 'place' in that world. From then you might explore the place more deeply or move on to other places which are linked. Many surveys have been done to help us understand why people use the Web. According to Rodgers and Sheldon (2002), there are four primary motives for Internet use: researching (in the most general sense), shopping, socializing and generalized surfing (for enjoyment).

Shehan (2002) carried out a cluster analysis of types of Internet sessions, finding that 'I need to find some information' was a significantly stronger motivation than all others. Visiting news sites, using search engines, searching for product information and using online databases together accounted for 34 per cent of users' online time. Searching for product information alone accounted for 7 per cent of online time, compared with only 1.7 per cent spent e-shopping. Eighty-five per cent of all Internet traffic comes from 13 major search engines (Gehan, 2003). Information search is important for consumers and it is important for e-retailers too: in a US study, the use of the Internet to search for information was the strongest predictor of e-shopping intention. In addition, information search improved shoppers' attitudes towards e-retailing a nd helped overcome the perceived barriers to e-shopping. Similarly, Fink and Laupase (2000) carried out an experiment with 30 Australian and 30 Malaysian participants who evaluated selected websites. They found evidence of a relationship between products and services and news stories. The authors argued that the impact of products and services displayed could be maximized through the presence of news stories providing information about recent developments. We referred briefly to our study investigating shoppers' motivations in e-shopping (Dennis and Papamatthaiou, 2003; discussed in more detail in *e-Economy: Rhetoric or Business Reality?*, in the same series as this book; Dennis and Richardson, 2004). The respondents were a sample of 150 undergraduatestudents. Enjoyment was one of the main motivations and 'involvement' was one of the most important enjoyment dimensions. In line with previous work drawing attention to 'variety seeking' (Rohm and Swaminathan, 2004), the most popular sites were Amazon (www.amazon.co.uk), CD WOW (www.cd-wow.co.uk) and eBay (www.ebay.co.uk), i.e. 'hedonic' e-retailers (Childers *et al.*, 2001).Amazon and eBay are the UK's top two sites in terms of audience numbers.

It is particularly strong on involvement, with visitors spending on average 1 hour and 11 minutes on the site, one of the longest of UK e-retailers. Visitors return to the site frequently to check on items they are buying or selling. There is also a feedback feature on sellers that helps to build trust, and eBay is one of few UK e-retailers to achieve over one billion page views per month. Such sites enthusiastically embrace the 'involvement' aspect of enjoyment with features such as chat rooms, bulletin boards, customer written stories and product reviews, suggestion boxes and personalization of the website offers. In short, many of the features that make these sites involving, enjoyable and successful are based on satisfying shoppers' needs for information in one form or another. Some e-retailers use surfers' needs for information as a successful method of directing traffic to their sites. For example, outdoor equipment supplier L L Bean (www.llbean.com) provides information on national parks, and chemist/ drugstore Boots specializes in nutrition and health information.

SEARCHING AND FINDING ON THE WEB

Shoppers, then, spend a lot of time *searching*, and e-retailers are, of course, most interested in what they *find* ('Seek, and ye shall find!'). They would like shoppers to find information on their products and services at their virtual store, and to find (and execute) ordering and payment processes. They thus need to understand what technologies the shoppers use, and how they use these technologies, in order to improve the chances of sales and services on the Web. Thus, e-retailers who can help satisfy surfers' wants for information have a head start in selling to those customers.

THE AVERAGE WEB SESSION

Let us consider what average users do in an average Web session:

- The users sit down and start their Web browser, often set up so that the initial screen (the home page) points to some major website, and it displays a list of links to other sites and services. For example, the home page might be set to the Yahoo! main page (www.yahoo.com). Possibly they might decide to *focus* immediately on some site they know about and type in the Web address (URL) or use 'favourites' or 'bookmarks' to access that site.

- Otherwise, they look through the home page visually and *evaluate* the list, and make some decision based on what they are interested in.
- They might then decide to access a *search engine*, for example Google, (www.google.com) and, by entering suitable search phrases and hitting the Search button, instruct the engine to produce a list of relevant web pages with a brief summary of their contents. Having got that list, it is then scanned and evaluated.
- They might decide to examine a *directory system* related to their search goals, and scan through that and evaluate items.
- The process of scanning through lists for relevant items and/or using search engines is repeated until the relevant items are found. If nothing suitable is found, the search is refocused or *abandoned* at any point, or the search goals may be refocused from information retrieved, deliberately or not (some advertisement might pop up). The users might even go directly to some site, even if it does not come up on a directory or search-engine list, if they know the Web address (URL).

Several important concepts arise from the above considerations. Let us now examine these in more detail.

They are:

- Focus
- Directories
- Search engines.

FOCUS

Suppose you want to purchase some hair conditioner. If you go down to the local town centre and locate a major shopping mall or high street area, you have expectations as to what you might find there and the ways you can quickly locate items of interest. For example, you would expect to be able to find a chain pharmacy store in a few minutes - in the United Kingdom, a branch of Boots or Superdrug. Having found such a store, you would expect to locate quickly a section with hair products and, equally quickly, a range of shampoos and conditioners. What you might also do is use some sort of directory (possibly the Yellow Pages) to locate stores of interest.

Compared with the bricks experience, an e-shopper on the Web operates in a rather different way. On the Web, a user starts up a Web browser with some initial page, perhaps that of their Internet service provider. They then start searching for the item required, following appropriate links. Almost certainly they will use some sort of Web search engine.

Obviously, we need to design web pages so that they are usable and attractive to the user. Nielsen (2000) has written extensively on website usability, and has pointed out a number of important considerations. A prime component of making sites usable is clarity and focus. If the user finds the site difficult to use, and the design messy and unfocused, they will abandon the site and turn to searching elsewhere. Neilsen suggests some standards to create user consistency, good design and relevance, leading to a unified user experience across the site.

DIRECTORIES

People like lists, from the Seven Wonders of the Ancient World to the Top 20 pop songs. Directories are lists compiled around some specific topic, such as the telephone directory and trade directories. In the early days of the Web, people (editors) compiled lists of the most popular sites. As the number of sites grew, the lists became rather long. To improve accessibility, they were split into categories and sub-categories. Well-known Web directories include Yahoo! (www.yahoo.com) and MSN (www.msn.com).

Let us consider Yahoo! in a little detail. Yahoo! is compiled by human editors who also create a short description that is shown alongside the link to the Web address. The editors categorize the topics logically, in a way a search engine does not. For example, a category listed on the Yahoo! main page might be *Shopping*. This might lead to *Electronics*, which might lead to *Cell Phones*. This might point to a list of cell phone items e-shoppers might be interested in.

This hierarchical arrangement ensures that shoppers can fairly quickly get to items in which they are interested.

Improvements in search engines mean that directories are losing some value, but they are still useful for locating groups of relevant websites on a similar topic. It should be noted that directories of this nature can be very wide in scope, or they could be more focused, in the nature of a trade directory. To ensure contact with potential customers, e-retailers might consider something much more focused.

One point: note that Yahoo!, for example, is rather more than just a directory. It includes a search engine (formerly, the Google engine), and a range of services such as mail and instant messaging. Such a service, which acts as a 'port' to many other Web and Internet services, is known as a *portal*. Portal owners hope that users will use their portal as their home page and point of departure, hence making them targets for selective advertising and other delights. This does make portal sites attractive (if expensive) places to place web banners and other advertising material. The big portals are hard at work implementing a 'Search, Find and Obtain' model across information, shopping and entertainment channels. The effectiveness can be demonstrated by usage figures: MSN and Yahoo! are the most popular websites worldwide, each with 83 million users (eMarketer, 2003).

SEARCH ENGINES

Search engines on the Internet have been around some time. The first ones actually did a 'live' search of remote file systems holding documents (FTP servers), looking for filenames which matched search terms. When the Web became popular, researchers built Web search engines to try out new software and hardware on the huge amounts of data that became available. Later on, these experimental systems were commercialized. Well-known commercial search engine systems are Google (www.google.com) and AltaVista (www.altavista.com.). There are actually *two* sorts of search engine involved.First, programs called 'crawlers' gather information about websites. This is done by starting with a list of 'well-known sites' and from there searching the sites they reference. This is an automatic process. The HTML (HyperText Markup Language) code corresponding to each web page is scanned for links to other sites. In the HTML, such a link will appear like this:

If this link is followed, the corresponding web page will also have links, and these too are followed. This process is continued, until millions of web pages are accessed. Each page is analysed for content. What this means is all the information in the page HTML - the title, the text of the body of the page and any additional information tagged on to the page (metainformation) - is extracted and examined for relevance, according to rules set up by the owner of the crawler. All this information is then put into a database (also called a catalogue or index). This process is repeated at regular intervals, possibly every two weeks.The database is indexed on content, and is made available to the e-shopper via a Web interface. Given some *search term*, such as 'shampoo', the database is searched for matching terms and the corresponding page URLs are retrieved, together with the page titles and summaries of the page contents. This information is then formatted into a web page which is returned to the e-shopper. So the user inputs the word 'shampoo' and obtains a page of references to websites involving that term.A few technical points:

- Following of links from any one page is only done to a certain 'depth', which means that it is important to put significant information on the Home Page or just a little 'below'.
- *Web crawlers* see a web page split into 'frames' as a number of pages, and therefore explore these less deeply than pages without frames. Frames are best avoided if you want Web crawlers to extract as much information as possible from your pages.

- Web crawlers are not clever enough to deal with databases (for example, catalogues) which might be accessed from your pages. Really significant information should be able to be accessed as plain HTML pages, rather than by using some catalogue systems. Catalogues are really meant for human users.

Note that the process of database construction is automatic, but guided by concepts such as *well-known sites* and *relevance*. It is also possible to notify a search-engine system of a site for inclusion, which again guides the crawler. Websites that meet the criteria are added to the index whether they have been submitted for inclusion or not.

Popular Search Engines

Google (www.google.com) is the world's most popular search site, accounting for 60 per cent of all searches (Gehan, 2003). Google compiles its catalogue of over four billion web pages very week or so. Despite being faster, larger and more efficient than competitors, even Google indexes only a fraction of the total web pages available. However, the coverage is very wide. Although most e-shoppers use search engines, the typical user is usually not willing to spend much time formulating search terms, and often gets rather frustrated if the information they require is not returned. They might abandon the search, or perhaps try another search engine. Many systems offer Boolean searching, which means that search terms and phrases can be linked, for example:

Digital camera AND Canon AND inexpensive

Some systems also offer the option of fine-tuning the results by allowing the user to input terms used to rank (put in some order of precedence) the returned results. The average e-shopper is not usually willing to learn how to set up these more sophisticated queries. They want a reasonable set of results with as little work formulating the query as possible. Otherwise, they tend to give up and try some other method.

They might use *metacrawlers*, which bring together results from various search engines and directories. Coverage is wide but operation can be cumbersome, with little fine-tuning possible, so these are not that popular.

The most useful systems as far as many e-shoppers are concerned are systems that allow natural language, for example a query such as:

Where I can buy inexpensive Canon digital cameras?

Systems such as *AskJeeeves* (www.ask.com) specialize in such natural language queries. Observation by the authors shows that users often pose their questions in natural language whatever the system! They do this because no one has ever told them that they cannot, and because reasonable results are often returned, since many search engine systems filter *noise words* (such as 'the', 'and' and 'but') and use the remaining words as search terms and for ranking the results. Systems such as Google also make suggestions in an attempt to correct spelling results.

Growth in Search Engine Activity

Most of the growth in e-shopping (according to the *New York Times*, 4 December 2003) is being driven by search engines like Google and other sites like the online marketplace eBay. Improved search quality, pioneered by Google, has made search engines an easy and efficient way for people to find things online - and for advertisers to find customers. At the same time, eBay, a haven for small businesses, has become the fastest-growing major shopping site, and much of Amazon's growth has come from serving as an intermediary for independent retailers. Another example is that of Visa, which noted that online sales, including travel, have increased considerably, much more than sales using Visa cards with traditional retailers.

According to eMarketer, a firm that compiles Internet research, online sales are rising by nearly 30 per cent per year, and soon 100 million people a year are expected to make online purchases. A PricewaterhouseCoopers survey indicates that:

not only are search capabilities and product information important to online shoppers when selecting an online shopping site, but they can help e-retailers turn shoppers into buyers and make the online shopping experience more like the on-land one. Search functions are the most popular online shopping feature.

The majority of online shoppers - 77 per cent - have used a search function while shopping online and most of these users are satisfied enough with search functions to use them on a regular basis. In addition to being the most popular features, survey results indicate that search capabilities and product information are most important to online shoppers when selecting an online shopping site. Search functionality and product information are ranked as the most important online shopping features by 43 per cent and 40 per cent of online shoppers, respectively.

(PricewaterhouseCoopers, 2003)

MINI CASE STUDY 5.1: POSTOPTICS - WEB ADVERTISING REVENUES

Postoptics is a small firm but is the UK's leading mail-order contact-lens supplier. Contact lenses by post are a niche focus market; they are used by only 6 per cent of the population, and at any one time only 3 per cent of those are looking for a new pair. Boss Trevor Rowley faced the problem of communicating with this small proportion of the population.

Rowley had tried conventional media advertising, but found that the most cost-effective results have come from 'pay-per-click' advertising with search engines such as Google, Yahoo!, Lycos and others. Pay-per-click is now the fastest growing form of Web advertising and, according to Google, generates five times as many hits as other types of online advertising. The advertising consists of listings that appear to the side of or above the list of websites generated by the search. Advertisers bid for keywords that are relevant to their businesses - the higher the bid, the higher in the listings. Bids may range from as low as £0.10 for specialist terms like 'multi-focal contact lenses' up to double figures in pounds to be highly placed for broad terms such as 'finance' or 'insurance'. This type of advertising can be ideal for small firms because it allows them to compete with larger companies on a level playing field.

The important thing for the advertiser is to find the right keywords. For example 'optical' might get many leads, but 'disposable contact lenses' would be a less expensive search term. A mix of generic and specific words is probably best. Some small companies like Postoptic bid on 20 or so terms; big companies can use 1,000 or more.

The benefit for the advertisers is that they only pay for customers who click through to their website from sponsored links. Postoptic has used listing companies such as Overture (the US pioneer) and Espotting (UK) to provide listings on sites such as MSN and eBay and also has had good results with Google. As a result, about 60 per cent of Postoptic's £5 million sales are now online. It costs an average of £12 to acquire a customer and the typical order value is £50 to £60.

MINI CASE STUDY 5.2: DAVID STEAD ORCHIDS (WWW.ORCHID-GUIDE.CO.UK/~DAVIDSTEAD)

David Stead Orchids is a small to medium-sized supplier of orchid plants and orchid-related sundries, based in Leeds, UK. Its website was created by a local Web developer.

Focus

The firm has a (fairly) memorable URL, which they quote in their advertisements in the orchid press. The site has an internal database, which the e-shopper can use to home down on what they require.

Directories

The firm appears in a number of directories, for example The Wedding Network (www.wsn-uk.co.uk/England/West_Yorkshire/Flowers), Easy Exotics (www.easyexotics. co.uk) and the Stephen H. Smith Garden Centre (www.shrubs. co.uk).

Search engines

All pages are correctly titled, and meta-information is used (description and key-words). Searches on the phrase 'David Stead Orchids' gave 39 hits on Google and 39 hits on AltaVista. Using the metacrawler Dogpile (www.dogpile.com) gave 49 hits!

The site is an example of how a small, local company can achieve international visibility by using the three main techniques mentioned.

MONITORING THE USE OF YOUR WEB PAGES

Having set up your site, you need to monitor what use is made of it. The simplest approach is to add a page counter to each major page. The information from this can be rather limited, but at least you can find out how many visits ('hits') have been made over a given period.

Every time a web page is accessed, information is recorded in a log file on the Web server. These logs can be provided to you by either your IT personnel or by the company that 'hosts' your pages (sometimes at an additional cost). The log stores information about the page URL, the time and date of access, the type of browsers used for access, (possibly) the location of the user and so on. By themselves, the logs are quite difficult to process, but there are log analysis programs which can produce useful tables and charts which summarize activity. By examining the logs, it is even possible to see what Web crawlers are accessing your system! You might get a few surprises here, and read information about visits from experimental crawlers at universities, and from Web crawlers run by institutions like the US Defence Department.

SOME PRACTICAL CONCLUSIONS

A number of things can be done to make your website more visible.

First, encourage shoppers to *focus* on your site. There are a number of aspects of the concept of focus that have arisen from the above discussion. Nielsen (2000) considers focus in the context of web-page design and suggests retaining the attention of users by building consistent style ad pages, built to good design standards, and with relevant content.

Advertisements, which can be added on to directory and Web search engine web pages are a means of changing the focus of a user's search towards your pages. Make it easy for users to get to your site by choosing a memorable URL, for example www.gardenplants.com (not www.somesite.com/gardens/). Advertise your website URL in your conventional advertising (magazines, flyers and so on). Winemakers have printed the URL on their bottles in order to bring the site to the attention of users.

Make shoppers want to look at your website by constantly changing the information. One way to do this is to link the site to a product catalogue database, so that shoppers can search for the latest up-to-date product information.

Ensure your website is well designed. Use a professional website designer. Do *not* use your computing staff - they can build you a site but are (probably) not professionals in human-computer interaction.

Submit your website URL to major Web directory systems. But be careful of offers you may receive to list your web page URLs in directories. Some of these are like offers to list your profile in a directory of 'World Business Leaders'. It might be that the only people who ever access these directories are the subscribers who have paid a substantial fee!

Link Popularity Engineering

Ensure that your URL appears in listings relevant to your product area. This approach is sometimes called *Link popularity engineering*.Search engines use link popularity in locating and ranking sites - the term refers to both the number of other sites linking to **This section summarized and adapted from www.webpromote.com, originally from Internet Marketing Challenge.*

the measured site and especially the importance and relevance of the linking sites. Improving link popularity raises a site in search engine rankings. To measure your own site on Alta Vista, Google and Hotbot, visit www.linkpopularity.com. View a comparison of your site's link popularity relative to your competitors and to other well-known sites at www.marketleap.com/publinkpop. Some ideas for engineering higher link popularity ratings on search engines follow below.

Instead of a single site that covers many different keywords, separate each product or service into groupings. Use related specialist sites that all link to the 'mother site' and to each other. Each should cover its own niche based on a core theme. The sites should be about the same size, say around five pages. Ideally, locate each on a different ISP. A sample matrix can be viewed at www.market-ingchallenge.com/chronicles/278/matrix.gif.

'Seed' your website Home Page with meta-information. At the beginning of a web page, it is possible to add extra information about the content of the page. This information does not get displayed, but is used by the Web crawlers to rank and index your pages. The information is basically a description of the web page and a set of key words provided to assist the indexing process. For example, the Norwegian wood-carver's site at sherpe.com/carving/ index.html has key words, which suggests a marketing function for specific products: meta name='keywords' content='ale, ale bowl, art, bowl, carving, chip, chip carving, craft, family, hand-carved, mangle board, norsk, norwegian, Norway, ole, Ostrem, sherpe, skjerpe, Tomtengson, Wang, wood'.

Isle of Man Kippers (www.isleofmankippers.com/kippers-main.htm) introduces terms such as 'cooking' and 'recipes', which implies that they are going beyond marketing into an educational function: kippers, herring, specialist food, gourmet food, fish, smoked fish, sea fish, Isle of Man, Manx, Manx kippers, Irish Sea, cooking, recipes.

Title all your pages. The title line is always used by Web crawlers for indexing. If it is missing, the page might be ignored.

Get a listing in Yahoo! It can be difficult to achieve but can be worth a paid listing: deadlock.com/promote/search-engines/yahoo.html.

Get a listing in the Excite/LookSmart paid inclusion programme. As with Yahoo!, other search engine managers consider that, if you are listed in LookSmart, your site must be worth listing. A single step submits your page to both, and also supplies results to AltaVista, MSN and iWon:

listings.looksmart.com/?synd= none&chan=lshomebus. Get a listing in top directories such as the free Open Directory Project: www.dmoz.org/add.html.

Start an affiliate programme. Affiliates earn a commission when a visitor to their site clicks the link to your sales page and then makes a purchase. Concentrate on sites with related content.

Get links to and from similar high-traffic, quality sites. Look for sites that serve the same audience as your site but are not competitive. Also contact sites that link to your competition.

In late 2003, a graphic and amusing illustration of the power of link popularity engineering could be seen by entering '*weapons of mass destruction*' into the Google search engine (www.google.com). The top link went to what looked like a standard 'This link cannot be displayed' message, but, on reading, was actually 'These weapons of mass destruction cannot be displayed', followed by witty and satirical text at the expense of government(s) apparently unable at the time to find weapons of mass destruction. At the bottom of the page there was a link to 'Get the WMD 404 tee shirt'. This linked to www.coxar.pwp.blueyonder.co.uk/about.htm, where you could indeed buy the T-shirt and also WMD mug, mouse mat and boxer shorts. There was also a link directly to books from Amazon such as *The Battle for Iraq*.

So how did the WMD site achieve its top Google rating? The answer is a combination of viral marketing and link popularity engineering. The author e-mailed friends and asked them to link their sites to the WMD site, and to pass on the message to their own friends. The network quickly grew to carry enough links to gain top rating on the search term. The WMD story thus illustrates the importance of link popularity engineering, even when based only on links (which may be on reciprocal deals) with virtually no financial investment needed.

CASE STUD: AUBUCHON

When searching Google for 'Christmas light sets', the second-ranked link to appear was Aubuchon Hardware, a family-run New England chain of 140 New England hardware stores. As a result, Aubuchon now sells more light sets in California than in Massachusetts, its home state. 'Search engines are great because we have so many different products', said William E. Aubuchon IV, who runs the website. Aubuchon uses two strategies to have its name appear for any of the 40,000 products. With the help of iProspect, a firm that helps companies improve visibility in search engines, it has tweaked the wording on its web pages to make them closer to the top of search engine results. It also buys text advertisements, typically called sponsored listings, which appear above and to the side of the actual search engine results. Now over 50 per cent of Aubuchon's online business comes from search engines.

'We're not a destination site, like Home Depot [the US leading hardware company], but search engines help people find us when they are looking for a specific product such as Christmas light sets', said Mr Aubuchon. 'Instead of us chasing customers around, on search engines the customers chase us around.' According to Aubuchon, search engine marketing will help the company double its online sales this year.

CASE STUDY: L L BEAN (WWW.LLBEAN.COM)

In the US, L L Bean has been a pioneer of mail order, selling goods to rural farmers since way back in the mid-1800s. Today, the company has put a reputation for customer responsiveness, helpfulness, cheerfulness and reliability to use in becoming world leader in e-retailing outdoor equipment and clothing, with an efficient, award-winning site. But the L L Bean site is not just about selling - it is packed with useful information about the outdoors. For example, when someone searches for a campground (or campsite in UK parlance), say in British Columbia (Canada), L L Bean comes high up the listings. The link will go immediately to a huge, easily accessible amount of information not just on camping, but also on trails (walks) and activities in national parks all over the world. For instance, the 'Park search' link is ideal to 'Plan your next adventure with ... 2200 worldwide park listings'.

The home page links easily to clothing, maps, books, camping and outdoor equipment, and outdoor information is always high on the agenda, with, for example, 'Preserving Acadia: L L Bean helps protect Maine's National Park'.

The moral seems to be that a good site does not necessarily do 'hard' selling, and that useful related information can lead surfers to shop from an e-retail site.

MAIN CONCERNS IN INTERNET BANKING

In a survey conducted by the Online Banking Association, member institutions rated security as the most important issue of online banking.

There is a dual requirement to protect customers' privacy and protect against fraud. Banking Securely: Online Banking via the World Wide Web provides an overview of Internet commerce and how one company handles secure banking for its financial institution clients and their customers. Some basic information on the transmission of confidential data is presented in Security and Encryption on the Web. PC Magazine Online also offers a primer: How Encryption Works. A multi-layered security architecture comprising firewalls, filtering routers, encryption and digital certification ensures that your account information is protected from unauthorised access:

- Firewalls and filtering routers ensure that only the legitimate Internet users are allowed to access the system.
- Encryption techniques used by the bank (including the sophisticated public key encryption) would ensure that privacy of data flowing between the browser and the Infinity system is protected.

- Digital certification procedures provide the assurance that the data you receive is from the Infinity system.

Claus Nehmzow, a Principal in the Information Technology Group in London at Booz Allen & Hamilton, writes of some compelling research findings and offers his projections for European banks in The Internet Will Shake Backing's Medieval Foundations.

He believes the low transaction cost will make banking on the Net irresistible, but also that this will require institutions to carefully consider and plan customer relations programs.

- It is believed that everything will be determined by content and context, and where execution will be key. From a customer and service provider perspective, this is where the world is moving-it is going to be real-time, on-line, personalisation for both marketing and the service experience. If existing banks don't want to disappear, it is this challenge of Integration that they need to embrace in order to win and survive. The more things change, the less they change. In the months and years-ahead are going to be how Service Providers integrate and market their offerings across different channels. The strategic and executional battles of the future are going to be fought for Channel Integration. What does Channel Integration means? It means that an institution presents an identical face to the customer-be it in the branch, on the web, at an ATM or for that matter, through a sales representative or a broker. An identical face, an identical message. Or better still, messages that reinforce each other. If a sales representative tries to sell you a housing loan, you get e-mail a day later reminding you about the loan. That's called Integrated Sales, which results in incremental economic activity and improved efficiencies of communications. Channel Integration across the phone web can clearly lead to a gain of several percentage points of GDP. The beauty of this approach is that one channel does not displace another. They feed on each other to create incremental value for the customer, as well as the institution. The incremental value comes from two distinct sources. Firstly, you reduce inefficiencies. You don't send people junk mail because you know that they are not likely to buy a particular product or service today. That results in net saving for the economy. Secondly, you persuade people at the right time (the right time from the customer's perspective, not from the service provider's perspective) to opt for a tailor made offering. This too increases value. Actually, this has to do with the Internet itself, and more to with the underlying technologies of the Internet which allow incremental efficiency, and empowers the customer to make more enlightened and timely choices.

- Lastly the product range is another issue which becomes important. It will take a technological revolution to make available advanced banking products on the net and given the rate at which the technology is developing we can expect this to happen in near future.

STRATEGIES TO BE ADOPTED BY INDIAN BANKS

Internet banking would drive us into an age of creative destruction due to non-physical exchange, complete transparency giving rise to perfectly electronic market place and customer supremacy. The question to be asked right now is "What the Indian Banks should do" Whatever is the strategy chosen and options adopted, certain key parameters would determine the bank's success on web:

1. For long term success, a bank may follow:
   - Adopting a webs mindset
   - Catching on the first mover's advantage
   - Recognising the core competencies
   - Ability to deal multiplicity with simplicity
   - Senior Management initiative to transform the organisation from inward to outward looking
   - Aligning roles and value propositions with the customer segments
   - Redesigning optimal channel portfolio
   - Acquiring new capabilities through strategic alliances.
2. The above can be implemented in four steps:
   - Familiarising the customer to new environment by demo version of software on bank's web site. This should contain tour through the features which are to be included. It will enable users to give suggestions for improvements, which can be incorporated in later versions wherever feasible.
   - Second phase provides services such as account information and balances, statement of account, transaction tracking, mail box, check book issue, stop payment, financial and customised information.
   - The third phase may include additional services such as fund transfers, DD issue, standing instructions, opening fixed deposits, intimation of loss of ATM cards.
   - The last step should include advanced corporate banking services like third party payments, utility bill payments, establishment of L/Cs, Cash Management Services etc. Enhanced plan for the customers in future can include requests for demand drafts and pay orders and many more to bring in the ultimate in banking convenience.

All the above strategies will help banks in translating their traditional business model into an Internet one, falling into three main categories

- One stop shop
- Virtual one-stop-shop
- Best of breed supplier.

Internet Banking in India - Guidelines

[RBI has accepted the recommendations of the 'Working Group on Internet Banking' to be implemented in a phased manner. Following recommendations are to be adopted by all banks offering Internet banking services, with immediate effect. These recommendations are applicable, in general, to all forms of electronic banking]

I. Technology and Security Standards:

II. Legal Issues:

III. Regulatory and Supervisory Issues:

Internet Banking - Abbreviations

ANSI: American National Standards Institute
ASCII : American Standard Code for Information Interchange
ATM : Asynchronous Transfer Mode
CERT: Computer Emergency Response Team
DBA: Database Administrator
DES: Data Encryption Standard
EDI: Electronic Data Interchange
FTP: File Transfer Protocol
GUI: Graphical User Interface
HTML: Hypertext Markup Language
HTTP: Hypertext Transfer Protocol
IC Card: Integrated Circuit Card
ISDN: Integrated Services Digital Network
ISO/OSI: International Organization for Standardization/Open Systems Interconnection
ISP: Internet Service Provider
LAN: Local Area Network
NIST: National Institute for Standards and Technology
FIPS: Federal Information Processing Standards
OSP: Online Service Providers
PIN: Personal Identification Number
POS: Point of Sale
SET: Secure Electronic Transaction
SHTTP: Secure Hypertext Transfer Protocol
SSL: Secure Socket Layer
SMTP: Simple Mail Transfer Protocol
SQL: Structured Query Language
TCP/IP: Transmission Control Protocol/Internet Protocol

URL: Uniform Resource Locator or Universal Resource Locator
WAN: Wide Area Network
web, www: World Wide Web

INTERNET BANKING SERVICES

The advantages of Internet banking are obvious. Business people can access their personal and business account information while saving a trip to the bank. You can check your balance whenever you need to, even if the bank is closed. Not only that, but you can pay your bills online as well, which saves both time and money on postage. Another advantage of Internet banking is the ability to easily compare services offered by different banks. You can buy financial products and apply for loans online, and in doing so, you can compare your options to ensure that you get the best possible services. You can even buy insurance online through Internet banking services. Stocks and bonds and other investments can be managed with online banking from your home or office independent of a financial intermediary like a stockbroker. The number one tip for banking online is to be very aware of Internet banking security. Identity theft is a real and growing problem today. As such, you need to be highly protective of your personal account information whenever doing transactions online. Make sure you never give personal information out over the Internet unless you are connected to a secure site.

Also, store your access information in a secure place. Routinely check your computer for spy ware and viruses, protecting your identity this way as well. Anther important security feature you will want to make sure is in place with your online bank is encryption. Verify that the banking portal has high-end encryption software in place. If not, it might be advisable to choose a different banking option. You can verify this by looking for the graphic, which is usually located at the bottom right of the browser that signifies the encryption is in place. Another tip about Internet banking is to remember that some procedures are still affected by the business hours of the bank. Even if you transfer a balance at 8:00 PM, it may not show up on your account until the next business day. Plan your transactions accordingly if you are working on a tight budget. Use the Internet to shop for the best banking options. Check interest rates on loans and savings accounts online. The Internet can be a great tool in helping you secure the best possible banking services to meet your needs. The history of Internet banking has come a long way over the last six years, and it is only going to get better! Get connected to Internet banking today. You can be in complete control of your finances with the click of a mouse!

Internet Opens New Vistas for Indian Banks

Indian banks have a chequered history. The British legacy left behind a host of large and small privately-held banks. The late 60s saw the nationalisation of banks, leading to the emergence of the public sector banks. The 90s saw the banking industry embracing technology in a massive way, led in particular by the new private banks and MNC banks. Among these series of technology innovations, Internet banking for the retail segment is a recent phenomenon that has generated a lot of interest in the Indian banking industry. Private and foreign banks have been the early adopters while the PSU banks are also beginning to latch on to the bandwagon. As per IDC estimates, the total number of registered users for Internet banking in India is over two million.

India has a little less than a million active Internet banking users. And though this is just 0.096 percent of the total population, it represents 15 percent of the India's Internet user population. Thus indicating that the concept of Internet banking is surely catching on. Impressive as these figures might be, the truth is that India lags behind other countries in Internet banking. In the US, the number of commercial banks with transactional websites is 1,275 or 12 percent of the total number of banks. Of these, seven could be called 'virtual banks.' Ten traditional banks have established Internet branches or divisions that operate under a unique brand name. At present, in the US approximately 78 percent of all commercial banks with assets more than $5 billion, 43 percent of banks with $500 million to $5 billion in assets, and 10 percent of banks under $500 million in assets have transactional websites. From the Asian market experience, it is clear that Internet banking is here to stay and will be a major channel to acquire and service customers. Markets like Korea and Singapore have nearly 10 percent of their population banking over the Internet. Though, these markets are way ahead of India both in terms of Internet penetration and online banking penetration, India is a big potential market and is fast catching up with its Asian counterparts.

Technology Innovations and PSU Lethargy

As in all forms of technology innovations, PSU banks have remained laggards in the race for adopting Internet banking practices. There are very few nationalised banks like State Bank of India, Bank of Baroda, Allahabad Bank, Syndicate Bank and Bank of India, that offer Internet banking services. Some others like Union Bank of India, Canara Bank and Punjab National Bank are on the verge of doing so. SBI's Internet banking initiative, launched in July 2001, is in fact doing quite well and has over 18,000 registered customers across 150 branches. The enthusiastic response has encouraged the SBI management to extend the service to an additional 500 branches. But despite positive news like this, PSU banks still have a lot of catching up to do on the Internet banking services front. DD Krishnamoorthy, deputy general manager, information technology, Bank of India says that the primary reason preventing PSU banks from introducing online banking services, has been the absence of a legal framework to back up, and regulate Internet banking operations in the country.

Though the Information Technology Act 2000 attempted to address a number of e-commerce regulatory issues, he feels that there still are several grey areas which have neither been spelt out properly, nor have the courts suggested workable modes of implementation.

Though Internet banking is only an extension of traditional banking services, there are several instances which contradict the legal framework for this banking in India provided by a set of enactments like the Banking Regulations Act, 1949, the Reserve Bank of India Act, 1934 and the Foreign Exchange Management Act, 1999. However, not many are willing to buy the argument that it's the lack of regulations that is preventing the PSU banks from taking the Internet plunge. Says an industry analyst, "More than a lack of regulatory framework, it is lack of zeal and a mindset attuned towards resisting any new technology that is holding back the nationalised banks. On top of this, the highly politicised unions are also an impediment as they feel that Internet banking would expose the low productive levels of the workforce." The average customer profile of PSU banks is also comfortable with the traditional banking system and is not too keen on adopting an online model. Typically, most PSU banks have the majority of their customer base in the smaller cities or towns and even in remote villages.

Even in bigger cities, a large proportion of their customers are either senior citizens or at least 50+ who have a natural aversion towards adopting new technology. This not the case with private or MNC banks, where the clientele is mostly urban-based falling in the 20-40 age group and who have a higher exposure to technology. Even the IDC survey seems to confirm this premise. Among the elite Internet banking users, that is, those customers who belong to Socio-Economic Class A1 (SEC A1) in the top five cities, it has been found that people access their account through the Internet once every week. Similarly users visit their ATM centre on an average of two times per week. The workplace happens to be the most favoured place to access Internet for banking purposes. The home comes a close second while cybercafes take the third place. ATM in the close vicinity to the office is the most preferred place among users for banking.

Insignificant Internet Banking

In contrast, Indian banks have an insignificant Internet banking record. ICICI Bank kicked off online banking way back in 1996 and a host of other banks soon followed suit. But even for the Internet as a whole, 1996 to 1998 marked the adoption phase, while usage increased only in 1999—due to lower ISP online charges, increased PC penetration and a tech-friendly atmosphere. Reveals Anup Bagchi, head, Internet Banking, ICICI Bank, "We had launched the Internet banking service even before the RBI had formulated its guidelines. Fortunately, as it was a comparatively new concept, the regulating authorities were extremely cooperative with us." After ICICI, Citibank, IndusInd Bank and HDFC Bank and Timesbank (now part of HDFC Bank), were the early ones to bite the technology bullet in 1999. Says C N Ram, head, information technology, HDFC Bank, "Our vision was very clear, we were not enamoured by the concept of Internet banking but looked at it more as an add-on service which our customers should gradually adopt." In line with this strategy, initially the Net banking facility was provided in order to meet the information requirements of the customers and gradually it ventured into fund transfers and third party transfers.

Though adoption of Internet banking by Indian banks and their customers would not set the Arabian Sea on fire, no one can deny the obvious benefits that this service offers. Costs of banking service through the Internet amount to a fraction of the costs through conventional methods. Industry estimates assume teller cost at Re 1 per transaction, ATM transaction costs at Re 0.45, phone banking at Re 0.35, debit cards at Re 0.20 and Internet banking at Re 0.10 per transaction. Says V K Ramani, president, information technology, UTI Bank, another of the early adopters, "No wonder, the cost-conscious banks in the country are now actively considering using the Internet as a channel for providing services. People were sceptical about even ATM at the beginning, but look how it has picked up today."

However, he warns that banks cannot expect instant returns, unless the Internet population itself does not reach a critical mass. Besides, he also feels that fully computerised banks, with better management of their customer base are in a stronger position to cross-sell their products through this channel. Nitin Chopra, head, consumer banking, ABN-AMRO Bank, feels that the prohibitive costs of real estate would always make Internet banking a much more viable option in the long run than physical banks. In today's environment besides their physical branches, banks need to grow non-branch delivery networks as a part of their growth strategy. ATMs are currently the hot favourite for most banks, but Internet banking definitely has the potential to leave the rest behind. Therefore, on the whole, Internet banking increases operational efficiencies and reduces costs, besides giving a platform for offering value added services to the customer, thereby fulfilling all the essential prerequisites for a flourishing banking industry.

ISSUES IN INTERNET BANKING

Financial institutions, their card associations, and vendors are working to develop an Internet payment infrastructure to help make electronic commerce secure. Many in the banking industry expect significant growth in the use of the Internet for the purchase of goods and services and electronic data interchange. The banking industry also recognizes that the Internet must be secure to achieve a high level of confidence with both consumers and businesses.

Sound management of banking products and services, especially those provided over the Internet, is fundamental to maintaining a high level of public confidence not only in the individual bank and its brand name but also in the banking system as a whole. Key components that will help maintain a high level of public confidence in an open network environment include:

- Security
- Authentication
- Trust
- Nonrepudiation
- Privacy
- Availability

Security is an issue in Internet banking systems. The OCC expects national banks to provide a level of logical and physical security commensurate with the sensitivity of the information and the individual bank's risk tolerance. Some national banks allow for direct dial-in access to their systems over a private network while others provide network access through the Internet.

Although the publicly accessible Internet generally may be less secure, both types of connections are vulnerable to interception and alteration. For example, hardware or software "sniffers" can obtain passwords, account numbers, credit card numbers, etc. without regard to the means of access. National banks therefore must have a sound system of internal controls to protect against security breaches for all forms of electronic access. A sound system of preventive, detective, and corrective controls will help assure the integrity of the network and the information it handles. See appendix C for a discussion of online attacks. Firewalls are frequently used on Internet banking systems as a security measure to protect internal systems and should be considered for any system connected to an outside network. Firewalls are a combination of hardware and software placed between two networks through which all traffic must pass, regardless of the direction of flow. They provide a gateway to guard against unauthorized individuals gaining access to the bank's network.

The mere presence of a firewall does not assure logical security and firewalls are not impenetrable: firewalls must be configured to meet a specific operating environment and they must be evaluated and maintained on a regular basis to assure their effectiveness and efficiency. Individuals who are technically competent must perform the installation, configuration, evaluation, and maintenance of firewalls. The specific risks involved may require a broad range of security controls. Appendix A contains a more detailed discussion of firewalls and associated controls.

The *IS internet banking* discusses other logical and physical security controls applicable to Internet banking environments. Examiners should be familiar with these controls before conducting a Internet banking examination.

Authentication is another issue in a Internet banking system. Transactions on the Internet or any other telecommunication network must be secure to achieve a high level of public confidence. In cyberspace, as in the physical world, customers, banks, and merchants need assurances that they will receive the service as ordered or the merchandise as requested, and that they know the identity of the person they are dealing with. Banks typically use symmetric (private key) encryption technology to secure messages and asymmetric (public/private key) cryptography to authenticate parties. Asymmetric cryptography employs two keys — a public key and a private key. These two keys are mathematically tied but one key cannot be deduced from the other.

For example, to authenticate that a message came from the sender, the sender encrypts the message using their private key. Only the sender knows the private key. But, once sent, the message can be read only using the sender's public key. Since the message can only be read using the sender's public key, the receiver knows the message came from the expected sender. Internet banking systems should employ a level of encryption that is appropriate to the level or risk present in the systems. OCC is aware that stronger levels of encryption may slow or degrade performance and, accordingly, management must balance security needs with performance and cost issues.

Thus, a national bank should conduct a risk assessment in deciding upon its appropriate level of encryption. The OCC does not mandate a particular strength or type of encryption. Rather, it expects management to evaluate security risks, review the cost and benefit of different encryption systems, and decide on an appropriate level of encryption as a business decision. Management should be able to explain the supporting analysis for their decision.

A common asymmetric cryptography system is RSA, which uses key lengths up to 1,024 bits. By using the two forms of cryptography together, symmetric to protect the message and asymmetric to authenticate the parties involved, banks can secure the message and have a high level of confidence in the identity of the parties involved. See appendix B of this for examples of how this technology works. Biometric devices are an advanced form of authentication.

These devices may take the form of a retina scan, finger or thumb print scan, facial scan, or voice print scan. Use of biometrics is not yet considered mainstream, but may be used by some banks for authentication. Examiners should evaluate biometric activities based on management's understanding of risks, internal or external reviews, and the overall performance of these devices. Trust is another issue in Internet banking systems. As noted in the previous discussion, public and private key cryptographic systems can be used to secure information and authenticate parties in transactions in cyberspace. A trusted third party is a necessary part of the process. That third party is the *certificate authority*.

A certificate authority is a trusted third party that verifies identities in cyberspace. Some people think of the certificate authority functioning like an online notary. The basic concept is that a bank, or other third party, uses its good name to validate parties in transactions. This is similar to the historic role banks have played with letters of credit, where neither the buyer nor seller knew each other but both parties were known to the bank. Thus the bank uses its good name to facilitate the transaction, for a fee. *See* OCC Bulletin 99-20, "Certification Authority Services," for more information on this topic.

Banks also may need a way to validate themselves in cyberspace, as theft of identity has taken place. According to GAO testimony (GAO/T-66D-99-34), perpetrators have copied legitimate brokerage-firm Web sites, altered addresses for customers to contact (and send checks), then put the fraudulent Web site back on the Internet. Except for the post office box and possibly the URL, everything on the Web site could appear legitimate. Banks will have to guard against a variety of frauds and scams as banking on the Internet becomes more prominent. A proper mix of preventive, detective, and corrective controls can help protect national banks from these pitfalls. Digital certificates may play an important role in authenticating parties and thus establishing trust in Internet banking systems.

Nonrepudiation is the undeniable proof of participation by both the sender and receiver in a transaction. It is the reason public key encryption was developed, i.e., to authenticate electronic messages and prevent denial or repudiation by the sender or receiver. Although technology has provided an answer to nonrepudiation, state laws are not uniform in the treatment of electronic authentication and digital signatures. The application of state laws to these activities is a new and emerging area of the law.

Privacy is a consumer issue of increasing importance. National banks that recognize and respond to privacy issues in a proactive way make this a positive attribute for the bank and a benefit for its customers. Public concerns over the proper versus improper accumulation and use of personal information are likely to increase with the continued growth of electronic commerce and the Internet. Providers who are sensitive to these concerns have an advantage over those who do not. *See* OCC Advisory Letter 99-6, "Guidance to National Banks on Web Site Privacy Statements," for a more complete discussion of this topic.

Availability is another component in maintaining a high level of public confidence in a network environment. All of the previous components are of little value if the network is not available and convenient to customers. Users of a network expect access to systems 24 hours per day, seven days a week. Among the considerations associated with system availability are capacity, performance monitoring, redundance, and business resumption. National banks and their vendors who provide Internet banking products and services need to make certain they have the capacity in terms of hardware and software to consistently deliver a high level of service. In addition, performance monitoring techniques will provide management with information such as the volume of traffic, the duration of transactions, and the amount of time customers must wait for service. Monitoring capacity, downtime, and performance on a regular basis will help management assure a high level of availability for their Internet banking system. It is also important to evaluate network vulnerabilities to prevent outages due to component failures. An entire network can become inoperable when a single hardware component or software module malfunctions. Often national banks and their vendors will employ redundant hardware in critical areas or have the ability to switch to alternate processing locations. The latter is often referred to as contingency planning. This topic is covered at length in the *IS*.

In addition to these issues, appendix D contains some discussion points examiners can use in national banks that are contemplating engaging in Internet banking.

2

Internet Banking Risks

Internet banking creates new risk control challenges for national banks. From a supervisory perspective, risk is the potential that events, expected or unexpected, may have an adverse impact on the bank's earnings or capital. The OCC has defined nine categories of risk for bank supervision purposes. The risks are credit, interest rate, liquidity, price, foreign exchange, transaction, compliance, strategic, and reputation. These categories are not mutually exclusive and all of these risks are associated with Internet banking.

INTERNET BANKING

Two distinct trends can be discerned in the realm of Internet Banking. On one hand, Banks and Financial Institutions are trying to enter into new areas and consolidate their hold on the entire financial sector. On the other hand, new Dot Coms are entering the financing business and challenging the banks. It could be said that two opposite things are happening at the same time. The banks, via their consolidation moves are trying to preserve their strongholds, while the Dot Coms are trying to fragment the market by providing superior services. Banks and Financial Institutions are trying to leverage their Brands and their position in the industry. While, the Dot Coms are using their competency in superior service design and experience of competing in this highly unstable environment. All the players share the same objectives: acquiring customers, providing them with new financial information, services, and products, and doing so in a way that enhances the value proposition of their products and services.

Internet Banking allows the Banks (and other Financial Service providers) to overcome the tradeoff between content and reach. With the use of Internet, banks can provide their services to a much wider audience then they could do without it. Even before the coming of Internet, competition had shifted from products to services. This was due, in large part, to the advent of Private Sector Banks.

Before the entry of these banks, the retail banking was more of a commodity with hardly any differentiation on the basis of products or services. Banks offered similar products and similar service. But the new private sector banks changed the scenario by differentiating on the basis of service. They started providing Telephone based banking and introduced the concept of home banking. The superior service being provided by these banks was the main reason for their rapid growth. But their reach was limited due to logistics of setting up branches and increasing the reach of their service. Any attempt to increase the branch network would have increased their overheads and any attempt to widen the areas being served by a branch was likely to lead to deterioration in the service levels. In other words, these banks were caught in a dilemma as they faced the Reach and content tradeoff. With the advent of Internet these banks have been able to overcome this tradeoff.

By using the Internet, these banks can expand their reach as well as maintain the standards of their services.

ELECTRONIC BILL PAYMENT

From the point of view of Banks, Electronic Bill Payment (EBP) represents something of a threat, in that it could lead to customer attrition and reduce revenue. Among other revenue streams, the following sources of funds for the banks could be affected:

- Float associated with processing in the physical form,
- Cash Management Services

The Banks can protect itself by providing this service to their customers. But EBP also has an important strategic dimension, as it can become an integral part of a bank's portfolio of services. EBP can attract customers to the bank by making transactions more efficient and enabling customers to access their financial information more easily. Moreover, online interactions allow use of such tools as e-CRM to create a more intimate relationship with the customer and promote and deliver other online products and services.

If the Banks do not establish control on EBP, they are likely to loose customers to the new providers of financial services, thus affecting other sources of revenue.

In India, HDFC Bank, ICICI Bank and Citibank are trying setup an EBP portal. ICICI has already started a portal called BillJunction.com. Banks are planning to use the Net for payment of utility bills. They are entering into tie-ups with utilities like MTNL, Airtel, Orange, and BPL Mobile etc. Right now, a customer who's received a bill in the physical form logs into the network in order to make an online payment. In the future, these bills will be sent to customers through the Net.

Consumers and Businesses can derive economic benefit on account of reduction in transaction costs and a reduction in the float resulting from physical processing of the Bills. In addition, many are likely to adopt it mainly for the convenience. They can pay bills electronically in the same way they do today, but by consolidating their bills, they can reduce the effort involved in the whole process. They can also access their account at the same time. They can conveniently access all billers from a single portal that also provides them banking facilities. This would enable them to view their account balance while paying bills. For portals or the intermediaries that consolidate bills from multiple billers at a single online location EBP is a tool to acquire customers and provide them other financial services also. Dominance of the EBP market can lead to an entry into other financial services markets such as credit or debit card payments, or indeed into a much broader range of e-commerce markets, such as payments gateways.

ONLINE BROKERAGE

Online Broking is emerging as another field where traditional service providers are likely to face tough competition from the Dot Coms. In Taiwan and Korea, 30% of the stock trading has already moved online. This is posing a threat to the traditional Full-Service Brokerages. By leveraging the power of the web, Charles Schwab has emerged as a major threat to Full-Service brokers like Merrill Lynch. In order to preempt the moves into these areas by new players, many Banks have already tied up with Online Brokerages.

The Banks have entered the e-trading business. Since many banks are also Depositary participants, they have tied up with e-traders so that a customer is able to buy or sell shares online and make and receive payments through the Net.

In India, HDFC Bank has tied up with Investsmart.com and is offering its services to all the clients of the brokerage. ICICI Bank has gone a step ahead and launched ICICIDirect.com. These banks have become exclusive providers of banking and depositary/custodial services to the clients of these online brokerages.

ONLINE DELIVERY OF FINANCIAL PRODUCTS

The Banks have started offering banking services like checking your account status fund transfer, ordering demand drafts and writing out cheques, via the net. Soon these will form only a small part of the total array of services being offered by them. These Banks have embarked on a number of new initiatives to protect their stronghold and to leverage the net. They are offering value-added services to their customers and at the same time are trying to get into B2C and B2B e-commerce. They are even trying to get their finger into various transactions between the Government on one side and the business and the customer on the other. Banks are trying to become a part of the online value chain. For example, they are trying to tie up with corporates so as to become a part of their supply chain and enable electronic transfer of funds between the different components of the Supply Chain. They are doing this by acting as an intermediary between the corporations and their vendors by enabling online transactions at one place.

Some Banks are trying to setup portals for routing payments like Excise Duty and Sales Tax. Not content with that Banks are setting up secure payment gateways to tap the B2C online market.

Banks have taken the application process for personal loans, car loans, and mortgage, online. They plan to offer other financial products like Bonds and Mutual Funds through their financial service portal. This strategy is aimed by pre-empting the entry of new startups into this business.

Another bit of the Net strategy, involves providing infrastructure for B2C as well as B2B e-commerce. Banks are setting up secure payment gateways that will allow online retail shops to obtain instant credit card verifications. Once the buyer hits the pay button at a B2C portal, the buyer's credit card details will get encrypted and travel securely to the Visa or MasterCard approval system through the bank's payment gateway.

The banks are also setting up their own shopping portals. HDFC has a stake in a portal called easy2buy.com where HDFC bank customers can buy using their bank account number. Federal Bank has similar arrangements with Rediff.com and Fabmart.com. ICICI has setup Magiccart.com, an e-tailing site.

At the B2B end, Banks are offering Net Banking service that allows electronic fund transfers among a company, its vendors and dealers. Another service being targeted at this segment is cash management. This will reduce the float, which is present in physical processing of the payments.

The Banks are also trying to integrate their systems with the ERP/Supply Chain system of their clients. This will enable the bank to benefit from the movement towards e-procurement. E-Procurement involves making transactions online and processing the payment electronically.

Internet Banking in India

The Internet banking is changing the banking industry and is having the major effects on banking relationships. Even the Morgan Stanley Dean Witter Internet research emphasised that Web is more important for retail financial services than for many other industries. Internet banking involves use of Internet for delivery of banking products & services. It falls into four main categories, from Level 1 - minimum functionality sites that offer only access to deposit account data - to Level 4 sites - highly sophisticated offerings enabling integrated sales of additional products and access to other financial services- such as investment and insurance. In other words a successful Internet banking solution offers

- Exceptional rates on Savings, CDs, and IRAs
- Checking with no monthly fee, free bill payment and rebates on ATM surcharges

- Credit cards with low rates
- Easy online applications for all accounts, including personal loans and mortgages
- 24 hour account access
- Quality customer service with personal attention

DRIVERS OF CHANGE

Advantages previously held by large financial institutions have shrunk considerably. The Internet has leveled the playing field and afforded open access to customers in the global marketplace. Internet banking is a cost-effective delivery channel for financial institutions. Consumers are embracing the many benefits of Internet banking. Access to one's accounts at anytime and from any location via the World Wide Web is a convenience unknown a short time ago. Thus, a bank's Internet presence transforms from 'brouchreware' status to 'Internet banking' status once the bank goes through a technology integration effort to enable the customer to access information about his or her specific account relationship. The six primary drivers of Internet banking includes, in order of primacy are:

- Improve customer access
- Facilitate the offering of more services
- Increase customer loyalty
- Attract new customers
- Provide services offered by competitors
- Reduce customer attrition

INDIAN BANKS ON WEB

The banking industry in India is facing unprecedented competition from non-traditional banking institutions, which now offer banking and financial services over the Internet. The deregulation of the banking industry coupled with the emergence of new technologies, are enabling new competitors to enter the financial services market quickly and efficiently.

Indian banks are going for the retail banking in a big way. However, much is still to be achieved. This study which was conducted by students of IIML shows some interesting facts:

- Throughout the country, the Internet Banking is in the nascent stage of development (only 50 banks are offering varied kind of Internet banking services).
- In general, these Internet sites offer only the most basic services. 55% are so called 'entry level' sites, offering little more than company information and basic marketing materials. Only 8% offer 'advanced transactions' such as online funds transfer, transactions & cash management services.

- Foreign & Private banks are much advanced in terms of the number of sites & their level of development.

EMERGING CHALLENGES

Information technology analyst firm, the Meta Group, recently reported that "financial institutions who don't offer home banking by the year 2000 will become marginalized." By the year of 2002, a large sophisticated and highly competitive Internet Banking Market will develop which will be driven by

- Demand side pressure due to increasing access to low cost electronic services.
- Emergence of open standards for banking functionality.
- Growing customer awareness and need of transparency.
- Global players in the fray
- Close integration of bank services with web based E-commerce or even disintermediation of services through direct electronic payments (E- Cash).
- More convenient international transactions due to the fact that the Internet along with general deregulation trends, eliminate geographic boundaries.
- Move from one stop shopping to 'Banking Portfolio' i.e. unbundled product purchases.

Certainly some existing brick and mortar banks will go out of business. But that's because they fail to respond to the challenge of the Internet.

The Internet and it's underlying technologies will change and transform not just banking, but all aspects of finance and commerce. It represents much more than a new distribution opportunity.

It will enable nimble players to leverage their brick and mortar presence to improve customer satisfaction and gain share. It will force lethargic players who are struck with legacy cost basis, out of business-since they are unable to bring to play in the new context.

GROWTH IN INTERNET BANKING

Numerous factors — including competitive cost, customer service, and demographic considerations — are motivating banks to evaluate their technology and assess their electronic commerce and Internet banking strategies. Many researchers expect rapid growth in customers using online banking products and services. The challenge for national banks is to make sure the savings from Internet banking technology more than offset the costs and risks associated with conducting business in cyberspace.

Marketing strategies will vary as national banks seek to expand their markets and employ lower cost delivery channels. Examiners will need to understand the strategies used and technologies employed on a bank-by-bank basis to assess the risk. Evaluating a bank's data on the use of their Web sites, may help examiners determine the bank's strategic objectives, how well the bank is meeting its Internet banking product plan, and whether the business is expected to be profitable.

Some of the market factors that may drive a bank's strategy include the following:

Competition — Studies show that competitive pressure is the chief driving force behind increasing use of Internet banking technology, ranking ahead of cost reduction and revenue enhancement, in second and third place respectively. Banks see Internet banking as a way to keep existing customers and attract new ones to the bank.

Cost Efficiencies — National banks can deliver banking services on the Internet at transaction costs far lower than traditional brick-and-mortar branches. The actual costs to execute a transaction will vary depending on the delivery channel used. For example, according to Booz, Allen & Hamilton, as of mid-1999, the cost to deliver manual transactions at a branch was typically more than a dollar, ATM and call center transactions cost about 25 cents, and Internet transactions cost about a penny. These costs are expected to continue to decline.

National banks have significant reasons to develop the technologies that will help them deliver banking products and services by the most cost-effective channels. Many bankers believe that shifting only a small portion of the estimated 19-billion payments mailed annually in the U.S. to electronic delivery channels could save banks and other businesses substantial sums of money. However, national banks should use care in making product decisions.

Management should include in their decision making the development and ongoing costs associated with a new product or service, including the technology, marketing, maintenance, and customer support functions. This will help management exercise due diligence, make more informed decisions, and measure the success of their business venture.

Geographical Reach — Internet banking allows expanded customer contact through increased geographical reach and lower cost delivery channels. In fact some banks are doing business exclusively via the Internet — they do not have traditional banking offices and only reach their customers online. Other financial institutions are using the Internet as an alternative delivery channel to reach existing customers and attract new customers.

Branding — Relationship building is a strategic priority for many national banks. Internet banking technology and products can provide a means for national banks to develop and maintain an ongoing relationship with their customers by offering easy access to a broad array of products and services.

By capitalizing on brand identification and by providing a broad array of financial services, banks hope to build customer loyalty, cross-sell, and enhance repeat business. Customer Demographics — Internet banking allows national banks to offer a wide array of options to their banking customers. Some customers will rely on traditional branches to conduct their banking business. For many, this is the most comfortable way for them to transact their banking business.

Those customers place a premium on person-to-person contact. Other customers are early adopters of new technologies that arrive in the marketplace. These customers were the first to obtain PCs and the first to employ them in conducting their banking business. The demographics of banking customers will continue to change. The challenge to national banks is to understand their customer base and find the right mix of delivery channels to deliver products and services profitably to their various market segments.

Types of Internet Banking

Understanding the various types of Internet banking products will help examiners assess the risks involved. Currently, the following three basic kinds of Internet banking are being employed in the marketplace:

- Informational — This is the basic level of Internet banking. Typically, the bank has marketing information about the bank's products and services on a stand-alone server. The risk is relatively low, as informational systems typically have no path between the server and the bank's internal network. This level of Internet banking can be provided by the bank or outsourced. While the risk to a bank is relatively low, the server or Web site may be vulnerable to alteration. Appropriate controls therefore must be in place to prevent unauthorized alterations to the bank's server or Web site.
- Communicative — This type of Internet banking system allows some interaction between the bank's systems and the customer. The interaction may be limited to electronic mail, account inquiry, loan applications, or static file updates (name and address changes). Because these servers may have a path to the bank's internal networks, the risk is higher with this configuration than with informational systems. Appropriate controls need to be in place to prevent, monitor, and alert management of any unauthorized attempt to access the bank's internal networks and computer systems. Virus controls also become much more critical in this environment.
- Transactional — This level of Internet banking allows customers to execute transactions. Since a path typically exists between the server and the bank's or outsourcer's internal network, this is the highest risk architecture and must have the strongest controls. Customer transactions can include accessing accounts, paying bills, transferring funds, etc.

Internet Banking Risks

Internet banking creates new risk control challenges for national banks. From a supervisory perspective, risk is the potential that events, expected or unexpected, may have an adverse impact on the bank's earnings or capital. The OCC has defined nine categories of risk for bank supervision purposes. The risks are credit, interest rate, liquidity, price, foreign exchange, transaction, compliance, strategic, and reputation. These categories are not mutually exclusive and all of these risks are associated with Internet banking.

Credit Risk

Credit risk is the risk to earnings or capital arising from an obligor's failure to meet the terms of any contract with the bank or otherwise to perform as agreed. Credit risk is found in all activities where success depends on counterparty, issuer, or borrower performance. It arises any time bank funds are extended, committed, invested, or otherwise exposed through actual or implied contractual agreements, whether on or off the banks balance sheet. Internet banking provides the opportunity for banks to expand their geographic range. Customers can reach a given institution from literally anywhere in the world. In dealing with customers over the Internet, absent any personal contact, it is challenging for institutions to verify the bonafides of their customers, which is an important element in making sound credit decisions. Verifying collateral and perfecting security agreements also can be challenging with out-of-area borrowers. Unless properly managed, Internet banking could lead to a concentration in out-of-area credits or credits within a single industry. Moreover, the question of which state's or country's laws control an Internet relationship is still developing.

Effective management of a portfolio of loans obtained through the Internet requires that the board and management understand and control the bank's lending risk profile and credit culture. They must assure that effective policies, processes, and practices are in place to control the risk associated with such loans. *See* the "Loan Portfolio Management," booklet of the for a more complete discussion of credit risk.

Interest Rate Risk

Interest rate risk is the risk to earnings or capital arising from movements in interest rates. From an economic perspective, a bank focuses on the sensitivity of the value of its assets, liabilities and revenues to changes in interest rates. Interest rate risk arises from differences between the timing of rate changes and the timing of cash flows (repricing risk); from changing rate relationships among different yield curves affecting bank activities (basis risk); from changing rate relationships across the spectrum of maturities (yield curve risk); and from interest-related options embedded in bank products (options risk). Evaluation of interest rate risk must consider the impact of complex, illiquid hedging strategies or products, and also the potential impact that changes in interest rates will have on fee income. In those situations where trading is separately managed, this refers to structural positions and not trading portfolios. Internet banking can attract deposits, loans, and other relationships from a larger pool of possible customers than other forms of marketing. Greater access to customers who primarily seek the best rate or term reinforces the need for managers to maintain appropriate asset/liability management systems, including the ability to react quickly to changing market conditions.

Liquidity Risk

Liquidity risk is the risk to earnings or capital arising from a bank's inability to meet its obligations when they come due, without incurring unacceptable losses. Liquidity risk includes the inability to manage unplanned changes in funding sources. Liquidity risk also arises from the failure to recognize or address changes in market conditions affecting the ability of the bank to liquidate assets quickly and with minimal loss in value. Internet banking can increase deposit volatility from customers who maintain accounts solely on the basis of rate or terms. Asset/liability and loan portfolio management systems should be appropriate for products offered through Internet banking. Increased monitoring of liquidity and changes in deposits and loans may be warranted depending on the volume and nature of Internet account activities.

Price Risk

Price risk is the risk to earnings or capital arising from changes in the value of traded portfolios of financial instruments. This risk arises from market making, dealing, and position taking in interest rate, foreign exchange, equity, and commodities markets.

Banks may be exposed to price risk if they create or expand deposit brokering, loan sales, or securitization programs as a result of Internet banking activities. Appropriate management systems should be maintained to monitor, measure, and manage price risk if assets are actively traded.

Foreign Exchange Risk

Foreign exchange risk is present when a loan or portfolio of loans is denominated in a foreign currency or is funded by borrowings in another currency. In some cases, banks will enter into multi-currency credit commitments that permit borrowers to select the currency they prefer to use in each rollover period. Foreign exchange risk can be intensified by political, social, or economic developments. The consequences can be unfavorable if one of the currencies involved becomes subject to stringent exchange controls or is subject to wide exchange-rate fluctuations. Foreign exchange risk is discussed in more detail in the "Foreign Exchange," booklet of the Internet Banking. Banks may be exposed to foreign exchange risk if they accept deposits from non-U.S. residents or create accounts denominated in currencies other than U.S. dollars. Appropriate systems should be developed if banks engage in these activities.

Transaction Risk

Transaction risk is the current and prospective risk to earnings and capital arising from fraud, error, and the inability to deliver products or services, maintain a competitive position, and manage information. Transaction risk is evident in each product and service offered and encompasses product development and delivery, transaction processing, systems development, computing systems, complexity of products and services, and the internal control environment.

A high level of transaction risk may exist with Internet banking products, particularly if those lines of business are not adequately planned, implemented, and monitored. Banks that offer financial products and services through the Internet must be able to meet their customers' expectations. Banks must also ensure they have the right product mix and capacity to deliver accurate, timely, and reliable services to develop a high level of confidence in their brand name. Customers who do business over the Internet are likely to have little tolerance for errors or omissions from financial institutions that do not have sophisticated internal controls to manage their Internet banking business. Likewise, customers will expect continuous availability of the product and Web pages that are easy to navigate. Software to support various Internet banking functions is provided to the customer from a variety of sources. Banks may support customers using customer-acquired or bank-supplied browsers or personal financial manager (PFM) software. Good communications between banks and their customers will help manage expectations on the compatibility of various PFM software products.

Attacks or intrusion attempts on banks' computer and network systems are a major concern. Studies show that systems are more vulnerable to internal attacks than external, because internal system users have knowledge of the system and access. Banks should have sound preventive and detective controls to protect their Internet banking systems from exploitation both internally and externally. *See* OCC Bulletin 99-9, "Infrastructure Threats from Cyber-Terrorists" for additional information.

Contingency and business resumption planning is necessary for banks to be sure that they can deliver products and services in the event of adverse circumstances. Internet banking products connected to a robust network may actually make this easier because back up capabilities can be spread over a wide geographic area. For example, if the main server is inoperable, the network could automatically reroute traffic to a back up server in a different geographical location. Security issues should be considered when the institution develops its contingency and business resumption plans. In such situations, security and internal controls at the back-up location should be as sophisticated as those at the primary processing site. High levels of system availability will be a key expectation of customers and will likely differentiate success levels among financial institutions on the Internet. National banks that offer bill presentment and payment will need a process to settle transactions between the bank, its customers, and external parties. In addition to transaction risk, settlement failures could adversely affect reputation, liquidity, and credit risk.

Compliance Risk

Compliance risk is the risk to earnings or capital arising from violations of, or nonconformance with, laws, rules, regulations, prescribed practices, or ethical standards. Compliance risk also arises in situations where the laws or rules governing certain bank products or activities of the bank's clients may be ambiguous or untested. Compliance risk exposes the institution to fines, civil money penalties, payment of damages, and the voiding of contracts. Compliance risk can lead to a diminished reputation, reduced franchise value, limited business opportunities, reduced expansion potential, and lack of contract enforceability. Most Internet banking customers will continue to use other bank delivery channels. Accordingly, national banks will need to make certain that their disclosures on Internet banking channels, including Web sites, remain synchronized with other delivery channels to ensure the delivery of a consistent and accurate message to customers.

Federal consumer protection laws and regulations, including CRA and Fair Lending, are applicable to electronic financial services operations including Internet banking. Moreover, it is important for national banks to be familiar with the regulations that permit electronic delivery of disclosures/notices versus those that require traditional hard copy notification. National banks should carefully review and monitor all requirements applicable to electronic products and services and ensure they comply with evolving statutory and regulatory requirements.

Advertising and record-keeping requirements also apply to banks' Web sites and to the products and services offered. Advertisements should clearly and conspicuously display the FDIC insurance notice, where applicable, so customers can readily determine whether a product or service is insured. Regular monitoring of bank Web sites will help ensure compliance with applicable laws, rules, and regulations. *See* the "Consumer Compliance Examination" booklet of the , OCC Bulletin 94-13, "Nondeposit Investment Sales Examination Procedures," and OCC Bulletin 98-31, "Guidance on Electronic Financial Services and Consumer Compliance" for more information.

Application of Bank Secrecy Act (BSA) requirements to cyberbanking products and services is critical. The anonymity of banking over the Internet poses a challenge in adhering to BSA standards. Banks planning to allow the establishment of new accounts over the Internet should have rigorous account opening standards. Also, the bank should set up a control system to identify unusual or suspicious activities and, when appropriate, file suspicious activity reports (SARs).

The BSA funds transfer rules also apply to funds transfers or transmittals performed over the Internet when transactions exceed $3,000 and do not meet one of the exceptions. The rules require banks to ensure that customers provide all the required information before accepting transfer instructions. The record keeping requirements imposed by the rules allow banks to retain written or electronic records of the information.

The Office of Foreign Asset Control (OFAC) administers laws that impose economic sanctions against foreign nations and individuals. This includes blocking accounts and other assets and prohibiting financial transactions. Internet banking businesses must comply with OFAC requirements. A bank needs to collect enough information to identify customers and determine whether a particular transaction is prohibited under OFAC rules. *See* the *FFIEC Information Systems Examination* (*IS*) for a discussion of OFAC.

Strategic Risk

Strategic risk is the current and prospective impact on earnings or capital arising from adverse business decisions, improper implementation of decisions, or lack of responsiveness to industry changes. This risk is a function of the compatibility of an organization's strategic goals, the business strategies developed to achieve those goals, the resources deployed against these goals, and the quality of implementation. The resources needed to carry out business strategies are both tangible and intangible. They include communication channels, operating systems, delivery networks, and managerial capacities and capabilities. The organization's internal characteristics must be evaluated against the impact of economic, technological, competitive, regulatory, and other environmental changes.

Management must understand the risks associated with Internet banking before they make a decision to develop a particular class of business. In some cases, banks may offer new products and services via the Internet. It is important that management understand the risks and ramifications of these decisions. Sufficient levels of technology and MIS are necessary to support such a business venture. Because many banks will compete with financial institutions beyond their existing trade area, those engaging in Internet banking must have a strong link between the technology employed and the bank's strategic planning process.

Before introducing a Internet banking product, management should consider whether the product and technology are consistent with tangible business objectives in the bank's strategic plan. The bank also should consider whether adequate expertise and resources are available to identify, monitor, and control risk in the Internet banking business.

The planning and decision making process should focus on how a specific business need is met by the Internet banking product, rather than focusing on the product as an independent objective. The bank's technology experts, along with its marketing and operational executives, should contribute to the decision making and planning process. They should ensure that the plan is consistent with the overall business objectives of the bank and is within the bank's risk tolerance. New technologies, especially the Internet, could bring about rapid changes in competitive forces. Accordingly, the strategic vision should determine the way the Internet banking product line is designed, implemented, and monitored.

Reputation Risk

Reputation risk is the current and prospective impact on earnings and capital arising from negative public opinion. This affects the institution's ability to establish new relationships or services or continue servicing existing relationships. This risk may expose the institution to litigation, financial loss, or a decline in its customer base.

Reputation risk exposure is present throughout the organization and includes the responsibility to exercise an abundance of caution in dealing with customers and the community. A bank's reputation can suffer if it fails to deliver on marketing claims or to provide accurate, timely services. This can include failing to adequately meet customer credit needs, providing unreliable or inefficient delivery systems, untimely responses to customer inquiries, or violations of customer privacy expectations.

A bank's reputation can be damaged by Internet banking services that are poorly executed or otherwise alienate customers and the public. Well designed marketing, including disclosures, is one way to educate potential customers and help limit reputation risk. Customers must understand what they can reasonably expect from a product or service and what special risks and benefits they incur when using the system. As such, marketing concepts need to be coordinated closely with adequate disclosure statements. A national bank should not market the bank's Internet banking system based on features or attributes the system does not have. The marketing program must present the product fairly and accurately.

National banks should carefully consider how connections to third parties are presented on their Web sites. Hypertext links are often used to enable a customer to link to a third party. Such links may reflect an endorsement of the third party's products or services in the eyes of the customer. It should be clear to the customer when they have left the bank's Web site so that there is no confusion about the provider of the specific products and services offered or the security and privacy standards that apply. Similarly, adequate disclosures must be made so that customers can distinguish between insured and noninsured products.

National banks need to be sure that their business continuity plans include the Internet banking business. Regular testing of the business continuity plan, including communications strategies with the press and public, will help the bank ensure it can respond effectively and promptly to any adverse customer or media reactions.

SIGNIFICANCE OF INTERNET BANKING

Internet banking (or E-banking) means any user with a personal computer and a browser can get connected to his bank -s website to perform any of the virtual banking functions. In internet banking system the bank has a centralized database that is web-enabled. All the services that the bank has permitted on the internet are displayed in menu. Any service can be selected and further interaction is dictated by the nature of service. The traditional branch model of bank is now giving place to an alternative delivery channels with ATM network. Once the branch offices of bank are interconnected through terrestrial or satellite links, there would be no physical identity for any branch. It would a borderless entity permitting anytime, anywhere and anyhow banking.

The network which connects the various locations and gives connectivity to the central office within the organization is called intranet. These networks are limited to organizations for which they are set up. SWIFT is a live example of intranet application.

Internet banking in india

The Reserve Bank of India constituted a working group on Internet Banking. The group divided the internet banking products in India into 3 types based on the levels of access granted. They are:

(i) Information Only System: General purpose information like interest rates, branch location, bank products and their features, loan and deposit calculations are provided in the banks website. There exist facilities for downloading various types of application forms. The communication is normally done through e-mail. There is no interaction between the customer and bank's application system. No identification of the customer is done. In this system, there is no possibility of any unauthorized person getting into production systems of the bank through internet.

(ii) Electronic Information Transfer System: The system provides customer- specific information in the form of account balances, transaction details, and statement of accounts. The information is still largely of the 'read only' format. Identification and authentication of the customer is through password. The information is fetched from the bank's application system either in batch mode or off-line. The application systems cannot directly access through the internet.

(iii) Fully Electronic Transactional System: This system allows bi-directional capabilities. Transactions can be submitted by the customer for online update. This system requires high degree of security and control. In this environment, web server and application systems are linked over secure infrastructure. It comprises technology covering computerization, networking and security, inter-bank payment gateway and legal infrastructure.

Automated Teller Machine (ATM)

ATM is designed to perform the most important function of bank. It is operated by plastic card with its special features. The plastic card is replacing cheque, personal attendance of the customer, banking hours restrictions and paper based verification. There are debit cards. ATMs used as spring board for Electronic Fund Transfer. ATM itself can provide information about customers account and also receive instructions from customers - ATM cardholders. An ATM is an Electronic Fund Transfer terminal capable of handling cash deposits, transfer between accounts, balance enquiries, cash withdrawals and pay bills. It may be on-line or 0ff-line. The on-line ATN enables the customer to avail banking facilities from anywhere. In off-line the facilities are confined to that particular ATM assigned. Any customer possessing ATM card issued by the Shared Payment Network System can go to any ATM linked to Shared Payment Networks and perform his transactions.

Credit Cards/Debit Cards

The Credit Card holder is empowered to spend wherever and whenever he wants with his Credit Card within the limits fixed by his bank. Credit Card is a post paid card. Debit Card, on the other hand, is a prepaid card with some stored value. Every time a person uses this card, the Internet Banking house gets money transferred to its account from the bank of the buyer.

The buyers account is debited with the exact amount of purchases. An individual has to open an account with the issuing bank which gives debit card with a Personal Identification Number (PIN). When he makes a purchase, he enters his PIN on shops PIN pad. When the card is slurped through the electronic terminal, it dials the acquiring bank system - either Master Card or VISA that validates the PIN and finds out from the issuing bank whether to accept or decline the transactions. The customer can never overspend because the system rejects any transaction which exceeds the balance in his account. The bank never faces a default because the amount spent is debited immediately from the customers account.

Smart Card

Banks are adding chips to their current magnetic stripe cards to enhance security and offer new service, called Smart Cards. Smart Cards allow thousands of times of information storable on magnetic stripe cards. In addition, these cards are highly secure, more reliable and perform multiple functions. They hold a large amount of personal information, from medical and health history to personal banking and personal preferences.

You can avail the following services through E-Banking.

Bill Payment Service

You can facilitate payment of electricity and telephone bills, mobile phone, credit card and insurance premium bills as each bank has tie-ups with various utility companies, service providers and insurance companies, across the country. To pay your bills, all you need to do is complete a simple one-time registration for each biller. You can also set up standing instructions online to pay your recurring bills, automatically. Generally, the bank does not charge customers for online bill payment.

Fund Transfer

You can transfer any amount from one account to another of the same or any another bank. Customers can send money anywhere in India. Once you login to your account, you need to mention the payees's account number, his bank and the branch. The transfer will take place in a day or so, whereas in a traditional method, it takes about three working days. ICICI Bank says that online bill payment service and fund transfer facility have been their most popular online services.

Credit Card Customers

With Internet banking, customers can not only pay their credit card bills online but also get a loan on their cards. If you lose your credit card, you can report lost card online.

Railway Pass

This is something that would interest all the aam janta. Indian Railways has tied up with ICICI bank and you can now make your railway pass for local trains online. The pass will be delivered to you at your doorstep. But the facility is limited to Mumbai, Thane, Nashik, Surat and Pune.

Investing through Internet Banking

You can now open an FD online through funds transfer.Now investors with interlinked demat account and bank account can easily trade in the stock market and the amount will be automatically debited from their respective bank accounts and the shares will be credited in their demat account. Moreover, some banks even give you the facility to purchase mutual funds directly from the online banking system.

Nowadays, most leading banks offer both online banking and demat account. However if you have your demat account with independent share brokers, then you need to sign a special form, which will link your two accounts.

Recharging your Prepaid Phone

Now just top-up your prepaid mobile cards by logging in to Internet banking. By just selecting your operator's name, entering your mobile number and the amount for recharge, your phone is again back in action within few minutes.

Shopping

With a range of all kind of products, you can shop online and the payment is also made conveniently through your account. You can also buy railway and air tickets through Internet banking.

Advantage of Internet Banking

As per the Internet and Mobile Association of India's report on online banking 2006, "There are many advantages of online banking. It is convenient, it isn't bound by operational timings, there are no geographical barriers and the services can be offered at a miniscule cost." Through Internet banking, you can check your transactions at any time of the day, and as many times as you want to. Where in a traditional method, you get quarterly statements from the bank. If the fund transfer has to be made outstation, where the bank does not have a branch, the bank would demand outstation charges. Whereas with the help of online banking, it will be absolutely free for you.

Security Precautions

Customers should never share personal information like PIN numbers, passwords etc with anyone, including employees of the bank. It is important that documents that contain confidential information are safeguarded.

PIN or password mailers should not be stored, the PIN and/or passwords should be changed immediately and memorised before destroying the mailers.

Customers are advised not to provide sensitive account-related information over unsecured e-mails or over the phone. Take simple precautions like changing the ATM PIN and online login and transaction passwords on a regular basis. Also ensure that the logged in session is properly signed out.

Banking & Insurance Sector

The economic reforms undertaken in the last 15 years have brought about a considerable improvement in the health of banks and financial institutions in

India. The banking sector is a very important sector of the Indian economy. The sector has made a marked improvement in the liberalization period. There has been extraordinary progress in the financial health of the commercial banks with respect to capital adequacy, profitability, asset quality and risk management. Deregulation has opened new doors for banks to increase revenues by entering into investment banking, insurance, credit cards, depository services, mortgage, securitization, etc.

The limit for foreign direct investment in private banks has been increased from 49% to 74%. In addition, the limit for foreign institutional investment in private banks is 49%. Liberalization and globalization have created a more challenging environment in the banking sector as well as in the other segments of the financial sector such as mutual funds, Non Banking Finance Companies, post offices, capital markets, venture capitalists, etc. Now the challenges faced by the sector would be gaining profitability, reinforcing technology, maintaining global standards, corporate governance, sharpening skills, risk management and, the most important of all, to establish 'Customer Intimacy'.

The insurance business is one of the most rapidly growing areas in the financial sector. As an economy grows over the years, insurance sector intensifies and broadens its reach. Every practical and futuristic individual would want himself, his family and his assets to be insured. Insurance deals mainly with life and general insurance. India has a large insurance market commensurate with its population. The IRDA Act 1999 (Insurance Regulatory and Development Authority of India Act) has given new opportunities to private players to enter into the market on the fulfillment of certain prerequisites. The IRDA is the licensing authority in the sector; the current FDI cap/Equity in the sector stands at 26 percent. There is no doubt the challenges ahead will become tougher with more companies competing both in general and life Insurance. Also mortgage insurance will soon be coming into the industry. New players have contributed to the launch of innovative products, services and value-added benefits. Major foreign players have entered the country and announced joint ventures in both life and non-life areas. These include New York Life, Aviva, Tokio Marine, Allianz, Standard Life, Lombard General, AIG, AMP and Sun Life among others.

Commercial banks are coming up with more and more vacancies, and the banking sector now has more new jobs than any other sector. Right from the branch level to the highest level, there is tremendous range of opportunities available in the sector. Jobs in this sector can be both rewarding and enjoyable, as you get opportunities to learn about business, interact with people and build up clientele. The same is the case with insurance, as it is the fastest growing industry under the financial sector. Both government and private players are currently offering a plenty of jobs in this sector. So, this is great news for you if you are thinking to go into the banking & insurance streams.

CREDIT RISK IN INTERNET BANKING

Credit risk is the risk to earnings or capital arising from an obligor's failure to meet the terms of any contract with the bank or otherwise to perform as agreed. Credit risk is found in all activities where success depends on counterparty, issuer, or borrower performance. It arises any time bank funds are extended, committed, invested, or otherwise exposed through actual or implied contractual agreements, whether on or off the banks balance sheet. Internet banking provides the opportunity for banks to expand their geographic range. Customers can reach a given institution from literally anywhere in the world. In dealing with customers over the Internet, absent any personal contact, it is challenging for institutions to verify the bonafides of their customers, which is an important element in making sound credit decisions. Verifying collateral and perfecting security agreements also can be challenging with out-of-area borrowers. Unless properly managed, Internet banking could lead to a concentration in out-of-area credits or credits within a single industry. Moreover, the question of which state's or country's laws control an Internet relationship is still developing.

Effective management of a portfolio of loans obtained through the Internet requires that the board and management understand and control the bank's lending risk profile and credit culture. They must assure that effective policies, processes, and practices are in place to control the risk associated with such loans.

Interest Rate Risk

Interest rate risk is the risk to earnings or capital arising from movements in interest rates. From an economic perspective, a bank focuses on the sensitivity of the value of its assets, liabilities and revenues to changes in interest rates. Interest rate risk arises from differences between the timing of rate changes and the timing of cash flows (repricing risk); from changing rate relationships among different yield curves affecting bank activities (basis risk); from changing rate relationships across the spectrum of maturities (yield curve risk); and from interest-related options embedded in bank products (options risk).

Evaluation of interest rate risk must consider the impact of complex, illiquid hedging strategies or products, and also the potential impact that changes in interest rates will have on fee income. In those situations where trading is separately managed, this refers to structural positions and not trading portfolios. Internet banking can attract deposits, loans, and other relationships from a larger pool of possible customers than other forms of marketing. Greater access to customers who primarily seek the best rate or term reinforces the need for managers to maintain appropriate asset/liability management systems, including the ability to react quickly to changing market conditions.

Liquidity Risk

Liquidity risk is the risk to earnings or capital arising from a bank's inability to meet its obligations when they come due, without incurring unacceptable losses. Liquidity risk includes the inability to manage unplanned changes in funding sources. Liquidity risk also arises from the failure to recognize or address changes in market conditions affecting the ability of the bank to liquidate assets quickly and with minimal loss in value. Internet banking can increase deposit volatility from customers who maintain accounts solely on the basis of rate or terms. Asset/liability and loan portfolio management systems should be appropriate for products offered through Internet banking. Increased monitoring of liquidity and changes in deposits and loans may be warranted depending on the volume and nature of Internet account activities.

Price Risk

Price risk is the risk to earnings or capital arising from changes in the value of traded portfolios of financial instruments. This risk arises from market making, dealing, and position taking in interest rate, foreign exchange, equity, and commodities markets. Banks may be exposed to price risk if they create or expand deposit brokering, loan sales, or securitization programs as a result of Internet banking activities. Appropriate management systems should be maintained to monitor, measure, and manage price risk if assets are actively traded.

Current and Prospective Risk

Transaction risk is the current and prospective risk to earnings and capital arising from fraud, error, and the inability to deliver products or services, maintain a competitive position, and manage information. Transaction risk is evident in each product and service offered and encompasses product development and delivery, transaction processing, systems development, computing systems, complexity of products and services, and the internal control environment. A high level of transaction risk may exist with Internet banking products, particularly if those lines of business are not adequately planned, implemented, and monitored. Banks that offer financial products and services through the Internet must be able to meet their customers' expectations.

Banks must also ensure they have the right product mix and capacity to deliver accurate, timely, and reliable services to develop a high level of confidence in their brand name. Customers who do business over the Internet are likely to have little tolerance for errors or omissions from financial institutions that do not have sophisticated internal controls to manage their Internet banking business. Likewise, customers will expect continuous availability of the product and Web pages that are easy to navigate. Software to support various Internet banking functions is provided to the customer from a variety of sources. Banks may support customers using customer-acquired or bank-supplied browsers or personal financial manager (PFM) software. Good communications between banks and their customers will help manage expectations on the compatibility of various PFM software products. Attacks or intrusion attempts on banks' computer and network systems are a major concern. Studies show that systems are more vulnerable to internal attacks than external, because internal system users have knowledge of the system and access.

Banks should have sound preventive and detective controls to protect their Internet banking systems from exploitation both internally and externally. Contingency and business resumption planning is necessary for banks to be sure that they can deliver products and services in the event of adverse circumstances. Internet banking products connected to a robust network may actually make this easier because back up capabilities can be spread over a wide geographic area.

For example, if the main server is inoperable, the network could automatically reroute traffic to a back up server in a different geographical location. Security issues should be considered when the institution develops its contingency and business resumption plans. In such situations, security and internal controls at the back-up location should be as sophisticated as those at the primary processing site. High levels of system availability will be a key expectation of customers and will likely differentiate success levels among financial institutions on the Internet. National banks that offer bill presentment and payment will need a process to settle transactions between the bank, its customers, and external parties. In addition to transaction risk, settlement failures could adversely affect reputation, liquidity, and credit risk.

Foreign Exchange Risk

Foreign exchange risk is present when a loan or portfolio of loans is denominated in a foreign currency or is funded by borrowings in another currency. In some cases, banks will enter into multi-currency credit commitments that permit borrowers to select the currency they prefer to use in each rollover period. Foreign exchange risk can be intensified by political, social, or economic developments. The consequences can be unfavorable if one of the currencies involved becomes subject to stringent exchange controls or is subject to wide exchange-rate fluctuations. Foreign exchange risk is discussed in more detail in the "Foreign Exchange," booklet of the Internet Banking. Banks may be exposed to foreign exchange risk if they accept deposits from non-U.S. residents or create accounts denominated in currencies other than U.S. dollars. Appropriate systems should be developed if banks engage in these activities.

Violations of Compliance Risk

Compliance risk is the risk to earnings or capital arising from violations of, or nonconformance with, laws, rules, regulations, prescribed practices, or ethical standards. Compliance risk also arises in situations where the laws or rules governing certain bank products or activities of the bank's clients may be ambiguous or untested. Compliance risk exposes the institution to fines, civil money penalties, payment of damages, and the voiding of contracts. Compliance risk can lead to a diminished reputation, reduced franchise value, limited business opportunities, reduced expansion potential, and lack of contract enforceability. Most Internet banking customers will continue to use other bank delivery channels. Accordingly, national banks will need to make certain that their disclosures on Internet banking channels, including Web sites, remain synchronized with other delivery channels to ensure the delivery of a consistent and accurate message to customers.

Federal consumer protection laws and regulations, including CRA and Fair Lending, are applicable to electronic financial services operations including Internet banking. Moreover, it is important for national banks to be familiar with the regulations that permit electronic delivery of disclosures/notices versus those that require traditional hard copy notification. National banks should carefully review and monitor all requirements applicable to electronic products and services and ensure they comply with evolving statutory and regulatory requirements. Advertising and record-keeping requirements also apply to banks' Web sites and to the products and services offered. Advertisements should clearly and conspicuously display the FDIC insurance notice, where applicable, so customers can readily determine whether a product or service is insured. Regular monitoring of bank Web sites will help ensure compliance with applicable laws, rules, and regulations. "Nondeposit Investment Sales Examination Procedures," and OCC Bulletin 98-31, "Guidance on Electronic Financial Services and Consumer Compliance" for more information.

Application of Bank Secrecy Act (BSA) requirements to cyberbanking products and services is critical. The anonymity of banking over the Internet poses a challenge in adhering to BSA standards. Banks planning to allow the establishment of new accounts over the Internet should have rigorous account opening standards. Also, the bank should set up a control system to identify unusual or suspicious activities and, when appropriate, file suspicious activity reports (SARs). The BSA funds transfer rules also apply to funds transfers or transmittals performed over the Internet when transactions exceed $3,000 and do not meet one of the exceptions. The rules require banks to ensure that customers provide all the required information before accepting transfer instructions. The record keeping requirements imposed by the rules allow banks to retain written or electronic records of the information. The Office of Foreign Asset Control (OFAC) administers laws that impose economic sanctions against foreign nations and individuals. This includes blocking accounts and other assets and prohibiting financial transactions. Internet banking businesses must comply with OFAC requirements. A bank needs to collect enough information to identify customers and determine whether a particular transaction is prohibited under OFAC rules.

Current and Prospective Impact of Reputation Risk

Reputation risk is the current and prospective impact on earnings and capital arising from negative public opinion. This affects the institution's ability to establish new relationships or services or continue servicing existing relationships. This risk may expose the institution to litigation, financial loss, or a decline in its customer base. Reputation risk exposure is present throughout the organization and includes the responsibility to exercise an abundance of caution in dealing with customers and the community. A bank's reputation can suffer if it fails to deliver on marketing claims or to provide accurate, timely services.

This can include failing to adequately meet customer credit needs, providing unreliable or inefficient delivery systems, untimely responses to customer inquiries, or violations of customer privacy expectations. A bank's reputation can be damaged by Internet banking services that are poorly executed or otherwise alienate customers and the public. Well designed marketing, including disclosures, is one way to educate potential customers and help limit reputation risk.

Customers must understand what they can reasonably expect from a product or service and what special risks and benefits they incur when using the system. As such, marketing concepts need to be coordinated closely with adequate disclosure statements. A national bank should not market the bank's Internet banking system based on features or attributes the system does not have. The marketing program must present the product fairly and accurately. National banks should carefully consider how connections to third parties are presented on their Web sites. Hypertext links are often used to enable a customer to link to a third party.

Such links may reflect an endorsement of the third party's products or services in the eyes of the customer. It should be clear to the customer when they have left the bank's Web site so that there is no confusion about the provider of the specific products and services offered or the security and privacy standards that apply. Similarly, adequate disclosures must be made so that customers can distinguish between insured and noninsured products. National banks need to be sure that their business continuity plans include the Internet banking business. Regular testing of the business continuity plan, including communications strategies with the press and public, will help the bank ensure it can respond effectively and promptly to any adverse customer or media reactions.

Current and Prospective Impact of Strategic Risk

Strategic risk is the current and prospective impact on earnings or capital arising from adverse business decisions, improper implementation of decisions, or lack of responsiveness to industry changes. This risk is a function of the compatibility of an organization's strategic goals, the business strategies developed to achieve those goals, the resources deployed against these goals, and the quality of implementation. The resources needed to carry out business strategies are both tangible and intangible. They include communication channels, operating systems, delivery networks, and managerial capacities and capabilities. The organization's internal characteristics must be evaluated against the impact of economic, technological, competitive, regulatory, and other environmental changes. Management must understand the risks associated with Internet banking before they make a decision to develop a particular class of business. In some cases, banks may offer new products and services via the Internet.

It is important that management understand the risks and ramifications of these decisions. Sufficient levels of technology and MIS are necessary to support such a business venture. Because many banks will compete with financial institutions beyond their existing trade area, those engaging in Internet banking must have a strong link between the technology employed and the bank's strategic planning process. Before introducing a Internet banking product, management should consider whether the product and technology are consistent with tangible business objectives in the bank's strategic plan. The bank also should consider whether adequate expertise and resources are available to identify, monitor, and control risk in the Internet banking business. The planning and decision making process should focus on how a specific business need is met by the Internet banking product, rather than focusing on the product as an independent objective. The bank's technology experts, along with its marketing and operational executives, should contribute to the decision making and planning process. They should ensure that the plan is consistent with the overall business objectives of the bank and is within the bank's risk tolerance. New technologies, especially the Internet, could bring about rapid changes in competitive forces. Accordingly, the strategic vision should determine the way the Internet banking product line is designed, implemented, and monitored.

FUTURE OF INTERNET BANKING

What will the future of Indian banking and insurance look like? Will the reform in banking and insurance sectors face the same fate as in power and telecom? It is increasingly evident that the economy offers opportunities but no security! Therefore, the future will belong to those who develop good internal controls, checks and balances and a sound market strategy. Business Growth, Cost Efficiency and Evolution are therefore regarded as key drivers which will have to be addressed. It is by now well recognized that India is one of the fastest growing economies in the world after over a decade of financial and banking sector reforms since 1991. Evidence from across the world suggests that a sound and evolved banking system is required for sustained economic development. India has a better banking system in place vis-à-vis other developing countries, but there are several issues that need to be ironed out.

The course of banking evolution and growth has gone through innumerable twists and turns in the post independence era. Retail banking segment in the banking industry is continuously undergoing innovations, product reengineering, adjustments and alignments. Given the size advantages, diverse customer base and scope for future expansion, there is a need for evolving a systematic approach to retail banking.

Retail Banking- Meaning and Scope

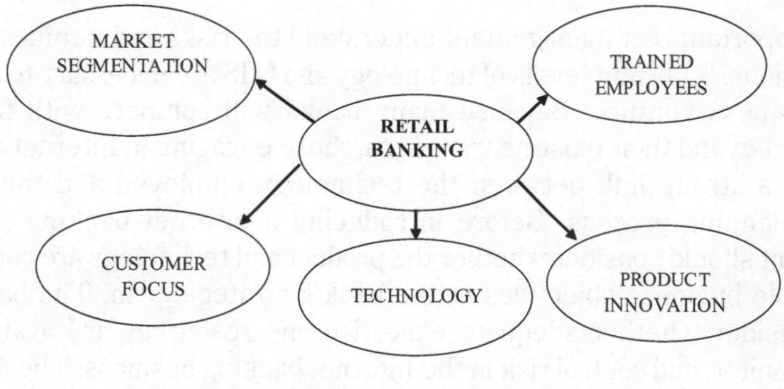

Fig. Factors influencing Retail Banking in India

Most of the Indian banks have been retail banks in their business composition. The term 'Retail Banking' encompasses various financial products (different types of deposit accounts, housing-consumer-auto and other types of loan accounts, demat facilities, insurance, mutual funds, Credit and Debit Cards, ATM and other technology-based services, stock-broking, payment of utility bills, reservation of railway tickets, etc.,) catering to diverse customer groups, offering a host of financial services, mostly to individuals. Simply speaking, it takes care of the diverse banking needs of an individual. The purpose if this paper is to try and identify the parameters on which the retail banking thrives and try to build insight into *the dynamics of the various parameters* and how they can pose a prospect or a problem in future.

The number of personal loan accounts with Scheduled Commercial Banks (SCBs) in India went up by almost 50 per cent between March 1997 and March 2002, as per CMIE data. Personal loan outstanding, however, went up by more than 130 per cent during the same period. The result was that the average personal loan outstanding increased from Rs. 24,668 in 1997 to Rs. 47,000 in

2002. Housing Loans, which accounted for about 28 per cent of personal loans outstanding in 1997, went up to 40 per cent in 2002. The following table gives a clear picture of the above:

Total personal loans outstanding increased from Rs. 28,000 crores in 1997 to more than Rs. 82,000 crores in 2002. On account of these personal loans, as distinct from loans to agriculture, trade, and industry, shot up from a little more than 20 per cent in 1997 to over 31.2 per cent in 2002. And that too over a period when total SCB outstandings shot up from Rs. 284,000 crore to Rs. Rs. 656,000 crores; an increase of more than 130 per cent. Data on Credit Cards are probably not included, given that there is no evidence that anyone, either in the RBI or in the Ministry of Finance, keeps track of credit cards. This, if true, is surprising news since credit cards account for a large and rapidly growing share of 'money supply', which RBI closely monitors in order to keep inflationary pressures in check.

RBI's Report on Trend and Progress of Banking in India, 2003-04 reveals some new trends in growth of credit. There is an upsurge in retail credit as against corporate advances, which may reveal itself in accumulating non-performing assets in banking sector and may accentuate the indebtedness of households in the medium term. However, with several counter-cyclical measures in place and a vigilant central bank , there is little need for alarm, as per Minna Kumar of Sify Finance in his study titled "Retail lending takes the lead" in November 2004.

Retail lending has been the key profit driver for banks in recent times with retail portfolio constituting 21.5 per cent of the total outstanding advances as on March 2004. On the other hand, stronger corporates strengthened their balance sheets by resorting to sizeable accruals as well as external commercial borrowings.

Current Scenario in Indian Retail Lending: Even though non-performing assets in the banking industry fell from 4.4 per cent in 2003 to 2.9 per cent in 2004, a hike in the percentage of retail lending may also pose a risk of poor asset quality of banks given that bad or 'impaired loans from from 2.5 per cent of total loans outstanding. Of the total retail loans, impaired housing loans constituted 1.9 per cent. The highest was in the consumer durable segment at 6.6 per cent. The retail segment's share in total loans for the period stood at 21.5 per cent, with housing loans constituting 48 per cent of the retail portfolio. The share of the housing loan portfolio out of total loan book of banks has grown from 3 per cent in 1993 to 7 per cent 2004. The following table gives details of Bank Credit to Retail Sector.

Nowadays, retail lending is the buzzword in banks in India. According to RBI's latest monetary policy, out of the total credit flow between April and August 2004, two-thirds had gone to retail loans. Most banks have retail loans of around 20% of their total lending portfolio and these loans are growing at an unnatural rate of 30 to 35% per annum. Housing loans constitute around 50% of the retail lending portfolio. Despite the fact that the housing loans portfolio grew only at 42% in 2003-04 compared to 55% the previous year, one analyst said "Due to shortage of around 1.9 million housing units, demand for the housing loans may shoot up significantly in the near future".

However, the rate at which the banks are disbursing the housing loans etc., caused concern to the Reserve Bank of India as this might lead to increase of bad loans. In its latest Trend and Progress of Banking in India 2004, RBI mentioned "The rising proportion of retail loans in the total lending portfolio may impair the quality of assets in this segment, thus, increase in the NPAs". To avoid any such bubble in this segment, RBI has increased the risk weightage on Home Loans from 50 to 75% and for Consumer Loans including Personal Loans and Credit Cards, from 100 to 125%. Around 2.5% of the retail loans are bad debts as on March 31, 2004 while this average is at 7.4% for all types of loans. It is even less for Housing Loans at 1.9%, and the obvious conclusion is that Retail Loans are safer.

But, to maintain this level of quality and avoid any kind of bubble in the making, banks should adopt sufficient risk management strategies. The following table gives more data on this aspect.

The Potential for Retail Banking in India:

An insight into the following paragraphs will justify the immense underlying potential for the Indian retail baking industry.

While the total outstanding retail loans in Taiwan is around *41% of its GDP*, the figure in India stands at *less than 5%.* The comparison with the West is even more staggering. Another situation that is natural when comparing retail sectors is the use of credit cards. Here also, the potential lies in the fact that of the consumer expenditure in India in 2001, *less than 1%* was through plastic, the corresponding US *figure standing at 18%.*

Hence, The Indian players are bullish on the retail business and this is not totally unfounded. *Two primary reasons are as follows*:

It is now undeniable that the face of the Indian consumer is changing. This is reflected adequately in a change in the urban household income pattern. The direct fallout of such a change will be the consumption patterns and hence the banking habits of Indians, which will now be skewed towards Retail products.

- Going by international standards, a large portion of the Indian population is simply not "bankable" - taking profitability into consideration. On the other hand, the financial services market is highly over-leveraged in India. Competition is fierce, particularly from local private banks such as HDFC Bank and ICICI Bank, in the business of home, car and consumer loans. There, precisely lie the pitfalls of such explosive growth. All banks are targeting the fluffiest segment i.e. the upwardly mobile urban salaried class. Although the players are spreading their operations into segments like self-employed and the semi-urban rich, it is an open secret that the big city Indian yuppies form the most profitable segment. Over-dependence on this segment is bound to bring in inflexibility in the business. Hence the challenge for various banks is to tap the underlying potential of the tapped and specifically the untapped market by developing sophisticated financial behaviour and spreading the scope to all over the country.

Prospects of Retail Banking in India

The conventional scenario of Banks is fast changing. The Banking Institutions have started revisiting their Visions. Should they have thousands of C class Accounts or a few A and B class Accounts? They have come to the conclusion that it is not economical to service the C class Accounts. Even in India, banks are raising the bar on deposits. Some Banks have even increased the minimum balance in Savings accounts so that they are out of reach of the small man. Why is this so? This is a natural corollary to the competencies that are being built up at a significant speed in all banks. Examining them one by one will help us know where the banks are heading, in the near future.

4 a. Customer Focus

All along, the word "Customer" used to denote any person who is having an account with a branch of a Bank or using the services of a Branch. Now, we are seeing a new definition for customer. A customer is no more a customer of the Branch; he is the Customer of the BANK. With the advent of *'AAA Banking' (Anytime, Anywhere,*

Anyhow Banking) the new definition of customer has become relevant. Technology enables the customer to "help himself" through Internet Banking, ATM Banking, Telephone Banking, Online Banking, Mobile Banking, or e-Banking, etc. Moreover the concept like *Know Your Customer (KYC)* reinforced when Reserve Bank of India recently urged banks to improve customer focus as a strategic initiative for effective management of profitability, risk and customer satisfaction as well as customer delight!

4 b. Segment focus

Banks are obviously for customer service. But banks are finding that they too need to segment and target High Networth Individuals (HNIs) and companies if they have to satisfy the needs of their stakeholders. Therefore, Banks are generally moving towards products that are focused on their targeted end customers. And this target is specifically the high end customers; as they do not find any leverage from the small accounts. But there is a strong trend in terms of consolidation in terms of the business segmentation. The general pattern of the banks is to cater to all segments – from agriculturists to high net worth individual to corporate banking to international banking. An analysis of the current scenario indicates that in future, each bank will decide on its core competency and cater only to selected segments. For example, the Deutsche Bank in India operates only in the corporate banking and it has turned as a market leader in this segment.

4 c. Product focus

Banks have been offering various asset products (Loans) and liability products (Deposits), taking the customers' general needs like fixed amount loans or running Cash Credit / Overdraft accounts or Fixed Deposit or Cumulative Deposit or Recurring Deposit as liability products. Now, the time has come for the Customer to demand a product that is not currently available in the Banker's kitty and the Bank has to literally create customer-specific products. Here comes the Banker in the role of a Financial Engineer.

Financial Services: Then and Now

Old Economy	New Economy
Confined market place	Unlimited market space
Competition between banks	Competition from brands
Limited product line	Extensive product breadth
One-size-fits-all products	Customisation and innovation
Branch-focused	e-Enabled, multi-channel players
Focus on business growth	Focus on revenue growth as well as cost-reduction
Revenues through margin	Revenue generated through fees and value-added services

Existing products and services are changing way for value-added ones thanks to the one-upmanship game among competing banks, sparked off by soaring consumer-demands.

4 d. Technology focus

As banks face the mutually interdependent forces of competition, regulation, technology, and customer expectations, a picturesque setting for the tremendous upheaval and opportunity emerges. This interdependency, in turn, is built upon mutually dependent technological trends.

- *Increase processing power*
- *Increase in networking*
- *Increase in flexibility in defining business standard*:
- *Increase in modularity of software*

These four trends are impacting irreversibly the business of banking, outsourcing, insourcing, analytics, and payment systems. Given these factors the banks are being more technology focused and driving the use of internet to help meet the requirements of their customers through segmentation.

(i) Internet banking: The trend in banking is changing from computerization of branches to laying a uniform platform by having core banking solution in all the branches. At the same time, banks are looking at internet banking. While a start has been made in the Internet banking in India, the number of transactions through this mode is extremely negligible (less than 1%). A study group appointed by the RBI has suggested that for Internet banking, there should be robust system keeping a log of all network activities and analyzing the same. RBI has gone on to suggest various technical features essential for having such a robust system. This should be in place within the next 2 years. Hopefully, the retail banks will see a surge/splurge in the usage from 1% to at least 10% in the next couple of years. Passing of Information Technology Act, 2000 gave enough relief to the users assuring of proper use of technology in banking.

(ii) Shared ATMs Till the year 2003, each bank was interested in opening its own ATMs to provide access and anytime banking to its customers. Cost of Installation of ATM is about Rs. 15 lacs with an additional maintenance cost of Rs.1.5 lacs per month. To break even, 300 transactions are to be put through each ATM per day. The cost of transaction in the branch of the Bank is approximately Rs. 60 while it is Rs. 10 if carried out through an ATM. To take advantage of this lower transaction cost, there is need for banks to induce customers to use more and more ATMs. In view of the huge investment cost of ATMs, Banks have now come to an understanding by which the customer of one Bank can use the ATMs of other Bank/s. This is in the right direction. Already SBI, HDFC Bank, ICICI Bank and others have started offering such a facility at a nominal payment per transaction, for which the customers are readily agreeable.

(iii) Outsourcing The challenge of managing the diverse services in a networked environment has caused the banks to introspect on what should be considered as their core skills and primary roles.

In future, banks will need to focus on value-differentiating services by keeping in-house their competitive advantages while partnering with others who complement its services-making the argument for best-of-breed integration a necessity.

(iv) In sourcing In sourcing is a model wherein banks perform operations that are originally done by their customers/other banks. Corporate clients may outsource activities like receivable management, accounting and risk management of corporate investments to banks. New product offerings will emerge as a combination of existing products and the new in sourced activities Banks, with their established processing capacities, are ideal partners for insurance and other

financial service firms in their pursuit of customer reach and service provision.

(v) *Analytics:* As they realize that product and related services by themselves cannot provide sustainable competitive advantage, banks are paying more attention to relationship with their customers and the way they manage risk, determine price, and allocate capital.

Hence, going forward, banks will attempt to augment their behavioral and economic views of the customer, preferably captured at the "Point of Contact" in addition to existing transactional and demographic data (in-house and external). Banks will require use of analytics to effectively manage their customer relationships, conduct detailed analysis that help more accurately model, and predict future customer behaviour and lay a quantified foundation for strategic decision-making.

On the other hand, banks often face the tricky task of asset allocation and pricing. In the last decade, investments in risk management and related systems have increased multifold, albeit made with a compliance objective towards identifying, measuring and funding risk. The future will see increasing investments in risk analytics as part of an integrated framework supporting asset pricing, performance measurement, and asset allocation models.

(vi) *Payment systems:* In recent years, alternate money transmission avenues, especially the development of electronic money schemes, have been gaining currency. Gradual expansion of Western Union Money Transfer in India through alliances with Banks, Post Offices, etc., is a thing to note in this direction. While electronic money has the potential to take over from cash for making small-value payments, making such transactions are becoming easier and cheaper for both consumers and merchants. This raises policy issues for central banks in its role as the guardian of the payment network and implementer of the monetary policy. The emergence of peer-to-peer money transmission mechanisms poses a challenge to current role of banks as gatekeepers to traditional payment systems. Robust payment systems, therefore, are a key requirement in maintaining and promoting financial stability with technology playing both a facilitating and disruptive role in them.

(vii) *Real Time Gross Settlement (RTGS):* In the last one decade, thanks to continuous thrust on computerization in the banking system, RBI took initiative for bringing in Electronic Funds Transfer (EFT), Electronic Clearing System (ECS), ATMs and Internet Banking. Cross selling of various financial products has been possible due to ATMs and Internet Banking. Investment climate has also geared up in volumes with Dematerialisation facility introduced by setting up of NSDL and CDSL after formation of National Stock Exchange in Mumbai. Clearing Corporation of India Ltd., (CCIL) has also made remarkable impact on funds settlement mechanism. Very soon Cheque Truncation system is going to be spearheaded by RBI in a phased manner.

RTGS is a payment system in which processing and settlement takes place in real-time (continuously). In this system, funds would flow freely from one market to another leading to better integration of the Domestic Financial Markets among themselves, and with International Financial Markets as well. RTGS, as a settlement process will minimize settlement risks by settling individual payments in real time in the books of accounts held by the RBI. RTGS will be a mode for large value Inter-Bank settlement, to be widely used, for enhancing risk control measures, for faster and efficient settlement of liabilities for better customer services for the ultimate users in the value chain.

RTGS would eliminate the time lag between the debit to an account of customer and its corresponding credit to another customer in a different bank. RTGS requires implementation of a 2 Level Gateway- one at the individual bank level and the other at the RBI level. Significant contribution made by Institute for Development and Research in Banking Technology (IDRBT), Hyderabad in this regard is commendable.

4 e. Employee focus

Earlier, there were premises where the branch of a Bank is located and there were three categories of staff to attend to the customers viz., Supervisory, Clerical and Sub-ordinate staff. With the disappearance of big ledgers and registers, the need for Sub-ordinate staff is also getting reduced.

The role of supervisory staff would increase and not in the sense of controlling the staff working with them but in different areas of delivering competitive services. Awareness about productivity, customer focus, competition, grievance/ complaint redressals, market surveys, etc among the bank staff has gone up very high. The VRS scheme introduced in the year 2000 by the Banks was to reduce the redundant staff consequent to computerization. It is felt that one more VRS would be needed for the Banks to shed their excess flab and make them fit and trim. Henceforth, the role for clerical staff would have to undergo a change from sitting under the roof in a branch to moving into the field and market various financial services offered by their Bank and not only attract new customers and retain existing clientele but also retrieve the customers lost to competitors. In a nutshell the trend is towards sophisticated well trained customer orientation.

Banking Hours

Bank hours were fixed so far. Now the fact is that almost all banks are moving towards any time/any where/home banking. Again, a closer look at this will reveal that Banks are moving away from the traditional customer to the customer who is extra busy. Who is this? Again, the high net worth individual and the highly profitable companies. For example ICICI bank has started 8 to 8 banking where the banking hours are 8 a.m. to 8 p.m. looking at this competitive market we may witness *24 hours banking*, very soon.

4 f. Others

(i) The Basel II effect: Essentially, the rules evolved by Basel Committee for Bank Supervision (BCBS) and adopted by RBI tell the banks how much capital the banks should have to cover up for the risk that their loans might go bad. The rules set out by Bank for International Settlements (BIS) in 1988 led the banks to differentiate among the customers it lent out money to. Different weightages were given to various forms of assets, with zero percentage weightings being given to cash, deposits with the central bank/govt etc, and 100 per cent weighting to claims on private sector, fixed assets, real estate etc. The summation of these assets gave us the risk-weighted assets. Against these risk weighted assets the banks had to maintain a (Tier I + Tier II) capital of 9 per cent i.e. every Rs100 of risk assets had to be backed by Rs 9 of Tier I + Tier II capital. To put it simply, the Indian banks had to maintain a Capital Adequacy Ratio (CAR) of 9 per cent as at present.

The problem with these rules is that they do not distinguish within a category i.e. all lending to private sector is assigned a 100 per cent risk weighting, be it a company with the best credit rating or company which is in the doldrums and has a very low credit rating. This is not an efficient use of capital. The company with the best credit rating is more likely to repay the loan vis-à-vis the company with a low credit rating. So the banks should be setting aside a far lesser amount of capital against the risk of a Company with the best credit rating defaulting vis-à-vis the company with a low credit rating.

With the rules being revised by BCBS and RBI, BASEL-II norms are to take place in the year 2007, the banks can decide on the amount of capital to set aside depending on the credit rating of the borrowing company.

Credit risk is not the only type that banks face in course of their business. These days, the operational risks that banks face are huge. The various risks that come under operational risk are competition risk, technology risk, casualty risk, crime risk etc. The original BASEL rules did not take into account the operational risks. Besides, there are other risks like Interest Rate Risk, Exchange Risk, etc. As per the BASEL-II norms, banks will have to set aside 15 per cent of net income to protect themselves against operational risks.

So to be ready for the new BASEL rules, the banks all over including in India will have to set aside more capital because the new rules could lead to Capital Adequacy Ratios of the banks falling. How the banks plan to go about meeting these requirements is something that remains to be seen. A few banks are planning initial public offerings / share issues to have enough capital on their books to meet these new norms. Recent examples are Dena Bank, Punjab National Bank, SBI, Andhra Bank, ICICI Bank, etc.

(ii) Consolidation –the future wave: In the recent past, there has been a lot of talk about Indian Banks lacking in scale and size. The State Bank of India is the only bank from India to make it to the list of Top 100 banks, globally. Most of the PSBs are either looking to pick up a smaller bank or waiting to be picked up by a larger bank. The buzz word in banking circles these days is, in particular, consolidation (mergers) of Public Sector Banks for good although facing stiff resistance from various corners.

The central government also seems to be game about the issue and is seen to be encouraging PSBs to merge or acquire other banks. Global evidence seems to suggest that even though there is great enthusiasm when companies merge or get acquired, majority of the mergers/acquisitions do not really work. So in the zeal to merge with or acquire another bank, the PSBs should not let their common sense take a back seat. Before a merger is carried out cultural issues should be looked into. A bank based primarily in North India might want to acquire a bank based primarily in South India to increase its geographical presence but their cultures might be very different. So the integration process might become very difficult. Technological compatibility both for software and hardware, besides trained work force, is another issue that needs to be looked into in detail, before any merger or acquisition is carried out.

The banks must not just merge because everybody around them is merging. As Keynes wrote," *Worldly wisdom teaches us that it's better for reputation to fail conventionally than succeed unconventionally*". Banks should avoid falling into this trap.

3

E-Commerce and Internet Banking

E-COMMERCE

Even though started as network primarily for use by researchers in defence and scientific community, with the introduction of WWW in early 1990s, use of Internet for commerce has grown tremendously. E-commerce involves individuals and business organizations exchanging business information and instructions over electronic media using computers, telephones and other telecommunication equipments.

Such form of doing business has been in existence ever since electronic mode of data/ information exchange was developed, but its scope was limited only as a medium of exchange of information between entities with a pre-established contractual relationship. However, Internet has changed the approach to e-commerce; it is no longer the same business with an additional channel for information exchange, but one with new strategy and models.

A business model generally focuses on:

- Where the business operates, that is, the market, the competitors and the customers,
- What it sells, that is, its products and services
- The channels of distribution, that is, the medium for sale and distribution of its products and
- The sources of revenue and expenditure and how these are affected.

Internet has influenced all the four components of business model and thus has come to influence the business strategy in a profound way. The size of the market has grown enormously as technically, one can access the products and services from any part of the world. So does the potential competition. The methods of reaching out to customers, receiving the response and offering services have a new, simpler and efficient alternative, now, that is, Internet.

The cost of advertisement, offer and delivery of services through Internet has reduced considerably, forcing most companies to rework their strategies to remain in competition. A research note by Paul Timmers of European commission had identified eleven business models, which have been commercially implemented. These are e-shop, eprocurement, e-auction, e-mall, Third-party market place, Virtual communities, Value chain service providers, Value chain integrators, Collaboration platforms and Information brokers. He classified business models along two dimensions, i.e, degree of innovation and extent of integration of functions.

The innovation ranged from the electronic version of a traditional way of doing business (e-shop) to more innovative ways by offering functions that did not exist before. The second dimension, i.e, extent of integration ranges from a single function business model (like e-shop) to fully integrated functionality (value chain integrator). In the top end of the graph are models, which cannot be implemented in a traditional way and are critically dependent upon information technology and creating value from information flow. Business models, in between these two limits are a combination of both dimensions in different degrees and have some degree of analogy in traditional firms. There are two types of e-commerce ventures in operation: the old brick and mortar companies, who have adopted electronic medium, particularly Internet, to enhance their existing products and services, and/ or to offer new products and services and the pure e-ventures who have no visible physical presence.

This difference has wider ramifications than mere visibility when it comes to issues like customer's trust, brand equity, ability to service the customers, adopting new business culture and cost. Another way of classifying the e-commerce is by the targeted counterpart of a business, viz, whether the counterpart is a final consumer or another business in the distribution chain. The two broad categories are: Business-to-Consumer (B2C) and Business-to-Business (B2B).

BUSINESS-TO-CONSUMERS (B2C)

In the B2C category are included single e-shops, shopping malls, e-broking, eauction, e-banking, service providers like travel related services, financial services etc., education, entertainment and any other form of business targeted at the final consumer. Some of the features, opportunities and concerns common to this category of business irrespective of the business segment, are the following.

OPPORTUNITIES

Internet provides an ever-growing market both in terms of number of potential customers and geographical reach. Technological development has made access to Internet both cheaper and faster. More and more people across the globe are accessing the net either through PCs or other devices. The purchasing power and need for quality service of this segment of consumers are considerable. Anybody accessing Internet is a potential customer irrespective of his or her location. Thus, any business targeting final consumers cannot ignore the business potential of Internet. Internet offers a unique opportunity to register business presence in a global market.

Its effectiveness in disseminating information about one's business at a relatively cost effective manner is tremendous. Time sensitive information can be updated faster than any other media. A properly designed website can convey a more accurate and focussed image of a product or service than any other media. Use of multimedia capabilities, *i.e.*, sound, picture, movies etc., has made Internet as an ideal medium for information dissemination. However, help of other media is necessary to draw the potential customers to the web site. The quality of service is a key feature of any e-commerce venture.

The ability to sell one's product at anytime and anywhere to the satisfaction of customers is essential for e-business to succeed. Internet offers such opportunity, since the business presence is not restricted by time zone and geographical limitations. Replying to customers' queries through e-mail, setting up FAQ pages for anticipated queries, offering interactive help line, accepting customers' complaints online 24 hours a day and attending to the same, etc. are some of the features of ebusiness which enhance the quality of service to the customers.

It is of crucial importance for an e-venture to realise that just as it is easier to approach a customer through Internet, it is equally easy to lose him. The customer has the same facility to move over to another site. Cost is an important issue in an e-venture. It is generally accepted that the cost of overhead, servicing and distribution, etc. through Internet is less compared to the traditional way of doing business.

Although the magnitude of difference varies depending on the type of business and the estimates made, but there is unanimity that Internet provides a substantial cost advantage and this, in fact, is one of the major driving forces for more number of traditional business adopting to e-commerce and pure e-commerce firms to sprout. Cost of communication through WWW is the least compared to any other medium. Many a time one's presence in the web may bring in international enquiries, which the business might not have targeted. The business should have proper plans to address such opportunities.

CONCERNS

There are a number of obstacles, which an e-commerce venture needs to overcome. Trust of customers in a web venture is an important concern. Many customers hesitate to deal with a web venture as they are not sure of the type of products and services they will receive. This is particularly true in a B2C venture like e-shop, e-mall or e-auction site. Traditional business with well established brands and goodwill and having a physical presence face less resistance from customers in this regard than a pure e-venture. Many B2C ventures have ultimately to deliver a product or service in physical form to the customer for a deal contracted through Internet. This needs proper logistics, an efficient distribution network, and control over quality of product or service delivered. These issues are not technology related and any let off in this area can drive the customer away to the competitor or from e-commerce. The privacy of information on the customer's preferences, credit card and bank account details etc. and customers' faith in a system where such privacy is stated to be ensured are important issues to be addressed. These are mainly technological issues, but human factor is important both at the business and at the customers' end and also in building the trust in the system. Security of a transaction, authenticity of a deal, identification of a customer etc. are important technological and systems issues, which are major sources of concern to ecommerce. Equally important are questions of repudiation of a deal, applicability of law, jurisdiction of tax laws etc.

These are important to all forms of e-commerce, whether B2C or B2B and all segments of business, i.e, manufacturing, services and finance and are addressed in different chapters of this book. Accessibility to Internet by the consumers is an important issue in B2C domain. This is particularly so in countries like India where penetration of PCs and other devices to households for access to Internet is minimal. Also important are availability of bandwidth and other infrastructure for faster and easier access. Considering that ecommerce aims at global market, deficiencies of these kinds in the developing world are no longer concerns confined to these areas, but are global e-commerce concerns.

BUSINESS TO BUSINESS (B2B)

As opposed to B2C e-commerce, in B2B domain, the parties to a deal are at different points of the product supply chain. Typically, in a B2B type domain, a company, its suppliers, dealers and bankers to all the parties are networked to finalize and settle all aspects of a deal, online. Perhaps, only the goods in different stages of processing physically move from the supplier to the dealer. This scenario can be extended to include the shipper, providers of different ancillary services, IT service provider and the payment system gateway, etc., depending on the degree of sophistication of the available systems. Another important feature of a B2B domain, as distinct from B2C, is that business information/ data is integrated to the back office systems of parties to a deal and the state of straight through processing (STP) or near STP is achieved.

This is a very significant aspect of B2B model of e-commerce, which results in improved profits through lowering cost and reducing inventories. For example, in a B2B environment, typically, the back office system of a company controls inventory requirement with reference to the order book position updated regularly on the basis of orders received from dealers through Internet. At the optimum level of inventory it raises a purchase order with the supplier, whose system in turn, processes the order and confirms supply. Buyer company's system issues debit instructions on its bank account for payment to the supplier. The buyer's bank credits seller's bank with the cost of sale though a payment gateway or through RTGS system. Similar series of transaction processes are also initiated between the company and its dealers and their respective banks.

Once e-commerce relationship is established between the firms, the transactions of the type can be processed with minimal human intervention and on 24 hours a day and 7 day a week basis. New business models are emerging in B2B domain. There are portals which offer a meeting ground to buyers and sellers of different products in supply chain, more like a buyer-seller meet in international business. This has enabled relatively smaller companies to enter the global market. Banks in the portal offer financial services for deals settled through the portal. Technology and networking are important constituents of a B2B type of business domain. Earlier, only large firms could have access to such technology and they used private networks with interface to each other for information flow and transaction processing.

A major concern used to be compatibility of EDI platforms across different B2B partners. Internet with WWW and other standard technology have offered opportunity to relatively smaller and medium sized firms to integrate their operations in B2B model and take advantage of the benefits it offers. It has also led to standardization of software platforms. Other new forms of business models in B2B domain are Application Service Providers (ASP) and Service Integrators. ASPs offer application software online to ecommerce companies who pay for the same according to the use without owning it. Often entire back office processing is taken care of by ASPs and other service integrators.

However, the utility of such service providers will to a large extent depend on the business strategy of the e-venture. The concerns of B2B e-commerce are similar to those of B2C, discussed earlier. The security issues are more pronounced because of high value transfers taking place through the net. So also are the issues relating to privacy of information, law, tax repudiation etc. The other issues of importance to a B2B firm are the choice of appropriate technology, the issue of build or outsource, maintenance and training of personnel, etc., since they involve large investments and are critical to success. Several studies have attempted to assess the relative importance of B2B and B2C business domains.

There is wide difference in estimates of volume of business transacted over Internet and its components under B2C and B2B. However, most studies agree that volume of transactions in B2B domain far exceeds that in B2C. This is expected result. There is also a growing opinion that the future of e-business lies in B2B domain, as compared to B2C. This has several reasons some of which are already discussed earlier, like low penetration of PCs to households, low bandwidth availability etc., in a large part of the world. The success of B2C ventures depends to a large extent on the shopping habits of people in different parts of the world. A survey sponsored jointly by Confederation of Indian Industries and Infrastructure Leasing and Financial Services on e-commerce in India in 1999 made the following observations. 62% of PC owners and 75% of PC non-owners but who have access to Internet would not buy through the net, as they were not sure of the product offered.

The same study estimated the size of B2B business in India by the year 2001 to be varying between Rs. 250 billion to Rs. 500 billion. In a recent study done by Arthur Anderson, it has been estimated that 84% of total e-business revenue is generated from B2B segment and the growth prospects in this segment are substantial. It has estimated the revenues to be anywhere between US $ 2.7 trillion to over US $ 7 trillion within the next three years.

THE GROWTH OF INTERNET BANKING AND COMMON PRODUCTS

Internet Banking is a product of e-commerce in the field of banking and financial services. In what can be described as B2C domain for banking industry, Internet Banking offers different online services like balance enquiry, requests for cheque books, recording stop-payment instructions, balance transfer instructions, account opening and other forms of traditional banking services. Mostly, these are traditional services offered through Internet as a new delivery channel. Banks are also offering payment services on behalf of their customers who shop in different e-shops, emalls etc. Further, different banks have different levels of such services offered, starting from level-1 where only information is disseminated through Internet to level-3 where online transactions are put through. Hence, I-banking concerns in B2B domain are discussed.

Considering the volume of business e-commerce, particularly in B2B domain, has been generating, it is natural that banking would position itself in an intermediary role in settling the transactions and offering other trade related services.

This is true both in respect of B2C and B2B domains. Besides, the traditional role of financial intermediary and settlement agents, banks have also exploited new opportunities offered by Internet in the fields of integrated service providers, payment gateway services, etc. However, the process is still evolving and banks are repositioning themselves based on new emerging e-commerce business models. In B2B scenario, a new form of e-commerce market place is emerging where various players in the production and distribution chain are positioning themselves and are achieving a kind of integration in business information flow and processing (STP or near STP) leading to efficiencies in the entire supply chain and across industries. Banks are positioning themselves in such a market in order to be a part of the financial settlements arising out of transactions of this market and providing wholesale financial services.

This needs integration of business information flow not only across the players in the supply chain, but with the banks as well. With the integration of business information flow and higher degree of transparency, the banks and other financial services institutions have lost some of the information advantage they used to enjoy and factor in to pricing of their products. However, such institutions have the advantage of long standing relationships, goodwill and brand, which are important sources of assurance in a virtual market. Banks are in fact, converting this goodwill into a business component in e-commerce scenario in providing settlement and other financial services. Some banks have also moved to providing digital certificates for transactions through e-markets. Banks' strategies in B2B market are responses to different business models emerging in e-commerce. A recent study by Arthur Andersen shows that banks and financial service institutions generally adopt one of three business models to respond to e-business challenges.

In the first place, they treat it as an extension of existing business without any significant changes other than procedural and what technology demands. The second strategy takes the same approach as the first but introduces structural changes to the underlying business. In the third approach banks launch e-business platform as a different business from the existing core business and as a different brand of product. There is no definite answer as to which approach is appropriate. Perhaps it depends on the type of market the bank is operating, its existing competencies and the legal and regulatory environment. It is, however, sure that e-banking is evolving beyond the traditional limits of banking and many new products/ services are likely to emerge as ecommerce matures.

E-COMMERCE DEVELOPMENT

The literature onf *e-service* has by and large followed the commercial thrust of Internet marketing development. Initially, the most common application by firms and use by users was through the website itself, often a basic overview of the company and more in keeping with having a public relations 'presence' in the e-commerce world.

The next most common application was to post more detailed information about products, and conversely this was the second most common use by users. The third wave of application is the now dominant interest in e-selling, that is, the use of the Web to sell or buy goods. This takes us to the fourth and emerging wave, one that is still greatly underutilized, namely e-service.

Essentially, e-service offers the potential for some of the more advanced applications of Internet technology. For example, firms could use intelligent agents to provide extraordinary service, by tracking and datamining previous histories through Internet sites and developing known patterns of users' requirements. Customer relationships can be developed, based on prior 'modelled' understanding of which offers a consumer is likely to respond to.

This is a special case of market segmentation to a market of one. As another application of work by Brookes *et al.* referred to in Cravens *et al.* (2000, p. 4), a manufacturer of washing machines could include in its warranty agreement the electronic capability of monitoring the ongoing usage of the machine.

Suppose that, after the machine has been bought, the household has a new baby. If detergent dosage or load patterns place strain on the motor, the machine could have the built-in communication capability to automatically page the manufacturer's service depot. The depot receives a message for a service representative to visit the household and adjust the washing machine before it becomes a problem. In this way, while both the information technologies and the servicing component are largely unobtrusive to the household, they are nonetheless essential to maintaining customer satisfaction and potential loyalty.

The literature has started to discuss e-service, but it is somewhat unstructured. For this reason, a review of the literature plays a particularly important front-end role and we provide a simple classification of the literature to assist. We have included a separate section debating whether self-service is a myth for e-service. Our own position on this matter is made clear. We follow the literature review with a proposed, more systematic, typology of e-service, which could be useful to readers.

THREE APPROACHES TO E-SERVICE

We have identified three types of e-service literature. The first is what we call the *macro* or *very broad view* of e-service, namely that e-service is effectively synonymous with e-commerce. An *intermediate view* of e-service is that we can study the provision of *specialist services* made available by *specialist service providers* that help service Internet users (both individuals and companies). The third perspective on e-service is what we term a *micro perspective*, namely the provision of particular and varied detailed customer services within a site as *part* of the website - user interface.

At the broadest level is the view that e-commerce per se is an electronic service to customers - one that provides greater convenience. This view places e-commerce as an option available to customers, providing another channel of distribution or information. For example, instead of spending, say, an hour to physically access and purchase from a bookstore, the customer has the option to purchase the same electronically. As a further example, a company may use the Web to provide information about the company's offering to assist consumers in their product search, without necessarily enabling the consumer to purchase through the Web.

A related macro view of e-service is the *services marketing* perspective on e-retailing. They argue that e-retail offerings are service offerings and exhibit many of the same characteristics as other non-Internet-based services. They further argue that Internet services can be evaluated by similar criteria, such as responsiveness, empathy and the establishment of trust through courtesy and competency. The principal service provided by e-retailers is a search and evaluation facility that potentially saves time and effort for the consumer. The task of the e-retailer is to provide a website design that caters to different shopping styles, provides evidence to reduce risk and also educates the user in a shopping mode that may differ to what they are used to in conventional retail shopping.

There is now a considerable number of papers that have applied the macro perspective of e-service to a specific industry. For example, Muir and Douglas (2001) have studied how service delivery has changed in legal services with the rise of e-commerce. They argue that the quality of service is potentially improved with the Web. A Web presence allows legal practices to be more transparent and to offer greater access to information for customers by way of improving their services. It is suggested that this improved communication may lead to a reduction in complaints against solicitors.An *intermediate perspective* of e-service is the provision of *electronic services* from *specialist providers* to users of the Internet and intranets. Thus we have a market (external or internal) in which key electronic services are similar to products and sold or exchanged in a market to general users of the Web. here is a huge variety of specialist firms that offer their services (products) to Web users.

Web designers form a stereotypical group in this category, but also included are all types of suppliers of a wide range of Internet services, such as portal providers or providers of any specific link in the Internet network. For example, consider the commercial services offered by Compuserve, Prodigy, America Online and e-world. The pages of the national financial newspapers are filled with the advertisements of companies offering such Web-enabling services, some claiming to offer an integrated service.Electronic trust services are specialist e-services that provide reassurance and trust to the financial and privacy security of Internet information flow. There is a number of third-party commercial service providers who guarantee protection of either the financial security or the personal confidentiality of information flows.

A special case of this situation is the role of the electronic signature, an issue discussed by Travers (2001), who is particularly concerned with the status, planning and implementation of electronic signatures, in the context of the UK Electronic Communications Act 2000. He argues that electronic signatures can be considered within a knowledge management framework and proposes a six-part system that incorporates people, clients, knowledge matters, business development and training. Travers notes that the Electronic Communications Act provides:

- An approvals scheme for businesses providing cryptography services such as electronic signature services and confidentiality services;
- For the legal recognition of electronic signatures and the process under which they are verified; and

- For the removal of obstacles in other legislation to the use of electronic communications and storage in place of paper.

A somewhat unusual example of a specialist e-service is the provision of electronic money (Buck, 1997), which could be redefined as a trust-service, but Buck did not do so in his paper. He notes that there is a range of online payment systems, including credit systems (e.g. Payflow Pro), debit systems (e.g. BankNet), token-based mechanisms (e.g. Digicash) and electronic cash schemes (e.g. Mondex). Such mechanisms vary considerably in terms of safety, privacy protection and trustworthiness.

An example of a specialist e-service within an internal market is that of an e-mail-mediated help service (Hahn 1998). Hahn analysed 265 help-service responses from service logs and found, among other things, that users and help-service staff held different internal models for ideal e-mail communication. Users desired a fairly simple exchange of communication, that is, a clear question followed by a quick, simple response. Staff, on the other hand, envisaged the need for a more complex interrelationship, over several messages.

This takes us to the third perspective of e-service, namely the *micro* approach. Perhaps the dominant element in this field is the role of information. Some authors see information-based marketing as a potential competitive advantage. Other scholars see the Web as important for tracking and gathering customer feedback (Sampson, 1998; Sen *et al.*, 1998). Still other writers focus on the role of e-information as an aid to facilitating consumer search.

It is particularly in Merrilees (2002) that a broader perspective is given to interactivity. He embraces a more multi-dimensional approach to the concept of interactivity. Included factors are two-way communication between the e-retailer and the user; the ability of each party to communicate with the other including through e-mail; the ability to personalize the situation for the individual user; and the ability of the individual to control the communication and learn from it.

Finally, there are numerous other Internet studies that emphasize particular aspects of e-service besides information or interactivity. For example Mols (2000), in his study of Danish retail banking, examined the role of more individualized services for consumers and their need for a close relationship with the bank. As a final example of a difficult-to-classify study of providing services on the Internet see Mathur (1998) who takes a financial accounting approach to the topic.

In summary, we have used our three-part classification of macro, intermediate and micro as an initial way of structuring the literature, as it exists. This is not to say that we endorse all perspectives of the literature. In particular we have reservations about the macro perspective. In a sense, the use of the World Wide Web by a retailer to market its organization as an online e-retailer is no more a services marketing exercise than the use of catalogues makes

Lands End a services marketer. The *service component for an e-retailer* is the sum total of the ancillary support mechanisms provided by the retailer and the channel intermediaries to aid the Web prospective buyer to select, pay for and receive the merchandise.

The e-retailer may provide services for the consumption of the prospective buyer through the Web channel, but this still does not make the channel a service unto itself. Thus we prefer the intermediate and micro perspectives of initial classification and our empirical research design is more in keeping with the micro perspective. A more refined taxonomy of e-services is developed below.

BRITISH LIBRARY (WWW.BL.UK)

This is a free service provided by the British Library in London that includes a 'turn the page' function. This technology is new to websites and is only available for three articles at the time of going to press. The home page offers a range of services provided by the library and is easy to use with simple menu selection and navigation.

Of interest is the 'turn the pages' of Leonardo da Vinci's notebook. This technology displays a scanned image of the original notebook and allows the user to turn pages using the cursor in a way similar to a real book. To enter this site, select 'turn the pages' on the home page and follow the instruction. To use this facility a Shockwave driver is required and can be downloaded free in two minutes from the same site. This is an interesting site for those who are interested in history.

A SECOND TAXONOMY OF E-SERVICE

We initially used a three-way classification of the e-service literature, namely macro, intermediate and micro, as a way of sorting the literature in this fragmented domain.

Our thinking on this topic has progressed to another proposed taxonomy of e-service. Not all of the aspects covered in this taxonomy are addressed in the empirical part. Taxonomy is put forward as an initial framework that can be debated by interested academics or practitioners.

THE SELF-SERVICE MYTH

Before leaving the literature, it is useful to discuss a crucial issue in the e-service area referred to by Moon and Frei (2000). They give the example of customers visiting a typical airline website and being confronted by a self-service search engine. If they know exactly when and where they want to travel, the website will generate a list of feasible flights. However, the search process becomes complex if they wish to find the cheapest airfare and are flexible on the dates and destinations. Moon and Frei are sceptical of the usefulness of the self-service approach to e-service and suggest that the customer is likely to have a much more satisfying experience if they call the airline's call centre for handling more complex situations.

Co-production is proposed by Moon and Frei (2000:26) as a better model than self-service for e-commerce. In the co-production model the company undertakes many of the tasks in shopping and buying, relieving the burden on the customer. The new model recognizes that, although customers like having choices, they do not want too many and appreciate pre-screened alternatives geared to their needs. Co-production also understands that customers want to state their preferences only once. Moon and Frei conclude that e-commerce firms should focus on customer service *not* self-service, and give illustrative examples of companies like Dell Computer Corporation. Dell performs a host of back-end transactions that are invisible to customers, such as grouping products by customer segments and displaying only in-stock items.

The current authors tend to endorse the sentiment of Moon and Frei in that we agree that it would be foolish for owners of e-sites to provide a minimalist infrastructure and simply to let users do their own thing. Our only objection is what to call the 'co-production model'. We are content to keep calling it a *self-service model*, but one that is designed appropriately and optimally.

Indeed, we believe that the challenge is for e-commerce firms to strive for an optimal self-service design capability. For a very interesting and relevant study, see Dabholkar (2000). His review of research into what consumers want from technologically-based self-service options suggests that speed, control and privacy are generally required. However, two additional attributes that positively influence the attitude of consumers towards computer technology are ease of use and fun or enjoyment. Web designers searching for the most effective design are advised to consult Dabholkar (2000).

We should point out that the same issue has been debated with conventional retailing. Some *weak* retailers have taken the view that *self-service* equals *no service* and have provided very little help to consumers, using the opportunity to reduce their costs (in particular fewer sales staff). This approach will only leave consumers frustrated and unable to find what they want and so they are likely to leave the store very unhappy. In contrast, as Merrilees and Miller (1996) note, for better-performing stores 'self-service' does not mean 'no service'. The best self-service stores, like IKEA, Wal-Mart and many superstores, appreciate that self-service needs to be designed in such a way that it delivers good service, albeit of a kind other than personalized service.

Thus *good self-service design* in *conventional retailing* includes a well-organized store, with good layout, good signage, helpful visual displays and ready access to product information. Merrilees and Miller (2001) have argued that the approach taken by superstores represents a new self-service paradigm of retail service. Broadly speaking, the same good self-service design principles readily transfer from conventional retailing to e-retailing.

E-SERVICE PERFORMANCE

Knowing what is meant by e-service is an important first step in managing an e-retail business. However, it is necessary to take another step, namely the measurement of how well an organization is performing in each e-service activity. At this point it is clear that we only have a limited understanding of which e-service functions are important to consumers and how well e-retailers deliver these services. Some much-needed new research, namely a study of critical incidents in e-service delivery. Our critical incident analysis is followed by an examination of the role of e-service metrics as a management tool. In turn we discuss an alternative measure of e-service performance, namely e-retail service quality.

A CRITICAL INCIDENT APPROACH TO E-SERVICE PERFORMANCE

This section outlines the results of new research initiated especially for this book. A content analysis of 138 e-retail sites was undertaken by four judges in order to assess the nature and effectiveness of e-service across those sites. It was suggested that a good way of getting started might be with book, music, gift and department store sites, because these represent a high share of the e-selling transaction activity. The final discretion as to sites chosen was left to the individual judges. The main criterion for selection as a judge was expertise in analysing e-retailer websites.

Notwithstanding each judge's expertise, further controls were built into the evaluation process through careful briefing and training of the judges. This briefing included careful instruction to make sure that all items were fully understood by each judge and that all judges had the same meaning for each. Another instruction was that each judge was to spend about 10 to 15 minutes moving through the site to understand its features and its content before answering the various set questions. Each site was analysed in the same way.

A survey instrument (protocol) was designed for each judge to use with each site. A wide number of site attributes were assessed on a Likert scale of 1 to 7, depending on whether the judge agreed or not that the site performed well on a particular attribute. There was also an open-ended section of the survey instrument where the focus was on the overall level of e-service for the site, based on a 1 to 7 Likert scale. On the same page the judge was asked to describe up to three important critical incidents/areas that positively contributed to their assessment of the overall level of e-service. Additionally, up to three important critical incidents could be listed that detracted from the level of e-service.

POSITIVE CRITICAL INCIDENTS

Initially we present the incidents that positively contributed to e-service. We do this in two ways. First we can note those positive facilitators to e-service across the *total* sample of 138 sites. We also break the results into *high-service sites* and *low-service sites*. High-service sites are those sites that were rated highly on the basis of the perceived overall level of e-service, that is, those sites that scored a 5, 6 or 7 out of 7. Those sites that scored 1 to 4 were called low-service sites. Across the total 138 sites, the three most positive incidents that contributed to e-service were:

- Interactivity and communication (56 per cent of all sites);
- Special offers (33 per cent);
- information (20 per cent).
- The next most important batch included:
- Variety of items for sale (14 per cent);
- Frequently asked questions (FAQs) (a separate type of interactivity) (12 per cent);
- Ease of use (12 per cent).

Other less important facilitators of e-service included security/privacy references (8 per cent), goods delivery (7 per cent) and returns policy (4 per cent). If we compare high-service and low-service sites, we more or less get a similar picture of what is important. One key difference is that the number of positive incidents of good e-service is a lot lower in low-service sites. Thus interactivity and special offers remain the highest two facilitators of good e-service, but the rate of incidence is about twice as much in high-service sites.

For example, in low-service sites there is a 27 per cent incidence of interactivity (compared to 72 per cent in high-service sites) and a 20 per cent incidence of special offers (compared to 39 per cent in high-service sites). A number of key determinants of e-service in high-service sites are downgraded in low-service sites. These include information, FAQ, security/privacy and returns.

NEGATIVE CRITICAL INCIDENTS

Apart from coding those elements of e-service that contribute to the overall level of e-service of a site, we have also analysed those elements that have reduced the overall level of e-service. We have retained the same classification of elements, but now we refer to negative critical incidents. That is, interactivity now refers to a lack of interactivity or a low level of service from this element. The same applies to the other eight elements of e-service.

The pecking order of negative critical incidents that affect overall e-service. The two most important negative incidents are a narrow variety of goods for sale (15 per cent of sites had this problem) and poor delivery service (14 per cent of sites). Other problem areas of e-service included interactivity (11 per cent), information (10 per cent), ease of use (8 per cent) and returns policy (8 per cent). The other three elements, FAQ, security/privacy and special offers, were rarely mentioned as a negative incident.

We have extended this analysis to a comparison of high-service and low-service sites. As we would expect, the number of negative incidents is almost thrice as great in the low-service sites. Variety and delivery were the top biggest problem areas for both types of sites, but had an incidence rate of less than 10 per cent in the high-service sites (compared to more than a quarter of the low-service sites). For the rest of the e-service elements, the most notable difference in the rankings is that of ease of use. It was the equal third highest problem area among low-service sites, but the lowest (and almost non-existent with a 1 per cent incidence) among the high-service sites.

LOGISTIC REGRESSION OF HIGH-LOW SERVICE SITES

We can extend our analysis from an enumeration of the critical incident elements (as a form of Pareto analysis), to a binary logistic regression analysis in which we can predict which sites fall into the high-service or low-service categories. The dependent variable is binary (either one type of site or the other). The independent variables are the nine dummy variables denoting positive critical incidents and the nine dummy variables denoting negative critical incidents.

Overall the degree of explanation is high, with an adjusted coefficient of determination of 0.53. Nine of the dummy variables were significant at the 5 per cent level. The model predicts very well, with an 88 per cent hit rate. The six major e-service elements that shunt a firm into either a high-service or low-service category were:

- Positive interactivity incidents
- Negative information incidents
- Negative delivery incidents
- Negative interactivity incidents
- Negative ease of use incidents
- Positive FAQ incidents.

In addition, less important influences were positive information incidents, positive special deals and negative variety of items for sale incidents.

Multiple Regression Analysis of Overall Service Rating

Given that we have recorded the actual overall service rating of the site, on a 1 to 7 scale, we can also analyse the data with conventional multiple regression analysis, with the overall service rating as the dependent variable and the same independent variables as before. This is another way of testing the robustness of our results, although the logistic regression and the multiple Ordinary Least Squares (OLS) are testing slightly different models and therefore we would not expect exactly the same results to be produced. the results. The adjusted coefficient of determination is good, at 0.56. Eight variables were significant. The six most important e-service elements explaining the overall service rating were:

- Positive interactivity incidents
- Negative delivery incidents
- Negative ease of use incidents
- Negative information incidents
- Positive information incidents
- Negative interactivity incidents.

Additionally, positive variety of the offerings had a marginal influence on overall service rating, while positive deals and negative variety of items were not quite significant.

If we compare we see that essentially the same elements are at work. However there are slight differences, with some elements appearing in one table only, and the pecking order changing marginally. For example, a positive FAQ service might elevate an e-retailer into the high-service category, but did not have any discernible influence on the overall rating regression.

E-SERVICE METRICS: A MANAGEMENT TOOL

Our research in the previous section revealed that interactivity was overwhelmingly important for achieving a perception of high e-service. This finding is even stronger when we add frequently asked questions (FAQs) to its role because this is a form of interactivity. In a sense the emphasis on interactivity is akin to the importance of personal service in the conventional literature. Interestingly, personal service was found to be the most important type of customer service in conventional retailing. Interactivity in the e-context includes two-way communication, the ability of the e-retailer to communicate to the user and the ability of the user to communicate with the e-retailer, responsiveness in answering questions (including the special case of FAQ) and personalization of the process.

Even without measurement, interactivity is clearly a good candidate as a capstone element in a powerful e-service programme. Similarly, we recommend that an e-retailer should audit its interactivity every year or so, along the lines suggested in the previous section (using, say, a critical incident analysis). If interactivity is found to be too low or not as high as desired, then steps can be undertaken to increase it, through, for example, increased customization or other means.

A second key finding of our research study is that interactivity needs to be supported by special offers, information, variety of items for sale and ease of use, as part of an integrated approach to e-service. An e-service audit of an e-retail site should incorporate all components of e-service.

A third key finding of our research is also very important for the practice of good e-service. We have shown that it is not sufficient to create and manage *positive e-service experiences*. Equally, the firm's e-commerce strategy needs to be able to handle *negative critical incidents*. The first point is that *even high-*

service sites experience periodic problems in e-service. Show that high-service sites, while generally having a very high (72 per cent) positive incidence of interactivity, nonetheless had a 6 per cent (that is, non-zero) incidence of negative interactivity. The same pattern occurs in the areas of product variety and delivery. Firms need to take steps to continuously improve (that is, lower) the rate of negative incidents. Ideally, more interactivity may need to be built in if all other aspects of interactivity fail - this is the ultimate approach to service-failure recovery. Perhaps it is a toll-free phone service that is needed as a service in the last resort?

A fourth key finding of our research that needs to be carefully considered by websites is that the solution for sites attempting to increase their e-service capability is not simply to *add* more information, an FAQ service or similar facility. Such actions are a necessary, though insufficient condition to becoming a high-service site. Take information, for example. Information incidents, both positive and negative, were important in determining membership of the e-retailer in a high-service or low-service category and the overall level of e-service of the site. Yet there was only a slight difference (and one that was *not* statistically significant) in the quantity of information across high-service and low-service sites. This suggests that the problem for some sites is not the *quantity* of information, but rather the *quality* and *relevance* of information. Thus the high rate (20 per cent) of negative incidents about information on the low-service sites may be due to overemphasis on the wrong information, that is, the wrong details, rather than the lack of information in general.

In summary, we suggest that e-retailers should regularly monitor or audit all of their e-service, at least as frequently as annually. The critical incident approach is a simple way of doing this and the method is robust because it captures both positive and negative incidents in e-service. Notwithstanding the merit of this approach, there are alternative ways of evaluating e-service and we turn to one of those in the next section.

E-RETAIL SERVICE QUALITY: AN ALTERNATIVE PERFORMANCE METRIC

Retail service quality entails the application of service quality as both a concept and measure to retailing. The landmark study in this respect is Dabholkar *et al*. (1996). One advantage of using a measure of (retail) service quality is that it represents a composite measure, pulling together a number of components of service, such as personal service, store design and problem-solving. So, instead of having to say that six or seven or whatever components of service are performing at the individual service level, we can combine our assessment into a composite service quality measure.More recently, researchers have extended their scope of retail service quality from conventional retailing to also include Internet or e-retailing. These studies include Zeithaml *et al.* (2000), Francis and White (2002a; 2002b), Janda *et al.* (2002) and Wolfinbarger and Gilly (2002). Each study uses slightly different dimensions (or items under each heading) of e-retail service quality, but generally the dimensions include:

- Website design
- Security
- Ordering system
- Delivery system
- Communication.

The five dimensions of e-retail service quality provide an umbrella approach for e-retailers wishing to use an alternative measure of e-service performance. We offer no view as to whether this approach or the critical incident approach is better. Indeed, e-retailers could quite easily use both sets of metrics to evaluate their e-service, as they complement each other.At the time of going to press a major new article on e-retail quality has appeared, namely Wolfinbarger and Gilly (2003). This article seems to be the most comprehensive and methodical of all of the articles in this field and so we should highlight its findings. Four components of e-retail quality were identified, namely:

- Website design (navigation, order processing, personalization);
- Fulfilment/reliability (receipt of correct goods, delivery on time);
- Privacy/security (security of credit card payments and privacy of shared information);
- Customer service (responsive to customer inquiries).

In terms of the predictive power of these four components, two of them (website design and fulfilment) were found to be the most important in contributing to overall quality, satisfaction and return purchases.

ADDITIONAL GUIDANCE ON PRACTICAL E-SERVICE PROVISION

A number of practical tools that could help the improved delivery of e-service for e-retailers. First, key concepts, such as interactivity and delivery, have been highlighted as having special importance. Second, the idea of e-service metrics is another practical tool ready for actual use by e-retailers. In addition to these ideas and tools, the reader might wish to consult a number of 'how to' books, including Sterne (1996), Cusack (1998) and Zemke and Connellan (2001).

We have analysed the total number of websites in the sample as well as sub-samples of *high-service* and *low-service* websites. We have also contrasted *positive* critical incidents from *negative* critical incidents. Perhaps an unexpected result, we found that the main e-service elements that drive positive e-service are *not* the same as the elements that cause negative critical incidents in e-service. Interactivity in particular, strongly supported by special offers and information about the product and firm, was the key component of positive e-service. In contrast, negative e-service experiences were most often associated with a lack of variety of items for sale and poor delivery arrangements.

We have suggested that interactivity could be the key capstone element for e-retailers trying to build a powerful e-service programme, with support from information, ease of use, variety and special offers. There is also a need to manage *service-failure recovery*, that is, the myriad of negative critical incidents. This may lead to the ultimate form of interactivity - namely an interactive service that handles the collective failure in all the other interactive mechanisms.

Two different taxonomies or classifications were used to explore the nature of e-services. We also argued that self-service is not a myth for e-services and should not be taken for granted. It needs to be properly designed to genuinely help the e-customer. Further, evaluating e-service performance is important for e-retailers, if they are to fully understand what attributes are needed by customers. Two different ways of measuring e-service performance were given, namely a critical incident approach and an e-retail service quality approach.

CASE STUDY : LEGAL SERVICES: BELL LEGAL GROUP (WWW.BELLLEGAL.COM.AU)

This is a legal services site of the Bell Legal Group on the Gold Coast, Australia, that offers a full range of legal services from corporate to individual issues. The site is typical of a service provider with a professional appearance and an abundance of information on the services that they provide. This site differs from many others due to the music and voice commentary on the home page.

The menu offers: our people, a group that lists employees' qualifications and experience with portrait photographs. It has the usual menu selection for contacts and queries with linked pages to a large range of predominantly Government websites related to legal matters ranging from privacy codes to taxation issues. The notion of providing an extra service through linkages to established sites is a fairly easy and cost-effective way of adding value to customers. Essentially it is a public service that is an option available to any e-commerce firm.

MOTORING ORGANIZATION: RAC (WWW.RAC.CO.UK)

This is a UK motoring organization that offers a range of services from breakdown to insurance coverage. The site is representative of a large organization that offers a multitude of services and requires careful navigation to locate particular information. This is made even more difficult with the amount of linked advertising and special deals scattered over the pages. If followed carefully the menu items on each page are self-explanatory and will lead to the desired location. The site is typical of similar motoring organizations worldwide that offer online services and information on their core and related products. While some of the site is intended to gain customers, there are some parts could be seen as public service, such as traffic conditions.

The home page includes connection to localities, insurance for vehicles, property and holidays, motoring information for breakdown, technical reports and car care, holiday information, accommodation deals, vehicle hire, ship/airline bookings and tours. It also covers a range of finance options for loans and insurances as well as legal matters. The site is interesting enough, with standout colours, and is complemented with related photographs, coupled with an abundance of graphic deals.

ARCHITECTURE OF E-COMMERCE SYSTEMS

The buying and selling of products and services over the Internet is termed 'online trading'. Online trading or e-Commerce is important to businesses because it provides a flexible source of trading with customers, and with business partners. To enable online trading, companies need to combine existing computerized transaction processing systems and information systems with Internet and Web technology. Existing computerized systems, databases, and Internet and Web technology are the basic components of online trading and form the architecture of e-Commerce systems. Computer system architecture consists of hardware and software components that are configured in terms of the needs of organizations.

Companies connect computers to a LAN, WAN and the Internet, using TCP/ IP, based on client-server architecture, to share computer software, printers or scanners. Basic Internet tools such as e-mail, browsers, search engines and protocols such as file transfer protocol (FTP) and Telnet are combined to form the system architecture for e-Commerce.

The systems architecture for a company will depend on its trading activities. A retail company will have a different architecture from a manufacturing company or a service company. As a company changes and evolves its mission or objectives, its e-Commerce system architecture will need to change too. Alternatively, the stimulus to change may come from competitors who use the most modern e-Commerce technology.

INTERNET, E-COMMERCE SYSTEMS AND INFORMATION SYSTEMS

Some of the terms used to describe a company's involvement with the Internet are that it has 'an online presence' or it has 'a Web site'. Such terms hide the complex IT and IS that form the infrastructure that underpin e-Commerce systems.

An information system is the application of a computer to capture and process data to provide information for managers and executives for the purposes of decision making and management. A company will normally have various information systems, such as an airline reservation system or an inventory control system. These systems will be linked to a corporate database that stores relevant data, like product or customer details. A company's Web site is connected to such information systems and databases to provide the essential product or service information for customer and employee use.

Companies' existing client-server technology and its IS/IT infrastructure is connected to the Internet to form part of an e-Commerce architecture. The e-Commerce architecture is based on a company's business model, consisting of the basic logic of what it wants to produce or sell, how it will market it, how it defines its customers and other fundamental business issues. IT is combined with Internet technology to enable a company to personalize its service to a customer.

DATABASES

A computer database consists of records on specific items of interest, for example customers' contact details or the products they have bought. It is a collection of data that can be queried for specific purposes such as targeting a particular customer for certain products. Databases are used to market products and services. This is termed *database marketing*. Databases are used to store data on the purchasing habits of customers and enable a company to develop a tailored relationship with its customers. The data are then processed to provide tailored information on individual customers' preferences that are then sent information about products or services relevant to their current buying habits. Data-mining techniques are used to reprocess existing data in databases to extract previously unrealized information of potential commercial use.

E-COMMERCE SYSTEMS AND THE CUSTOMER

e-Commerce systems that interface with the customer need to be pragmatic. The selection and evaluation of Internet technology need to be appropriate to both the company's needs and the customer's ability to use the system. A good business model will assume that the customer has little interest in technology and avoid the technology trap.

Avoiding the technology trap. It is not user-friendly to use over-complex Internet and Web technology in e-Commerce systems. The technology needs to be appropriate to prevent prolonging the time it takes for customers' commands to be executed by the system.

WEB SITE EVALUATION SOFTWARE

It is possible to measure the popularity of a company's Web site using evaluation software that generates log files. Such log files record the number of visitors to the site or page impressions. They record which parts of the Web site are most popular, the times of the day people visit, record which search engines are being used by visitors and how long they spend on the site, known as the 'stickiness' of the site. These log files can subsequently be used to evaluate the performance of the site from a business perspective and the information can be used to make it easier for customers to make transactions.

INTERNET SERVICE PROVIDERS

A company wanting to trade over the Internet has to agree a contract with an Internet service provider (ISP). ISPs provide communication and hosting services for individuals and companies wanting to access the Internet. ISPs provide access to the Internet and enable Internet commerce by connecting individuals and companies to the Internet. There are thousands of ISPs that a company can choose from, all of them providing domain name services and electronic mail. The two most popular ISPs are UUNET Technologies and AT&T World Net. Other organizations, like a bank with mainframe computers, may also act as an ISP.

ISPs also provide hosting services for Web sites by installing and operating the server computers and software for a company. The computers and software are located at the ISP's site. Transaction services such as payment systems or order capture and fulfilment are also provided by ISPs.

EXAMPLE OF E-COMMERCE ARCHITECTURE

The important considerations for designing e-Commerce architecture are the customer, the company, the company's existing information systems and how payment will be made. For example, a company with a Web site that includes an order form would need a Web server that can provide a catalogue, whose details would be retrieved from a catalogue database, and order form.

It would need to interface with an existing database to collect and record the order details entered by the customer. The payment might be transacted with a credit card whose details would be captured on the order form utilizing standard security features available on the Web.

This example shows that an e-Commerce system is composed of existing information systems, databases and Internet technology. Other sophisticated e-Commerce architectures are possible for companies that need distributed transaction processing. For example, the Open Buying Consortium (OBI) has proposed a system architecture consisting of six fundamental system components split into buy-side, the customer and sell-side activities. These components are: Browse, Request, Approve, Fill, Receive and Pay.

E-COMMERCE SECURITY TECHNOLOGY

The success of e-Commerce depends on the security of data like personal details and credit card numbers transmitted over the Internet. The domain name system Internet protocol that makes IP addresses readable by humans is insecure. Security measures need to be taken in e-Commerce systems to prevent compromising the systems. Some of these measures include building firewalls, incorporating cryptography and authentication, and using secure connections.

Firewall

A firewall is hardware and software that are used to secure a private computer network system from uninvited intruders. A firewall is used to control whether a client is permitted to connect to the private network it protects.

Cryptography

Cryptography is a science that provides secure communication over vulnerable channels. Cryptography is fundamental to the success of the Internet and e-Commerce. Governments regulate cryptographic technology because of its importance to national security.

In cryptography a message, like a credit card number, is encrypted using a key and the encrypted message is transmitted. The receiver uses the key to decrypt the message and convert it back to its original form. The basic elements of a cryptographic system are algorithms, protocols and key management. An example of key management is the secret-key encryption algorithms. These algorithms are 'secret' because only the receiver and sender know the secret key.

Cryptography is used to provide secure transmission of data over the Internet. Private data like credit card details or digital signatures are encrypted and then transmitted over the Internet. Cryptography can keep a message secret and act as a gateway for identifying senders and receivers. It provides the secure electronic transaction technology for credit card transactions on the Internet.

Authentication

Authentication procedures are used to establish the identity of an individual or another computer system. Authentication procedures can be hardware-or software-based. Authentication procedures make use of personal items of knowledge or possession such as secret names or birth dates. Good authentication systems make use of two-factor authentication, such as a place name and memorable date known to the user. Some banking systems make use of three-factor authentication before allowing customers to make online account transfers.

Secure Socket Layer

The secure socket layer (SSL) is a layer of security between the application and the transport protocol. The purpose of SSL is to enable secure and reliable data transmission and communication over the Internet. The SSL provides private connection, making use of encryption and secret-key cryptography.

Authentication in SSL is achieved using public-key cryptography, which consists of a private key that is never made public chosen by one participant in the data exchange, and a public key chosen by the other participant in the exchange. Either key may be used for encryption. Reliability of data transmission is achieved by using secure hash functions like SHA or MD5. Secure hash functions check the integrity of a message. SSL is commonly used in e-Commerce systems.

INTERNET BANKING ON BANK

Internet technology holds the potential to fundamentally change banks and the banking industry. An extreme view speculates that the Internet will destroy old models of how bank services are developed and delivered. The widespread availability of Internet banking is expected to affect the mixture of financial services produced by banks, the manner in which banks produce these services and the resulting financial performances of these banks.

Whether or not this extreme view proves correct and whether banks take advantage of this new technology will depend on their assessment of the profitability of such a delivery system for their services. In addition, industry analysis outlining the potential impact of Internet banking on cost savings, revenue growth and risk profile of the banks have also generated considerable interest and speculation about the impact of the Internet on the banking industry. Banking through internet has emerged as a strategic resource for achieving higher efficiency, control of operations and reduction of cost by replacing paper based and labour intensive methods with automated processes thus leading to higher productivity and profitability.

However, to date researchers have produced little evidence regarding these potential changes. Nonetheless, recent empirical studies indicate that Internet banking is not having an independent effect on banking profitability, although these findings may change as the use of the Internet becomes more widespread. More recently in India too, a wider array of financial products and services have become available over the Internet, which has thus become an important distribution channel for a number of banks. Banks boost technology investment spending strongly to address revenue, cost and competitiveness concerns. For some activities, banks hope to see a near-term impact on profitability. Other investments are motivated more by a desire to establish a competitive position or avoid falling behind the competition.

The purpose of present study is to analyse such effects of Internet banking in India, where no rigorous attempts have been undertaken to understand this aspect of the banking business. The primary aim is to advance the understanding of how Internet banks are different from the non-Internet banks in terms of profitability, cost efficiency, asset quality and other characteristics by examining bank financial statements from year end 1998 to year end 2006.

The present study tests not only whether the Internet delivery channel affected the financial performance of the commercial banks in our sample, but also how these changes happened. The study examines a comprehensive set of 10 measures of financial performance that allow us to "look inside the black box" of bank performance. By developing a deeper understanding of these phenomena, we can draw more insightful inferences about the impact of the Internet on banking business strategies, production processes and financial performance. Increasing this type of knowledge is vital for both academic literature and also for bank marketers who cannot count on the initial success achieved by the Internet banking investment.

REVIEW OF EXISTING LITERATURE

A few empirical studies exist in the literature, which have examined the relative performance of banks offering Internet banking services. The table also includes the studies which have examined the financial performance of Internetonly banks that do not operate any physical branches. Egland was the first important study, which estimated the number of US banks offering Internet banking and analysed the structure and performance characteristics of these banks. It found no evidence of major differences in the performance of the group of banks offering Internet banking activities compared to those that do not offer such services in terms of profitability, efficiency or credit quality. However, transactional Internet banks differed from other banks primarily by size.

In contrast to the results of Egland, Furst found that banks in all size categories offering Internet banking were generally more profitable and tended to rely less heavily on traditional banking activities in comparison to non-Internet banks.

An exception to the superior performance of Internet banks was the de novo Internet banks, which were less profitable and less efficient than non-Internet de novos.

The authors concluded that Internet banking was too small a factor to have affected banks' profitability. Sullivan found that click and mortar banks in the 10th Federal Reserve District incurred somewhat higher operating expenses but offset these expenses with somewhat higher fee income.

On average, this study found no systematic evidence that banks were either helped or harmed by offering the Internet delivery channel. Similar to the results of Furst *et al.*, this study also found that de novo click and mortar banks performed significantly worse than de novo brick and mortar banks. Using information drawn from banks in Italy, Hasan found that the Internet banking institutions were performing significantly better than the non- Internet groups. Additionally, the risk variables associated with the Internet group continued to be lower relative to the non-Internet group.

The asset-liability variables revealed that on average the banks in this Internet group were larger and had significantly higher trading and investment activities and less dependent on retail deposits (both demand and saving deposits) relative to the non-Internet group. The only category where the Internet group showed a lower performance was the noninterest expense category. It found a significant and positive link between offering of Internet banking activities and banks' profitability and a negative but marginally significant association between the adoption of Internet banking and bank risk levels particularly due to increased diversification. Hernando and Nieto examined the performance of multichannel banks in Spain between 1994 and 2002. The study found higher profitability for multichannel banks through increased commission income, increased brokerage fees and (eventual) reductions in staffing levels and concluded that the Internet channel was a complement to physical banking channels.

In contrast to earlier studies, the multichannel banks in Spain relied more on typical banking business (lending, deposit taking and securities trading). The adoption of the Internet as a delivery channel had a positive impact on banks' profitability after one and a half years of adoption. It was explained by the lower overhead expenses and in particular, staff and IT costs after the same period. Sathye investigated the impact of the introduction of transactional Internet banking on performance and risk profile of major credit unions in Australia. Similar to the results of Sullivan, the Internet banking variable didn't show a significant association with the performance as well as with operating risk variable.

Thus, Internet banking didn't prove to be a performance enhancing tool in the context of major credit unions in Australia. It neither reduced nor enhanced risk profile. DeYoung observed the change in financial performance of Internet community banks in U.S. during 1999-2001. The results found that Internet adoption improved community banks' profitability, particularly through increased revenues from deposit service charges. Internet adoption was also associated with movements of deposits from checking accounts to money market deposit accounts, increased use of brokered deposits and higher average wage rates for bank employees.

It found little evidence of changes in loan portfolio mix. The findings suggested that Internet adoption was associated with an economically and statistically significant improvement in bank profitability. DeYoung analysed systematically the financial performance of pure-play Internet banks in U.S. The study found relatively lower profits at the Internet-only institutions than the branching banks, caused in part by high labour costs, low fee based revenues and difficulty in generating deposit funding.

However, consistent with the standard Internet banking model, the results indicated that Internet-only banks tended to grow faster than traditional branching banks. Internet-only banks have access to deeper scale economies than branching banks and because of this, they are likely to become more financially competitive over time as they grow larger. Delgado found similar results for Internet-only banks in the EU. Nevertheless, the magnitude of technology based scale economies found in Delgado was substantially larger than that estimated by DeYoung studies.

The evidence of the impact of the adoption of Internet as a delivery channel on financial performance is mixed at both sides of the Atlantic. Nevertheless, the latest studies seem to find a positive relationship with profitability. It can be argued that as the intensity and experience in the usage of Internet increases, the financial performance of multichannel banks is likely to improve. In Indian context, many publications throw light over the importance of Internet banking and also its prospects for the Indian banking industry.

However these studies don't depict any empirical relationship between banks' profitability and Internet banking. The purpose of this paper is to study the same correlation applicable in Indian context. This paper also proposes and tests the existence of financial gaps between Internet banks and non-Internet banks in India.

DATA

The primary data set comes from the publicly available data source on bank's financial statements and income-expense reports sent to the regulators and banking associations. The Reserve Bank of India (RBI), provided the data. The data was matched with Indian Banking Associations data source, IBA Bulletin and Center for Monitoring Indian Economy (CMIE) data source PROWESS, for additional variables.

The Internet related details were drawn from a survey of commercial banks' Websites during the period of June 2007. The banks whose home pages were not discovered despite of best efforts were assumed to be banks with no Website.

The data set is limited to the banks that are operating as commercial banks as on March end 2006. In doing so, the banks that are acquired by other banks or have closed down their operations during the period are not included. Finally, a panel data of 85 commercial banks turned out to be the sample of the study over the period 1998-2006 which represented nearly 39 per cent of total scheduled commercial banks in India.

As all the banks in sample are not observed in the entire period, the study has used an unbalanced panel data for the empirical work. The 85 banks consisted of 28 public sector banks (8 banks in State Bank of India (SBI) group) and 20 nationalized banks), 28 private sector banks (21 old and 7 new private sector banks) and 29 foreign banks. The sample includes 49 Internet banks and 36 non-Internet banks. Table reports the description of sample banks.

Table. Adoption Rates of Internet banks

Bank Banks Banks	Number of Banks percentage	Number Internet	Number of banks as a Websites	Internet of with of banks in category
Private Sector				
Banks	28	27	17	60.7
New[1]	7	7	7	100.0
Old[2]	21	20	10	47.6
Public Sector				
Banks	28	28	26	92.8
SBI Group[3]	8	8	8	100.0
Nationalized[4]	20	20	18	90.0
Foreign Banks	29	29	6	20.7
All Banks	85	84	49	57.6

The survey results reveal that, during the period of June 2007, 84 banks in India had Web sites, of which 49 allowed transactions to be initiated through the Internet. However, the adoption rates across individual bank categories are not uniform. Adoption rates for transactional Web sites are highest in public sector and are lowest in foreign banks. Among the sub-categories, the adoption rates for transactional Web sites are highest in new private sector banks and SBI group.

INTERNET AND NON-INTERNET BANKS: COMPARISON OF PERFORMANCE

Evaluating bank performance is a complex process that involves assessing interaction between the environment, internal operations and external activities. In general, a number of financial ratios are usually used to assess the performance of banks. Financial performance has been studied under different yardsticks of performance *i.e.*, size, profitability, financing pattern, economic efficiency, operational efficiency, asset quality, diversification and cost of operations. This section reports the results of univariate analysis to differentiate the Internet and non-Internet banks.

The null hypothesis regarding the financial performance of Internet and non-Internet banks is: H1: The financial performance of banks adopting Internet banking is not different from those of banks choosing not to adopt Internet banking, in terms of size, profitability, operating capability, financing, asset quality, diversification and cost of operations. The decision to accept or reject null hypothesis is made on the basis of the value of the test statistic obtained from the data at hand.

In the present study, the statistical significance of the means of various test statistics is determined by using the two independent samples t-statistic. A probability (p) value is provided for the hypothesis that the means in the

Internet and non-Internet samples are the same. A lower p-value indicates a greater likelihood that the two figures compared represent real differences between the two categories of banks (Internet vs. non-Internet, etc.).

The Internet group as well as the non-Internet group across 10 financial performance measures. The performance of an Internet group with non-Internet banking group and separately for public sector banks (SBI group and nationalized banks), private sector banks (new and old private sector banks) and foreign banks has been analysed.

PROFITABILITY, OPERATING EFFICIENCY AND FINANCING

On an average, Internet banks are more profitable than non-Internet banks and are operating with lower cost as compared to non-Internet banks, thus, representing the efficiency of the Internet banks.

Internet banks in public sector, particularly, in nationalized bank category are more profitable than non-Internet banks. Comparatively, both the categories of private sector Internet banks are less profitable than non-Internet banks but the difference is not statistically significant. The lower profitability of these banks may be due to higher operating expenses, both fixed cost as well as labour cost.

Table: Profitability, Operating Efficiency and Financing Pattern of Internet and Non-Internet Banks (1998-2006)

	Profitability (Return on Assets) (%)			Operating Efficiency (Operating Cost) (%)			Financing Pattern (Deposits) (%)		
	Mean (N_1)	Mean (N_2)	"t"	Mean (N_1)	Mean (N_2)	"t"	Mean (N_1)	Mean (N_2)	"t"
All Banks (N_1=143) (N_2=596)	.898	.697	2.06** (0.039)	50.790	56.448	-3.07*** (.002)	77.441	71.144	4.17*** (.000)
Public Sector (N_1=58) (N_2=187)	.935	.647	4.65*** (.000)	48.766	59.764	-7.25*** (.000)	82.177	85.354	-2.00** (.050)
SBI Group (N^1=17) (N_2=55)	.870	.924	-.76 (.450)	47.885	51.680	-1.97* (.054)	80.419	79.863	.69 (.491)
Nationalized (N_1=41) (N_2=132)	.962	.531	5.35*** (.000)	49.132	63.132	-7.28*** (.000)	82.907	87.643	-2.15** (.037)
Private Sector (N_1=58) (N_2=180)	.714	.694	.162 (.871)	53.584	55.320	-.57 (.567)	79.095	86.182	-4.36*** (.000)
New Private (N^1=35) (N_2=15)	.806	.866	-.24 (.809)	51.772	44.859	1.17 (.247)	74.154	79.086	-1.81* (.076)
Old Private (N_1=23) (N_2=165)	.575	.678	-.56 (.575)	56.340	56.271	.01 (.988)	86.614	86.827	-.215 (.830)
Foreign Banks (N_1=27) (N_2=229)	1.212	.740	1.83* (.070)	49.136	54.626	-1.35 (.176)	63.714	47.720	5.03*** (.000)

Note: N_1 = No. of observations for Internet banks

N_2 = No. of observations for non-Internet banks

*** = significant at the 1 per cent or better level;

** = significant at the 5 per cent level; and

* = significant at the 10 per cent level.

Table also shows major financing characteristics of Internet and non-Internet banks. The Internet banks in India are able to generate more deposits or customer accounts than non-Internet banks. The results are consistent with Hernando and Nieto. Internet banks in India rely more on traditional source of financing *i.e.* deposits as compared to borrowing financing which is inconsistent with previous studies.

As far as categories of the banks are concerned, the private sector Internet banks fund less of their assets from traditional sources, such as deposits. Internet banks in public sector, particularly in nationalized bank category have also shown the same preference. It appears as these banks have begun to view the addition of Internet banking as a way to offer products that will reduce their dependence on core deposits. On the other hand, foreign Internet banks rely more on generating deposits, consistent with overall results.

4

Technology in Mobile Banking

Some banks are making significant investments in mobile systems to deliver a range of types of business value, from increased efficiency and cost reduction, to improved operational effectiveness and customer service to provide a competitive advantage. A factor that has contributed to this development has been the extended availability and capacity of mobile communications infrastructure around the world. The number of types of mobile devices has been increasing rapidly and the functionality available has also improved.

The shrinking costs of data transmission and, due to the intense competition from suppliers, the reduced costs of devices have catalysed the distribution of mobile technologies and amplified the growth of the worldwide mobile market. In those countries where traditional telecommunication infrastructure is not well developed, mobile technologies is transforming accessibility to the Internet based services. Mobile banking may be described as the newest channel in electronic banking to provide a convenient way of performing banking transaction using mobile phones or other mobile devices.

The potential for mobile banking may be far greater than typical desk-top access, as there are several times more mobile phone users than online PC users. Increasingly "mobile life styles" may also fuel the growth of anywhere, anytime applications. There are two main types of technologies available for use in mobile Banking: Wireless Application Protocol (WAP) and Wireless Internet Gateway (WIG). WAP is an application environment and set of communication protocols for wireless devices designed to enable manufacturer, vendor, and platform independent access to the Internet and advanced telephony services. WIG is a Short Message Service (SMS)-based service, in which a menu of available banking options is initially downloaded from the bank to the phone device.

This enables users to browse bank accounts and conduct other banking related tasks. Mobile banking was offered in the UK by the banks such as The Woolwich during early 2000s, but it failed to achieve a critical mass of users. The same story has been repeated in many other counties with mixed results.

The main hurdle in development of mobile banking is low consumer adoption due to a number of factors discussed below:

- *Internet connectivity costs*: Although connection costs from mobile phones is steadily declining it is still high enough in many countries to deter customers from using their mobiles for applications such as e-banking.
- *Difficult user interface*: Human Computer Interface (HCI) issues are a key factor in mobile technology acceptance. HCI includes the use and context of computers, human characteristics, computer systems and interface architecture, and the development process. A general rule is that the easier and more adoptable the interface, the greater is the user acceptance. HCI issues in mobile working are different in the mobile working context than in the traditional office environment. Kristoffersen identifies three key elements that define mobile work contexts and explain how they differ from the office setting:
  - Users' hands are often used to manipulate physical objects, as opposed to users in the traditional office setting, whose hands are safely and ergonomically placed on the keyboard.
  - Users may be involved in tasks ("outside the computer") that demand a high level of visual attention (to avoid danger as well as monitor progress), as opposed to the traditional office setting where a large degree of visual attention is usually directed at the computer.
  - Attention span of a mobile device user is much shorter than a desktop computer user so design of mobile systems interfaces need to be much simpler with very limited amounts of text. Systems navigation needs to be very easy too.
  - Methods to ease the burden of input and spread the requirements of processing output over all the human senses, while still maintaining data integrity are of importance
  - Speech and handwriting recognition are two growing forms of input. The benefits of speech recognition include minimal user attention input, direct system entry, remote microphone capabilities, and faster speed of operation compared to other competing input methods. These technologies need to be incorporated into mobile devices to improve the user's interface.
- *Lack of awareness amongst customers*: Many banking customers are not even aware of availability of mobile banking or associated benefits. As with other technologies, awareness increases with time and needs considerable promotional efforts.
- *Limitations in functionality of mobile devices*: Mobile technologies are still dogged by limitations such as limited battery life, unreliable

network connections, volatile access points, risk of data loss, portability, and location discovery. Even in the developed world, until recently, wireless communications were very limited with regards to functionality of devices and speed of communications. Constraints such as screen size, memory, and storage capabilities as well as data transfer rates averaging 14.4 Kilo Bytes Per Second (KBPS), limited the amount of data that could be both displayed and accessed. These limitations are still one of the biggest barriers to the adoption of mobile working in many countries.

- *Accessibility issues*: High speed public Internet access is offering opportunities to get and stay connected in more locations. Today, hotels that cater to business travellers frequently offer in-room high speed Internet access. As these high speed access networks ramp up, mobile applications are growing in popularity. It may take several years to reach that 'always connected' goal, and connectivity in less populous areas will lag behind high tech corridors.
- *Security concerns*: Mobile technology still suffers from questionable security. So it may not be suitable for transfer of highly confidential financial information. Mobile devices are increasingly becoming a target for virus writers, hackers, and short message service (SMS) spammers. Tower Group's research, over 200 mobile phone viruses have been identified since phones have been able to support PC-like applications such as e mail, instant messaging and Web browsing, and the number is doubling every six months. The resulting disruption of service and data theft can cause many problems for consumers, including lost revenues and customer dissatisfaction for mobile operators. However, the greatest loss may be absorbed by banks providing mobile access, as in almost all cases of fraud banks suffers from the losses. This factor may be making many banks hesitant in providing mobile banking. To be successful in mobile banking the industry must develop an ability to effectively contain the malware problems to a level that is at least on part with that of the existing Internet channels.
- *Organisational changes*: To offer mobile banking many organizations will need to change their business processes, ways in which information is provided and accessed, working practices and work relationships, working styles and most important of all, changes in roles, responsibilities and management structures. It may be a manageable task in some organizations but a very difficult one in others'.
- *Small number of choices (only a few banks offer mobile banking)*: There are a bewildering number of options when it comes to providing

mobile banking. It is possible to spend anything from a few thousand to several millions of pounds on any combination of mobile hardware, software and networks without realising many real benefits. With falling prices of mobile technology one may perceive that mobile working is cheap to implement. However, it is important to remember that technology costs are only a small proportion of the likely total costs. As a rule of thumb, these costs account for 30% of a typical mobile project, with the remaining 70% including items such as training, maintenance, security, management and integration (Flood date?). This implies that the real cost of mobile working could be much greater than promised savings.

- *Technology overload*: The proliferation of personal information devices such as home computers, mobile phones and digital organizers, coupled with the rise of new media such as e-mail and the World Wide Web, have forever altered the way in which information consumers work and play. These fragmented information channels often result in inefficient working patterns as users switch from device to device and between different media which may result in mobile savvy customers unable to use their devices for day to day tasks such as e-banking.

To promote adoption, customers need to be made aware of the advantages mobile banking offers over other channels. Customers should be provided with opportunities to try out mobile banking or see demonstrations, maybe at branches or through electronic media, of how this channel operates. This would raise awareness, and give people a better understanding of mobile banking options. In addition, services being offered should be widely advertised to the target market, such as young people who tend to be early adopters of innovative services. Perceptions of risk, as with many innovations need to be addressed by limiting customers' liability and implementation of latest security technologies. New versions of WAP use encrypted digital signature to enhance security.

The functionality and user interface of mobile devices is improving all the time whereas the cost of Internet connectivity in the developed world is decreasing. These developments mean that the prospects of widespread mobile banking adoption now looks brighter than ever. An example of a mobile phone banking system is reported by Geach. Named M-pessa, the system is developed by mobile phone operator Safaricom in Kenya. It was launched to improve the efficiency of Microfinance by using mobile technology to make financial transactions cheaper, quicker and accessible to much wider population than currently was the case. M-Pessa is a fully operational service available to phone users in Kenya. The ideas and systems were adopted from South Korea and proved to be especially useful for people with no access to banking or Internet through their computers. Basically, M-pessa is a financial services application installed on a mobile phone. A new generation SIM card is needed with M-pessa software embedded. Upgrades to older SIM cards are available free of charge and works on most mobile phone sets so users don't have to buy a new handset to access it.

Financial services available at present include:

- Person to person (P2P) transfers
- Individual to business transfers
- Cash withdrawals at the registered outlets
- Receipt or payment of loans
- Balances in real time and ordering of statements.

All of which are executed by SMS text message. The transfer facility works in a similar way to PayPal. An area where M-pessa differs from PayPal is that Pay- Pal requires users to have a bank account or credit card to transfer funds to their PayPal account and to obtain the funds on withdrawal from the PayPal account. Arguably, M-pessa could therefore, be better in terms of increased commercial transactions as people without any account or card such as under 18s could use it to make purchases. In the case of M-pessa, a customer must have an account with Safaricom in which to pay cash into initially.

The customer then selects the option he/she wants, for example 'Send Cash' and enters the phone number for the individual or business that they wish to transfer the funds to. The amount is then entered followed by the user's PIN. A message appears asking for confirmation; by selecting 'OK' an SMS will be sent to M-pessa. Soon after that the customer will then receive an SMS from M-pessa confirming that the funds have been sent, and a code for the recipient to use. The recipient will also receive an SMS stating they have been sent funds from the names person/business. To withdraw cash the recipient needs to go to the nearest registered outlet with the code that the funds sender sends directly to the individual, and identification.

The transfer process would take just a few hours in most cases. This or a similar system can easily be implemented in advanced countries such as the UK, US or Australia. The registered outlet could be a post office, a bank, a mobile phone retailer or a local grocery shop. The main advantage is that no access to a bank is needed by either party; all that is needed is traditional cash to pay into the service provider's (such as Safaricom) account. by the person wishing to send the funds. This means that service would be especially useful for people without a local bank or without a bank account at all. The Mpessa technology is therefore, a viable alternative to the traditional financial system. M-pessa provides fairly low cost service in Kenya. Benefits for businesses are that the potential customer base is increased by providing another means of payment and an easy access to funds that for some people currently do not exist. This has the potential, therefore, to help maintain and increase trade in local shops – a much needed respite for them from increasing competitive pressures from supermarkets. Security of such a system could be a problem.

The mobile phone itself could be stolen, potentially allowing the thief to transfer or withdraw funds. The phone could be hacked into, akin to what is done in desktop environments. In the case of a stolen phone the built in PIN and authentication provisions of M-pessa should mean that provided these security details are not held with the phone the thief should not have the chance to use the phone for fraudulent purposes. Extra security could come from CCTV at the registered outlets or phone can be blocked by the network providers. Anti-virus software could also be provided to financial service users at low cost to counter the threat of hacking and viruses. Recent trends suggest that, with the arrival of more functionality and user friendliness in mobile technologies, these technologies might be ready for the delivery of financial services. Riivari's research on mobile banking found that mobile banking is accelerating around Europe and beyond. Laforet and Li's research on mobile and Internet banking claimed that younger consumers were more interested in online and mobile banking than older consumers, and use of mobile banking amongst this segment is growing fast.

To cash in on improved prospects, at least in the developed world, some banks such as Citibank in the US have re-introduced the mobile (or wireless device as they call it) banking. This new service will allow mobile phone or other wireless devices such as BlackBerry users to enter a six digit pin to access a wide range of financial services. Experiments are also underway, mainly in Japan, Norway and US, to turn these mobile devices into payment tools. Often called 'Contactless Payments' it involves swiping an enabled mobile phone near a point-of-sale terminal to make payments which could be a bill or purchase of goods. These efforts to develop such systems often have support from credit card vendors who are looking for new ways to make payment processes more convenient.

THE MOBILE INTERNET

The growth of the mobile Internet now exceeds that of the PC version. Mobile communications offer considerable potential to marketers because of their unrivalled combination of:

- Instant response;
- Personalized content (as each customer has a unique telephone number);
- Scope for geographical location tracking.

The potential for mobile networks is particularly high in developing countries that do not have an established wired telephone network and hence no established PC-based Internet services. In the Philippines, for example, SMS messaging has recently taken off rapidly, and mobile Internet services therefore offer huge marketing opportunities in these emerging markets.There has been a lot of hype recently about the potential of location-based technology in particular. However, current services are very basic, and it is important to remember that there is some way to go before they become sufficiently reliable and useful to have a broad appeal. For example, variations on the scenario whereby a customer is called on their phone and advised of a special breakfast offer just as they walk to work past a Starbucks outlet, have been heralded as the ultimate in personalized promotional campaigns. There are a number of practical difficulties, though, such as customers' reluctance to be bombarded with intrusive advertising messages and the challenge of communicating effectively with the wide range of mobile devices and standards currently in use.The usefulness of wireless devices has recently been improved by new standards such as Jini and Bluetooth that connect wireless devices to other electronic products:

- Jini (www.jini.com) allows mobile phones, PCs and personal digital assistants (PDAs) to collaborate as part of an intelligent network, without the need for the correct device driver to be added to the operating system before a new device can be used.
- Bluetooth (www.bluetooth.com) is particularly useful for linking mobile devices because it does not require any wire connections. For example, it could allow a user on a mobile in a car to transfer data from an office PC directly to a home printer.

Keynote systems (www.keynote.com) recently launched a mobile performance measurement service to compare the services offered by all the major UK networks. It can measure delivery times, network comparisons, handset performance and geographic availability, thereby allowing content providers, networks or manufacturers to judge how successful their services have been. It also allows consumers to benchmark performance and make informed purchase decisions. In addition, for a detailed comparison of the characteristics of different mobile technologies, see Smith and Chaffey.

Mobile phones are now rapidly evolving and becoming 'pocket portals' that provide a range of personalized services including email and text messaging with just one monthly bill. Before discussing some of the recent and pending innovations in this area, we shall review developments over the past two or three years.The first mobiles to offer Internet access, using Wireless Application Protocol (WAP), were introduced in 1999. The information displayed had to be especially formatted for a small screen area, and the limited functionality fell well short of the often extreme levels of industry hype. The telecommunications industry broke one of the central rules of marketing, which states that promotional campaigns should 'under-promise' and 'over-deliver' rather than the other way round. Users found that navigating between pages on a mobile phone could be an extremely laborious process, for which they were paying by the minute for connection charges. During 2000, many early users abandoned mobile commerce after disappointing experiences. While mobile commerce is useful for 'distress' purchases such as parking, actually browsing the Web on a mobile phone is hardly a straightforward and stress-free experience. However, there have been successes to date, notably with mobile banking and gambling services.'Second-generation' mobile phones introduced early in 2001 offer faster connection speeds and are starting to carry advertising. High response rates are currently enjoyed by advertisers (perhaps owing to the novelty factor!), and the most successful campaigns have been run by companies such as the *Sun* newspaper, which has used the mobile channel to advertise competitions being run in the paper itself.

In other words, the *Sun* is using online advertising to drive its traditional core business - which is offline newspaper sales. Mobile advertising still represents a very small percentage of company promotional spend in comparison with more traditional media such as radio and television, but the figure is increasing. Business services via mobile channels are currently few and far between, but early experiments are under way with order placing, stock-checking availability and order tracking to facilitate supply chain integration.The much-hyped but still awaited third generation of mobile communications (3G) is expected to deliver sound and images and be 'always on'. Auctions held in 2000 for the licences to operate 3G services netted the UK government over £20 billion, but since then the share prices of the 'successful' telecommunication firms that purchased them have been severely dented.The technology competing with WAP is called Short Message Systems (SMS), and it is currently by far the more successful in terms of user numbers. SMS is a derivative of numeric paging technology, which has been in existence for many years, updated for two-way communication. To illustrate the rapid growth of SMS, consider the following figures:

- In 1998, mobile phones had a 20 per cent market penetration in the UK and some *1 million* text messages were sent.

As with the growth of the PC-based Internet, it seems that communications with staff and customers are currently adding most value at this early stage, while the widespread acceptance of mobile transactions is still some way away. One must also bear in mind that not all these applications will be relevant to all companies all the time, and in most cases they will complement rather than replace existing channels. The key skill for marketers is to focus on the particular aspects of mobile marketing that will add value to customers in their specific industry contexts. We will now examine each of these areas in turn, drawing upon a number of examples to illustrate this important point.

CONTENT PROVISION AND ADVERTISING

Mobile advertising is expected to grow exponentially following a slow start in the difficult economic conditions of 2000-1. The long-anticipated 3G technology will offer far more scope for creative advertising than the small black and white text-only screens that have dominated the market until recently.

It seems to be commonly accepted that busy professional people do not want their important business interrupted by marketing messages on their mobile phones. However, we all at least tolerate advertisements while watching movies ... so firms that specialize in placing advertisements on mobile firms are at the moment focusing their advertisement placement on mobile entertainment services rather than on business ones. Placing adverts in mobile games that users are playing when they have time to spare is likely to be more acceptable than if a user is interrupted while trying to link up remotely to a company for business purposes. In exchange for the entertainment value in the game, it is reasonable to expect that the customer will tolerate (and, companies of course will hope, respond to) the advertising message. For example, Stone reports that Mobliss, a US-based wireless marketing agency, worked with Tribune Media in turning its 'Jumble' brand (a scrambled-word game) into a multi-player wireless game. It was also an effective advertising tool because the words used in the puzzles could be directly related to the advertiser's company or product. The advertisements can be displayed as either graphical images or text and themed to correlate with the creative campaign that the advertiser is running offline. In either case, with mobile Internet access, customers also have the ability to click a button and be connected directly to the advertiser's call centre. Mobliss has also launched a snow report system at www. mysnowreport.com where customers can go online and build in their preferences for particular resorts. Then a text message detailing snow conditions can be sent to the customer's phone. By forming partnerships with companies like the travel agency Moguls that are trying to reach the skier demographic (high income, high expenditure), a customer is able to check out the snow conditions at a resort, and then follow an advertiser's link that is offering a discounted package trip to that resort.

Then another link will connect the customer to the call centre to speak to a ski-travel agent. In these circumstances, the customer is more likely to perceive the advertisement as a benefit rather than as just a nuisance. Targeting is very effective because if a user is enquiring about snow conditions, then almost by definition they are themselves a skier. In addition, the fact that the overwhelming majority of people currently using mobile Web services are males aged 20-39 with incomes over £30,000 is of course very appealing to advertisers.Traditional magazines have been experiencing a fall in advertising revenues over the past couple of years due to the global economic slowdown. The ability to offer interactivity through SMS can make a publication more appealing to companies seeking to place advertisements, while at the same time winning new readers for the magazine itself. So, for example, a company seeking to run a mobile advertising campaign to promote its brand could:

- First, rent a database of readers of a particular magazine that fit the demographic profile of their target group;
- Second, send text messages promoting a competition linked to the brand that is set out in the paper-based magazine.

Stone (2002) reports that a few companies have begun sending coupons as messages to wireless devices in order to unload 'perishable' services such concert seats or restaurant tables. He describes the example of PlanetHopper, a small company based in New York, which is focusing upon the entertainment industry.

It has partnered General Cinemas, theatres and Shecky's guide to bars and clubs to provide the wireless coupons. By advertising in cinemas and in some 200 New York bars and restaurants, it drew some 20,000 users who opted in to get the promotional messages. The key to success is 'opt in' messaging, as people's tolerance of spam messages falls. *The Economist* (2001) recommends that to avoid giving offence, mobile advertisements must:

- Be optional (meaning actively requested by users);
- Be personalized;
- Be moderate in volume;
- Be free to the recipient;
- Offer a means to unsubscribe.

The article goes on to report on a recent initiative by a mobile advertising company called the Mobile Trial, in which advertisements as text messages had an average response rate of 10-20 per cent. This is much higher than usual rates for direct mail (3 per cent) and Internet banner advertisements (less than 1 per cent).

MOBILE COMMERCE

Mobile commerce - meaning the actual purchase of items from the mobile Internet - is expected to grow rapidly over the next few years.

(www.forrrester.com) suggests that worldwide revenues could reach $200 billion by 2005. Be warned that we have heard wild projections before - in connection with the potential revenues likely to be generated by dotcoms, for example - so do not read too much into these figures. Before getting carried away in another round of Internet euphoria, think about the recent high level of negative publicity about mobile theft, which highlights the problem of security. Steps have recently been taken by the major market players to address this issue. In early 2002, a common database of stolen phone numbers was established so that the handsets could be disabled to prevent unauthorized purchases being made. Remember also that many people are still reluctant to undertake PC-based commerce, let alone transact through a mobile phone.

Growth in mobile commerce is likely to be driven by alliances between banks and telecommunications companies. Both parties have particular strengths which if brought together can add considerable value. Banks have a banking licence, credit verification skills and an established retail network. Mobile operators provide a modern brand image and the infrastructure of a mobile network. Both have a large customer base upon which to draw. While some companies (notably Vodafone) have made public their objective to provide financial services when restrictions on the allocation of banking licences are lifted (in 2002), others believe that the partnership route is the way forward. So far, banks have taken a cautious approach and built their mobile capabilities for small numbers of customers on a trial basis.

They now face the challenge of scaling up the infrastructure to cope with larger volumes of users. Abbey National, for example, offers e-Banking via the Genie mobile portal, which can be accessed by WAP phones over any service network. According to Bansal (2001), the bank's strategy is to develop partnerships that enable it to offer electronic banking across all technology platforms. These alliances offer customers the security of dealing with an established brand, which can be significant in building the necessary trust for mobile banking to really take off.

INTERNAL COMMUNICATIONS

Remote workers can use wireless devices to access office systems and marketing information held on the corporate intranet. Such services are useful for logistics companies needing to keep track of their drivers' location and also to send SMS messages with reminders and alerts, for example of schedule changes or traffic problems. Salespeople operating in the field can update customer records or request specific information automatically. Although the potential for the mobile Internet to enhance communications between staff or between staff and customers is considerable, adapting the corporate security systems to allow access through the mobile environment can be a significant headache, as can the practicalities of integrating mobile channels with existing IT systems more generally.

MOBILE CHALLENGES

Leung and Antypas (2001) note how the current mobile landscape resembles the first-generation Internet in the mid-1990s in terms of the key business challenges:

- *Bandwidth*. Many innovative services such as real-time video streaming will not be feasible, given the limited bandwidth currently available, and will remain what the authors refer to as 'pipe dreams' for the foreseeable future. The problem may be eased somewhat - although by no means fully addressed - by the arrival of 2.5G and 3G handsets promised for 2002.
- *Interperability*. Cellular carriers currently have different systems and standards that are not compatible with each other. GSM (Global

Service for Mobile), TDMA (Time Division Multiple Access) and CDMA (Code Division Multiple Access) are available on different carriers in different areas, meaning that communications with customers may need to be channelled through each carrier for its specific area.

- *Equipment*. The mobile cannot compete with the desktop in terms of display, computing power and keyboard facilities. The displays are currently available only in black and white, and support very limited animation. There are no cookies to recognize passwords and personalize greetings, and if the Internet connection is broken, then access cannot be resumed from where it was last used because the application will restart.

Case Study: The Mobey Forum

The Mobey Forum, (www.mobeyforum.org) was established in May 2000 to develop and promote mobile technology in financial services, in search of a secure and customer-friendly solution to the issue of mobile payments. The Forum aims to ensure that users will be able to pay for goods and services as easily with their phones as they can with credit or debit cards today. Its mission is to encourage the use of mobile technology for services such as remote banking and share-dealing. The Forum advocates a 'dual chip' phone, one for the mobile service and one for banking transactions. This means that the financial services provided will be independent of the telecom provider. Users are expected to treat the phone as they would a wallet, as it will encompass facilities for:

- Receipt storage;
- Electronic ticketing;
- Promotional coupons;
- Making payments.

A series of trials are currently under way. By working closely with European standardization bodies, the Mobey Forum aims to avoid fragmentation of the mobile commerce market by a multitude of competing standards. It is also putting across the message that if mobile payment services are to thrive, the key customer needs of security, convenience and usability must be central to developers' agendas.

Case Study: Is the Future of E-commerce Mobile?

In Japan, most business people have to commute every day and will spend a good part of their working days in densha or chikatetsu, the Japanese public transport system. As a result, mobile communication devices such as PHSs (Personal Handyphone System), mobile phones and pagers have become very popular and are being supplied in a wide variety of models. The PHS, developed by Japan's NTT, is a lightweight portable wireless phone that can function as a cordless phone at the user's home and as a mobile phone elsewhere. It can handle voice, fax and video signals. Users can send and receive email and even develop their own Web pages on tiny mobile handsets.

At the Information Technology Conference in Taiwan held in June 2000, Tadashi Sekizawa, the CEO of Fujitsu, claimed that the mobile Internet - defined as an intelligent transmitting system that can link with any Internet-accessible hardware or satellite system - will gradually replace personal computers as the most important application in the electronic commerce era. Japan is an exceptional player in the mobile field, having developed its own unique hardware system. The service is not delivered via desktop personal computers, laptop computers or digital televisions, but by using mobile phones and PDAs.

NTT Mobile Communication network, Japan's leading mobile phone operator, and its competitors Nippon IDO Tsushin and DDI Cellular Group, are already providing mobile data services such as home banking, news headlines, restaurant guides, weather reports, cinema schedules and fortune-telling to the Japanese market. NTT DoCoMo, one of the most advanced companies in the telecommunication's industry today, is currently introducing the first 3G mobile phone service. The 3G mobile phone service will be the first step for Japan into the 'Evernet' (a Japanese term for universal access to the Internet, irrespective of place, time and equipment). NTT DoCoMo is using a technology called FOMA (Freedom of Mobile Multimedia Access) which will provide more freedom in terms of speed and quality than the WAP technology developed in the West. The company has already begun offering its hit 'i-mode' wireless Internet service to the US market through its partner AT&T Wireless. The service will be tested first in the Seattle area before being expanded nationwide early in 2002. It will allow US users to exchange email, check stock prices and find restaurants, movies and other information from their cell phones.

NTT DoCoMo is set to expand rapidly, having bought a 16 per cent stake in AT&T Wireless in 2000, as well as minority stakes in KPN Mobile NV of Netherlands, Hutchinson 3G UK Holdings, Taiwan's KG Telecom and Hutchinson Telecom of Hong Kong. Kiyoyuki Tsujimuru, Managing Director in charge of global strategy, was confident the i-mode would be a hit overseas: 'Cell phones in the United States and Europe are still like 13-inch black and white TV sets. There is a huge gap in technology. People see colour displays and are stunned.' US users will be able to access a wide variety of i-mode sites such as CNN for news or Disney for their characters. There are already 40,000 i-mode sites operational in Japan. The variety and the quality of the information displayed makes NTT DoCoMo one of the first in the world able to offer advanced forms of wireless technology allowing for video, audio and other data-rich transmissions.

DIGITAL TELEVISION

Interactive Digital Television (iDTV) looks similar to PC-based Internet but is delivered through a television set and can be operated using a remote control. From a standing start in 1999, market penetration by 2002 is currently around 40 per cent of UK households and is projected to rise to 95 per cent by 2010, according to a Netpoll survey. Leading providers include Sky Digital, ON Digital, Telewest and NTL. One of the key drivers for this surprisingly rapid growth has been the provision of free set-top boxes by these platform providers. Services currently provided include home shopping, email, video, banking and travel. Forrester Research (2001) predicts that more people will access the Internet through a television than through a PC by the end of 2004.

Advertising through this mechanism can be interactive, as viewers can respond immediately to request further information or to sign up for a promotion. Digital television has helped increase the fragmentation of viewers, as there are over 200 channels now available in the UK. This means that advertising can be easily targeted to tighter niche audiences, for example through exposure on sports, cooking or health channels. Advertisers can develop their own television channels in order to incorporate content provision and communicate with their customers less intrusively. For example, the PC version of Boots' digital health channel, Wellbeing, is also automatically accessed if you type in 'www.boots.co.uk'. Specialist digital television channels also provide more focus for sponsorship deals. Domino's Pizza, which is represented on satellite, cable and the Web, is one of the early success stories of iDTV. e-Commerce transactions represent 4 per cent of its total business. Management credit the firm's sponsorship of *The Simpsons* as pivotal in building Domino's iDTV business. This activity has given Domino's a brand recognition figure of 98 per cent in multi-channel homes.

The UK government is currently pushing for total digital television penetration, and there has been talk of switching off the analogue signal by as soon as 2010. By the end of 2001, the number of digital television owners in the UK reached the same level (36 per cent) as the number of Internet users in the country for the first time, according to e-MORI's Technology Tracker (www.e-mori.co.uk). While the number of new users seeking Internet access is levelling off, digital TV ownership more than doubled in 2001. In social groups AB and C1, PC-based Internet access far outweighs digital television ownership, but the ratio shifts in social groups C2 and DE, in which twice as many households have digital television as have Internet access via PC. The relationship between social class and choice of Internet access mechanism is illustrated in Figure 7.5. Fewer than half of digital television owners have so far used interactive services such as shopping, banking, gaming or email. This is because PCs have been traditionally viewed as information tools and are a logical choice for accessing the Internet and using online consumer services. The television, however, is viewed as an entertainment tool, and the biggest driver for digital adoption so far has been improved picture quality and a greater choice of channels, with little attention being paid by consumers to the advantages of interactive services.Smith and Chaffey (2002) note the following advantages of iDTV to marketers:

- Direct-response mass-market advertising;
- Highly targetable;
- Moving buyers through the complete buying process;
- Audience engagement through interaction;
- Brand-building and positioning reinforcement;
- Brand-building through community-building;
- Customer service - reduction of bottlenecks;
- Security – less risk associated with TV than Web sites;
- Controllable - highly measurable;
- Cost savings.

These authors go on to recommend five key steps to making iDTV work in practice:

- Start small; test out advertisements first on a small scale and see what reaction is gained.
- Develop your own content area or micro Web site linked to iDTV.
- Design for the lowest common denominator to maximize the number of people who can make use of your service.
- Grow your offer over time to include purchasing or personalization.
- Form partnerships or build a team for the future to ensure that the necessary skills are available.

However, despite the rapidly increasing volume of viewers, actual purchase transactions have been slow to take off. Forrester Research notes that many retailers currently using iDTV as a channel to market are planning to pull out when their contracts come up for renewal. The main reason for their dissatisfaction is weak sales.

The Forrester Research report points to a poor visitor-to-purchase ratio of only 2 per cent. Also problematic is the location of transactional sites within 'walled gardens', which are dedicated interactive channels that are separate from programme content. The challenge is to find ways and means of driving consumers to these interactive channels and encouraging them to carry out transactions. Although a shake-out of unprofitable business is probably inevitable, the iDTV medium is slowly evolving, costs are falling and interactivity becoming less 'clunky', suggesting that opportunities will present themselves to companies prepared to take the longer view.

'Push' technology is the name given to a broad spectrum of products that automate the delivery of information to the user. Many Web sites are currently based upon 'pull' models, whereby users seek out the information in which they are interested. In contrast, push technologies create automated communications relationships whereby products can be aimed at users who have expressed an interest and given permission to be sent targeted material.

V-Commerce (short for 'voice') allows users to conduct self-service transactions alternately using the web and the telephone. This initiative is being led by the V-Commerce Alliance, which consists of a number of Internet and telecom companies. For example, a consumer would be able to make an airline reservation over the Web, and then later call a specific number to obtain departure gate or frequent-flyer information - or, before ordering a new computer online, speak to a customer service representative to check which model would be most suitable for their requirements.

Speech recognition is becoming increasingly common in US call centres, particularly in the banking and airline industries. It is also being adapted as a 'hands-free' input device for cars in Europe and Japan, as the motor industry recognizes that voice is the safest way for drivers to interact with in-car technologies (The Economist, 2001b). Nissan already sells a premium model that uses voice instruction to control audio, temperature, navigation and lighting. The new technologies promise to deliver access to information and services on a permanent basis anywhere that there is a telephone connection.

It is only in the past year or so that the necessary computing power has become small and cheap enough to fit into mobile devices in a cost-effective way. In addition, the (admittedly slow) spread of broadband access to the Internet in public places is fuelling the demand for instant information. What is also generating interest is the way in which speech recognition is improving the quality of information services by eliminating the need for telephone queuing and badly designed menu-driven voicemail systems.

Apart from call centres, other opportunities for telephone-based services using speech recognition include:

- Self-service banking;
- Catalogue ordering;
- Weather and stock market reports;
- Email collection;
- Virtual personal assistants (VPAs).

In order for the telephone and the Internet to be merged effectively, common industry standards need to be achieved so that Web pages can handle voice. In October 2001 the World Wide Web Consortium (www.w3.org) - a voluntary organization that sets international standards - released a draft version of VoiceXML for this purpose. At the same time, however, a new platform was created by such key players as Microsoft, Intel and Philips to develop a rival standard called SALT (Speech Application Language Tags). It remains to be seen which of these will prevail.

Virgin plans a new service (www.virginunlimited.com) that aims to sell everything from cars and toasters to holidays at big discounts. It will offer postcode-specific advice on financial services and household utilities at the lowest prices. In order to provide this service, the company has established partnerships with a number of consumer durable wholesalers and also providers of specialist niche products. Consumers will be able to ask product providers to compete for business by stating their requirements. The company that offers the best price and terms will win the order.

Consumers are often frustrated at having to deal with different service providers for each channel, which necessitates separate billing arrangements, passwords and email addresses. Consequently, they will migrate to services that allow them to personalize a single service for use on multiple devices. Looking ahead, Java TV (still at a very early stage of development) will bring together television and computing technologies to enable broadcasters to deliver value-added services to a range of Java-enabled devices. This means that the Internet will be rendered 'device independent' and customers will be able to switch their viewing from television to PC or mobile - anywhere and at any time - as their circumstances dictate. The organizational challenges associated with developing and integrating effective multiple channel operations should not be underestimated.

CHALLENGES OF MULTI-CHANNEL MARKETING

The usage of various Internet access mechanisms has developed over the past few years. At this early stage, companies need to address a number of challenges when considering the development of multi-channel strategies that allow customers to access online content from a range of devices:

- The extent to which they should invest in these relatively untried technologies, with little indication of likely customer demand or long-term prospects for making money.
- The need to 'repurpose' content for each tool. For example, trying to display a Web site on a WAP screen means that graphics and pictures are lost, and different coding is required. Smith and Chaffey also note that switching between PC and iDTV is problematic because Web sites are designed to be viewed in 'lean-forward mode' from two feet away, but iDTV in 'laid-back mode' from more like eight feet away. Navigating with a mouse is also very different from navigating with a remote control device.
- The unique properties of each medium in terms of the user experience delivered. For example, mobile transactions are likely to be for low-value or distress purchases, because the amount and quality of information that can be displayed to the customer on screen is limited. In contrast, the PC allows huge volumes of data to searched and displayed, and so is best suited to situations where the customer wants to carry out extensive research before making a purchase. Digital television offers yet another dynamic; although it is still in its infancy, early usage suggests that purchases may take place in a more

collaborative, impulsive and social context than through the other channels.

- Whether they should offer all their products or services across each medium (and if so, the extent to which customization is necessary and/or appropriate) or 'mix and match' according to the characteristics of each channel and the specific message to be delivered.
- The need for *integrated* online and offline marketing campaigns. Smith and Chaffey (2002) describe how MTV asked viewers to send in SMS text messages to provide comments and vote for their favourite video. MTV then played the winning video together with the comments live. The event was promoted through offline magazines read by the target audience, and the paper-based advertisement demonstrated a text message on a phone explaining how to take part.
- How to manage the necessary internal information processing that will allow the company to achieve a unified view of customer activity across all channels. For this to work, a central database is necessary to provide up-to-date customer details to all channel operators. Remember that customers' expectations are continually rising and they may expect to use a combination of channels to effect just one single purchase ...

It should be clear from this brief discussion that the technical ability to offer multi-channel access is just the starting point. Considerable investment needs to be made in the back-office computer systems and business process integration necessary to actually make it work in practice. The difficulties are even greater for small firms with limited financial resources, or those with legacy computer systems that cannot be easily integrated. However, for those that succeed, the potential for combine multi-channel offerings with *personalized* content provides an enormous marketing opportunity.

THE GENIE MOBILE INTERNET PORTAL

Genie was launched in 2001 as the world's first exclusively online mobile service. Genie's UK mobile service operates on the BT Cellnet network and is therefore now part of O2. BT Cellnet is one of the largest UK mobile networks, with over 8 million customers, and offers 99 per cent coverage of the UK population.

Genie is the UK's leading mobile Internet company, with over 3 million registered users of the Genie Internet portal. It provides free text messaging and free access to WAP. The mobile Internet is the technology that allows users to view information, play games and manage personal email via a WAP phone. WAP stands for Wireless Application Protocol and is the worldwide standard enabling WAP mobile phones to access the Mobile Internet. Genie Mobile Internet provides a number of services available on WAP phones:

- Email - the ability to read, reply and forward emails;
- M-Commerce - you can now buy books and CDs;
- Information - the latest sports scores, current news and gossip;
- Enquiries - flight times, cinema times;
- Entertainment - games, competitions and reviews.

Mobile phone and Internet services are integrated so that customers can access information on a PC or via mobile phone.

The Genie portal itself runs at significant loss, but its services appeal to the key market segment of early-adopter mobile phone users. Members of this group are predisposed to purchasing new gadgets, understand the rapidly developing terminology and issues surrounding mobile developments, and also happen to spend the most money on mobiles. Any mobile user can register on the site - they do not necessarily have to be using O2 networks. By permission-based marketing to these registered Genie visitors, special deals can be offered to get them to switch to the O2 network. At this stage of market development, the key selling points as far as users are concerned relate to content (in the form of information and alerts about share prices, skiing conditions, sports results, etc.) rather than transactional commerce.

The Genie brand has high awareness ratings despite low advertising spend. According to *Campaign's* dotcom weekly awareness survey, Genie is ranked tenth in the UK, with an awareness rating of 27 per cent, just behind the Easy Group on 32 per cent and ahead of Wellbeing on 20 per cent. Genie is promoted on the major portals such as Google, MSN and Yahoo!, and pays for prominent placements on search engines so that a banner is invoked should a surfer conduct a search for 'mobile phone', for example.

Genie aims to leverage value from its mobile services by offering customers special deals through partnerships with banks and ISPs as part of a 'closed' network. This business model is superior to many 'open' network portals because partner firms will either pay for preferential access to Genie customers or at least provide content for free. Genie customers who want to access services from companies outside the partner network have to pay extra for the privilege. To illustrate how this works, consider the example of mobile banking. Genie provides secure links to eight leading banks to enable customers to access their bank accounts via their mobile phones on the O2 network. Within the next twelve months, customers will also be able to trade stocks in this way. Hence there is scope for the major stockbrokers to be 'plumbed in' to the partnership to make the entire contact, share purchase and payment transaction from the bank account a seamless and immediate process for the customer. If such a service is available, why would a customer want to look elsewhere for a stockbroker? Stockbrokers, therefore, will pay for a preferential placing in the Genie portfolio, and indeed several may compete with each other - with the best positions on the listing commanding the highest fees.From the partner firms' perspective, there are three key drivers for associating with Genie:

- To obtain additional revenue from existing customers by offering an alternative channel to access the company;
- To expand the customer base by appealing to new market segments (for example people who use their mobile phone to bet with Ladbrokes through the Genie gateway have a very different demographic profile from that of Ladbroke's traditional customer base relying upon the firm's network of betting shops);
- To reduce the costs of servicing their customer base. This is the key driver for banking partners, for example.

To illustrate the potential of mobile services to reduce costs (and in some cases change the partner firm's entire business model), consider the example of a recruitment agency for temporary staff. In the past, such a firm would rely upon a team of office-based employees to make telephone calls to perhaps hundreds of registered individuals to advise them of newly received employment opportunities and sign people up as required. This could be an expensive and time-consuming exercise if large numbers of staff were required. By sending a text message simultaneously to the entire labour pool database requesting those interested to call in and sign up for the job, the entire cost structure of the business is altered. The staff employed to recruit would only have to answer calls from people accepting the work, rather than make a large number of outgoing calls touting for business. In the near future, the acceptance procedure will also become Web based, thereby reducing the need for human intervention still further.

MOBILE BANKING IN INDIA

India has about 207 MM (September' 2007 TRAI Data) mobile phone subscribers, a number that is larger than the number of bank accounts or Internet users. Given the mobile tele-density of about 20% and development of secure mobile technology solutions, banks are well-positioned bridge the digital divide and introduce the unbanked sector to the financial mainstream

You may be aware that Reserve Bank of India had set up the Mobile Payments Forum Of India (MPFI), a 'Working Group on Mobile Banking' to examine different aspects of Mobile Banking (M-banking). The Group had focused on three major areas of M-banking, i.e., (i) technology and security issues, (ii) business issues and (iii) regulatory and supervisory issues. A copy of the Group's report is enclosed. RBI has accepted the recommendations of the Group to be implemented in a phased manner. Accordingly, the following guidelines are issued for implementation by banks. Banks are also advised that they may be guided by the original report, for a detailed guidance on different issues. However to start with , we must understand who the various stakeholders are and what there expectation are:

Stakeholders are as follows

(a) Consumers
(b) Merchants
(c) Mobile Network operators
(d) Mobile device manufacturers
(e) Financial institutions and banks
(f) Software and technology providers
(g) Government

Each stakeholder group has the following expectations:

(a) To meet the following Consumer expectations:

- Personalized service
- Minimal learning curve
- Trust, privacy and security
- Ubiquitous – anywhere, anytime and any currency
- Low or zero cost of usage
- Interoperability between different network operators, banks and devices
- Anonymity of payments like cash
- Person to person transfers

(b) To meet the following Merchant expectations:

- Faster transaction time
- Low or zero cost in using the system
- Integration with existing payment systems
- High security
- Being able to customize the service
- Real time status of the mobile payment service
- Minimum settlement and Payment time

(c) To meet the following Telecom Network Providers expectations:

- Generating new income by increase in traffic
- Increased Average Revenue Per User (ARPU) and reduced churn (increased loyalty)
- Become an attractive partner to content providers

(d) To meet the following Mobile Device Manufacturers expectations:

- Large market adoption with embedded mobile payment application
- Low time to market
- Increase in Average Revenue Per User (ARPU)

(e) To meet the following Banks expectations:

- Network operator independent solutions
- Payment applications designed by the bank
- Exceptional branding opportunities for banks
- Better volumes in banking – more card payments and less cash transactions
- Customer loyalty

(f) To meet the following Software and Technology Providers expectations:

- Large markets

(g) To meet the following Government expectations

- Revenue through taxation of m-payments
- Standards

  The overall security framework should ensure.
- Encrypted messaging / session between consumer's phone and third party service provider / telecom company. Minimum encryption standards to be specified to make the transaction banking grade (E.g. Min 128 bit SSL)
- All subsequent routing of messages to the bank's servers must be with the highest level of security with dedicated connectivity like leased lines / VPNs.
- If any sensitive information is stored in third party systems, banks must ensure that access to this information is restricted with appropriate encryption and hardware security standards.
- All transactions that affect an account (those that result in to an account being debited or credited, including scheduling of such activity) should be allowed only after authentication of the mobile number and the mPIN associated with it. Transactions only for information such as balance enquiry, mini statements, registered payee details, etc may be allowed with either mobile number or PIN.
- Unless fool proof security is used in compiling and deploying the mobile banking applications, the PIN number should not be allowed to be stored in the mobile banking application on the phone. As, generally the application installed on the phone would be developed in Java, it may be possible to decompile it extract the mPIN. Alternatively, the application should be so compiled that it should not be feasible to extract the PIN on decompilation.
- All accounts, credit or debit cards allowed to be transacted through the mobile phones should have the mobile phone number linked to the account, credit or debit card. This mobile number should be used as the second factor authentication for mobile transactions.
- During the transaction, the PIN should not travel in plain text. Doing this, there is risk of the PIN being snooped out of the phone from sent items and also it being exposed at the SMSC level. Also, it may be able to snoop out the PIN during transmission, although, this is very difficult in cellular communications.
- Proper level of encryption should be implemented for communicating from the mobile handset to the mobile payments

service provider's server. It has been assumed that proper security checks would be made by the banks to ascertain the security levels of the service providers. This may include PCI DSS certification in addition to bank's own audits.

- Proper system of verification of the phone number should be implemented, wherever possible. This is so as to guard against spoofing of the phone numbers as mobile phones would be used as the second factor authentication.
- It is also recommended that Internet Banking login ids and passwords may not be allowed to be used through the mobile phones. As fraudsters get more sophisticated, the chances of phishing attacks on mobile phones would become more probable. Allowing Internet banking login id and password usage on the mobile phone may compromise their usage on the Internet banking channel. This restriction may be communicated to the customers through an industry wide effort so as to ensure that Internet banking passwords are not compromised through mobile phones.
- The payment authorisation message from the user's mobile phone should be securely encrypted and checked for tampering by the service provider or the bank. It should not be possible for any interceptor to change the contents of the message.
- Provided the above security recommendations are reviewed, the mobile payment service could use any of the preferred mode of communication viz., SMS, IVRS, WAP/GPRS, USSD and NFC. There are couple of security issues in some of these modes of communications, which are listed below:
  - SMS is the simplest form of communication, but is vulnerable to tampering. As long as there is a second level of check on the details of the transaction so as to guard against data tampering and the mPIN does not travel in plain text, this mode of communication can be used.
  - IVRS is also a simple mode of communication and therefore does not have any inbuilt security measures. The system should be capable of encrypting the DTMF tone entries, if required to be stored or transmitted.
  - USSD communication uses its inbuilt encryption technology to talk between the cell phone and the operator's server. However, the decryption of the information happens at the cell phone operator's server. Vulnerability of data may exists at this point. This information should be re-encrypted and transmitted to the service provider.

- Any of the following modes of user interface may be used, provided the above listed security measures are taken into consideration:
  a. SMS
  b. Menu driven application
  c. Menu driven USSD application
  d. WAP/GPRS website
- Formats need to be specified for exchange of information between banks. On the debit/credit card front, the exiting ISO 8583 message format may be used for communication between bank switches. However, for account number based mobile transfers, a message format may need to be frozen.
- Banks should designate a network and database administrator with clearly defined roles as indicated in the technology Group's report
- Banks should have a security policy duly approved by the Board of Directors. There should be a segregation of duty of Security Officer / Group dealing exclusively with information systems security and Information Technology Division which actually implements the computer systems. Further, Information Systems Auditor will audit the information systems.
- Banks should introduce logical access controls to data, systems, application software, utilities, telecommunication lines, libraries, system software, etc. Logical access control techniques may include user-ids, passwords, smart cards or other biometric technologies
- At the minimum, banks should use the proxy server type of firewall so that there is no direct connection between the Internet and the bank's system. It facilitates a high level of control and in-depth monitoring using logging and auditing tools. For sensitive systems, a stateful inspection firewall is recommended which thoroughly inspects all packets of information, and past and present transactions are compared. These generally include a real time security alert.
- All the systems supporting dial up services through modem on the same LAN as the application server should be isolated to prevent intrusions into the network as this may bypass the proxy server.
- The information security officer and the information system auditor should undertake periodic penetration tests of the system, which should include:
  - Attempting to guess passwords using password-cracking tools.
  - Search for back door traps in the programs.
  - Attempt to overload the system using DDoS (Distributed Denial of Service) & DoS (Denial of Service) attacks.
  - Check if commonly known holes in the software, especially the browser and the e-mail software exist.

  - The penetration testing may also be carried out by engaging outside experts (often called 'Ethical Hackers')
- Physical access controls should be strictly enforced. Physical security should cover all the information systems and sites where they are housed, both against internal and external threats.
- Banks should have proper infrastructure and schedules for backing up data. The backed-up data should be periodically tested to ensure recovery without loss of transactions in a time frame as given out in the bank's security policy. Business continuity should be ensured by setting up disaster recovery sites. These facilities should also be tested periodically

MOBILE BANKING BUSINESS MODELS

A wide spectrum of Mobile/branchless banking models is evolving. These models differ primarily on the question that who will establish the relationship (account opening, deposit taking, lending etc.) with the end customer, the Bank or the Non- Bank/Telecommunication Company (Telco). Models of branchless banking can be classified into three broad categories - Bank Focused, Bank-Led and Non Bank-Led.

BANK-FOCUSED MODEL

The bank-focused model emerges when a traditional bank uses non-traditional lowcost delivery channels to provide banking services to its existing customers. Examples range from use of automatic teller machines (ATMs) to internet banking or mobile phone banking to provide certain limited banking services to banks' customers. This model is additive in nature and may be seen as a modest extension of conventional branch-based banking

BANK-LED MODEL

The bank-led model offers a distinct alternative to conventional branch-based banking in that customer conducts financial transactions at a whole range of retail agents (or through mobile phone) instead of at bank branches or through bank employees.

This model promises the potential to substantially increase the financial services outreach by using a different delivery channel (retailers/ mobile phones), a different trade partner (Telco/ Chain Store) having experience and target market distinct from traditional banks, and may be significantly cheaper than the bankbased alternatives.

The bank-led model may be implemented by either using correspondent arrangements or by creating a JV between Bank and Telco/non-bank. In this model customer account relationship rests with the bank.

NON BANK-LED MODEL

The non-bank-led model is where a bank does not come into the picture (except possibly as a safe-keeper of surplus funds) and the non-bank (*e.g.* Telco) performs all the functions.

MOBILE BANKING SERVICES

Banks offering mobile access are mostly supporting some or all of the following services:

- Account Information:
  - Mini-statements and checking of account history
  - Alerts on account activity or passing of set thresholds
  - Monitoring of term deposits
  - Access to loan statements
  - Access to card statements
  - Mutual funds/ equity statements
  - Insurance policy management
  - Pension plan management
- Payments and Transfers:
  - Domestic and international fund transfers
  - Micro-payment handling
  - Mobile recharging
  - Commercial payment processing
  - Bill payment processing
- Investments:
  - Portfolio management services
  - Real-time stock quotes
  - Personalized alerts and notifications on security prices
- Support:
  - Status of requests for credit, including mortgage approval, and insurance coverage
  - Check (cheque) book and card requests
  - Exchange of data messages and e mail, including complaint submission and tracking
- Content Services:
  - General information such as weather updates, news
  - Loyalty-related offers
  - Location-based services

One way to classify these services depending on the originator of a service session is the 'Push/Pull' nature. 'Push' is when the bank sends out information based upon an agreed set of rules, for example your banks sends out an alert when your account balance goes below a threshold level. 'Pull' is when the customer explicitly requests a service or information from the bank, so a request for your last five transactions statement is a Pull based offering. The other way to categorize the mobile banking services, gives us two kind of services – Transaction based and Enquiry Based. So a request for your bank statement is an enquiry based service and a request for your fund's transfer to some other account is a transaction-based service. Transaction based services are also differentiated from enquiry based services in the sense that they require additional security across the channel from the mobile phone to the banks data servers. Based upon the classifications, we arrive at the following taxonomy of the services listed before.

	Push Based	Pull Based
Transaction Based		• Fund Transfer • Bill Payment • Other financial services like share trading.
Enquiry Based	• Credit/Debit Alerts. • Minimum Balance Alerts • Bill Payment Alerts	• Account Balance Enquiry • Account Statement Enquiry • Cheque Status Enquiry. • Cheque Book Requests. • Recent Transaction History.

TECHNOLOGIES BEHIND MOBILE BANKING

Technically speaking most of these services can be deployed using more than one channel.

Presently, Mobile Banking is being deployed using mobile applications developed on one of the following four channels:

- IVR (Interactive Voice Response)
- SMS (Short Messaging Service)
- WAP (Wireless Access Protocol)
- Standalone Mobile Application Clients

IVR – INTERACTIVE VOICE RESPONSE

IVR or Interactive Voice Response service operates through pre-specified numbers that banks advertise to their customers. Customer's make a call at the IVR number and are usually greeted by a stored electronic message followed by a menu of different options. Customers can choose options by pressing the corresponding number in their keypads, and are then read out the corresponding information, mostly using a text to speech programme.

Mobile banking based on IVR has some major limitations that they can be used only for Enquiry based services. Also, IVR is more expensive as compared to other channels as it involves making a voice call which is generally more expensive than sending an SMS or making data transfer (as in WAP or Standalone clients). One way to enable IVR is by deploying a PBX system that can host IVR dial plans. Banks looking to go the low cost way should consider evaluating Asterisk, which is an open source Linux PBX system

SMS – SHORT MESSAGING SERVICE

SMS uses the popular text-messaging standard to enable mobile application based banking. The way this works is that the customer requests for information by sending an SMS containing a service command to a pre-specified number. The bank responds with a reply SMS containing the specific information. For example, customers of the HDFC Bank in India can get their account balance details by sending the keyword 'HDFCBAL' and receive their balance information again by SMS.

However there have been few instances where even transaction-based services have been made available to customer using SMS. For instance, customers of the Centurian Bank of Punjab can make fund transfer by sending the SMS 'TRN (A/c No) (PIN No) (Amount)'. One of the major reasons that transaction based services have not taken of on SMS is because of concerns about security.

The main advantage of deploying mobile applications over SMS is that almost all mobile phones are SMS enabled. An SMS based service is hosted on a SMS gateway that further connects to the Mobile service providers SMS Centre. There are a couple of hosted IP based SMS gateways available in the market and also some open source ones like Kannel.

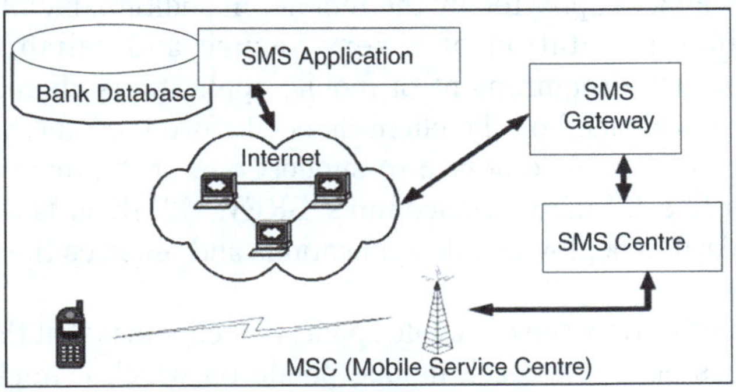

Fig. SMS Network Architecture

WAP – WIRELESS ACCESS PROTOCOL

WAP uses a concept similar to that used in Internet banking. Banks maintain WAP sites which customer's access using a WAP compatible browser on their mobile phones. WAP sites offer the familiar form based interface and can also implement security quite effectively.

Bank of America offers a WAP based service channel to its customers in Hong Kong. The banks customers can now have an anytime, anywhere access to a secure reliable service that allows them to access all enquiry and transaction based services and also more complex transaction like trade in securities through their phone A WAP based service requires hosting a WAP gateway. Mobile Application users access the bank's site through the WAP gateway to carry out transactions, much like internet users access a web portal for accessing the banks services.

The following figure demonstrates the framework for enabling mobile applications over WAP. The actually forms that go into a mobile application are stored on a WAP server, and served on demand. The WAP Gateway forms an access point to the internet from the mobile network.

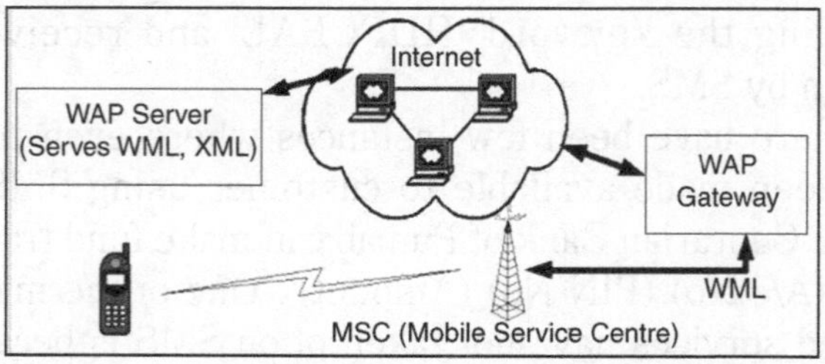

Fig. WAP Network Architecture for Mobile Applications

STANDALONE MOBILE APPLICATION CLIENTS

Standalone mobile applications are the ones that hold out the most promise as they are most suitable to implement complex banking transactions like trading in securities. They can be easily customised according to the user interface complexity supported by the mobile. In addition, mobile applications enable the implementation of a very secure and reliable channel of communication. One requirement of mobile applications clients is that they require to be downloaded on the client device before they can be used, which further requires the mobile device to support one of the many development environments like J2ME or Qualcomm's BREW. J2ME is fast becoming an industry standard to deploy mobile applications and requires the mobile phone to support Java.

The major disadvantage of mobile application clients is that the applications needs to be customised to each mobile phone on which it might finally run. J2ME ties together the API for mobile phones which have the similar functionality in what it calls 'profiles'. Out of J2ME and BREW, J2ME seems to have an edge right now as Nokia has made the development tools open to developers which has further fostered a huge online community focused in developing applications based on J2ME. Nokia has gone an additional mile by providing an open online market place for developers where they can sell their applications to major cellular operators around the world.

Quite a few mobile software product companies have rolled out solutions, which enable J2ME mobile applications based banking. One such product is Wireless Ibanco. The mobile user downloads and installs the wireless I-banco application on their J2ME pone. The J2ME client connects to the wireless I-banco server through the service providers GSM network to enable users to access information about their accounts and perform transactions. One of the other big advantages of using a mobile application client is that it can implement a very secure channel with end-toend encryption.

However countries like India face a serious obstacle in the proliferation of such clients as few users have mobiles, which support J2ME or BREW. However, one of the biggest CDMA players in the Indian telecom industry, Reliance Infocomm has about 7.01 million users all of which have handsets, which support J2ME. Reliance has unveiled one of the most ambitious data services deployment programme in the country. On the other hand a country like South Korea with its tech-savvy population has a widespread adoption of the higher-end mobiles, which support application development.

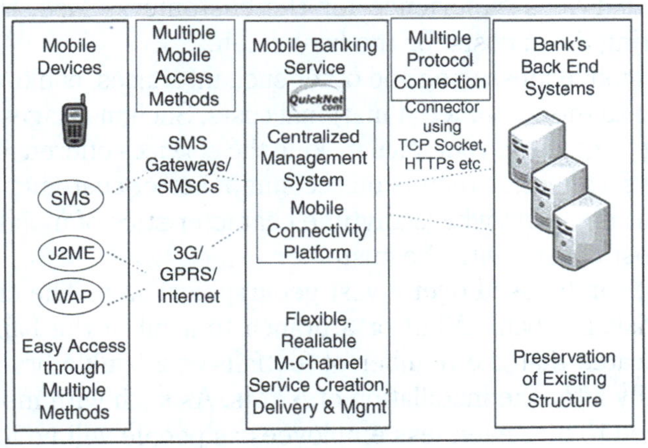

ADVANTAGES OF MOBILE BANKING

The biggest advantage that mobile banking offers to banks is that it drastically cuts down the costs of providing service to the customers. For example an average teller or phone transaction costs about \$2.36 each, whereas an electronic transaction costs only about \$0.10 each. Additionally, this new channel gives the bank ability to cross-sell up-sell their other complex banking products and services such as vehicle loans, credit cards etc. For service providers, Mobile banking offers the next surest way to achieve growth. Countries like Korea where mobile penetration is nearing saturation, mobile banking is helping service providers increase revenues from the now static subscriber base.

Service providers are increasingly using the complexity of their supported mobile banking services to attract new customers and retain old ones. A very effective way of improving customer service could be to inform customers better. Credit card fraud is one such area. A bank could, through the use of mobile technology, inform owners each time purchases above a certain value have been made on their card. This way the owner is always informed when their card is used, and how much money was taken for each transaction.

Similarly, the bank could remind customers of outstanding loan repayment dates, dates for the payment of monthly installments or simply tell them that a bill has been presented and is up for payment.

The customers can then check their balance on the phone and authorize the required amounts for payment. The customers can also request for additional information. They can automatically view deposits and withdrawals as they occur and also pre- schedule payments to be made or cheques to be issued. Similarly, one could also request for services like stop cheque or issue of a cheque book over one's mobile phone. There are number of reasons that should persuade banks in favour of mobile phones. They are set to become a crucial part of the total banking services experience for the customers. Also, they have the potential to bring down costs for the bank itself.

Through mobile messaging and other such interfaces, banks provide value added services to the customer at marginal costs. Such messages also bear the virtue of being targeted and personal making the services offered more effective. They will also carry better results on account of better customer profiling. Yet another benefit is the anywhere/anytime characteristics of mobile services. A mobile is almost always with the customer.

As such it can be used over a vast geographical area. The customer does not have to visit the bank ATM or a branch to avail of the bank's services. Research indicates that the number of footfalls at a bank's branch has fallen down drastically after the installation of ATMs. As such with mobile services, a bank will need to hire even less employees as people will no longer need to visit bank branches apart from certain occasions. With Indian telecom operators working on offering services like money transaction over a mobile, it may soon be possible for a bank to offer phone based credit systems.

This will make credit cards redundant and also aid in checking credit card fraud apart from offering enhanced customer convenience. The use of mobile technologies is thus a win-win proposition for both the banks and the bank's customers. The banks add to this personalized communication through the process of automation. For instance, if the customer asks for his account or card balance after conducting a transaction, the installed software can send him an automated reply informing of the same. These automated replies thus save the bank the need to hire additional employees for servicing customer needs

SUCCESS STORIES : LG TELECOM, SOUTH KOREA

In terms of the evolution of services being offered on mobile applications, South Korea is showing the way. The big push came when LG Telecom Ltd., the smallest of Korea's three mobile service providers teamed up with the Kookmin bank to launch the 'Bank on' service. Under this scheme mobile users were able to use smart chips embedded in cell phones for accessing all of the transaction and enquiry based services. The chip-based service automated the authentication of users when they accessed their bank's financial services to make the whole process much faster and convenient. The icing on the cake came with the ability of these chip enabled cell phones to be used simultaneously as cash cards. By October 2004 there were already about 100,000 infrared readers adapted to take payment directly from mobile phone handsets in Korea. Users can now use their cell phones to pay for everything, from restaurant bills, travel tickets, merchandise and even haircuts.

RELIANCE INFOCOMM, INDIA

When Reliance Infocomm, India rolled out its CDMA network, (at the time the mobile market in India was still in its infancy, and data services were almost never heard off) it made sure that all handsets supported Java.The Reliance application platform, also known as R-World brought Java compatibility even to the lower end phones. Reliance used a novel way to overcome the memory limitations of lower-end mobile phones, which hampered deploying of multiple standalone J2ME based clients. Instead of storing applications statically on their cell phones, users access a single menu based application called R-World, which connects them to the Reliance servers.

Using the menu based user interface, mobile users select the application, which they want to run and download them over-the-air to their cell phones. These applications are then executed locally on the mobiles. From mid-2004 Reliance tied up with two of the popular private sector banks, HDFC and ICICI, to provide a host of their enquiry and transaction based mobile banking services through its R-World environment.

ABN AMBRO, INDIA

ABN AMRO Bank brings to the convenience of mobile banking using an application called MPOWER. It allows customers to access their account for enquiry and transactions using simple SMS messages.

	ICICI Bank	HDFC Bank	IDBI Bank	HSBC	Bank of America	Citibank	ABN Ambro
Balance enquiry	✓	✓	✓	✓	✓	✓	✓
Last few transactions	✓	✓	✓	✓	✓	✓	✓
Cheque payment status			✓	✓	✓	✓	✓
Stop payment of cheques		✓					
Statement request	✓	✓	✓	✓	✓	✓	
Cheque book request	✓		✓				✓

One can do the following using MPOWER:

- Balance and Transaction Enquiry
- Share Holdings in Demat Account
- Funds Transfers to ABN AMRO and other banks
- Bill Presentment and Payment
- Cheque Enquiry and Stop Cheque
- Online Fixed Deposit Opening
- Request for Cheque Book and Statement
- Request for new PIN and change PIN online

CITIBANK

Banks are hoping to extend mobile banking as technology improves. Citibank has two ongoing cell phone trials. The first is a partnership with MasterCard, AT&T, and Nokia that places chips in cell phones allowing Citi debit and credit to make payments by waving the cell phone at a participating store's register. Citi's other pilot is with Obopay that lets debit and credit customers transfer money between mobile phones. Analysts say even more revenue is possible in the coming years when more functions are added to cell phones like international transfers, and booking travel arrangements.

While mobile banking is relatively new, the service has shown some traction with customers. Citi Mobile says it had more subscribers than expected while the service was being piloted around the country in the spring. Wachovia Mobile says their service has been getting about 50,000 unique visitors a week since its launch. Celent predicts that by the end of 2010, 35% of all online banking households will be using mobile banking.

BACKEND SYSTEMS AND TECHNOLOGY

Banking is a complex business and the ICT systems supporting it are becoming increasingly complex.

PRODUCT APPLICATIONS

Most banks have several different computer applications for their products. In most cases these systems were developed decades ago so they are often labelled 'Legacy Systems'. There are many problems associated with such systems such as difficulties in integrating them with each other and with newer systems, inflexibility in terms of expansion or scaling down, and rising costs of maintenance. These problems often prevent even strategic level decision making such as forming partnerships with other banks or mergers, as integrating the legacy systems of two or more banks only multiplies the problem. Legacy systems often fall short in provision of business intelligence for compliance, sales and management needs, or management decision making. This is mainly due to fact that the data formats used are often incompatible with modern data mining tools, and without data from these core systems the resulting business intelligence would often be incomplete or misleading. New product development can also be a problem, as the systems would have to be "hard-coded" even just to make simple product or fee changes, which can be very time-consuming and costly. Good customer service for e-banking customers is also difficult to achieve because the systems do not offer a consistent look and feel to the customer. To improve customer service, the provision of information on timely bases, prevention of fraud, and to support new agile business models, banks need to deal with all the problematic issues associated with these legacy systems. One solution is, of course, replacement, but often high costs and unacceptable risks make this option unattractive.

Another alternative is to reengineer these systems first and then wrap them with new technology, which can provide functionality as a service to other systems and allow changes to the core systems without the need to redevelop all systems. Later systems can be divided and replaced/redeveloped on a piecemeal basis. This approach, if executed well, can help link a bank's infrastructure with modern business process driven applications. However, to implement it organizations may have at least to partially implement the Service Oriented Architecture. In addition, very good project management and support from top management in terms of provision of required resources would be crucial. Another solution is outsourcing, as there are standard software packages available to manage most banking products.

This option is often more risky and usually small or medium sized organizations take it up because they may not have enough resources to build these systems themselves. To mitigate the risks, software packages and more importantly vendors have to be chosen carefully to ensure best fit with the existing organization. Future changes in the organization and systems architecture in particular must also be taken into account. Whichever strategy is chosen, banks need to ensure that new systems are process and customer oriented rather than the transaction orientation more common with legacy systems. Integration with other systems which support different service delivery channels such as branches or the internet is also key to ensuring efficient enterprise-wide work flow information and to giving the bank a uniform look and feel. Security should always be a major priority when any changes in core systems is implemented.

To this end, core systems may have to work with new biometric technologies, whether that takes the form of retinal scans, fingerprints or voice recognition. Business continuity, that is implementation of disaster recovery systems, is another fast developing area and receiving much more attention now due to ever increasing risks from natural disasters and terrorism. In the US, for example, many financial institutions were directly affected by the destruction wrought by Hurricane Katrina in 2005. They learned the hard way how unprepared they really were.

The damage was so severe in certain regions that some banks couldn't bring up applications until six months after the hurricane. Likelihood of this kind of event means that many banks have renewed their focus on preparedness as they rethink their risk management strategies and bolster their business continuity plans. Costs of unplanned or even planned downtime is spiralling as 24 hours banking channels need to be available all the time. Continuity plans need to be revisited and updated every three months as a minimum, as one or more components of the continuity systems may not work when needed. Regular testing and simulation of disasters and mock recovery exercises are often needed to uncover any weak links. Every scenario and every possibility needs to be accounted for and drills need to be exercised and recovery plans need to be put into action. This will ensure that banks can get back to business quickly in the event of a disaster.

DATA WAREHOUSING

Information has always been a cornerstone of good business decision making. Its importance however is growing all the time as the amount of data which can be collected from customer interaction is increasing at a faster pace than ever. It is important for businesses to seek ways to access, store, maintain, and utilize the enormous data efficiently. This data, if collected and processed in the right way, can provide a meaningful insight into the purchasing behaviour and needs of individual customers. To do this organizations need modern technological tools such as data warehousing systems. Data warehouse technology can be described as collecting data from several dispersed sources to build a central data storage, so that users can use appropriate data-analysing tools to analyse it and convert this data into meaningful aids for decision making. Banking activities highly information intensive, therefore the need for data warehousing is greater in this industry than most others.

Data warehouse tools can collect daily transaction data both internally and externally, and then accumulate, categorize, and store data for further analysis. From an implementation point of view, it is important to carefully evaluate and plan ahead before implementing data warehouse technology, owing to the large amount of investment and organizational effort required. The implementation process needs skilled personal, proper project management, and involvement of most stakeholders. Information consultants may be used to provide fresh ideas about the most suitable technologies and sources of information. Outsourcing may be an attractive option if an organization doesn't have the necessary knowledge and skills in-house.

KNOWLEDGE MANAGEMENT SYSTEMS

A detailed review of knowledge management systems (KMS) is beyond the scope of this chapter. Given the importance of this topic we have dedicated a whole chapter to discussing various aspects of KM. However, a few KMS issues are included in this chapter. The key to understanding KMS is that not all knowledge can be codified and maintained in data or information management systems. Much of the knowledge we use on a daily basis is part of what we do as social beings – in KM terms, it is implicit rather than explicit.

As banks seek to move more towards e-banking solutions, the computerised information systems will perhaps be able to cope with explicit knowledge, but the incorporation of implicit knowledge requires systems which combine technology with human expertise. Whilst technical systems have been presented as perhaps the catalyst for much of e-banking development, it has been made clear that this cannot be successfully implemented without recognition of the organizational and human change which will of necessity accompany this. There are many sources to assist with this problem, and the reader might find initially referring to Lehaney a good starting point.

CUSTOMER RELATIONSHIP MANAGEMENT SYSTEMS (CRM)

CRM systems are technology enabled management tools which help manage an organization's relationship with its customers. CRM systems help gather/store customer data, analyse this data to enable customised marketing, and are often used to semi-automate customer services. The main purpose of CRM is often stated as 'enriching relationships' with customers to gain greater loyalty, but at times they are used to cut the costs of customer services processes.

In an e-banking context, CRM software can help move customers from expensive branch or phone-based services to self-help services over the internet. There have been numerous CRM successes and failures reported in the literature. As with other new technology and other type of change, success depends on how an organization manages the change process and implements the required processes. One example of successful implementation of CRM is TotalJobs Group. For the Totaljobs Group, a recruitment company, the decision to implement CRM throughout its workforce proved beneficial. The company originally introduced a hosted CRM system from Salesforce.com to its own sales force during 2001-2002.

Two years later, it rolled the system out to the rest of the organization, and it is now used by 268 of its 285 employees. The system gives each employee a single view of the customer, so that before a call he/she is able to appraise customer information. Whereas it is impossible to pinpoint the role that CRM has played in the rapid growth of Totaljobs, one useful indicator is the customer satisfaction survey, which regularly shows a continuing increase in customer satisfaction. The ability of CRM systems to segment customers also enables businesses to identify most profitable customers so that marketing efforts can be efficiently targeted at that segment. Failures in CRM can often be traced to rigid corporate structures and cultures rather than technology itself. Vendors can also over promise, so organizations planning to implement CRM systems need to evaluate their own needs first and then conduct a detailed evaluation of how these systems can meet those needs rather than relying on the sales pitch of the vendors.

A major reason why CRM systems may disappoint is that they do not overcome integration problems, as they often have to interface with problematic legacy systems. One example of CRM related failures is DELL. Dell is well known for its "direct" business model that bypassed computer retailers and enables customers to customise the products they purchase using online tools. It has recently lost market share and damaged its stock market reputation, in part because its much-lauded technology enabled processes had a flaw. When a delivery goes wrong or a product is found to be faulty, customers will be left struggling as the human element in the customer-facing function has been cut to a minimum.

The computer problems can often only be solved by humans with the necessary knowledge and authority. In Dell's case, customer frustration with the attention they received eventually found expression through a blog for the whole world to read. This case shows that technology itself cannot meet customer expectations. Only well motivated and trained staff, backed by the right business processes and technologies can do that. Another problem is that CRM can cost millions of dollars, and many of its benefits can be hard to quantify and justify in terms of return on investment.

These figures are often calculated on a cost saving basis, with the possible enrichment of customer relationships, which is invisible, being easily ignored. It does not mean that CRM investment should not be evaluated at all, instead the evaluation should be done taking multiple dimensions into account. These dimensions may include customer retention rates, acquisition of new customers, effectiveness of marketing campaigns and so on. These success dimensions should be defined before the start of CRM implementation. This will provide a focus to the implementation effort as well as preventing CRM being labelled a failure if it fails to live up to one success criterion (such as cost savings).

MIDDLEWARE TECHNOLOGY

Lack of integration with other systems is one of the most common reasons for the failures of the technologies. There are many ways of tackling the problem of integration, such as re-coding parts of existing systems or replacing them altogether, but one method, the use of middleware technologies, has attracted a lot of attention and widespread implementation. These technologies enable different types of systems to interact with each other, and make it easier to integrate new systems which a company may implement in the future to into the existing infrastructure.

There are many types of middleware technologies but one which is becoming increasing dominant is Services Oriented Architecture (SOA). Potential benefits, such as reduced IT costs, systems integration and greater business agility have persuaded many organizations to adopt SOA. SOA is different from other computer applications development paradigms such as object oriented software development. O'Donnel the advantages of SOA over other software development technologies is that by externalizing functionality into reusable components and organising them into a logical framework, it minimizes two of the greatest causes of delay – the need for exhaustive communication between the business and IT, and the need for IT to write code. In addition, unlike other IT paradigms, organizations can also re-use their legacy systems as SOA enables legacy systems to communicate with other systems.

In the context of SOA, services are self describing, platform-independent computer programmes that enable rapid and often low-cost composition of distributed IT solutions. Services perform functions, which can be anything from simple requests to complicated business processes. Services are offered by service providers or brokers – organizations that procure the service implementations, supply service descriptions, and provide related technical and business support. When an organization needs a service they look for it themselves using Internet based directories and contact a relevant provider/broker to purchase it. To use these services, organizations need to build an architecture based on universal standards so that new services can be added in a very quickly. That architecture is called 'Service Oriented Architecture'.

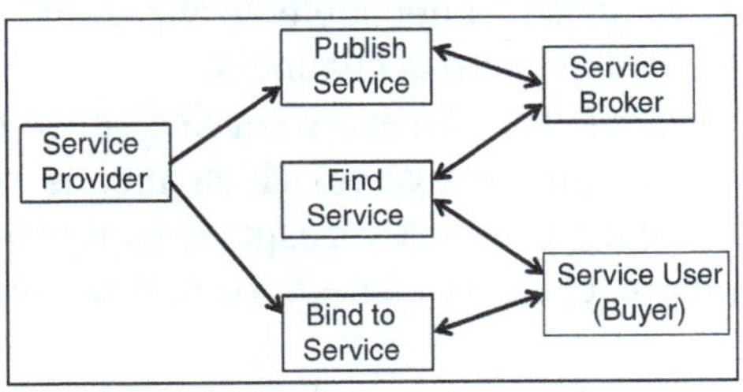

Fig. A Simple Model of Service Oriented Architecture

Knorr and Rist define SOA as a broad, standards-based framework, in which services are built, deployed, managed, and orchestrated in pursuit of new and much more agile IT infrastructure that responds swiftly to shifting business demands. SOA builds on the stacks of protocols such as Extensible Markup Language (XML), Simple Object Access Protocol (SOAP), Web Services Description Language (WSDL), and on the concept of Business Process Re-engineering (BPR). Typically a company would re-engineer its processes and use SOA to support those processes. Often viewed as a methodology, the SOA can be implemented across multiple projects, both internally and externally, eliminating the need to rebuild similar services for each project. Many vendors now offer SOA related products such as messaging solutions or business process management tools (BPM) that help implement SOA. However it remains a complex task, which requires considerable upfront investment, a high level of technical expertise and very careful change management.

Despite this, many organizations are adopting SOA because of the following benefits:

- *Integrating legacy systems*: SOA makes it easier to integrate new systems with old legacy systems under a single architecture. Integrating legacy into an SOA is relatively easy, as the IT department has only to build an interface to make the legacy application's data available in a standardised format that other SOA compliant systems can understand. Many retail banks are now focusing on understanding their customers and deepening the relationship with them. To do this they must achieve a single view of the customer so they can understand customer's needs. The SOA has potential to provide them by enabling end-to-end integration.
- *Service reuse*: Most components of SOA can be re-used several times. To fully benefit from this feature, organizations have to train, encourage and reward programmers to reuse existing services. This is the key reason given for claims that SOA is cheaper than its alternatives. In the banking industry, services are usually coupled within a particular process. Generally speaking, banks are unable to decouple the process, and the services held within each process need to be rebuilt to get the same services in another channel. SOA, however, allows banks to decouple services and make them modular so they can be reused across channels.
- *Shorter development cycle*: Greater service reuse often translates into accelerated development cycles which means that IT departments have greater ability to quickly respond to dynamic business needs. The development cycle is also shortened by the reduction in need for coding.
- *Long term cost savings*: Reusability of SOA components could also result in significant cost savings. Kobielus, the marginal cost of building new applications will continue to drop as the reuse rate climbs. When an application component is reused, SOA becomes more than 30% cheaper than traditional development approaches. Kobielus also points out that many of the SOA related savings come from its ability to consolidate silos of redundant application functionality and data throughout organizations.
- *Flexibility*: SOA offers considerably more flexibility than other architectures. Once an organization has built its systems using SOA, it becomes easier to add or replace one part without disturbing the other parts. This means than many business processes can be re-engineered or amended within a very short period of time.

A survey carried out by Information Week revealed that companies are getting or hoping to get many benefits from SOA adoption. These benefits include: IT platform standardisation, business processes automation, business flexibility, operational savings, systems integration and so on.

Whilst these benefits will persuade many businesses to implement SOA, there are barriers to its adoption:

- *Large upfront investment*: We discussed long-term cost savings. However, initially SOA will require significant investment, which some organizations may not be able to afford. Kobielus reports that Standard Life Group, an insurance company, maintains three SOA implementing development groups with about 500 people, about half of whom are delivering SOA services and applications. The company also has a staff of seven which just manages their SOA-enabling distributed application infrastructure. This type of operation is expensive, and the Return on Investment (ROI) can take long time to materialise. This issue is less of a problem for large organizations with large IT budgets, but for small and medium sized organizations it may be more problematic, and can be exacerbated by service reuse opportunities which are likely to be fewer than for large organizations.
- *Complexity*: Implementing SOA is not easy. Erlanger claims that SOA implementation is one of the most daunting projects that organizations can undertake because it represents a whole new of way of thinking which will change the way developers operate and interact with the business. This could mean that many organizations will not have enough or right kind of human resources to succeed in adopting SOA.
- *Lack of mature development tools*: Many SOA development tools are still in their early stages and it will be some time before the standards bodies develop universal standards for describing services and service platforms, along with delivering the management tools they will need. This could be a particular problem where an organization implements a multi-vendor solution.

These limitations create many problems for organizations in implementing SOA. An InformationWeek research survey, nearly a third of companies using SOA consider that they are falling short of expectations, a quarter have seen growing complexity in their IT systems, a third have been hit with higherthan- expected costs, and half report difficulties in integrating legacy systems into new software-development processes in a cost effective manner. These findings suggest that we may be far from the SOA benefits claimed by SOA technologies vendors. Implementing SOA is as much of management issue as a technological one.

The main management issues include:

- *Choosing a vendor*: Just like other IT systems, this is also a key question in the SOA context. Should an organization buy SOA related technologies from a single vendor or implement a best-of-breed solution? Knorr and Rist recommend best of breed (multi vendor) solutions to fully benefit from the flexible nature of SOA and to avoid lock-in with one vendor. However, lack of standards in services description could mean that organizations have to use considerable financial and human resources just to evaluate the various services on offer.

- *Governance*: As SOA is a new IT paradigm, any governance issues and ways to manage them are still in their earlier stages of development. Knorr and Rist define governance in an SOA context as a combination of workflow rules: who is responsible for what service, what happens when quality assurance uncovers problems, the management of service interface definitions, and so on.
- *Adoption*: Like many other technology implementations, SOA may also suffer employee resistance. Erlanger reports that Verizon's efforts only took off after it developed incentives for business units to adopt SOA. In addition to incentives, SOA education and getting people to understand new roles and responsibilities may also help.
- *Security*: SOA is based on open standards, making reusability and security critical issues. The industry has, however, agreed on a simple framework for securing XML messages, called WS-Security which is the most often used Web service specification after SOAP and WSDL.
- *Service management*: SOA should be managed like any other network resource. Knorr and Rist, several vendors offer dashboardlike solutions that monitor the health of services, maintain service levels, scale performance, set up failovers, handle exceptions and so on. Which of these solutions should be used depends on size of the SOA implementation budget.

These may include an objective evaluation of benefits and drawback of SOA, or studying best practice in adoption or implementation of SOA in order to recommend an easy to follow practical model. Impacts of SOA on organizational structures, culture and business processes also form an interesting research direction. In-depth research and evaluation is needed to avoid pitfalls and to maximise benefits from SOA.

M-SHOPPING

Retailing has seen many incarnations in the last 200 years. Shoppers have accessed retail merchandise through traditional stores, mail order, door-to-door distributors, telephone ordering, television shopping, the World Wide Web and now mobile shopping technology. A key to this evolution is not that the 'new' retail medium is the latest shopping incarnation available to the consumer but more the flexibility of accessing merchandise at a location that is complementary to the needs of the consumer at that time in their lives. If the Internet and Web gave the consumer the facility to shop *anytime* that suited their needs, mobile shopping approaches the added advantage of *anywhere* the consumer feels the need or want for merchandise.

As the early days of the Internet mediated shopping, many new terms were used to describe the emerging wireless electronic shopping environment. Examples of such terms are mobile commerce, m-commerce, m-business, mobile shopping and m-shopping. For this text we shall use the term m-shopping to define: Any retail purchase made from a mobile electronic device, such as a cellular phone through a wireless network; in most cases these transactions are made through an Internet-mediated facility.

Where store retail meant shopping at the store's address and Web shopping means shopping where the computer is wire connected to the Internet, m-shopping provides shopping access where the buyer is geographically located within a wireless network.

HOW HAS M-SHOPPING COME ABOUT?

In less than one decade the Internet has gone from a file transfer facility between academics around the world to a communications and entertainment medium for almost every person with a personal computer. Growth of Internet usage was exponential until recently when signs of a slowdown in the rate of new user uptake of the Internet became apparent.

This slowdown is partly explained by the Rogers (1971) adoption curve; the innovators and early adopters were quickly drawn to the Internet and slowly followed by the early majority. The statistics that indicate this slowing of usage uptake do not reflect usage popularity.

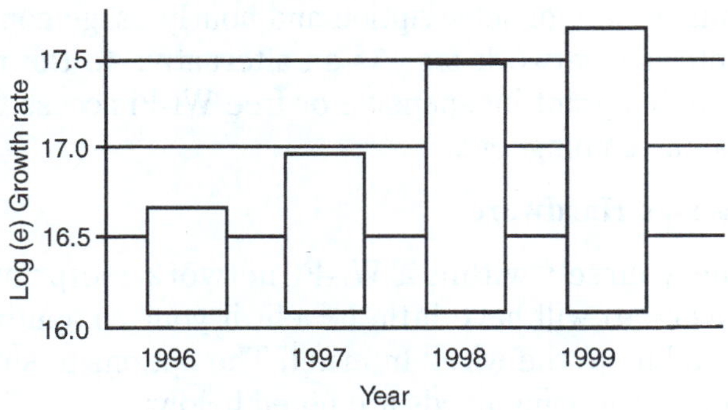

Fig. Internet hosts, growth rates 1996-1999

From e-mail correspondence and looking at news, to conducting banking and online shopping, Internet users are using the Internet longer when the access is readily available, as is the case with growing access to home broadband facilities. Where we access the Internet for personal usage is also changing. While initial private Internet usage was in the home, current Australian research identified that over 40 per cent of Internet usage in the workplace is for personal purposes (Strutt,). What is clear now is that users are becoming dependent upon the Internet and expect to have access when it is needed and not wait until access becomes available. The solution to 'anywhere' Internet access for any online activity including m-shopping is to supplement the cabled/wired Internet facilities with mobile/wireless Internet facilities.

WHAT IS NEEDED TO GO M-SHOPPING?

In the same context as accessing the Internet for the first time, a potential m-shopper requires certain platform elements. The principle platform elements of the m-shopping environment are a network and telecommunications hardware.

Network

Suppose you were conducting a meeting in a restaurant and subsequently needed to book travel. Certainly, you could book the travel over the Internet but there is no phone to plug in your modem or Ethernet socket for an *LAN* connection. Until recently your alternative was to link your notebook computer to the Internet through a cellular phone on the GPRS or GSM network. Drawbacks to this access method are the slow access speed of between 9,600bps and 68Kbits and the corresponding high telephone charges for the session. A better alternative is the increasingly available wireless fidelity (Wi-Fi) networks.

'Hotspot' locations delivering Wi-Fi in hotels, fast-food chains and airport lounges are being established by major telecommunications carriers in the US, Europe and Asia Pacific, e.g. Telstra (www.telsta.com.au) and Sprint (www. sprint. com). Emulating traditional consumer Internet access, entrée to these Wi-Fi networks is by way of subscription and hourly usage contracts - higher than a cabled Internet network fee. As an alternative to the major carriers, wireless communities grant inexpensive or free Wi-Fi access to the Internet for e-mail, shopping, gaming, etc.

Telecommunications Hardware

Establishing yourself within a Wi-Fi network footprint (the area of transmission coverage) will have little benefit if your computing devices are only configured to link to the wired Internet. The options to surf the wireless Internet and fulfil m-shopping needs are noted below:

Wi-Fi-enabled PC - linked to an Internet service provider (ISP) network:

- Notebook PCs are now being enabled by the manufacturers to include integrated wireless networking, e.g. Dell Inspiron 500M with Intel Centrino chip.
- Similar to adding a modem to a PC for Internet access, PC users may purchase a wireless access card for their desktop or notebook computers.

Wi-Fi- or *Bluetooth*-enabled Personal Digital Assistant (PDA). Bluetooth is a radio transmission service that links cellular phones and computer hardware in a similar manner to Wi-Fi, though over a much shorter distance and with slower transmission times. Such an enabled PDA may access the Internet through either:

- An ISP network; or
- Internet-linked PC network; or
- Cellular phone that is linked to GSM network.

Wi-Fi- or Bluetooth-enabled cellular phone that is linked to the GSM network. -231-

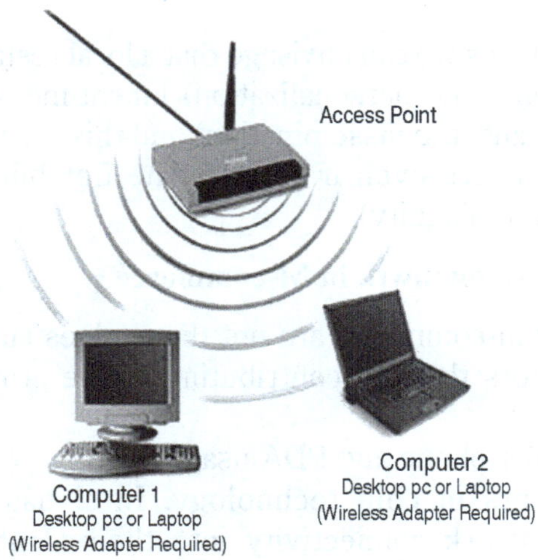

Fig. Wireless Networking Hardware

FEATURES THAT DISTINGUISH M-COMMERCE FROM TRADITIONAL E-COMMERCE

Though a component of e-commerce, m-commerce has its own distinguishing elements which are listed below:

- *Mobile* By its very nature, m-commerce is not restricted to a fixed telecommunications line (hard cable) that is linked to the Internet at a single location - m-commerce users may carry their mobile communications device (including cellular phone or personal digital assistant) and use this device to make a purchase in any region that provides mobile/wireless communication coverage.
- *Ubiquity* Mobile technology enables the user to access information wherever they are assuming the user is, within the mobile communication broadcast region.
- *Personalization* Due to the limited memory capacity of the current mobile hardware, internal software enables a finer degree of

information sorting and categorization to meet the mobile user's needs.

- *Flexibility and convenience* The mobility of the mobile hardware delivers the early promise of e-commerce, that is, 'anywhere anytime' shopping. For example, cellular phone handsets and PDAs permit users to conduct transactions and/or receive information even when the user is engaged in another activity such as travelling or working.
- *Dissemination and localization* Originators of information, for example local retailers, may use wireless networks to deliver specific information to some or all m-shopping users who enter the geographic region.

Using these features we can envisage that a local restaurant may broadcast their vegetarian menu (the personalization) lunchtime specials within a few blocks of the restaurant (the dissemination) and this message would reach m-commerce enabled users even if driving (the flexibility) in an unfamiliar geographic region (the ubiquity).

Contributors ot the Growthwth in M-commerce

The features of m-commerce are not themselves sufficient to expand its adoption. Other factors that are contributing to the growth of m-commerce include:

Growth in cellular phone and PDA usage.

- Improvements in chip technology. Intel has already integrated wireless network connectivity into their Centrino computer chip (www.intal.com/products/mobiletechnology/index.htm). Wireless modems for notebook and desktop computers have significantly dropped in price and are starting to become real alternatives to wired networking.
- Mobile communication devices are culturally entrenched. Cellular phones have evolved from costly commercial sales tools to personal communication facilities with voice and text (SMS and MMS). To improve the adoption rates, cellular phone companies such as Nokia and Siemens have developed a range of phones that are more fashion accessories than telecommunications hardware.

Declining costs of connectivity.

- Competitive pressures between the communications providers and improving production systems have reduced costs of telecommunications hardware and transmissions.

User incentives provided by telecommunications carriers.

- Discounted hardware to encourage network usage.
- Discounted airtime to increase network usage.

User equity.

- Potential m-shoppers who have a communication disability may use mobile devices to make a retail purchase using voice prompts, or a voice-navigated site.

AVANTGO.CO.UK

In the UK, AvantGo is the market-leading content provider for Internet phones and PDAs with a wide range of information and shopping, including: books, CDs/videos, computers, travel, electronics and clothing from over 200 suppliers. Based in California with over 350 employees, AvantGo has been supplying mobile Internet content since 1999. PDA sales are growing fast, with over seven million units sold per year in Europe. The chief use of AvantGo's content is to provide up-to-the-minute information. Financial information comes from sources such as Bloomberg and the Financial Times. News is from live feeds from the BBC and newspapers such as the Telegraph. Other important content includes mapping and sports. AvantGo is paid by content providers for hosting the content and also receives a share of the advertising revenue. Consumers pay subscriptions to use the content channels.

Shopping via PDAs is popular in the UK among young, male, educated, affluent shoppers. AvantGo's expertise is in providing Internet content in a suitable form for use on mobile phones and PDAs.

Using a PDA, a shopper can prepare orders at any convenient time - providing efficient use of, say, travel time. The orders are then sent automatically the next time the PDA is connected either via land line or mobile. This system provides great flexibility and many of the benefits of m-shopping without always needing the cost of mobile connection. Users of PDAs and mobile Internet are loyal and interactive - click-throughs are 10 to 20 per cent higher than for conventional Internet promotions. According to AvantGo, special offers redeemed by electronic bar code are achieving astonishing 5 to 8 per cent response rates.

PAYMENTS THROUGH M-COMMERCE

Using a mobile network device to make a payment is often referred to as a *micro-payment*. Depending upon the mobile device and available networks in the geographic region, a consumer has the option of making a micropayment in one or all of these modes:

- *Short Message Service (SMS) charges* The consumer keys in the SMS number that is assigned to the merchandise to be purchased and a charge appears on the billing consumer's account where SMS charges are normally listed. For example, some Coca-Cola beverage vending machines accept traditional coin payments and also display the SMS number for the particular machine. The beverage buyers call the SMS number from their own mobile device and, once the vending machine receives the SMS signal, the consumer may select the beverage to be dispensed. The charge for the beverage appears on the consumer's next SMS bill.

- *Direct charge billing to the account linked to the consumer's mobile device* Mobile network devices today are fitted with facilities to transmit data to another computerized device in close proximity without making a telephone call. These data transmission facilities range from inferred (IR) beams, Bluetooth and Wi-Fi transmissions. The owner of the mobile device transacts the purchase sequence as they would do traditionally, that is, select the merchandise to be purchased and take it to the sales counter/ checkout for payment. The only difference is that, instead of payment by cash, EFTPoS (Electronic Funds Transfer Point of Sale) or credit card, the mobile device owner transmits the account details using one of the data transmission facilities noted above.

Similar to the already described Coca-Cola SMS purchases, India's BPL mobile customer may send a message to 2233, which will be displayed on the LCD panel of the vending machine. The vending machine confirms the customer's mobile number, then asks for the choice of chocolate and, once selected, dispenses the chocolate. Finally, the customer receives an SMS confirming the transaction. The vending transaction cost is debited from a pre-paid card or added to the monthly bill of a post-paid customer.

- *Using a clearing house service* Intermediaries allow for payment authorities on behalf of the customer to pay for merchandise. One group, the Mobile Payment Services Association, is a coalition between Spain's Telefonica Moviles SA, Germany's T-Mobile AG and Britain's Orange SA and Vodafone Group PLC. The system of making payments through a mobile communications device is often referred to as a micropayment.

Micropayments

M-shopping-enabled technology permits the shopper to make payments in a variety of situations that may be grouped as:

- *Unmanned point of sale equipment*, i.e. food and beverage vending machines, parking meters, public transport ticketing systems (Editor, 2003b).
- *Manned shopping counters*, i.e. fast food and beverage providers.
- *Full-time cellular phone merchant connections*, i.e. SMS and WAP sites that automatically take payments by way of a cellular phone account rather than needing to enter credit card details.

The benefits of micropayment to retailers include:

- Billing the accounts linked to the mobile devices, e.g. the cellular phone does not carry the charges associated with the transfer of credit card funds.

- Reduced need to provide customers with change for vending machines.
- Bill fraud is reduced. When a mobile device is stolen, the communications carrier usually disables network access for that device and so it cannot be used to make further micropayments.
- Extends the frequency of impulse purchases for items of small value.

The benefits of micropayment to the mobile consumer include:

- Reduced dependence upon carrying cash and credit cards.
- Record of purchase appears on the account attached to the micropayment, e.g. cellular phone account.

PROFILING THE M-SHOPPER

The mobile shopping environment is still in its emergent stage of retailer development and shopper adoption. For retailers to tailor their market offering to the needs of the mobile shoppers, we should profile the current and intended adopters of m-shopping. As a contributor to this profiling we have incorporated the wireless shopping research of Fenech (2002, 2003). *Buying behaviour* Such individuals are frugal, enjoy shopping and take up new shopping facilities when they become available. In summary they are:

- Buying impulsive;
- Highly desirous of shopping convenience;
- Innovative in shopping;
- Positive in their attitude towards non-store marketing;
- Positive in their attitude towards shopping;
- Price conscious;
- Seekers of variety.

Use of mobile communication technology This individual already uses the functionality of their mobile technology; this is demonstrated by:

- Frequently Sending SMSs.

Shopping and communication environment This shopper is confident in the parties that contribute to the shopping process and desires the convenience of m-shopping. In summary they:

- Desire the convenience of mobile phone shopping;
- Enjoy mobile phone shopping;
- Have a low concern of financial risk from visited Web retailer;
- Have a low concern of privacy risk from ISP;
- Are satisfied with mobile phone carrier.

As surprising as the concept of Web-based e-retailing was in 1996, the concept of mobile shopping far from a phone jack or retailer must also be surprising in the beginning of this new millennium. Fortunately, we have already seen the benefits of e-retailing and this should significantly shorten the adoption rate of m-shopping.

E-BANKINGIN WEBSITE DEVELOPMENT ISSUES

In e-banking, a bank's website acts as a bank branch or front end. The main difference is that when customers login they do most of the work themselves without any assistance. Therefore creating a positive customer experience is more critical in the e-banking environment. E-banking websites and other related systems, without the benefit of human guidance, are expected to communicate effectively and enhance knowledge and understanding of the sometimes voluminous, and often technical, information involved in financial transactions. To create a positive experience, a great deal of planning, resources and expertise needs to be invested in the development and ongoing maintenance of websites.

To start with, a website must manage all the aspects that customers would expect from the buying process in a non-web environment. This requires a shift from website usability alone to interactivity and the ability to positively engage a customer. The focus should be on how the communication with customers can be improved by using the rich variety of available media. Giving more attention to the customer in the buying process could help in understanding the communication between customers and the bank, and subsequently lead to design and evaluation of websites that can stimulate the real-life buying experience more closely. Table suggests that in addition to the customer experience, e-marketing best practices and reliability/responsiveness of the website also play a major part in website success. Provision of decision aid tools such as interest rate calculators also helps create a positive impression.

The ability of a website to provide a bank with useful feedback about customer behaviour for marketing purpose is also becoming a must for bank websites. Some banks have also had positive experiences selling additional services. For example, Bank B bank in the U.K. provided new and used cars to customers looking for finance to buy a car. UBS sells Roman coins, United Overseas Bank offers discounts on restaurants, and Wells Fargo displays wanted posters. Many banks use their websites to market products, serve investors, inform the media, attract recruits, build the brand and much more.

Table. Web Site Design Strategy

Web Site Characteristic	Definition/	Promotion Measures/ Ways	Merits	Design
Informational/ communica- tional design	This approach is for companies to use the Web as a	• Putting banking services on-line. • Building broad awareness and image.	• Providing large quantities of information to customers. • Giving a company	

	supplement to traditional marketing, delivering additional benefits to customers and building relationships with them. automating	• Using the Web as a cost-effective way to augment their core products with related information and service function. • Obtaining cost savings from channel enabling routine customer services. cost.	an instant global presence and attracting people to one's ad, some of them are not the company's target market, but potentially will be. • Opening a new communication enrichement of relationships with customers. • All at a reasonable
On-line/ transactional design	This approach is for companies to use the Web to construct "virtual Business"– independent, profitable ventures that exist only on the Internet.	• Creating a retail presence larger than any physical presence could. • Creating a virtual business providing extra information in a form competitors cannot imitate. • Creating a virtual business that takes a specialty product or collectible and sells it worldwide. • Creating a virtual business that uses the Internet to produce superior economic benefits to customers that competitors cannot imitate. • Creating a virtual business providing convenience to customers that competitors cannot match.	• Providing a larger or more specialized selection of products than competitors can offer. • Providing higher quality and higher quantity information, more economic benefits, and more convenience than competitors can offer • Providing a sense of community for customers

Website development also suffers from problems encountered by traditional information systems. A view of website development as a purely technological domain is an inadequate one. Such a perspective reduces the complexity of the issues involved, and attempts to define it in terms of rules and procedures by which given inputs can be turned into predictable outputs. A human-centred approach is quite different. Human issues are 'complex' and 'adaptive', and cannot be fully described in terms of rules and procedures.

To understand such issues we may consult social theory. In the last two decades, information systems have become more fragmented and distributed, so the social issues have grown in importance. Arguably, the World Wide Web represents currently the most distributed form of technology-enabled system, in which a wide range of user types needs to be taken into account. It could be argued that the social issues are becoming much more important than technology related issues. Suffice it to say here that the web, for example, could be understood as a social, communicative, subjective phenomenon, in which the views and opinions of participants become fundamental to our approach to website development. Further, from a radical humanist, or critical perspective, the dominant, technological view of IS as functionalist, 'hard', problem solving, is seen to be an impoverished, over-focused on the use of technology. 'Soft' or human-centred methodologies are employed as a solution to this problem. But some question the ability of either 'hard' and 'soft' approaches to achieve much by themselves, and suggest the need to combine approaches under the umbrella of social theory.

One theory, radical humanism offers the potential to achieve this. This reconceptualisation of the system as a social system is an important part of any intervention, focusing debate not on a clearly defined technical or organizational problem to which a solution is to be developed as well as on the complex interaction of all the issues involved. The aim would be to change the focus from technology or organizational functions to the views and ideals of the stakeholder groups involved. The task becomes not one of how to engineer a solution to a known and agreed problem, but how to study and improve a problem situation made up of complex interacting issues. From the issues raised by boundary debate, it becomes possible to consider balanced strategies.

5

Risk Management in e-Banking

INTRODUCTION

As has been shown to be the case with information systems, it can be argued that the perception of knowledge seen as either a purely technical or purely social phenomenon is insufficient. This argument will be developed within this chapter, the aim being to answer the question: 'what kind of system is an e-banking system, when seen from a knowledge management perspective?' We begin by looking at organisations and their management, initially establishing a historical frame. Systems thinking, and its relationship to KM, is then reviewed, followed by a more in depth analysis of social systems philosophy and theory, and the domain of epistemology.

All of this points to a theoretical grounding on which to base the application of KM to e-banking in the philosophy and theory of Kant and Habermas, and in order to further develop this theme, social theory, and particularly critical social theory, is discussed. The outcome is an argument for social systems theory, and, more particularly, critical social theory, and for theories of communicative action to provide the grounding for e-business. A discussion then follows of what this means for the application of KM to e-banking, incorporating the concepts drawn from social theory.

E-BANKING SYSTEMS AS A WHOLE

The banking sector occupies an important position in the global economy. The sector has been subject to many external and internal forces. Of the external forces, technological change is likely to have the most far-reaching impact on the sector. Technology, in particular the Internet, is a key driver of these changes. In this sector computer systems in general, both backend and front end systems have largely remained centralised owing to the nature of the business and high security requirements.

This to some extent helped banks to automate key business processes by integrating their systems. Systems integration is essential to delivering the same information across all distribution channels such as e-banking, phone banking and branch banking. Despite some successes in e-banking implementation, many technological problems remain, as some banks still lag behind others mainly due to their inability to deal with their legacy systems problems. Diniz present two different classifications of e-banking systems. These two classifications are based on the level of interactivity of the site (weak, average, strong) and on the type of opportunities pursued by the bank (informational, transactional, client relationship). They found that that the type of technology to be used evolves with the interactivity and functionality of the Web site of the bank.

For example, an informational site is primarily based on a brochureware model, while an e-banking web site which is oriented towards the management of client relationships requires more sophisticated technologies like Customer Relationship Management (CRM). Mizrahi proposed another model of e-banking systems evolution in which IS integration depends on two variables: adequacy of the customer-channel relationship and capacity of managing information across channels. Availability of systems and security of data has always been an important issue, but is arguably even more critical in e-commerce, with 24 hours a day, seven days a week availability.

Any unauthorized access to data or unplanned 'downtime' of systems can result in a public relations disaster. At the same time, threats from computer viruses, frauds and terrorism are increasing. This all means that a considerable IT budget is spent on fraud prevention and disaster recovery systems, which may include investment in encryption technologies, other security measures and maintaining two parallel sets of systems to ensure all time availability.

The following are becoming an integral part of e-commerce related systems implementation:

- Capacity and 'stress' testing should be done regularly, as prediction of demand for e-commerce systems can be more difficult than for traditional systems;
- In the area of security, online systems opens up systems to the outside world. Investments in security related software/hardware will be a major expense;
- Identity theft and fraud in online environments are one of the major threats to the existence of e-commerce. Firms need to keep up with new and evolving sources of threat.

Although many of these risks are unique to e-commerce, the principles of general good IT risk management apply in most cases.

DEFINITION OF E-BANKING

For this booklet, e-banking is defined as the automated delivery of new and traditional banking products and services directly to customers through electronic, interactive communication channels. E-banking includes the systems that enable financial institution customers, individuals or businesses, to access accounts, transact business, or obtain information on financial products and services through a public or private network, including the Internet. Customers access e-banking services using an intelligent electronic device, such as a personal computer (PC), personal digital assistant (PDA), automated teller machine (ATM), kiosk, or Touch Tone telephone. While the risks and controls are similar for the various e-banking access channels, this booklet focuses specifically on Internet-based services due to the Internet's widely accessible public network. Accordingly, this booklet begins with a discussion of the two primary types of Internet websites: informational and transactional.

Informational Websites

Informational websites provide customers access to general information about the financial institution and its products or services. Risk issues examiners should consider when reviewing informational websites include:

Potential liability and consumer violations for inaccurate or incomplete information about products, services, and pricing presented on the website;

Potential access to confidential financial institution or customer information if the website is not properly isolated from the financial institution's internal network; Potential liability for spreading viruses and other malicious code to computers communicating with the institution's website; and Negative public perception if the institution's on-line services are disrupted or if its website is defaced or otherwise presents inappropriate or offensive material.

Transactional Websites

Transactional websites provide customers with the ability to conduct transactions through the financial institution's website by initiating banking transactions or buying products and services. Banking transactions can range from something as basic as a retail account balance inquiry to a large business-to-business funds transfer. E-banking services, like those delivered through other delivery channels, are typically classified based on the type of customer they support. The following table lists some of the common retail and wholesale e-banking services offered by financial institutions.

Table : Common E-Banking Services

Retail Services	Wholesale Services
Account management	Account management
Bill payment and presentment	Cash management
New account opening	Small business loan applications, approvals, or
advances	
Consumer wire transfers	
Investment/Brokerage services	Commercial wire transfers
Loan application and approval	Business-to-business payments
Account aggregation	Employee benefits/pension administration

Since transactional websites typically enable the electronic exchange of confidential customer information and the transfer of funds, services provided through these websites expose a financial institution to higher risk than basic informational websites. Wholesale e-banking systems typically expose financial institutions to the highest risk per transaction, since commercial transactions usually involve larger dollar amounts. In addition to the risk issues associated with informational websites, examiners reviewing transactional e-banking services should consider the following issues:

Security controls for safeguarding customer information;

Authentication processes necessary to initially verify the identity of new customers and authenticate existing customers who access e-banking services;

Liability for unauthorized transactions;

Losses from fraud if the institution fails to verify the identity of individuals or businesses applying for new accounts or credit on-line;

Possible violations of laws or regulations pertaining to consumer privacy, anti-money laundering, anti-terrorism, or the content, timing, or delivery of required consumer disclosures; and

Negative public perception, customer dissatisfaction, and potential liability resulting from failure to process third-party payments as directed or within specified time frames, lack of availability of on-line services, or unauthorized access to confidential customer information during transmission or storage.

E-banking Components

E-banking systems can vary significantly in their configuration depending on a number of factors. Financial institutions should choose their e-banking system configuration, including outsourcing relationships, based on four factors:

Strategic objectives for e-banking;

Scope, scale, and complexity of equipment, systems, and activities;

Technology expertise; and

Security and internal control requirements.

Financial institutions may choose to support their e-banking services internally. Alternatively, financial institutions can outsource any aspect of their e-banking systems to third parties. The following entities could provide or host (i.e., allow applications to reside on their servers) e-banking-related services for financial institutions:

Another financial institution,

Internet service provider,

Internet banking software vendor or processor,

Core banking vendor or processor,

Managed security service provider,

Bill payment provider,

Credit bureau, and

Credit scoring company.

E-banking systems rely on a number of common components or processes. The following list includes many of the potential components and processes seen in a typical institution:

Website design and hosting,

Firewall configuration and management,

Intrusion detection system or IDS (network and host-based),

Network administration,

Security management,

Internet banking server,

E-commerce applications (e.g., bill payment, lending, brokerage),

Internal network servers,

Core processing system,

Programming support, and

Automated decision support systems.

These components work together to deliver e-banking services. Each component represents a control point to consider.

Through a combination of internal and outsourced solutions, management has many alternatives when determining the overall system configuration for the various components of an e-banking system. However, for the sake of simplicity, this booklet presents only two basic variations. First, one or more technology service providers can host the e-banking application and numerous network components as illustrated in the following diagram.

In this configuration, the institution's service provider hosts the institution's website, Internet banking server, firewall, and intrusion detection system. While the institution does not have to manage the daily administration of these component systems, its management and board remain responsible for the content, performance, and security of the e-banking system.

Second, the institution can host all or a large portion of its e-banking systems internally. A typical configuration for in-house hosted, e-banking services is illustrated below. In this case, a provider is not between the Internet access and the financial institution's core processing system. Thus, the institution has day-to-day responsibility for system administration.

E-banking Support Services

In addition to traditional banking products and services, financial institutions can provide a variety of services that have been designed or adapted to support e-commerce. Management should understand these services and the risks they pose to the institution. This section discusses some of the most common support services: weblinking, account aggregation, electronic authentication, website hosting, payments for e-commerce, and wireless banking activities.

Weblinking

A large number of financial institutions maintain sites on the World Wide Web. Some websites are strictly informational, while others also offer customers the ability to perform financial transactions, such as paying bills or transferring funds between accounts.

Virtually every website contains "weblinks." A weblink is a word, phrase, or image on a webpage that contains coding that will transport the viewer to a different part of the website or a completely different website by just clicking the mouse. While weblinks are a convenient and accepted tool in website design, their use can present certain risks. Generally, the primary risk posed by weblinking is that viewers can become confused about whose website they are viewing and who is responsible for the information, products, and services available through that website. There are a variety of risk management techniques institutions should consider using to mitigate these risks. These risk management techniques are for those institutions that develop and maintain their own websites, as well as institutions that use third-party service providers for this function. The agencies have issued guidance on weblinking that provides details on risks and risk management techniques financial institutions should consider.

Account Aggregation

Account aggregation is a service that gathers information from many websites, presents that information to the customer in a consolidated format, and, in some cases, may allow the customer to initiate activity on the aggregated accounts. The information gathered or aggregated can range from publicly available information to personal account information (e.g., credit card, brokerage, and banking data). Aggregation services can improve customer convenience by avoiding multiple log-ins and providing access to tools that help customers analyze and manage their various account portfolios. Some aggregators use the customer-provided user IDs and passwords to sign in as the customer. Once the customer's account is accessed, the aggregator copies the personal account information from the website for representation on the aggregator's site (i.e., "screen scraping"). Other aggregators use direct data-feed arrangements with website operators or other firms to obtain the customer's information. Generally, direct data feeds are thought to provide greater legal protection to the aggregator than does screen scraping. Financial institutions are involved in account aggregation both as aggregators and as aggregation targets. Risk management issues examiners should consider when reviewing aggregation services include:

Protection of customer passwords and user IDs-both those used to access the institution's aggregation services and those the aggregator uses to retrieve customer information from aggregated third parties-to assure the confidentiality of customer information and to prevent unauthorized activity,

Disclosure of potential customer liability if customers share their authentication information (i.e., IDs and passwords) with third parties, and

Assurance of the accuracy and completeness of information retrieved from the aggregated parties' sites, including required disclosures Additional information regarding management of risks in aggregation services can be found in appendix D.

Electronic Authentication

Verifying the identities of customers and authorizing e-banking activities are integral parts of e-banking financial services. Since traditional paper-based and in-person identity authentication methods reduce the speed and efficiency of electronic transactions, financial institutions have adopted alternative authentication methods, including:

Passwords and personal identification numbers (PINs),

Digital certificates using a public key infrastructure (PKI),

Microchip-based devices such as smart cards or other types of tokens,

Database comparisons (e.g., fraud-screening applications), and

Biometric identifiers.

The authentication methods listed above vary in the level of security and reliability they provide and in the cost and complexity of their underlying infrastructures. As such, the choice of which technique(s) to use should be commensurate with the risks in the products and services for which they control access. Additional information on customer authentication techniques can be found in this booklet under the heading "Authenticating E-Banking Customers."

The Electronic Signatures in Global and National Commerce (E-Sign) Act establishes some uniform federal rules concerning the legal status of electronic signatures and records in commercial and consumer transactions so as to provide more legal certainty and promote the growth of electronic commerce. The development of secure digital signatures continues to evolve with some financial institutions either acting as the certification authority for digital signatures or providing repository services for digital certificates.

Website Hosting

Some financial institutions host websites for both themselves as well as for other businesses. Financial institutions that host a business customer's website usually store, or arrange for the storage of, the electronic files that make up the website. These files are stored on one or more servers that may be located on the hosting financial institution's premises. Website hosting services require strong skills in networking, security, and programming. The technology and software change rapidly. Institutions developing websites should monitor the need to adopt new interoperability standards and protocols such as Extensible Mark-Up Language (XML) to facilitate data exchange among the diverse population of Internet users.

Risk issues examiners should consider when reviewing website hosting services include damage to reputation, loss of customers, or potential liability resulting from:

Downtime (i.e., times when website is not available) or inability to meet service levels specified in the contract,

Inaccurate website content (e.g., products, pricing) resulting from actions of the institution's staff or unauthorized changes by third parties (e.g., hackers),

Unauthorized disclosure of confidential information stemming from security breaches, and

Damage to computer systems of website visitors due to malicious code (e.g., virus, worm, active content) spread through institution-hosted sites.

Payments for E-commerce

Many businesses accept various forms of electronic payments for their products and services. Financial institutions play an important role in electronic payment systems by creating and distributing a variety of electronic payment instruments, accepting a similar variety of instruments, processing those payments, and participating in clearing and settlement systems. However, increasingly, financial institutions are competing with third parties to provide support services for e-commerce payment systems. Among the electronic payments mechanisms that financial institutions provide for e-commerce are automated clearing house (ACH) debits and credits through the Internet, electronic bill payment and presentment, electronic checks, e-mail money, and electronic credit card payments. Additional information on payments systems can be found in other sections of the IT Handbook.

Most financial institutions permit intrabank transfers between a customer's accounts as part of their basic transactional e-banking services. However, third-party transfers-with their heightened risk for fraud-often require additional security safeguards in the form of additional authentication and payment confirmation.

Bill Payment and Presentment

Bill payment services permit customers to electronically instruct their financial institution to transfer funds to a business's account at some future specified date. Customers can make payments on a one-time or recurring basis, with fees typically assessed as a "per item" or monthly charge. In response to the customer's electronic payment instructions, the financial institution (or its bill payment provider) generates an electronic transaction-usually an automated clearinghouse (ACH) credit-or mails a paper check to the business on the customer's behalf. To allow for the possibility of a paper-based transfer, financial institutions typically advise customers to make payments effective 3-7 days before the bill's due date.

Internet-based cash management is the commercial version of retail bill payment. Business customers use the system to initiate third-party payments or to transfer money between company accounts. Cash management services also include minimum balance maintenance, recurring transfers between accounts and on-line account reconciliation. Businesses typically require stronger controls, including the ability to administer security and transaction controls among several users within the business.

This booklet discusses the front-end controls related to the initiation, storage, and transmission of bill payment transactions prior to their entry into the industry's retail payment systems (e.g., ACH, check processing, etc.). The IT Handbook's "Retail Payments Systems Booklet" provides additional information regarding the various electronic transactions that comprise the back end for bill payment processing.

The extent of front-end operating controls directly under the financial institution's control varies with the system configuration. Some examples of typical configurations are listed below in order of increasing complexity, along with potential control considerations.

Financial institutions that do not provide bill payment services, but may direct customers to select from several unaffiliated bill payment providers.

Caution customers regarding security and privacy issues through the use of on-line disclosures or, more conservatively, e-banking agreements.

Financial institutions that rely on a third-party bill payment provider including Internet banking providers that subcontract to third parties.

Set dollar and volume thresholds and review bill payment transactions for suspicious activity.

Gain independent audit assurance over the bill payment provider's processing controls.

Restrict employees' administrative access to ensure that the internal controls limiting their capabilities to originate, modify, or delete bill payment transactions are at least as strong as those applicable to the underlying retail payment system ultimately transmitting the transaction.

Restrict by vendor contract and identify the use of any subcontractors associated with the bill payment application to ensure adequate oversight of underlying bill payment system performance and availability.

Evaluate the adequacy of authentication methods given the higher risk associated with funds transfer capabilities rather than with basic account access.

Consider the additional guidance contained in the IT Handbook's "Information Security," "Retail Payment Systems," and "Outsourcing Technology Services" booklets.

Financial institutions that use third-party software to host a bill payment application internally.

Determine the extent of any independent assessments or certification of the security of application source code.

Ensure software is adequately tested prior to installation on the live system.

Ensure vendor access for software maintenance is controlled and monitored.

Financial institutions that develop, maintain, and host their own bill payment system.

Consider additional guidance in the IT Handbook's "Development and Acquisition Booklet."

Financial institutions can offer bill payment as a stand-alone service or in combination with bill presentment. Bill presentment arrangements permit a business to submit a customer's bill in electronic form to the customer's financial institution. Customers can view their bills by clicking on links on their account's e-banking screen or menu. After viewing a bill, the customer can initiate bill payment instructions or elect to pay the bill through a different payment channel.

In addition, some businesses have begun offering electronic bill presentment directly from their own websites rather than through links on the e-banking screens of a financial institution. Under such arrangements, customers can log on to the business's website to view their periodic bills. Then, if so desired, they can electronically authorize the business to "take" the payment from their account.

The payment then occurs as an ACH debit originated by the business's financial institution as compared to the ACH credit originated by the customer's financial institution in the bill payment scenario described above. Institutions should ensure proper approval of businesses allowed to use ACH payment technology to initiate payments from customer accounts.

Cash management applications would include the same control considerations described above, but the institution should consider additional controls because of the higher risk associated with commercial transactions. The adequacy of authentication methods becomes a higher priority and requires greater assurance due to the larger average dollar size of transactions. Institutions should also establish additional controls to ensure binding agreements-consistent with any existing ACH or wire transfer agreements-exist with commercial customers. Additionally, cash management systems should provide adequate security administration capabilities to enable the business owners to restrict access rights and dollar limits associated with multiple-user access to their accounts.

Person-to-Person Payments

Electronic person-to-person payments, also known as e-mail money, permit consumers to send "money" to any person or business with an e-mail address. Under this scenario, a consumer electronically instructs the person-to-person payment service to transfer funds to another individual. The payment service then sends an e-mail notifying the individual that the funds are available and informs him or her of the methods available to access the funds including requesting a check, transferring the funds to an account at an insured financial institution, or retransmitting the funds to someone else. Person-to-person payments are typically funded by credit card charges or by an ACH transfer from the consumer's account at a financial institution. Since neither the payee nor the payer in the transaction has to have an account with the payment service, such services may be offered by an insured financial institution, but are frequently offered by other businesses as well.

Some of the risk issues examiners should consider when reviewing bill payment, presentment, and e-mail money services include:

Potential liability for late payments due to service disruptions,

Liability for bill payment instructions originating from someone other than the deposit account holder,

Losses from person-to-person payments funded by transfers from credit cards or deposit accounts over which the payee does not have signature authority,

Losses from employee misappropriation of funds held pending access instructions from the payer, and

Potential liability directing payment availability information to the wrong e-mail or for releasing funds in response to e-mail from someone other than the intended payee.

Wireless E-banking

Wireless banking is a delivery channel that can extend the reach and enhance the convenience of Internet banking products and services. Wireless banking occurs when customers access a financial institution's network(s) using cellular phones, pagers, and personal digital assistants (or similar devices) through telecommunication companies' wireless networks. Wireless banking services in the United States typically supplement a financial institution's e-banking products and services.

Wireless devices have limitations that increase the security risks of wireless-based transactions and that may adversely affect customer acceptance rates. Device limitations include reduced processing speeds, limited battery life, smaller screen sizes, different data entry formats, and limited capabilities to transfer stored records. These limitations combine to make the most recognized Internet language, Hypertext Markup Language (HTML), ineffective for delivering content to wireless devices. Wireless Markup Language (WML) has emerged as one of a few common language standards for developing wireless device content. Wireless Application Protocol (WAP) has emerged as a data transmission standard to deliver WML content.

Manufacturers of wireless devices are working to improve device usability and to take advantage of enhanced "third-generation" (3G) services. Device improvements are anticipated to include bigger screens, color displays, voice recognition applications, location identification technology (e.g., Federal Communications Commission (FCC) Enhanced 911), and increased battery capacity. These improvements are geared towards increasing customer acceptance and usage. Increased communication speeds and improvements in devices during the next few years should lead to continued increases in wireless subscriptions.

As institutions begin to offer wireless banking services to customers, they should consider the risks and necessary risk management controls to address security, authentication, and compliance issues.

ETHICS OF E-BANKING

In this paper we aim to open up the debate on the ethics of E-banking by focusing on the activities of one case study company in the wholesale banking sector. Press and academic attention to the subject of online banking tends

to focus on consumer products (B2C) and the threat they pose to traditional branch operations if concerns about privacy and security can be adequately addressed. Writers have so far largely ignored ethical issues instigated by the enormous potential of the Internet in facilitating inter-bank transactions (B2B) in the wholesale market by reducing costs. The financial services industry has been through 'structural and operational tumult' since the mid-1990s, and innovative use of new information technology, electronic commerce and the associated cost reductions are driving ongoing changes in banking (Kalakota and Whinston, 1996). New technology brings benefits and risks and new challenges for human governance of the developments (Hamelink, 2000). Harnessing the technology necessary for E-banking is just the first of the challenges faced by the sector. Equally important is the development of the necessary management skills to ensure the sustained success of the new processes. Intertwined in the functional perspectives of marketing, human resource management and strategic planning are the ethical perspectives. One of the new management perspectives that will contribute to long-term success in electronic commerce is the associated moral responsibility of banking organisations and their stakeholders. Because electronic commerce is still developing and is rapidly changing, there is very little experience or agreement on its related ethical issues (Turbin, et al, 2000). However, one of the few perspectives to emerge in the early stages of development is that of trust.

In any transaction trust plays a key role. Face-to-face, transactions allow for the assessment of trust on the basis of physically observed information. This is not normally part of an electronic exchange. Trust may also be based on previous experience of successful transactions with predictable outcomes. This is not yet established in electronic commerce. Where there is no personal experience, the transaction partner might rely on reputation. Similarly, it is too early for electronic commercial activities to have built up a reputation in wholesale banking. The best the bank can hope for is to trade on its terrestrial reputation. High profile risks of electronic commerce such as security and privacy (Kelly and Rowland, 2000), the media and popular myths all act to confound the attempts of business to operate in cyberspace, not to mention the genuine imperfection of existing technology. Building high ethical standards and systems in which transaction partners can trust are imperative management requirements of the sustainable ethical enterprise.

Beyond functional issues there are ethical ideals to which the responsible businessperson should aspire. New information and communication technologies have provided the structure for the new economy (Castells, 2000) and a new economic order. Corporations often have more power and influence than public social institutions, their economic significance sometimes exceeding those of governments (Hamelink, 2000). This level of power must bring with it responsibility. We can no longer look to governments or even religion to guide our activities – we must take responsibility ourselves, whether we are individuals, companies, non-governmental organisations or cyber-networks. There is a clear need for further serious efforts to raise ethical consciousness and ethical behaviour in the 'networked economy' (Zonghao 2001).

From Medieval Trade Fairs to e-Banking

The development of money has been inextricably associated with the growth of trade and commerce. In Europe in the 1100s, rudimentary banking and foreign exchange institutions emerged as a direct product of the medieval trade fairs (Melamed, 1990). Monetary exchange and banking systems then developed rapidly as foreign and domestic trade expanded exponentially following the onset of the industrial revolution. Although commodity-based money dates back to antiquity, money in its present primarily token form (i.e., money that does not exist in any physical form but takes the form of financial claims on banks and other financial institutions) has only assumed predominance during the past 100 years (Chown, 1994).

International trade has grown significantly in the post-war period and with it the associated monetary flows. More recently, deregulation and globalization have led to a spectacular growth in the value of non-trade-related financial transactions. Every transaction whether trade-or non-trade-related gives rise to obligations that needs to be settled through a transfer of money between the parties involved. Settlement of non-trade-related and large value trade transactions is increasingly based on the electronic large value payment systems, which have been developed since the 1960s. Together this has led to a major expansion in payment and settlement systems which now handle payment volumes on a daily basis that collectively dwarf economic output in the main industrial countries. Electronic banking started with the use of proprietary software and private networks, but was not particularly popular until the emergence of the Web (Turbin et al 2000). The Internet and other global on-line networks have created new commercial opportunities for networked commerce. Development of an Internet electronic payment system provides opportunities for the creation of completely new sets of global and national trading relationships. The Internet offers the possibility of 'open systems' payment and settlement systems that operate in parallel to existing, more traditional bank-based networks. Electronic banking and electronic commerce are now seen as an inevitable aspect of financial services. The new global commercial market place permits goods to be ordered and paid for electronically irrespective of location. This requires new institutional structures as well as changes to existing outdated legal, commercial and ethical systems (Kalakota and Whinston, 1996). The changes brought about by electronic commerce are similar in scope to those experienced when medieval trade fairs were established in Europe in the 11th century. The comparison is particularly apt, since that period saw the emergence of many of the banking institutional structures and payment instruments, which are now being reformed by the spread of E-banking. The case study and subsequent discussion presented here represent the findings of a pilot study into the ethical implications of electronic commerce in the business-to-business context. Semi-structured interviews were conducted with managers playing key roles in the bank's electronic commerce strategy. The study should be regarded as 'work in progress' and a number of questions for further research have been raised.

Case Study

The ABC Bank Group is active worldwide with around 1,500 branches and over 50,000 employees in more than 70 countries, including all the major financial centres. Ranked by total assets, market capitalisation and size of customer base, ABC Bank is one of Europe's leading banking groups. This case study focuses on Investment Banking, which is one of the bank's four main divisions, and in particular the business area of foreign exchange trading run by the subsidiary XYZ in the City of London. As noted earlier, press and scholarly attention to the subject of online banking has tended to focus on consumer products while the enormous potential of the Internet in facilitating inter-bank transactions by reducing costs has been largely ignored. There are increasing numbers of people in the world who are classified by banks as 'high net worth' meaning they have more than $300,000 in liquid assets. All banks are chasing this business, from which they can earn high fees for arranging and managing investments. It is estimated that XYZ earns some 40% of its profits from just 12% of capital usage in this area.

There is absolutely no incentive for the bank to offer this group of customers web-based services that will cut out the banks intermediary and advisory role and hence reduce income by cannibalising the existing lucrative business. Prospective electronic commerce projects in this business area therefore stand little chance of internal acceptance and the associated financial support. Projects which are likely to result in job losses within the bank through their automation of paper-based tasks also require support from sufficiently powerful factions if they are to go ahead, and tend to result in considerable tensions between areas of the bank reliant on traditional processing and the electronic commerce development teams. In order for an electronic commerce project to be financially supported it must demonstrate the potential to generate a positive return or be deemed necessary to keep up with competitor innovation in the area concerned, and 'not tread on too many toes internally'.

One project that met these criteria was the development of a website which offered customers access to and information about the most important Internet applications concerned with investment banking. The service provides the latest news together with selected charts and useful links. Online trading in currencies is already possible, and additional transaction applications dealing with bonds, shares and derivatives will be online very shortly. Customers have their own personalised access to the world's capital markets online, and can see and respond to changes in global currency prices in real time. The system customers are tapping into is the same as that used by XYZ for trading in the markets on its own account, in other words it is a multi-million pound investment in state of the art technology with the latest security protections.

The bank has focused upon the foreign exchange transaction as its 'flagship' online product because such activity forms a natural starting point for capturing related business from customers. Very few international banking services do not involve the purchase or sale of currency, so from handling a customer's foreign exchange transactions it is relatively easy for XYZ to cross-sell other products or services. In many cases foreign exchange trading is offered to customers as a 'loss-leader' because of this potential.

Although start-up costs are incurred in 'plumbing in' customers' systems to that of the bank, by settling transactions online the trading costs incurred by XYZ are more than halved. Fewer trading staff are required and the customer is 'locked in' through the system plumbing in process, so it is therefore more likely to use XYZ for subsequent related investment banking services. If the anticipated volume of trading is high enough, XYZ can offer to 'plumb in' a customer free of charge and still save money. However, the real potential of such online trading for XYZ does not lie merely in automation, but in the 'white-labelling' of the foreign exchange service. This means that the online trading facility is made available to the clients of XYZ's customers, branded as if the service actually belonged to the client. For example, if XYZ's customer is an Italian regional bank, then foreign exchange transactions can be made between XYZ and all the Italian bank's clients worldwide. From the end customer's perspective, the system they use for trading appears to belong to the Italian bank, because it will be 'badged' appropriately. The advantage to XYZ is the extension the facility affords to its customer base, as money laundering regulations prevent an investment bank from accepting transactions from individuals in this area, so the Italian bank performs a useful intermediary function. For the Italian bank the attraction is the ability to 'piggyback' access to an expensive and sophisticated online system, thereby incurring prestige but none of the set up costs.

A potential problem with this system lies in the allocation of credit limits. If XYZ sets a ceiling of £20 million per transaction based on its assessment of the risk involved in dealing with the Italian bank, then the online trading system affords the same luxury to each of the Italian banks customers, who may be far less creditworthy. Consequently, XYZ developed an 'add on' system which allows the Italian bank to set appropriate sub-limits for each of its customers that are using the system. The system was developed in consultation with XYZ's Credit Managers and designed to replicate both the qualitative and quantitative judgements that were previously made manually. The expensive Credit Manager role within investment banks is now threatened because of the success of the online system, which is now being applied to XYZ's own account trading. Ethical overview Consideration of the ethics of eBusiness has tended to focus on areas relating to the fragility of information collected and held electronically and transferred via computer-mediated communication. These include privacy of information about individuals, accuracy of information, ownership of information and intellectual property and accessibility of information held. These perspectives focus very much on the individual consumer and disregard the significant area of electronic commerce that is business to business. In the B2B case privacy based issues around information control are less critical at the personal level. By looking at a business to business case, we identify the moral precepts relevant to the case which may form a basis for further consideration of ethics in this area. These relate to: freedom of choice; transparency; facilitating fraud (ethical/illegal activities of others). It should be noted however, that this choice of moral issues is inspired by this particular case.

There are likely to be other issues which would have risen from different sets of circumstances. Hence, while we think that these issues may have wider currency, we urge continued, systematic consideration of relevant ethical issues in this context. In this section we refer to some ethical theories to help identify rigorously observed notions of right and wrong. In particular, we identify discourse ethics as a potentially useful perspective to apply to electronic commerce. First though, on the positive side, the reduction of costs means that organisations can improve service and potentially generate more profits for shareholders and job security for employees. On the other hand, job losses are the means by which costs are cut and this has social implications for those in the firing line. The displacement of job opportunities away from face-to-face and back-office service roles to information system professionals is a common feature of the electronic commerce revolution (Turban et al 2000). Employment issues aside, however, there are also positive aspects of online trading for business customers and in turn consumers. As the case study points out, access to expensive online systems is enabled by 'piggybacking'. From an ethical point of view, this means that high quality systems are not held by an exclusive group but made available to those other than the wealthiest, hence opening up fair access. Access to sophisticated systems comes with a catch. The need for 'plumbing in' of software and hardware, which means that business customers are locked into XYZ's facilities, is a form of restriction of free choice. When we buy one product from a certain supplier, we do not normally expect that this means our future choices of supplier are restricted in practice. The key ethical issue here is that the business customer should be quite clear that there are significant implications for future freedom of choice of suppliers of foreign exchange and related services. In much the same way that Microsoft has been criticised for implicit locking in of customers to its software, electronic commerce through reliance on customising computer access to the specific service encourages, even forces, the user to come back to a supplier once used. As a customer –whether a business customer or consumer – once time and energy has been put into setting up the electronic access, psychological choice for alternatives are removed. This is both a clever marketing ploy, and a somewhat devious capturing of business if the customer is not entirely clear about the extent of commitment which they are making.

It is in this respect that transparency is so critical for ethical e-Banking. Cyberspace offers fantastic opportunities for disguise. This can be used for overcoming prejudices (Rogerson, 1999) but also for misleading either customer or supplier as to who you are and what you are offering. Clearly, outright fraudulent activities are to be condemned, but how far is it ethically acceptable for electronic commerce activities to convey ambiguously, by hint or absence of clarification, what it is they are offering? The white labelling aspect of our case study is illustrative here. Just like purchasing 'own label' products in a supermarket that are not actually made by the supermarket, there is an issue of misrepresentation. Branding theory demonstrates that we are drawn to products and producers that we recognise and trust (Ind, 2001). If the Italian banking consumers think that they are being supplied with the service by the Italian bank, not XYZ there is a basic problem of transparency. In the case of a packet of soap powder or cereal, there may be no real consequence other than discomfort at having been mislead. In cyberspace transactions, the consumer will be operating with significant capital as if they were dealing with the institution they know and trust when in fact it is a third party. Given the concerns about privacy and fragility of information mentioned above this could also have worrying consequences for the party whose details are gathered by XYZ in this case. Discourse ethics states that ethical actions are those that are reached by transparent, full, open discussion including all those who are connected in any way to a decision. Here we offer some details of its basic precepts (drawn from Spence 1998). Discourse ethics theory finds its origins in contemporary philosophers Karl-Otto Apel (1976) and Jurgen Habermas' (1992) theories of real communication. It focuses on the reaching of a consensus by a process of argumentation. Kettner (1996) defines this approach as following the principle that ethically sound arrangements are those governed by unrestrained, fully participative argumentative dialogue or discourse. He goes on to outline five constraints for the use of this theory in practice:

1. Autonomous articulation of need-claims;
2. Bracketing of power differentials of the participants;
3. Transparency;
4. Participants should have empathetic ability in relation to different roles;
5. There should be comprehensive inclusion of all who will be affected.

Steinmann and Lohr (1994) define the principles of discourse ethics, explaining its categorisation as a cognitive ethical theory thus: "such a claim assumes that when there are disputes about competing moral positions, universal, reasoned solutions can be reached through sensible application". Furthering the tradition of the Erlangen school, Steinmann and Lohr have developed a particular theory of discourse ethics drawing on what Lorenzen called 'dialogical argumentation', which he suggests is the means by which the problems of communal life can be mastered. This follows earlier notions of philosophical constructivism, which suggest that a person can only really understand something as true when they have had a part in constructing it (Cooper, 1996). Steinmann and Lohr (1996) propose the transcending of personal short-term objectives as the means by which to seek social peace, which they define as a general free consensus. They take trouble to point out that their position is not one of relativism. The normative element of their work is that peace must be held as the highest value, and social institutions must be designed to support the stability of peace. A successful exchange according to discourse ethics theory would be considered to be an argument, in the form of a thorough, constructive discussion, which enables the building of a new normative basis for a decision. Thus, through communication, an understanding of one's own and others' needs and normative groundings are reached, and then a new alternative built through consensus. Criticisms of discourse ethics are that it assumes too optimistically that participants are genuinely seeking the best outcome, that they can be persuaded by rational argument to change their original opinion and that they do not want to force their view on others. Further, concern has been expressed that participants need to have achieved a sophisticated level of moral reasoning, and would need to be familiar with both the process of discourse ethics and the culture of participants when attempting to reach a consensus with members of different countries. For discourse ethics theory to apply, the culture of an organisation must itself encompass values like tolerance, candour and constructive criticism, for consensus in companies to be a possibility. Adoption of a discourse ethics approach in E-Banking would mean that all transaction partners should be absolutely clear who they are dealing with and what the implications are. Where white labelling occurs, all concerned should be quite clear with whom they are doing business. The ideal circumstances of discourse theory will not of course always be possible, nevertheless the principles provide a benchmark against which action can be measured (Preuss, 1999).

We have already dismissed fraudulent activity as both illegal and unethical. What about the facilitating of fraudulent activity? How much responsibility do businesses have to prevent their products and services being used in the pursuit of illegal activity? In the US, for example, the selling and marketing of handguns emphasising the fact that the grip does not reveal fingerprints has been questioned in ethical terms (Brenkert, 2000). The Swiss banking system of confidentiality has repeatedly been challenged when criminal investigations are underway. XYZ is now enabling money laundering. While the bank itself can claim that it has not dirtied its hands, it is by implication responsible in some way. These questions require us to consider the role of business in society. Historical perspectives that the business of business is to maximise profit, are no longer acceptable in the light of limited government power to deal with the global welfare issues of which business is an inherent part. Social contract perspectives on new roles and responsibilities of business organisations encourage responsibility for actions and consequences in the B2B and B2C contexts.

In the XYZ case the issues are not limited to the B2B perspectives because of the apparent direct link to, for example, the Italian bank's customers. Here we see the features of e-Banking contributing to increasing depersonalisation, although corresponding standardisation of credit decisions. Ethically speaking, adding automatically applied rules to the allocation of credit limits can be viewed in two main ways.

First, Kantian theory is concerned with the duty of the individual to act in a way that is universalisable, reversible and demonstrates respect for persons. In practice this means that rules of action can be identified which are absolute and independent of context or consequences. Furthermore, utilitarianism is concerned with following that course of action that maximises the greatest good for the greatest number: rule utilitarianism is where the rule applied results consistently in the maximisation of utility. Hence, according to both Kantianism and rule utilitarianism, rather than allowing favouritism, poor judgement, even corruption and bribery to determine credit limits between the banker and the customer, standard, automated procedures mean that everyone gets the same treatment. Whether this treatment is just depends on the quality of the rules applied.

Second, taking the personal relationship out of responses to credit limit applications has the effect of dehumanising transactions in the banking sector. A client's relationship with a bank or credit manager can be established over years of loyal customer commitment. Boiling this down to boxes ticked and computer-generated numbers would, according to an ethic of care, result in the loss of the development of individual relationships, human touch and use of intuition. Such aspects may be viewed as heretical to the new electronic economy, but human networks are just as important a part of business practice as electronic networks.

Interestingly, however, as with the application of standard rules, the just response to credit applications by the credit manager is reliant on the quality of decision-making that the manager applies. The difference is that we would not necessarily expect the manager to make absolutely, clinically applied standard decisions each time. The manager may include sensitive, intangible aspects in the decision-making process.

SCIENTIFIC MANAGEMENT IN E-BANKING

Our study of organisation theory begins with Frederick Taylor's scientific management, initially formulated at the turn of the nineteenth to the twentieth century. Major subsequent developments have been administrative management theory, where the management process is defined and bureaucracy theory. Taylor's work may be loosely classified as time and motion or work study, and this adheres to the rational model, which views organisations mechanistically, seeing the attainment of maximum efficiency as achievable by putting together the parts in an effective way under the control of management. Hierarchy, authority and rational decision making are fundamental to this.

In the 1920s, as evidenced by the Hawthorn experiments, the human relations model began to gain ground, based on social structures of people at work and motivation. This model pointed to democratic, employee centred management. More recent developments have seen the growth of the systems model of organisations, where they are viewed systemically as open systems responding to environmental changes and maintaining a steady state. This systems approach links well with empirical research in socio technical systems, and contingency theory. Broadly, the systems model recommends that if an organisation is not functioning properly the sub-systems should be examined to see that they are meeting organisational needs, and the organisation examined to see that it is well adjusted to its environment.

These tasks are charged to a management sub-system. From a systems perspective, business organisations today may be characterised as complex, adaptive, human activity systems. In so far as such systems are devoid of human interaction, focus on a purely mechanistic approach may yield valuable results. As system complexity, and particularly the degree of human activity, increases, this approach is seen to break down, and human viewpoints need increasingly to be considered. There can be little doubt that this "micro-social" view of an organisation is highly relevant to e-business.

In e-banking we have a situation in which technology and human activity are increasingly integrated, with the whole "socio-technical" system becoming the key focus of attention. The systems perspective on management offers insights into this which are not available through alternative views. The following section investigates this perspective more fully, as a precursor to applying systems thinking and knowledge management to e-banking.

SYSTEMS THINKING

In common usage, the term 'system' has come to mean very little. How, for instance, are we to make sense of a single definition of 'system', when it is applied to such diverse objects as 'a hi-fi system', 'the railway system', or 'the system of planets and stars we refer to as the Universe'? Clearly, before the idea of a Knowledge Management system is investigated, we need a common definition of 'system': this is what this section aims to achieve.

To begin with, a system is more than a simple collection of components, since properties 'emerge' when the components of which systems are comprised are combined. So, for example, we may gather together all of the components that make up a bicycle, but only when they are assembled do we have the emergent property of a mode of transport. Further, all systems must have a boundary – try to envisage a system without a boundary, and it soon becomes clear that the concept is meaningless. When considering the nature and properties of any system, care should be taken when looking at the components of the system in isolation.

These parts, or sub-systems, interact, or are 'interdependent', and so need to be considered as a whole or 'holistically'. In addition, there is likely to be a discernible structure to the way sub-systems are arranged – in a hierarchy, for example. Finally, there need to be communication and control with the system, and it has to perform some transformation process.

So, in summary, a system may be defined according to its:

- Boundary

- Emergence
- Holism
- Interdependence
- Hierarchy
- Transformation
- Communication and Control

Further to this, and following Checkland, it is possible to conceive of a typology of systems divided into:

- Physical systems, which are either natural or designed; and
- Human activity systems.

Generally, whilst physical systems might be *complicated*, and require significant skill and expertise to construct or even understand, only human activity systems exhibit *complexity*. In essence, human activity systems are complex adaptive systems.

In order to relate this understanding to Knowledge Management, it is necessary to determine how organisational systems should be categorised. Are they designed physical or human activity systems, or some combination of the two? Designed physical systems are mechanistic or deterministic, requiring a view of the World that is mechanical or technical, and typically rule-based. By way of an example, think of an aeroplane.

It is clearly a designed physical system, whose design depends on the laws of aerodynamics. Construction of, arguably, this most complicated of all machines requires considerable skill and knowledge, but it all accords to a set of rules, most of which are well known. It is these properties that have led to such systems being seen as closed in relation to their environment. By contrast, organisational systems, whilst they might make use of designed physical or even natural systems, are made up of human actors. They are open, complex adaptive systems of activity.

Following this line of thought, Knowledge Management systems emerge as fundamentally systems of human activity, exhibiting voluntary behaviour. Such systems take an interpretivistic or subjective view of the World: a view which sees not 'objective reality', but a series of human perspectives and opinions. They are probabilistic rather than deterministic. However, whilst KM systems may be primarily human activity systems, they may also contain sub-systems which are technological or organisational, and these sub-systems may have a role in better enabling the KM to function.

A way of conceptualising this is to think of a KM system as a human activity 'lens' through which all knowledge activity is viewed, and in accordance with whose characteristics and properties that activity is interpreted.

Knowledge management and knowledge acquisition therefore consist fundamentally of human activity, and as a consequence are subject to human perception and agreement. The whole, bounded KM system which this is seeking to manage or interpret may contain technological and structural elements, but the purpose of these is simply to better enable the human activity system to function.

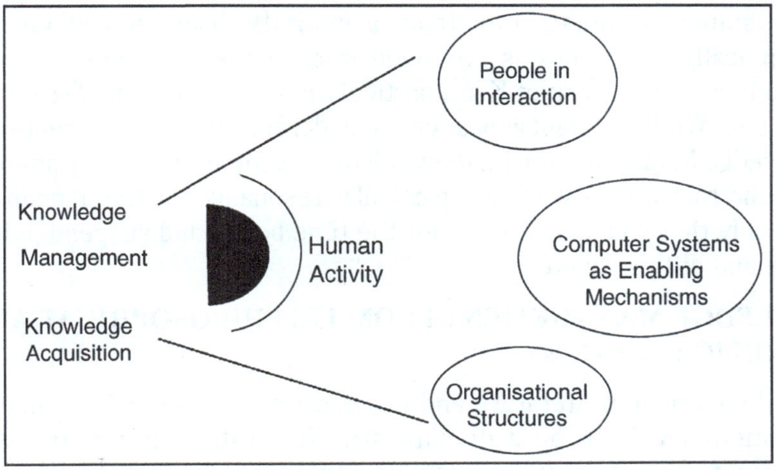

Fig. The Nature of Knowledge Management Systems

By seeing KM in this way, we move ever closer to a new viewpoint from which to observe, implement and manage e-business systems which, after all, we have posited as socio-technical. This view is supported by research that highlights the complexity of social systems, and the inappropriateness of studying such systems using scientific methods. In effect, in the social sciences, there is a complexity that stems from the introduction of human activity. Such activity is not absolutely predictable, being based on intended and unintended actions that do not easily lend themselves to study by the reductionist rules of repeatability and refutation.

Systems thinking, then, may be seen as fundamental to an understanding of KM and, hence, e-banking, which may be recast as a human activity, supported or enabled by structural and technological sub-systems. By way of a summary, each of the properties of systems can now be related directly to issues in KM.

THE PHILOSOPHY AND THEORY OF SOCIAL SYSTEMS

This is a section which some readers will find interesting and others may wish to avoid. We include it here for completeness, and because we see it to be of immense importance. Much of our research has focused in this area, with the aim of providing a sound foundation for the ultimately practical issues, which, in our view, need to be underpinned by significant philosophical and theoretical principles.

SOME PHILOSOPHICAL ISSUES

The philosophical and theoretical perspective on which this study is grounded sees the World as socially constructed, and therefore argues that human issues are best seen from a socially constructed viewpoint. Philosophically, this study is grounded in critical social theory, as derived specifically from the work of Kant, particularly as described in *The Critique of Pure Reason*. Whilst it might appear odd to underpin a twenty-first century study of Knowledge Management with the work of an eighteenth century philosopher, we contend that Kant's work has particular resonance for the domain of KM, and ask only that you bear with us for the time being, and suspend judgement until the end of this chapter.

KNOWLEDGE MANAGEMENT FROM ITS PHILOSOPHICAL AND THEORETICAL ROOTS

Information from literature and empirical evidence suggests knowledge management (KM) to be a domain still at a rather immature stage of development. One of the key reasons identified for this is that the concept of *knowledge* lacks a clear definition. This chapter lays out an approach to underpinning the concept of knowledge, and thereby KM, from philosophical and theoretical perspectives, and from this underpinning reframes the domain of KM.

The work is presented, not as a definitive study, but as something to promote what we see as an essential debate. Comments on the issues discussed here will be gratefully received by the authors. It is common to come across ideas of knowledge that categorise it according to: explicit or implicit; explicit or tacit; more than data or information and less than wisdom; and so on. Whilst of value in themselves, such definitions lack something fundamental, as is evidenced by the fact that they commonly give rise to selfreferential definitions. What seems to be happening here is that we are learning something about the nature of knowledge, having assumed that we already understand what it is *in its essence*. In this study we meet the problem head on, but first a word of caution! Attempt a once-and-for-all definition which will satisfy everyone on the question of knowledge as a concept.

We, as authors, would like to think that we can achieve the task of setting in motion an important debate, which will yield satisfactory outcomes to its participants: this chapter aims to be the beginning of that debate. So to the question 'what is knowledge?' To answer this, our research has been on two complementary dimensions: philosophical and theoretical. First we have undertaken a very brief review of the KM literature in order to determine a rationale for the study. Following this, the chapter looks at what we might learn from epistemology, with the explicit aim of determining what the theory of knowledge has to tell us about its management.

This particularly addresses how an understanding of such theory helps unravel the problem of what knowledge *is*, without which we argue that *management* of knowledge is impossible. We next take a deeper historical perspective on philosophical developments in the understanding of knowledge. Beginning with concepts taken from Greek philosophy, this history covers the thinking of early Western philosophers through to the most recent ideas of contemporary epistemology. Issues covered include scientific versus alternative forms of knowledge, knowledge as objective reality or subjective understanding, and Kant's transcendental philosophy.

Where relevant, specific philosophical positions are addressed, examples being Locke's definition of knowledge according to its source in intuition, reason or experience, and Hume's concept that knowledge is limited to sense experience. A review of pre-critical philosophy is used as a backdrop to the philosophical perspective which forms the basis of this research, grounded on Kant. Specific theoretical developments seen to be relevant to an understanding of Knowledge Management are then reviewed, including work by Habermas on the 'subject-knowerobject' problem, through which knowledge is defined both in relation to objects of experience and to the so-called *a priori* categories that the knowing subject brings to the act of perception. Through this and other theoretical perspectives, the social and reflective dimensions of knowledge are investigated in more depth.

The aim throughout is to relate these ideas to an understanding of knowledge that will inform contemporary Knowledge Management studies, and the final section of the chapter looks at the practical guidance for knowledge and its management which might be derived from these perspectives, and how this relates to selected recent approaches to KM.

A BRIEF REVIEW OF THE LITERATURE

The knowledge management (KM) literature seems, from our perspective, to lack certain fundamentals, which a review of some of the more recent publications will serve well to illustrate. There seems to be only a limited attempt to base the development of organisational KM systems on any explicit foundation. So, for example, in an otherwise excellent paper partially targeted at unearthing the 'conceptual foundations' of Knowledge Management, Alavi and Leidner discuss views of knowledge taken from IT and other literature, commenting that: *"The question of defining knowledge has occupied the minds of philosophers since the classical Greek era and has led to many epistemological debates. It is unnecessary for the purposes of this paper to engage in a debate to probe, question, or reframe the term knowledge ... because such an understanding of knowledge was neither a determinant factor in building the knowledge-based theory of the firm nor in triggering researcher and practitioner interest in managing organizational knowledge."* It is our contention that, by any reasonable standards, such a view is unsupportable.

It seems that what is being said could be characterised in any of the ways listed below, none of which seems to us to be acceptable:

- The philosophical and theoretical foundation for the study of knowledge has nothing to tell us about how we should manage it.
- Philosophy and theory is of no value to the debate
- That we should accept there being no more to say about the underpinning to the domain, and it is therefore acceptable to proceed on a conceptual or pragmatic basis.
- That all of the philosophical and theoretical issues raised in the past have been incorporated into current approaches.

However we should interpret this statement, it is our hope that, by the end of this chapter you will be closer to our view: that philosophy and theory are central to an understanding of how to manage knowledge. Not all writers exclude consideration of fundamental underpinning to the domain, but mostly the research can be characterised as eclectic and somewhat unconnected in character. So, for example, Sutton draws widely from philosophical and theoretical sources, including, for example, Heidegger and Wittgenstein. But the arguments and perspectives are presented in a rather disconnected manner.

For the most part, research in KM is primarily pragmatic or at best conceptual. In an essentially pragmatic study, Earl proposes a taxonomy of KM strategies. The problem is that, although the *practical* significance of the findings presented are without question of value, there seems to be nothing to tie the ideas together, with even the conceptual schema being strangely fragmented. Other recent publications on KM seem to follow a similar tack. These include a Journal of the Operational Research Society special issue, and a range of edited texts.

WHAT WE MIGHT LEARN FROM EPISTEMOLOGY

It seems perhaps curious that so much of the writings in KM ignore epistemology, or the theory of knowledge:

- "Philosophers have given a great deal of thought to ... what we can know – or mistakenly think we know – through perception or through other sources of knowledge, such as memory as a storehouse of what we have learned in the past, introspection as a way to know our inner lives, reflection as a way to acquire knowledge of abstract matters, or testimony as a source of knowledge originally acquired in others".

What seems to be put in play here is the dependence, for an understanding of the concept of knowledge, on its generation and retention from and within a number of sources. Certainly, any idea of managing knowledge that solely focuses on material stored, for example, in databases, seems insufficient even from this initial cursory inspection. Further to this, reason may also be seen as a source of *a priori* truths, though such an approach has been challenged by empiricist philosophers. Together with the position taken on these issues by this chapter, which is essentially Kantian. Finally, from the domain of epistemology, we have to consider the process of inference, by which basic knowledge is extended. Within the limits of a chapter of this length, as suggested, attempt to make sense of these issues and their relation to KM in our contemporary Western World. But before that, we would like to delve a little deeper from a philosophical and theoretical perspective.

ISSUES FROM PRE-CRITICAL PHILOSOPHY

Some of the earliest and most influential Western evidence of civilizations struggling with systems of thought is to be found in Greek philosophy, which, at its most basic, might be seen as a search for *certain* knowledge. Central to this is the concept that our senses may delude us, and a questioning of whether we have any basis for believing that sense experience brings us into contact with objective reality. This led early Greek philosophers to the central question of what the world consisted of. Socrates, for example, believed it possible to achieve objective knowledge through conceptual analysis.

It is here that we first see the division of knowledge into *what is* and *what ought to be*: factual and normative knowledge. Seeking knowledge through conceptual analysis led Socrates to his 'theory of ideas', which was further developed by Plato. In essence, Plato considered ideas to have objective reality, and knowledge to be gained by a continuous cycling between ideas and perceptions. Plato argued that whilst the objects of our knowledge do exist those objects cannot be attributed to anything in our world of perception. They existed in an ideal state in a world beyond our knowledge. Aristotle's approach to determining knowledge takes into account the philosophies of nature, mathematics and metaphysics. Here again we see the attempt to establish absolute truths through the process of reason. Moving forward to the beginnings of our modern age, the reawakening of interest in the ideas which had absorbed the Ancient Greeks led, during the Renaissance and beyond, into what might be characterised as arguments over method.

Emerging pre-eminent during the period of the Enlightenment was scientific method, within which knowledge was seen as objectively determined. To those espousing early scientific method, we live in a world which is realistic and deterministic, and which can be understood through reductionist method, using such approaches as induction, deduction and experimentation. Truth was to be determined through repeatability, refutation, verification and falsification. Into this world came Descartes as the first of the 'Continental Rationalists'. In terms of knowledge creation, the relevance of Cartesian method is that truth is judged according to rational criteria – even sense experience should be verified through reason. In opposition to this we might cast the British empiricists. Locke, as with the empiricists who followed him, accepted rationalism as giving an insight into *concepts*, but did not see that this necessarily gave an insight into *reality*. For the latter, acquisition of knowledge is attained in the empirical sciences. We thus reach a position where the concepts of knowledge production through rational and empirical processes are in opposition, and to the philosophy of Immanuel Kant.

A FOUNDATION IN KANTIAN CRITICAL PHILOSOPHY

Kant's critical problem, as first formulated in the letter to Herz, concerns the nature of objective reality. Prior to Kant, all philosophical schema took objective reality as a 'given', and sought to explain how it was that we could have knowledge of this reality. If this were taken as definitive, it is easy to see how we might build (empirical) knowledge in the way suggested by Locke: that we are born with a 'tabula rasa' or 'blank slate' on which impressions are formed through experience. This explains the pre-Kantian debate of reason versus experience as the source of our knowledge. The rationalist view was that, by reason alone, we are able to formulate universally valid truths; empiricists, by contrast. Kant's insight, and unique contribution, was to bring together rationalism and empiricism in his new critical transcendental philosophy.

The basis of this is his 'Copernican Revolution' in philosophy. Loosely stated, this says that objective reality may be taken as existing, but that, as human beings, we have access to this only through our senses: we therefore see this objectivity not as it is, but as we subjectively construct it. Unlike Berkeley, Kant does not claim that objects *exist* only in our subjective constructions, merely that this is the only way in which *we can know them*: objects necessarily conform to our mode of cognition. For this to be so, Kant's philosophy has to contain *a priori* elements: there has to be an object-enabling structure in our cognition to which objective reality can conform, and thereby make objects possible for us.

This is what lies at the heart of Kant's Transcendental Idealism:

- Whilst objects may exist (be 'empirically real'), for us they can be accessed only through their appearances (they are 'transcendentally ideal').
- Our cognition does not conform in some way to empirical reality, rather this 'objectivity' should be seen as conforming to our modes of cognition. In this way, we 'construct' our objective world.
- Objects of cognition must conform to our sense experience. So, in this sense, knowledge is sensible, or the result of experience.
- These objects must conform to the object-enabling structures of human cognition. The resultant transcendental knowledge is (at least) one stage removed from objective reality, and is, according to Kant, governed by *a priori* concepts within human understanding.

KANT AND KNOWLEDGE

The thinking with which Kant was grappling in trying to make sense of knowledge is well represented by the positions of Leibniz (1646-1716) and Hume (1711-1776). In effect, both saw knowledge as either necessary and *a priori*, or contingent and experiential. Kant's unique argument is that, whilst accepting these forms of knowledge, although all of our knowledge *begins with* experience, it does not follow that knowledge all *arises from* experience: in other words, experience may be simply the cue that gives rise to knowledge claims not derived from it.

One of these key non-empirical knowledge claims is the concept of freedom. A further claim made by Kant is that knowledge can be built only through the combined interactions of sensibility and intuition: *"Without sensibility no object would be given to us, without understanding no object would be thought. Thoughts without content are empty, intuition without concepts are blind. It is, therefore, just as necessary to make our concepts sensible, that is, to add the object to them in intuition, as to make our intuitions intelligible, that is, to bring them under concepts. These two powers or capacities cannot exchange their functions. The understanding can intuit nothing, the senses can think nothing. Only through their union can knowledge arise"*. Further, that which appears to us is not simply a collection of unconnected sensations: it consists of content as well as form, and without the latter would be meaningless.

Form is intuitive, and cannot arise out of the sensation – it must be *a priori*. A sequence of auditory sensations, when heard by us, becomes a tune; but the tune is not inherent in the original data (this would be equivalent to empirical data supplying its own form, and even if there is seen to be an inherent form supplied with the data, there is no reason why we should see it as such, this requires apprehension) – it must be supplied by us. *"What objects may be in themselves, and apart from all this receptivity of our sensibility, remains completely unknown to us. We know nothing but our mode of perceiving them – a mode which is peculiar to us ... Even if we could bring our intuition to the highest degree of clearness, we should not thereby come any nearer to the constitution of objects in themselves"*. Kant's philosophy has been the foundation for much of philosophical debate which continues to the present day, one of the primary themes of which is pursued below. Whilst Kant's work, even within this one text of *The Critique of Pure Reason*, is complex and extremely diverse, certain strands of relevance to KM can be drawn out. Primary amongst these is the need to take a position on the way in which we see the World.

As human beings, our viewpoint is essentially made up of two factors:

1. The concepts which we are born with, which Kant called *a priori* concepts. An example of this which seems particularly relevant to our research domain, given its dependence on communication, is the idea that we are born with an ability to communicate through language.

The actual language used is acquired empirically, but the ability to acquire it seems to be endemic to the human race.

2. An empirical understanding which we access through our senses. The relevance of this is that we do not have access to 'objective reality', only to that which our senses are able to show us (for Kant, this formed the basis of his theory of 'Transcendental Idealism', giving rise to 'objects for us' which differ from what objects might be 'in themselves').

Theoretically, this philosophical position leads to a grounding in those theories relevant to human understanding and interaction, which are to be found in the social and cognitive domains. Given that in KM we are seeking mutual understanding, those theories which best explain social interaction might be seen as especially relevant. Drawing again on the stream of social enquiry emanating from Kantian philosophy, this leads, through the critical social theory of the early twentieth century Frankfurt School, to contemporary social theorists such as Foucault and Habermas. It is to the latter that the fields of management science and, now, Knowledge Management, turned for support in the 1980s and beyond, and it is therefore strands of Habermasian theory that are used to underpin this study.

The detailed range of these theoretical perspectives is too great for inclusion in a chapter of this length, but the principles will show its relevance to KM. Habermasian critical social theory is concerned with issues such as social inclusion, participation, and a view of how we *ought to* undertake intervention in social domains.

A THEORETICAL PERSPECTIVE GROUNDED ON KANT

Critical philosophy has been fundamental to a stream of thinking in the 20th century to the present day, giving rise to forms of critical social theory, for which the primary contemporary theorist is Habermas. Habermas follows Kant in arguing that reliable knowledge is possible only when science assumes its rightful place as one of the accomplishments of reason. Whilst the achievements of scientific study are not disputed, the problem perceived through the route followed by Kant and Habermas is that the methods of science which have grown out of modernity are effectively self referential: that scientific study sets up rules and then tests itself against its own rules is a procedure which has given considerable advances to modern society, but to regard this as representing all knowledge is mistaken.

Habermas refers to the worst excesses of this as 'scientism': that we must *identify knowledge with science*. Habermas' argument is against the objectivistic illusion of unreflecting science (or otherwise modern positivism), in which, with (for example) approaches such as experimental method, rules are devised against which observations are then tested in an unreflective and self-supporting manner. Habermas argues that the scientistic (positivist) science community is unable to perceive self reflection as part of its process, and that such reflection must be built into an understanding of knowledge.

As with Kant, Habermas' challenge is whether knowledge is reducible to the properties of an objective world, leading him to a definition of knowledge which is based on perception, but only in accordance with *a priori* concepts that the knowing subject brings to the act of perception. Further, since the knowing subject is a social subject, all knowledge is mediated by social action and experience, leading to Habermas grounding his theories in communicative interaction, an issue we return to at the end of this chapter.

In essence, Habermas argues that these difficulties disappear once a scientific basis for our thinking is denied. For example, suppose science (as is suggested by Kant and Habermas) is seen as just one form of knowledge, which in any case is simply a convenient human perception of how the world works. Now, all human endeavour becomes mediated through subjective understanding.

However, this problem has been replaced with another, which may be stated as follows:

- Accepting all human actions as mediated through subjective understanding leads to the possibility of a basis for Knowledge Management in the universal characteristics of language.
- There is no longer a dichotomy between subject and object.
- The difficulty we are now left with is essentially a practical one, of how to incorporate these ideas into management practice.

To address this, Habermas' theory of communicative action presents a universal theory of language which suggests that all language is oriented towards three fundamental validity claims: truth, rightness and sincerity. What is most compelling about this theory, however, is that all three validity claims are *communicatively mediated*. This viewpoint is most radically seen in respect of the truth claim, where it is proposed that such a claim results not from the content of descriptive statements, but from the Wittgenstinian approach casting them as arising in language games which are linked to culture: truth claims are *socially contextual*. These ideas are taken forward to provide an approach to KM which is grounded theoretically and philosophically.

KNOWLEDGE MANAGEMENT AND ITS APPLICATION TO E-BANKING

Knowledge Management has been defined by some as the extraction and conversion of 'tacit' knowledge on an individual and organisational level into 'explicit' knowledge. Further, it is argued, this explicit knowledge often takes the form of specific electronic 'tools' or 'assets' which can be manipulated for competitive gain, examples being intranets, groupware and knowledge repositories. 'Tacit' knowledge, by contrast, is often described as the 'hunches, intuition and know-how' of people, or their 'skills, routines and competencies'. The aim of KM as regards tacit knowledge might be seen as an attempt to make this often highly subjective knowledge explicit, thereby facilitating its management through such enabling media as technology.

The link to e-banking here is clear: the target of most e-banking (and, indeed, e-business) technology is the systematic recording and management of information – or, perhaps, "explicit knowledge". A deeper study of KM shows us the limitations of such an approach, which should be replaced by techniques aimed at integrating e-banking systems into the socio-technical fabric of its existing and potential users. Additionally, a number of studies have called for a more holistic, systemic approach to KM. One such example is the division into the 'know-why, know-what, know-who, know-how' questions of KM. Know-how might be seen as technologically focused, know-who as socially constructed and depending on processes of debate, whilst know-why and know-what relate to issues of power and coercion in societal structures.

Finally, there are numerous classifications which aim to demistify KM. Included in these, for example, is the division into socialisation, externalisation, combination and internalisation. But what does 'managing knowledge' infer from the standpoints discussed in this chapter?

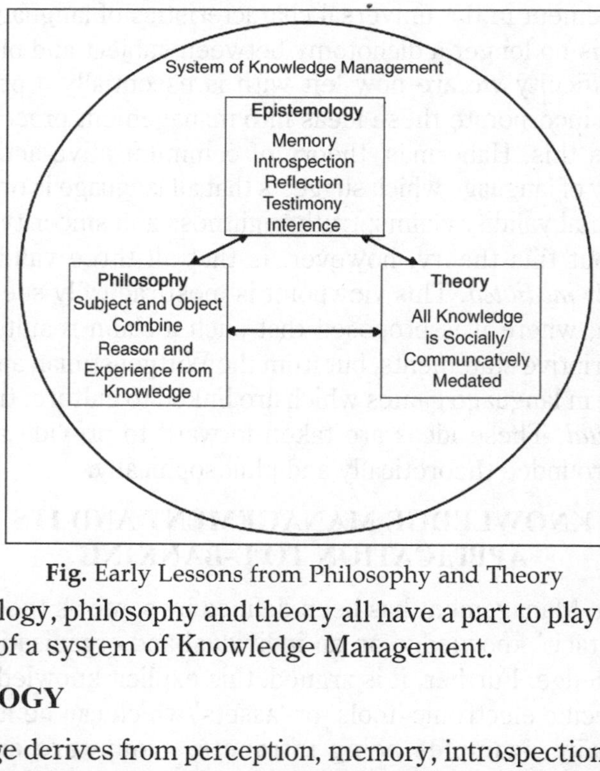

Fig. Early Lessons from Philosophy and Theory

Epistemology, philosophy and theory all have a part to play in determining the elements of a system of Knowledge Management.

EPISTEMOLOGY

Knowledge derives from perception, memory, introspection, reflection and testimony. It is subject to *a priori* concepts, and is extended by inference.

PHILOSOPHY

From the time of Greek philosophy, there have existed fundamental arguments regarding knowledge being a search for truth, or for normative agreement. Initially the argument raged between rationalism and empiricism, and one of Kant's unique contributions, through the 'Copernican revolution in philosophy', was to unite subject and object in knowledge production: subject and object, according to Kant, make each other possible.

THEORY

Following the thinking of Habermas, in which can be seen the echoes of Kant, science produces only one form of knowledge – believing all knowledge to be scientific is an 'objectivist illusion'. What Habermas does that is so helpful to us is he sites knowledge as mediated by social action, and subject to reflection, without which we end up with self-referential systems which are in danger of producing 'knowledge' based on disputable 'facts'.

To misquote an anonymous source:

- "The problem ain't so much what we know, as what we know that ain't so."

SUMMARISING THE ISSUES FROM PHILOSOPHY AND THEORY

The philosophical and theoretical investigation conducted in researching the content of this chapter indicates that knowledge is a human construct, inseparable from the *a priori* understanding that we, as human 'actors', bring to its formation. Epistemology shows us that, for example, 'knowledge as a storehouse' is at best a partial view, and one which, for the purpose of KM, must be supported by other knowledge sources and processes. So, as human 'actors', the *a priori* conceptual understanding we bring to the knowledge process, if omitted from the management of knowledge, leaves that management impoverished.

The primary philosophical concerns in relation to KM may be summarised as:

- We see knowledge both in terms of 'truth' and 'normative understanding'. Knowledge is not solely concerned with those irrefutable truths or facts which might be scientifically proven.
- Reason and experience contribute to our knowledge store and our understanding.
- The 'objectively real' and our 'subjective understanding' are interlaced, each providing the conditions for the other.

KM, therefore, must be addressed *through* a human perspective: there is no sense in a KM process focused only on the 'objectively real'. Following the Kantian stream of critical social theory into the twenty-first century, the most significant theorist, and one on whom much management systems development has been based, is Habermas. From Habermas' theoretical approach to communicative action, it is possible to see a way forward through knowledge derived from a communicatively mediated rationality, in which normative understanding is privileged ahead of 'objective truth'. The remaining objective of this chapter is therefore to ground KM in a more comprehensive view of social theory.

SOCIAL THEORY

This section is a search for the relevant theoretical underpinning to Knowledge Management research and practice, further expanding the philosophical and theoretical. Information is sought from two sources. In the first place, there is the underpinning social theory itself. Secondly, the holistic intent of Knowledge Management is pursued through a review of systems theory.

A study is undertaken of social theory, reviewing the paradigmatic arguments, and assessing potential future directions. To establish the theoretical underpinning, the relevant philosophical, ontological, epistemological and methodological issues are outlined, and placed in context with the development of the natural sciences and systems science. Difficulties encountered in management science are reviewed, providing a basis for development of the relevant theoretical underpinning to Knowledge Management. Critical social theory has been applied extensively in information management and offers potential as a way forward for Knowledge Management.

This chapter aims to determine a practical approach to Knowledge Management by exploring work already undertaken in the domain of management science, where the relevant ideas have been a subject of debate since the 1960s.

This exploration begins with an outline of the branch of critical social theory to be applied, and pursues this line of reasoning through critical systems thinking, relating each approach to the paradigm problems encountered. These views are then synthesised to produce an approach to Knowledge Management which is true to the principles of critical social theory

SOCIAL THEORY: THE PARADIGM PROBLEM

This section reviews the work of Burrell and Morgan, which is used to provide a framework for understanding the development of Knowledge Management within this chapter.

Burrell and Morgan positioned all social theories into one of four paradigms: functionalist, interpretivist, radical humanist and radical structuralist, according to the extent to which they were subjective versus objective or regulative versus radical.

The subjective-objective dimension can be seen in terms of four elements: an ontology, an epistemology, a view of the nature of human beings, and methodology. The ontological debate concerns the nature of reality, the two opposing extremes of thought being realism: that reality is external to the individual and is of an objective nature; and nominalism: that reality is a product of individual consciousness.

Epistemology is concerned with the grounds of knowledge, or how the world might be understood, and this understanding communicated as knowledge.

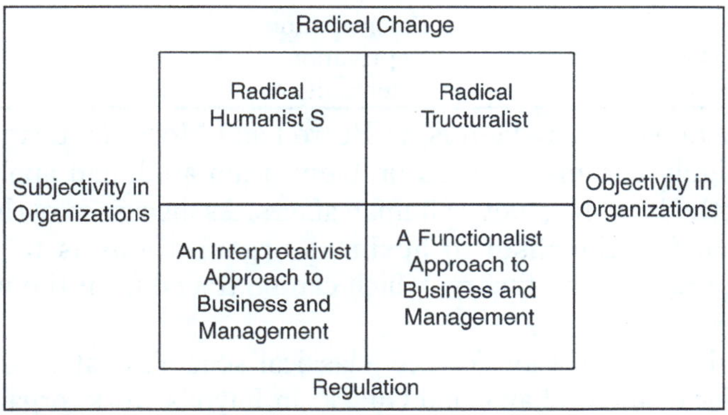

Fig. Four Paradigms for the Analysis of Social Theory

The two opposing extremes are positivism: knowledge is hard, real and capable of being transmitted in a tangible form; and anti-positivism: knowledge is soft, more subjective, based on experience and insight, and essentially of a personal nature. Human beings may be viewed on a scale from deterministic: determined by situations in the external world and conditioned by external circumstances; to voluntaristic: they have free will, and create their environment.

The view taken of ontology, epistemology and the nature of human beings directly influences the methodological approach which is adopted. A realist ontology, positivist epistemology and view of human beings as largely deterministic, leaves nomothetic methodologies as the appropriate choice.

Such methodologies are characterised by a search for universal laws that govern the reality that is being observed, leading to a systematic approach. A nominalist ontology, anti-positivist epistemology and view of human beings as largely voluntaristic, indicates ideographic methodologies as appropriate: the principle concern would be to understand the way an individual interprets the world, with a questioning of external 'reality'.

The regulation-radical change dimension was the result of Burrell and Morgan recasting the then prevalent order-conflict debate. The sociology of regulation emphasises a view of society based on preservation of the status quo, whilst the sociology of radical change is "concerned with man's emancipation from the structures which limit and stunt his potential for development."

Table. The Regulation—Radical Change Dimention

Ragulative Organization Theory with:	Radical Organization Theory is Concerned is Concerned with:
The status quo	Radical change
Social order	Structure conflict
Consensus	Modes of domination
Social intergration and cohesion	Contradiction
Solidarity	Emancipation
Need satisfaction	Deprivation
Actuality	Potentiality

The functionalist paradigm is, in Burrell and Morgan's terms, regulative in nature, highly pragmatic, often problem orientated, and applying natural scientific methods to the study of human affairs. As discussed earlier, the early application of functionalism to business organisations is to be found in functionalist organisation theory, which can be traced from the work of F.W. Taylor.

This laid the foundation for the 'classical school', contributors to which have been, for example, Fayol and Gulick. In Fayol's work, organisations are characterised in terms of a reality which can be investigated systematically, taking a highly mechanistic view of human beings, informed by an objectivist ontology and epistemology. Functionalist organisation theory can be identified anywhere from the most objective to the most subjective margin of the paradigm, and, from a social theoretical perspective, the objective-subjective dimension does not automatically imply ply a paradigm shift.

The relevance of this to e-banking goes back to the earlier arguments for e-banking as a human-centred domain. A functionalist approach to e-banking does not exclude human action, but risks functionalist issues such as structure becoming the main focus of attention: a 'real world' which is seen to exist independently of human perception. There is, of course, a real danger that, given the highly technological foundation of e-banking systems, the domain will be dominated by functionalism. The purpose of this chapter is to offer an alternative to this in order to avoid the critical problems of such a focus. As with the functionalist paradigm, the interpretative paradigm is also regulative, seeing social reality as "...little more than a network of assumptions and intersubjectively shared meanings." Burrell and Morgan argue that the ontological assumptions of interpretative sociologists lead them to seek an understanding of the existing social world from an ordered viewpoint, and do not allow them to deal with issues of conflict or coercion. Interpretivism suffers criticism from all sides.

Functionalists see it as finding out about problem situations without any means of solving problems or, in effect, producing any 'hard' output. Radical thinkers criticise interpretivism for its support of the status quo - the existing power base: interpretivism is fine for achieving consensus, provided the conditions required for consensus-seeking pre-exist; it has no means of overthrowing existing power structures or of resisting coercion. The radical humanist paradigm has much in common with the interpretative paradigm, being nominalist, anti-positivist, voluntaristic and ideographic, but unlike interpretivism "emphasises the importance of overthrowing or transcending the limitations of existing social arrangements." Radical humanism aims to help humans achieve their true potential.

The emphasis is on radical change and the attainment of potentiality through human emancipation, or release from 'false consciousness':

- ".. The consciousness of man is dominated by the ideological superstructures with which he interacts, and these drive a cognitive wedge between himself and his true consciousness. This. 'false consciousness' inhibits or prevents true human fulfilment"

Radical humanism is the position from which critical theory may be taken as a perspective. In relation to the earlier discussions, interpretivism offers an alternative to functionalism in so far as it does not accept there to be an objective reality but only socially constructed reality, but that its relativist stance makes it unable to view itself as the target for reflection. The radical humanist paradigm offers a way forward.

Through critical social theory there is the possibility of moving beyond a debate located firmly in the sociology of regulation to a critically reflective, radical position. Habermas provides the primary theoretical support which management science has taken to underpin interventionist approaches based on radical humanism. Habermas' Theory of Knowledge Constitutive Interests sees all human endeavour as undertaken in fulfilment of three knowledge constitutive or cognitive interests: technical, practical (in satisfaction of human interaction or communication) and emancipatory. Jackson follows the cognitive categories of Habermas, and argues that in Western industrialised society the technical interest has been accorded too much primacy. Jackson goes further in asserting, again after Habermas, that, in fact, practical questions are re-defined as technical ones, effectively blocking the separation of what we ought to do from questions of how we ought to be doing it.

The radical structuralist paradigm shows similarities with functionalist theory, but advocates radical change through structural conflict. Whilst a tenable view for organisational theorists, its value to this study is limited, since the aim is not revolution but gradual change. These paradigmatic considerations carry implications for an approach to e-business based on KM.

APPLYING KNOWLEDGE MANAGEMENT TO E-BANKING

So far in this chapter we have argued for a systems-based KM approach to e-banking, bringing together the social and technical elements of the domain in order to better balance the technology and human elements of e-banking systems. We begin building a perception of these as systems informed directly by social theory, in order to further enhance their foundation. In the study of social systems, where the key to the functioning of the system is human activity, functionalist views are therefore questioned. Experimentation is of limited value in such systems: the utility of problem solving, functionalist techniques, is diminished when dealing with ill-defined, highly complex human activity systems.

As a result, 'softer' methods of approaching the issues are seen to be of value. Social systems are therefore where the reductionist, functionalist approach meets its most severe challenges, and where systems views are seen to be of increasing relevance. Social science involves increasing complexity; a complexity which derives from the systemic nature of the objects of study and the introduction of human activity. The limitations of functionalism are demonstrated in the study of social systems, where predictive models may be seen to have only limited value. Social action does not lend itself to study by reductionist methods, but is determined by the meaning that individuals attribute to their actions.

This brings the discussion back to the functionalist - interpretivist debate, but now, with the support of social theory, this debate can be taken further and a foundation developed for e-banking. This is the direction which has been pursued by part of the systems movement, from its origins in the so called Singer/ Churchman/ Ackoff school, through to present day systems thinkers. Jackson has shown how the soft methods of Ackoff, Checkland and Churchman all adhere to some degree to the assumptions of the interpretative paradigm, and identifies a third position which distinguishes hard, soft and emancipatory systems thinking.

The argument is for a pluralist approach, which sees the strengths and weaknesses in each of the three areas and argues that each one must be respected for those strengths and weaknesses. All of this is mirrored in e-banking, where the argument, which from a Habermasian perspective is seen as a critical social problem, is wrongly cast within the sociology of regulation. E-banking is best perceived from a radical humanist perspective. Seen from social theory, for example, the concept of an e-banking system consisting of only the computer element might be seen as excessively functionalist, though perhaps with some evidence of interpretative analysis. But interpretative approaches alone would be seen as insufficient to deal with the complexity of human interaction, which critical social theory, whilst addressing the functionalist and interpretivist, also signals progression to a more radical approach.

Much work in this area has already been undertaken in the management science domain, and it is from here that further support will be sought in formulating an alternative framework for e-banking.

CRITICAL SOCIAL THEORY: THE THEORETICAL UNDERPINNING

Critical social theory can be traced from the work of Kant, through Marx and the Frankfurt School. The two most widely accepted modern theorists are Foucault and Habermas, and it is to the latter that management science turned in the 1980s in order to develop a more human-centred view of its domain. CSoT applied to the field of e-banking is appealing for its denial of a grounding in solely natural scientific principles.

Seen through a scientific framework, e-banking appears as objective: the same for all involved since it is independent of human perception. CSoT refutes this, seeing our understanding of the world as determined by *a priori* conditions which are uncritically accepted. Critical theory seeks to expose these, and thereby release human beings from their 'false consciousness' to a position from which true potentiality can be attained. An alternative to the current functionalist and interpretivist approaches to e-banking may be found in developments based on the work of Habermas, in particular his theory of knowledge constitutive interests.

Table. The Theory of Knowledge Constitutive Interests

Knowledge Constitutive Interest	Basis of Human Interest	Underlying Paradigm	Methodological Approach
Technical (Control)	Labour (Instrumental action)	Functionalist	Empiricism Rule-based
Practical (Understanding)	Communicative Interaction	Interpretative	Hermeneutics Human-Centred
Emancipatory (Freedom)	Authority (Power)	Radical/Critical	Critique Human-Centred with critical intent

Habermas' three cognitive interests, technical, practical, and emancipatory, are identified in labour, interaction and power, and provide conditions for the three sciences, empirical/analytic, hermeneutic, and critical. The empirical/analytic, served by the natural sciences, is therefore seen as satisfying only the technical interest. Since, as has been argued, traditional approaches to e-banking might be seen as having their roots in the natural sciences, or at best in an interpretative ontology, they appear from a Habermasian perspective as an insufficient basis for e-banking. What is needed in addition is critical science to deal with issues of power and domination, serving the emancipatory interest. From these roots came the development, in the domain of management science, of critical systems thinking.

CRITICAL SYSTEMS THINKING

Critical systems thinking (CST), it is argued, accepts the contribution of both hard and soft approaches, and, through critique, enhances awareness of the circumstances in which such approaches can be properly employed. The pragmatism of functionalist approaches and the lack of theoretical reflection in interpretivism allow CST to expose both as special cases with limited domains of application. The value of CST to e-banking can be demonstrated through the Burrell and Morgan grid. Burrell and Morgan's work, together with contributions from Oliga, may be interpreted as shown in Figure.

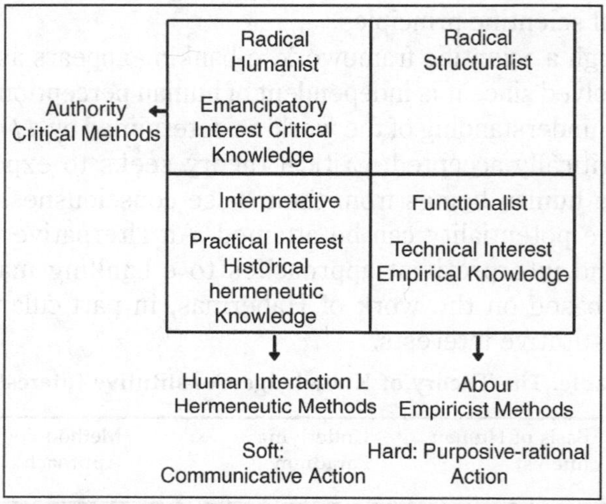

Fig. The Social Validity of Hard, Soft and Critical Approaches

This perspective further supports the view that traditional views of e-banking largely emerge as serving the technical interest, focusing on purposive-rational action. The alternative, evident in this domain since the 1970s but still limited in acceptance, is the service of the practical interest from the interpretative paradigm, relying on the communication of perceptions and consensus forming. The key to the value of critical systems thinking to e-banking rests on the value of an approach based on critical pluralist method.

A CRITICAL SYSTEMS FRAMEWORK FOR KNOWLEDGE MANAGEMENT IN E-BUSINESS

As has been argued, the foundations of a critical systems approach to organisational studies owes much to the work of Churchman which was built on foundations laid by Singer, and has been continued by Ackoff and other adherents to the systems school. In the rest of this chapter as suggested, attempt to draw together the issues from organisational theory, systems theory, social theory and philosophy, and critical theory, to provide a foundation for e-banking based on systems thinking and KM. In short, the objective is to construct a critical systems framework for e-banking.

The route we have chosen to this is a review of the progress in critical systems thinking within the domain of management. As the objective is an *action* framework, the initial approach is to assess the various means by which critical systems has been applied in management settings, before drawing this together at the end to form a framework for action. The work of Jackson and Keys proved a major turning point in the development of a critical framework which is true to the commitments of critical systems thinking.

By looking at the range of problem contexts and at the systems methodologies available for addressing these contexts, Jackson and Keys provided a unified approach which draws on the strengths of the relevant methodologies, rather than debating which method is best, and argued for a reconciliation focusing on which method to use in which context, controlled by a 'system of systems methodologies'.

SYSTEMS METHODOLOGIES IN E-BANKING

A convenient starting point is to be found in the work of Jackson and Keys and the 'system of systems methodologies'.

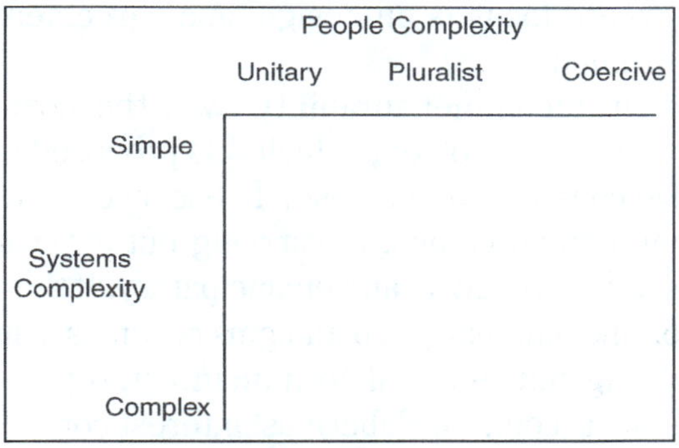

Fig. The System of System Methodologies

The SOSM is used as the basis for an argument that organisational intervention can be understood through determination of the problem contexts within which it is conducted. The SOSM is therefore, first and foremost, a problem context classification, through which it is argued that problem contexts can be categorised according to the extent to which they exhibit a 'people complexity', from unitary to coercive, and a 'systems complexity', from simple to complex. So, for example, a 'problem' may be seen as 'simple-unitary': 'simple' in the sense that it has few elements and few interactions between elements; 'unitary' in terms of people complexity in that there is only one agreed viewpoint. Such 'problems', it is argued, do not require discussion, and can be 'solved' using hard, scientific, 'design-based' methods. By contrast, a 'complex-coercive' context not only exhibits system characteristics of high complexity but also cannot be progressed until the power issues (hence high 'people complexity') dominating the context are resolved.

In use, this problem context classification forms a basis for determining the methodology to be used in the intervention. So, for example, a 'simple-unitary' problem context will demand the use of a methodology which focuses on design issues, and does not seek to address multiple viewpoints, since these are seen not to exist within the context identified. For e-banking, our earlier analysis would seem to place it at complex – pluralist/ coercive on this classification.

TOTAL SYSTEMS INTERVENTION AND THE COMPLEMENTARIST FRAMEWORK

In the early development of total systems intervention (TSI), the paradigm position taken by the SOSM was core to the approaches recommended. That is to say, it was accepted that different problem contexts 'inhabited' different paradigms, and further that communication across paradigms was difficult if not impossible. So, for example, a problem context characterised by high levels of disagreement among participants, in which debate might be seen as a way forward, might prove difficult to combine with a requirement to produce a technical system, where focus is on design, and agreement as to means and ends is typically assumed.

Whilst 'paradigm incommensurability' was the normal view in these approaches, a way out of the problem, which was proposed through Habermas' theory of knowledge constitutive interests. In essence, this theory was that, at a fundamental level, human beings, in carrying out any task, seek to satisfy three interests: technical, practical and emancipatory. If this could be shown to be so, then the incommensurability of paradigms becomes a human construction, rather than something fundamental to human activity, and by acceding to approaches which take account of Habermas' interest constitution theory, such incommensurability could be overcome.

By the early 1990s, the most comprehensive attempt at applying this theory to organisations was undertaken through total systems intervention, where 'complementarism' was promoted as a way forward, enabling methodologies from different paradigms to be used together in a single intervention, applied to the same problem situation. Total systems intervention (TSI), offered a 'critical complementarist' approach which was seen to be capable of resolving both the theoretical and practical difficulties. This Habermasian perspective sees the functionalist view of organisations as an insufficient basis, serving only the technical interest. What is needed in addition is social science, to service the practical (hermeneutic) interest in achieving communication and consensus, together with critical science to deal with issues of power and domination, serving the emancipatory interest.

Critique is applied in a Kantian sense, aiming to:

- Free participants from purely instrumental reason;
- Enable practical reason, to examine and re-examine assumptions made; and

- Inform the choice and mix of methodologies in relation to the changing nature of the problem contexts and the strengths and weaknesses of the available methodologies.

TSI is iterative and recursive. Iteration implies that the process is continuous, rather than a start-end method. The TSI ideology explicitly recognises the part played by both technical and human activities in organisations, and the extent to which human interpretation may in some instances so distort the so called 'real world' that study of the latter may become meaningless.

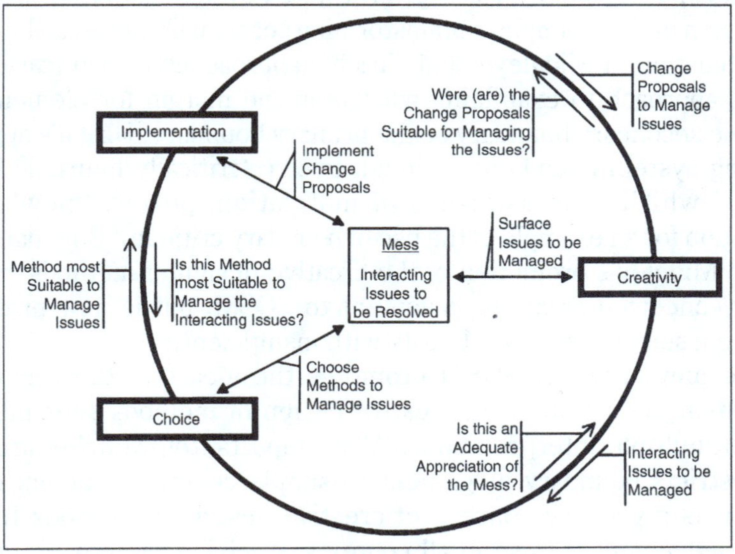

Fig. The Process of Total Systems Intervention(TSI)

TSI provides a critical framework within which choice and implementation of methodologies in an intervention can be managed pluralistically. The problem context is viewed as a 'mess' within which creativity is used to surface the issues to be managed; reflection on creativity then seeks to critically determine whether an adequate appreciation of the 'mess' has been gained. Originally, the SOSM was used to inform methodological choice. Latterly, it has been recommended that this be replaced by the complementarist framework.

In this, first metaphor is used to determine whether the key concern is one of design (technical), debate (practical) or disimprisonment (emancipation); then a methodology or mix of methodologies may be chosen to address the problem context, with critical reflection on whether these methodologies are indeed the most suitable being carried out prior to implementation.

THE CREATIVE DESIGN OF METHODS

Midgley and Ulrich focus on boundary critique as the key to mixing methods. Boundary critique has a long history, but it is from Ulrich and Midgley that the recommendation to critically challenge what should or should not be considered part of any system is drawn. Midgley's approach is to begin with a boundary definition which is accepted as arbitrary, and progress by "... looking for grey areas in which marginal elements lie that are neither fully included in, nor excluded from, the system definition." The critical choices made at the boundary are of truth and rightness: truth being represented by questions of what is, and rightness by questions of what ought to be. Critical assessment of the system boundary should be undertaken by a representative sample of participants in the system. Typically, an arbitrary system definition is presented for discussion in, for example, a brainstorming session. Critique can be informed by a combination of Midgley's and Ulrich's approaches to boundary critique: Midgley's approach to examining what is in the margin for elements which support the secondary boundary or the primary boundary; Ulrich's approach to challenging system boundaries through twelve 'critically heuristic boundary questions' which address issues of motivation, power, knowledge and legitimisation for an example of the use of boundary critique). Boundary critique has led to Midgley's promotion of the creative design of methods which was originally conceived as an improvement to SOSM, but is now promoted as addressing issues which SOSM deals with insufficiently.

For example, whilst SOSM promotes the idea that there is only one interpretation of each method, creative design of methods sees methods as subject to multiple interpretations. Also, importantly, Midgley argues that SOSM restricts boundary judgement to simple coercive problem contexts, whereas it is a primary concern of creative design of methods to free up boundary judgement for use in all contexts. Applying the creative design of methods requires that the interventionist maintain a multiplicity of participant viewpoints, together with the potential mix of methods or parts of methods required to address them, within an ongoing critical framework. The boundaries must be critically challenged throughout an intervention, and the approach will be continually changing in response to this and participant feedback.

DIVERSITY MANAGEMENT

Flood and Romm promote diversity management and triple loop learning as an improved way to deal with mixing methods. In essence, triple loop learning is seen as a way to manage the diversity of methodologies and theories available, in addressing the diversity of issues to be found in organisational intervention. In application, diversity management is about managing design, debate, and might-right issues, and so is a complementarist approach to the perceived hard, soft and critical factors which Flood and Romm see as pervading organisational problem contexts. The overall objective of diversity management might be seen as the enhancement of emancipatory practice.

CRITICAL SYSTEMS PRACTICE

In his most recent work, Jackson continues to promote critical pluralism, but now sees this in terms of developing TSI into critical systems practice. Pluralism in the use of methodology is advocated: ".. to make the best use of the methodologies, methods, models and techniques ... to tackle diverse and difficult problem situations while ... ensuring their continual improvement through research". This pluralism must: encourage flexibility in the use of methodologies, enabling practitioners to decompose approaches and tailor them, within a critical framework; encourage paradigm diversity: using methodologies from different paradigms in the same intervention. What is clear in Jackson's recommendations is his view that it is no longer possible to rely on Habermas, but, rather, pluralism calls for a meta-methodology, for which Jackson lays out nine "constitutive rules".

This "critical systems meta-methodology" is seen by Jackson as a "structured way of thinking which understands and respects the uniqueness of the functionalists, interpretative, emancipatory and post-modern theoretical rationales, and draws upon them to improve real-world problem situations." It is recommended that methods for enhancing creativity are applied, at least, from these perspectives, and that methodologies are used as appropriate. Critical systems practice, Jackson recommends, should be embedded within a systems and action research approach; should ensure a pluralism of 'clients', theoretical and methodological pluralism, pluralism in the modes of representation employed, and pluralism in the facilitation process; and should be sensitive to the organisational context in which it is operating.

Further, the claim to be using a generic system methodology, according to the particular theoretical rationale it is designed to serve, must be justified according to the principles and guidelines established for the use of each generic systems methodology. In essence, critical systems practice calls for an improved version of TSI, but it is as yet unclear how these ideas are to be applied. In essence, a set of constitutive rules are provided, but a framework within which these might be operationalised is not given.

CRITICAL PLURALISM

In critical pluralism, Mingers promotes what he sees to be missing in critical approaches to the use of a mix of methodologies: multi-paradigm multimethodology. From a discussion of current dilemmas in critical systems thinking, Mingers promotes emphasis on engagement with agents in a social context as the basis for his approach. The focus, he suggests, should be on the relationship between three notional systems seen to form the multimethodological context: the problem content system, or real world situation of concern; the intellectual resources system, or available theories and methodologies; and the intervention system, or agents undertaking the intervention. In theoretical terms, the work is strongly grounded on Habermas' theory of communicative action but with the added consideration of knowledge being linked to power. Mingers uses this thinking to develop a framework for mapping methodologies against the four phases of appreciation, analysis, assessment and action, based on Habermas' three worlds. The actual process of critical multimethodology, he argues, "will be a continual cycle of reflection, judgement, and action".

PRAGMATIC PLURALISM

Taket and White offer pragmatic pluralism as a means of mixing methods from an essentially postmodernist perspective. Their approach is strongly grounded theoretically, with the suggestion that guidelines, examples, stories and metaphors are of more value than prescribed frameworks for action. The approach is expressly holistic, and sees pluralism as a means of addressing diversity. Pluralism, they argue, should be applied to the roles of the interventionist, modes of representation, and the nature of the client.

It is explicit that work with the disempowered should be seen as fundamental within any intervention context. In application, it is argued that, in any intervention, there will be multiple rationalities to be managed, and that, whilst guidelines may be offered for addressing these, there is little to be gained from a prescriptive approach. The approach is therefore largely left open to the practitioner, who should follow a strategy of mix and match, operationalising what feels good in accordance with the guidelines provided: the interventionist should recognise differences in methodologies and match these with variety in the local context. Triangulation, the use of parts of methodologies in combination, a flexible and adaptive stance, and critical reflection, are all fundamental to the application of this approach. This completes the review of perspectives on KM.

DISCUSSION AND CRITIQUE

Each of the approaches has in common the aim of addressing diverse problem contexts with a diversity of methods. The system of systems methodologies originally presented an approach to matching problem context to methodologies seen to be applicable to that context, and was expressly based on Habermas' theory of knowledge constitutive interests (KCI). Total systems intervention initially operationalised SOSM into a process for intervention, similarly based on KCI; arguably, diversity management has continued this theme, being essentially an improved application of KCI.

With the creative design of methods came an approach which sought to develop the ideas of SOSM and TSI, enabling the use of parts of methodologies, synthesised to address a unique problem context, within an expressly critical framework. The creative design of methods also introduced the idea of a basis in Habermas' theories of communicative action, rather than the theory of knowledge constitutive interests. The recent critical systems practice advocated by Jackson also moves away from KCI, recommending instead that any claim to be using a methodology according to its theoretical rationale must be justified "according to the principles and guidelines established for the use of each ... methodology."

In this, Jackson might be seen as returning to the need to recognise the distinctive background and theory of each methodology. Pragmatic pluralism draws on a very broad theoretical range, but much is premised on critical social theory. Finally, critical pluralism provides a framework for intervention grounded on Habermas' theory of communicative action.

If we seek to summarise much of the work in KM in terms of theoretical development, the primary basis is to be found in critical social theory, with the main theories being applied in determining intervention approaches having been Habermas' theory of knowledge constitutive interests, and his theory of communicative action. Of these, communicative action seems the most promising arena in which to ground future development of the domain, and to apply KM to e-banking.

TERMS OF E-BANKING

The term Internet Banking or E-Banking Internet both are used as supplement. E-Banking is the one of the major part of E-Financing. Hertzum et al. (2004) defined E-Banking as web-based Banking. In other words E-Banking refers to the banking operations, which is done over World Wide Web. However, more comprehensive and well-established definition is given by the United Nations Conference on Trade and Development (UNCTAD). This definition covers almost all area of E-Banking.

Internet banking refers to the deployment over the Internet of retail and wholesale banking services. It involves individual and corporate clients, and includes bank transfers, payments and settlements, documentary collections and credits, corporate and household lending, card business and some others (UNCTAD, 2002). E-Banking information architecture is modelled as client-server architecture. A client operating through a PC linked to Internet opens the special E-Banking site of his bank and then, using a set of special secure numbers, gets access to his bank accounts and has the opportunity to consult them, as well as to make all necessary payments and transfers form his personal accounts. When the transaction number is exhausted the bank sends him a new set of numbers for his individual transfer sessions. In some cases the bank provides customized software. The bank software program can also be utilized offline, for example for preparing the payment orders offline and then making the actual order online. The client receives all numbers separately, mainly by mail. The bank also provide clients with similar facilities in its premises so that clients can use the bank equipment such as an ATM or a special facility linked to the main terminal facility called Multimat, permitting them to effect the same account examination, payment and transfer operations without consulting the bank staff.

Evolution

Since the late 1990s E-Banking has developed from virtual insignificance to tens of millions of users worldwide (OECD, 2001). However, E-Banking is the product of different generations of electronic transactions. The current web-based internet or E-Banking is the latest of several generations of systems: *Automated Teller machine (ATMs), Phone Banking, PC or House Banking.* Automated teller machines (ATMs) were the first well-known machines to provide electronic access to customers where as in phone banking, users call their bank's computer system on their ordinary phone and use the phone keypad to perform banking transactions. PC banking superseded phone banking and allowed users to interact with their bank by means of a computer with a dial-up modem connection to the phone network. Phone and PC banking entailed maintenance costs associated with keeping up to date with diverse modems and with avoiding prohibitively complex installation procedures. After those generations Deutsche Bank launched the very first Internet banking project in Latin

America in 1996 and Citibank has developed a special "e-toolkit" across all its branches worldwide (UNCTAD, 2002). E-Banking uses the web browser for the user interface and the Internet for data transfer and download of software, and so has a potential for reducing maintenance costs. For users, E-Banking provides current information, 24-hour s-a-day access to banking services. The primary services provided by e-banks are transferring money among one's own accounts, paying bills, and checking account balances. Loans, brokering, share trading, service bundling, and a host of other financial services are being added to these primary services. E-Banking is widely used in, among other places, the Nordic countries. In 2001, E-Banking was used by more than 25% of the population in Norway, Sweden, and Finland, and by 15% of the population in Denmark (OECD, 2001). In 2004, E-Banking usage in Denmark had grown to 45% (Statistics Denmark, 2004). Jeevan (2000) notes that with rigid controls giving way to deregulation, banks are gearing up their communications infrastructure to obtain a competitive edge from E-Banking, which is fast becoming a reality in India. Nair (1999) points out that E-Banking is fast becoming a strategic necessity for most commercial banks, as competition increases from private banks and NBFIs.

E-banking Opportunity and Challenges

According to the "E-Commerce beyond 2000", the banking and finance sector has been a rapid adopter of E-Commerce because its products could easily be virtualized and the product had priority over place (NOIE, 2000). Yerkes (1998) observes that banks can generate revenue through increased account access fees, and benefit from promotional opportunity to cross-sell products such as credit cards and loans. Whereas Stamoulis (2000) observed that banks initially promoted their core capabilities, such as products, channels and advice, through the Internet, Yerkes (1998) argues that, due to the relative newness of this rapidly growing industry, banks as well as consumers had serious concerns about the security of Internet access to client accounts, which was the biggest challenge (Denny 2000). The advances in Internet security and the advent of relevant protocols such as Integrion, OFX, SET, etc. has put banks in perspective again as financial intermediaries and facilitators of complete commercial transactions via electronic networks and especially via the Internet (Stamoulis, 2000). Consumers are increasingly looking for services they can access from a single entry point. As Denny (2000) observes, awareness of competition has motivated banks to move aggressively in seeking alliances and establishing joint ventures to maintain their claim to this part of the Ecommerce infrastructure. Like there are alliances in the ATM network, Group Network, Money Transfer Network etc.

This is also creating segmentation of networks where the customers of this networks sometimes unable to access to others' network. Seitz and Stickel (1998) note that consumer behaviour in banking changed partly as a result of changes in the amount of spare time available to individuals. Mobility, independence of time and place, and flexibility has become key words in consumer banking. Timmers (2000) supports this view, highlighting the key features of the Internet – such as 24 hour availability, almost immediate access, and the absence of physical borders. Indeed, the Internet has been one of the key drivers in promoting E-Commerce in the banking sector (Jeevan, 2000). The opportunities for banks in the Internet arena are varied (Stamoulis, 2000). Despite this plethora of opportunities, threats to the e-banks abound. One major threat to banks is the "Internet only" virtual banks. With US$ 2 million, one can set up a fully-functional, Internet Only bank and provide payment services on the Internet.

The Internet banks serve also as gateways offering identification and authorization services to a number of third party service providers. There are user-friendly opportunities for conducting business over the Internet with telephone companies, Energy Company, tax board and other institutions. Demand for those services influences also the usage rates of Internet banks. For example in 2002 in USA, 81867 private individuals submitted electronic tax declarations 79727 of them did it through Internet banks and 2140 through tax board's own home page.

(20.3% of declarations were submitted electronically). This is increasing the benefits of Internet banks for the consumers and is a win-win situation for the banks and service providers. Regulatory barriers in many countries are on the wane (Sathye, 1998).

As the Internet gains momentum, governments are under pressure to reduce the barriers to competitive activity in the financial sector still further, to allow existing banks to remain competitive with their newer rivals (Carew, 1998). It is evident that banks can obtain an advantage by exploiting their existing, E-Commerce-ready infrastructure, through leveraging it on the Internet (Fellenstein and Wood, 2000), but this opportunity must be seen in the context of a highly competitive, rapidly-moving market-place in which new rivals are emerging from many different directions. Several studies including Schultz et al. (2001) suggest that security measures that are inconvenient for users may weaken E-Banking prospect, for example because of lack of user acceptance or outright resistance. Dourish and Redmiles (2002) propose a distinction between theoretical and effective security. Theoretical security concerns the level of security that is technically possible; whereas effective security concerns the level of security achieved in practice, and is typically lower than theoretical security. Several studies including Jih et al. (2005) indicate that user adoption of E-Banking is affected by perceived security. This supports a view of security as crucial to the overall usability of E-Banking systems.

E-banking Competitiveness

E-Banking is developing gradually and it is getting acceptance globally. But, whether this field is lucrative for entry can be judged by industry and competitive analysis. Like other industry, Porter's Five Forces Model of Competition (Porter, 1985) can also be applied to understand e-Banking competitiveness.

Rivalry Among Competing Parties

As there is no single internet only bank exist in this world, the current rivalry among the competitor or banks in the banking industry should be considered. Banking institutions are countering their competitors by leveraging E-Commerce technologies and various service offerings online (Morath, 2000). This is a major shift from the early days of Electronic Funds Transfer (EFT), when large organisations introduced electronic banking to simplify the management of their salary and payroll problems. Stamoulis (2000) observes that the Internet is increasingly considered a strategic weapon by banks, which are leveraging it as a distribution channel to offer complex products at the same quality they can provide from their physical branches, at a lower cost, to more potential customers, without boundaries. E-Banking is used to augment their current value chain, offering new product and compete for the customers.

New Entrants

At present, the entry barriers to Internet banking appear to be much higher for new entrants than was the case during the early days of this type of banking. The barriers stem from customer attitudes and the very nature of banking services and products. The traditional banks with a strong customer base have a competitive advantage over newcomers. However, Li (1997) argue that one of the critical factors – barriers to entry – no longer exists in banking. Foster et al (1999) have also observed that competitors can come from any industry to “disintermediate” banks (i.e., eliminate banks as the interface between customers and suppliers). Product differentiation is very difficult for banks, since most of the products sold in retail banking are constrained by legal or industry regulations and, in any case, are readily imitated (Nemzow, 1999). Many countries have de-regulated their banking sector so government policies no longer form an entry barrier to banks’ competitors. Technological know-how in banking also provides low protection to existing banks (Stemper, 1990). As Li (1997) argues, the only significant entry barrier is likely to be the brand name of the service providers in retail banking.

Suppliers

Supplier has much bargaining power in this industry, as there are a small number of large players in the industry (Kotler and Armstrong, 1997). Dial (1995) observes that banking demonstrates the typical attributes of an oligopoly – such as risk avoidance and relatively undifferentiated customer service – which have made it susceptible to encroachment by software giants such as Microsoft, who are attempting to replace banks as intermediaries.

Buyers

As Mishra (2001) has noted, the Internet has levelled the playing field: the bargaining power of consumers is increasing, switching costs are becoming lower (with Internet banking gaining momentum), and consumer loyalties are harder to retain (Nemzow, 1999). Some specific factors that have conspired to create the new competitive environment for banking include: changing consumer needs and perceptions, globalisation, technological innovations, and competition from non-banking entities.

Though many banks offered ‘home banking services’ from a PC during the 1980s and 1990s, the concept was initially a failure due to the lack of a critical mass of PCs and computer literate customers, as well as to the somewhat limited user interfaces initially available (Lucia and Peters, 1998). Home banking, however, is gaining in popularity with increasingly literate consumers, a wider installed PC base and more generic features together with the user-friendly interface the Web enables.

Substitutes

The threat of substitutes to banking in terms of competition from the non-banking, financial, and micro credit sector is increasing rapidly. As Viermetz (1998) observes, the major credit card issuer in the US is not a bank but rather Dean Witter of Discover Card fame. Huggins (2001) points to the fact that traditional boundaries in banking are disappearing. Using EBusiness methods, major retailers and telecom providers are starting to offer financial services to their clients. Attitudes are also shifting from direct transactions to savings and investment, as the baby boomers reach their forties and fifties, and prepare for retirement (Carew, 1998). Increasingly, consumers expect online services from their financial institutions (Constantine, 2000). The trend toward electronic delivery of products and services is particularly important to the financial services industry, where the shift is partly a result of consumer demand, but is also partly a result of the ruthlessly competitive environment (Geyer, 1997).

The analysis of the current state of E-Banking reveals that the field is getting fierce day by day. Every member of this industry is participating to some extent in E-Banking. Substitute products by non-banking sectors, disintermediay issues, brand preference, increased buyer barging power, change of preference made the competitive environment unfavorable for the new entrants. However, to survive existing banking sectors must embrace E-Banking.

E-banking Strategy

Several model of E-Business were tried by different banks all over the world to get them involved in the E-Banking vicinity. The most used E-Business model were *Internet Only, Brick-and-Click or Click-and-Mortar.* However, 'Internet Only' model failed to survive. Security First Net Bank (SFNB) which was formed in 1996 in the US (Humphreys, 1998) and claims to be the first Internet-only bank in the world. But it was acquired by the Royal Bank of Canada in 1998 (Pratt, 2000; Arora 2000), suggesting that customers may still want the comfort of a physical presence. The present trend is 'Brick and Click' or 'Click and Mortar', where banks serve their customers through internet having physical operations simultaneously. Progress in information technology has reduced transportation costs (Vesala, 2000), transaction cost and thus Jeevan (2000) suggests that the Internet enabled banks to offer low-cost, high value-added financial services. Although price incentives can play significant role in getting customers online the service needs to be based on quality rather than price only. Developing technological solutions should was not done with a product or line of business in focus but with a customer relationnship focus with integrated delivery of products and services. Success or failure in Internet banking is greatly determined by the integration of technology infrastructure with the business processes.

LEGAL AND REPUTATIONAL RISK MANAGEMENT

To protect banks against business, legal and reputation risk, e-banking services must be delivered on a consistent and timely basis in accordance with high customer expectations for constant and rapid availability and potentially high transaction demand. The bank must have the ability to deliver e-banking services to all end-users and be able to maintain such availability in all circumstances. Effective incident response mechanisms are also critical to minimise operational, legal and reputational risks arising from unexpected events, including internal and external attacks, that may affect the provision of e-banking systems and services. To meet customers' expectations, banks should therefore have effective capacity, business continuity and contingency planning. Banks should also develop appropriate incident response plans, including communication strategies, that ensure business continuity, control reputation risk and limit liability associated with disruptions in their e-banking services.

A Brief History of Internet Banking

The main purpose that banks have been serving since their inception is keeping our money safe for us. While keeping our money safe, they also let us earn a certain amount of interest on the money deposited with them. Traditional banks have been doing this, and internet banks continue the same function. The only difference is in the way the transactions are made.

Online banking has been around for quite a few years. In fact, it was introduced in the 1980s and has come a long way since then. The last decade has seen a profuse growth in internet banking transactions. Several pieces of legislation have also been introduced in this area.

Though it began in the 1980s, it was only in the mid nineties that internet banking really caught on. What attracts customers to internet banking is the round the clock availability and ease of transactions. Studies estimate that internet banking still has a long way to go. There are several banks that have customers who prefer banking in the traditional ways. Statistics released by the FDIC show that only 40% of the banks in the U.S. offer internet banking facilities worth mentioning. All the others may have an online presence but do not have enough online transactions to justify their presence on the internet.

Some customers have been known to turn to internet banking due to dissatisfaction with standard procedures and practices. The total absence of human interaction appeals to some people. Some customers turn to internet banking facilities for security reasons. This is mainly because of customers being assured of banks' ability to keep transactions safe and secured.

Most online transactions are made using the Internet Explorer interface. The Internet Explorer has been around for more than ten years now.

We all know about internet banking and most of us use it quite often as well, but few of us actually understand about the history of internet banking and how it all came out. Knowing the history of internet banking can be incredibly useful, especially since it will allow you to have more respect for the little things that you take for granted.

How it All Began

Computers themselves have really come an enormous way since their initial establishment, as the earliest electronic computers were so large that they would take up the entire area of a room, while today some are so small that they can hardly be seen at all.

In today's world, computers play an incredibly large role in the way the world exists in general, and the majority of tasks could actually not be completed if not for the use of computers. Although there are certainly some areas and jobs that cannot yet be completed solely by computers and which thus still require actual manpower, for the most part, computers have helped to make life significantly easier, productive, and more convenient for us all.

The history of Internet banking obviously begins with the history of the Internet, which is notoriously known throughout the world now as a household name, but which actually did not even exist too long ago.

Although the term Internet was first adopted around the year 1974, it wasn't until the 1990s that the Internet became a really universal adoption. The Internet grew incredibly throughout the 90s, and as it continued to grow, various different search engines and Web directories were created in order to assist Web browsers, as well to track pages on the Web and allow people to find things more easily.

Internet banking has been around for quite a few years now, but has really only become prominent over the past year or so in particular. Internet banking offers an array of different advantages to the user, including: account balances and history including year-to-date information, the ability to transfer money from one account to another and to payees for bill payments, check history, reorders, and stop payments, check credit card balances and statements, complete online loan applications, secure interactive messaging with staff, and much more. Internet banking basically allows you to be able to do everything that you can in your regular banking institution, only with the benefit that you can do it all right from the convenience of your own home. Not only is this great because you can be comfortable and have peace of mind knowing that you can keep track yourself of all your banking issues, but as well it allows for more ease because you never have to worry about rushing out and making it to the bank in time, as you can complete Internet banking tasks around the clock.

Advantages of Internet Banking Services

The advantages of Internet banking are obvious. Business people can access their personal and business account information while saving a trip to the bank.

You can check your balance whenever you need to, even if the bank is closed.

Not only that, but you can pay your bills online as well, which saves both time and money on postage.

Another advantage of Internet banking is the ability to easily compare services offered by different banks. You can buy financial products and apply for loans online, and in doing so, you can compare your options to ensure that you get the best possible services. You can even buy insurance online through Internet banking services. Stocks and bonds and other investments can be managed with online banking from your home or office independent of a financial intermediary like a stockbroker.

The number one tip for banking online is to be very aware of Internet banking security. Identity theft is a real and growing problem today. As such, you need to be highly protective of your personal account information whenever doing transactions online. Make sure you never give personal information out over the Internet unless you are connected to a secure site. Also, store your access information in a secure place. Routinely check your computer for spy ware and viruses, protecting your identity this way as well. Anther important security feature you will want to make sure is in place with your online bank is encryption. Verify that the banking portal has high-end encryption software in place. If not, it might be advisable to choose a different banking option. You can verify this by looking for the graphic, which is usually located at the bottom right of the browser that signifies the encryption is in place.

Another tip about Internet banking is to remember that some procedures are still affected by the business hours of the bank. Even if you transfer a balance at 8:00 PM, it may not show up on your account until the next business day. Plan your transactions accordingly if you are working on a tight budget.

Use the Internet to shop for the best banking options. Check interest rates on loans and savings accounts online. The Internet can be a great tool in helping you secure the best possible banking services to meet your needs.

The history of Internet banking has come a long way over the last six years, and it is only going to get better! Get connected to Internet banking today. You can be in complete control of your finances with the click of a mouse!

BOARD AND MANAGEMENT OVERSIGHT

Because the Board of Directors and senior management are responsible for developing the institution's business strategy and establishing an effective management oversight over risks, they are expected to take an explicit, informed and documented strategic decision as to whether and how the bank is to provide e-banking services. The initial decision should include the specific accountabilities, policies and controls to address risks, including those arising in a cross-border context. Effective management oversight is expected to encompass the review and approval of the key aspects of the bank's security control process, such as the development and maintenance of a security control infrastructure that properly safeguards e-banking systems and data from both internal and external threats. It also should include a comprehensive process for managing risks associated with increased complexity of and increasing reliance on outsourcing relationships and third-party dependencies to perform critical e-banking functions.

Security Controls

While the Board of Directors has the responsibility for ensuring that appropriate security control processes are in place for e-banking, the substance of these processes needs special management attention because of the enhanced security challenges posed by e-banking. This should include establishing appropriate authorisation privileges and authentication measures, logical and physical access controls, adequate infrastructure security to maintain appropriate boundaries and restrictions on both internal and external user activities and data integrity of transactions, records and information. In addition, the existence of clear audit trails for all e-banking transactions should be ensured and measures to preserve confidentiality of key e-banking information should be appropriate with the sensitivity of such information.

Although customer protection and privacy regulations vary from jurisdiction to jurisdiction, banks generally have a clear responsibility to provide their customers with a level of comfort regarding information disclosures, protection of customer data and business availability that approaches the level they can expect when using traditional banking distribution channels. To minimise legal and reputational risk associated with e-banking activities conducted both domestically and cross-border, banks should make adequate disclosure of information on their web sites and take appropriate measures to ensure adherence to customer privacy requirements applicable in the jurisdictions to which the bank is providing e-banking services.

E-BANKING WORLD WIDE

Since its inception, Internet banking has experienced strong and sustained growth. World Bank report on leapfrogging in e-finance pointed out that the three countries with impressive progress in information technology in this sense are Estonia, Republic of Korea and Brazil (Claessens et al 2001). Creation of the world's leading electronic banking systems has been done at a remarkably low cost compared to other world-class internet banks (Sahlen 2002). As a result, Internet banking operations currently represent between 5 per cent and 10 per cent of the total volume of retail banking transactions both in the United States and in Europe. According to Jupiter Media, Internet traffic for all United States banks grew by 77.6 per cent between July 2000 and July 2001, compared with overall World Wide Web traffic growth of 19.8 per cent over the same period. Another source estimated that the share of United States households using Internet banking will increase from 20 per cent in 2001 to 33 per cent in 2005, and that by 2010 there might be 55 billion users. In the European Union, 60 million people, representing 18 per cent of the adult population, use online banking (Forrester Research 2003a). In France, the number of online banking accounts is recording an annual growth rate of 75 per cent. However, Estonia is a country that has become a leader in Internet banking (which now reaches 18 per cent of the population), not only among Eastern European countries but in world rankings, through a combination of easyto-use software, free-of-charge transactions and behaviour changes resulting from the influence of the Nordic countries' IT culture on Estonia. A sector in which Latin America is seems to be performing better than in other industries is online retail banking. Growth in this area has been driven by traditional banks, which have

used the online channel to generate customer loyalty and improve their operating margins. Two Brazilian banks, Bradesco and Banco do Brasil, have thus achieved more than 4 million online customers each (E-Marketer 2002b). Mexico is another leader of Internet banking in Latin America. It adopted legislation providing for the development of both E-Commerce and e-finance. In Mexico, the number of online bank users more than tripled from 700,000 in 2000 to 2.4 million in 2001, and it could reach 4.5 million in 2005 (E-Marketer 2002b). One reason for the success of Latin American banks' online ventures seems to be the attention they have paid to providing retail customers with multiple ways to access their accounts (Internet, telephone, wireless). However, given that the share of the total population that actually has a bank account is relatively small, the expansion of Latin American online banking may be facing a bottleneck.

According to the "Banking on the Internet" report (NOIE, 2000), Australia has a strong platform for E-Banking growth, with 37.7% of the population willing to engage in home Internet Banking. Statistics reveal that the largest increase for the period 1998-2000 was in the use of the Internet banking/bill payment category, which increased from 0.6% in May 1998 to 8% in May 2000 an increase of 81.0%. Banks in Australia have responded to customer demand by providing interactive services (NOIE, 2000) through account-monitoring and management services, other value-added services such as Insurance Management, online securities trading, foreign currency transactions and electronic reminders.

All banks offering E-Banking also offer security for transactions using firewalls, virus protection, 128 bit (or higher) encryption, verification by means of digital certificate and state limits to customer liability for unauthorized use of access codes. However, Batt (2001) argues that Internet banking is yet to reach a scale that offers material cost savings to banks. Compared with overall Internet usage estimated at 4.4 million in Australia, the major banks together have attracted only 1.2 million to online banking. The Internet is a global phenomenon and so is e-finance. Its deployment is not limited to developed countries, and indeed some developing countries – such as India and the Republic of Korea – are experiencing particularly strong growth in E-Banking. Thailand's e-payment strategy 2002–2004, under the leadership of the Bank of Thailand, has created an industry payment body to involve other stakeholders, in particular from commercial banks, which take leading responsibility for the development of e-payment systems and technologies. In Asia one of the most impressive records has been achieved by the Republic of Korea. Internet banking in that country has increased at a rapid pace, the number of online users having risen from 2 million in 2000 to 5.3 million in December 2001. The country is a leader in the region with 54 per cent of users having multiple online banking relationships (Korea Times Infotech, 2002).

The Republic of Korea is also leading in online brokerage and in mobile banking. In South-East Asia Internet banking is also developing rapidly in Thailand, Malaysia, and Singapore and to a lesser extent, in the Philippines. Jeevan (2000) notes that with rigid controls is giving way to deregulation, banks are gearing up their communications infrastructure to obtain a competitive edge from E-Banking, which is fast becoming a reality in India. A. Nair (1999) point out that E-Banking is fast becoming a strategic necessity for most commercial banks, as competition increases from private banks and NBFIs. Though deregulation may have had an impact on the banking industry in general, the Indian infrastructure itself is plagued by a lack of PC penetration (there is an estimated 2 million units for a population close to 1 billion according to Gupta and Storey, (1999) and low telephone penetration (19.1 million in 1999). Thus India has got low E-Banking adoption rates, low labour costs and "free" existing branches, there is a better price discovery process as more and more markets gain integrated real-time and improved access to these trading and data-dissemination platforms. At the same time, however, many changes are still required in technology, access infrastructure and banking regulation

In Bangladesh there is a large gap between the computerization of foreign banks and that of local commercial banks (the gap is particularly great in respect of local public commercial banks) and as regards the state of their intra-and inter-branch online networks. However, 75 per cent of local banks are planning to introduce E-Banking, which implies very dynamic improvements in their ICT use indicators. Virtually all banks use banking software at their head offices and during the past few years around one third of local banks has become SWIFT members. Credit card and point of sale services (POS) are already provided by a quarter of local banks, while ATM and internet banking are expanding rapidly especially in major cities (Raihan, 2001). Apart from North and South Africa the Sub Saharan Africa is the region that is seriously lagging behind in Internet banking, although it is giving to the rest of the world the good example of microfinance developments. The latest available estimates of African E-

Commerce were published in the E-Commerce and Development Report 2002. Those figures, which correspond to market research forecasts published in 2001, are $4 million of online retail in 2002, growing to $70.6 million in 2003 (Forrester Research 2001).

Conclusion and Recommendations

Web based banking service or E-Banking, the latest generation of electronic banking transactions, has opened up new window of opportunity to the existing banks and financial institutions. It permits business process re-engineering, serving borderless market, to achieve zero latency leading to improvements in customer service levels and better risk management because of real-time settlement. Since its evolution in 90th decade, it is having unprecedented growth. The growth rate is higher in Developed Countries, and comparatively lower in LDCs countries. The E-Banking sector is highly prohibitive for the new entrants although the inception cost is lower with high growth rate. The brand preference of the customer, existing network, physical existence, security and safety, supplier bargaining power, substitute product of non-banking sectors have made the way thorny. However, new comer with innovative idea and strategy definitely can make position in this sector. The analysis of the evolution and present status of E-Banking make us some room to make commandments for the government, new entrants and existing e-banks for effective utilization of the opportunity to accelerate the economic growth.

Internet penetration is a major factor for the growth of E-Banking. A research by OECD indicated that there is a strong positive correlation between Internet usage and E-Banking usage. The trend is usually logarithmic and the take off phase of Internet banking needs at least 30% Internet usage among the population (Christiansen, 2001). However, Internet penetration alone does not guarantee online banking penetration. In this situation, like Mexico, companies can give incentives, subsidizing the surfing cost, free training, multiple access facility (web, telephone, ATM etc.), motivation programs to the user and the population as a whole.

Standard or Common and Mature technology is always a problem in this Hi-Tech age. In Finland, for example, there are multiple technological standards for some E-Banking services that complicate fast spreading of these innovations (Kerem et al., 2002). Setting up electronic banking requires substantial investments and it is very complicated to move from old technologies to new ones. Thus banks can cooperate closely in the field of developing standards to offer services to third parties.

E-Banks must take aggressive marketing effort. It has been seen that the marketing efforts made to promote Estonian Internet banking have been continuous and aggressive in different media channels and in bank branches. Avlonitis et al (2000, p 37) have made a comprehensive research showing that innovative products, which have been promoted extensively, have a higher chance of success in the market than similar products without the communications support.

All of the efforts to establish an 'internet only' model E-Banking of business has not been succeed yet. Thus there must be a physical existence of the bank and E-Banking could be an extent to that operation. It will give the customers an impression of security and safety. Besides analysis showed that the senior citizens all over the world like to account with brick and mortar banks. Avoiding them, the e-banks would loose a large portion of their customers.

Using *State-of-Art* technology enables the organizations to avoid problems of legacy systems and any inefficiency. For example, rapid adoption of new technologies has helped the Estonian banks to leapfrog some of the traps that have slowed down the process of development in countries with better starting position.

E-Banks must try to expand their network as soon as possible. Because most of the cases customers uses E-Banking facility to pay bills, shopping etc. As more and more third party will involve in the network, they could attack more customers.

Governments' main role is enhancing the enabling environment, as it is known that the direct intervention into financial markets may have poor results. In general, the Estonian government has taken a laissez faire approach to the regulation and supervision of the

Last but not least, the e-banks must try to achieve critical mass. Achieving critical mass is key success factor in electronic banking development. This can be achieved when there is substantial Internet penetration and banks are able to provide services, which have very broad demand. In this case, the satisfied users will serve as endorsers and marketers of the service. The power of person-to-person communication and word of mouth can never be underestimated.

FUTURE OF E-BANKING

The ability to communicate by use of language is something that human beings bring to the world by nature of their existence: that is to say, it is not developed empirically, but is a priori. To the extent that any theoretical position can be grounded on such an a priori ability, then such a position may be seen as fundamental to us as communicative human actors. In so far as communication, at least partially, may be oriented towards mutual understanding, it might be argued as the foundation of knowledge creation and sharing.

In these terms, knowledge is not reducible to the properties of an objective world, but can be defined both objectively and according to the a priori concepts that the knowing subject brings to the act of perception. This knowing subject, being social, mediates all knowledge through social action and experience:

subject and object are linked in the acts of cognition and social interaction, and the so-called subjective and objective 'paradigms' may be represented as just a convenient tool for understanding, which has been accorded too much primacy as a form of reality. Rather, then, than relying on the concept of paradigms, this concept, and particularly the idea of paradigm incommensura-bility, should be opened up to challenge.

Consider the so-called subjective/ objective dichotomy. According to the paradigm argument, viewed from an epistemological perspective, one who sees a problem context as positivistic, and seeks, for example, a technological solution, will be unable to communicate and share knowledge with another who views the same problem context as existing in the views and opinions of those participants involved in and affected by the system of concern.

There are at least two fundamental difficulties with this:

1. It contradicts common human practice, and, dare it be suggested, common sense. Human participants in social groups commonly combine technical ('positivistic') and interpretative ('anti-positivistic') activity, seemingly denying the paradigm incommensurability thesis from an epistemological standpoint.
2. Theoretically, the paradigm incommensurability view seems to have dubious support. At its most basic level, it derives from the idea that technical, scientific, functionalist activity cannot be conducted together with interpretivistic, subjective activity. But if, theoretically, subjective and objective are inseparable, paradigm incommensurability becomes much less compelling.

In essence, then, it is the argument of this chapter that these difficulties disappear once a scientific basis for our thinking is denied. For example, suppose science is seen as just one form of knowledge, which in any case is simply a convenient human perception of how the world works. Now, all human endeavour becomes mediated through subjective understanding, and the paradigms as impenetrable barriers disappear. So, the problem of interest constitution theory being no longer defensible is resolved, since it is no longer being relied on.

However, this problem has been replaced with another, which may be stated as follows:

- Accepting all human actions as mediated through subjective understanding leads to the possibility of a basis for KM in the universal characteristics of language.
- The dichotomy between subject and object has gone, and with it, paradigm incommensurability.
- Organisational intervention is recast as an entirely communicative issue. For example, the so-called technical interest of knowledge constitution theory becomes instead an question of how technology

may further enable human interaction, all within a framework of human intercommunication.

- The difficulty which now arises is essentially a practical one, of how to incorporate these ideas into e-banking practice.

Work by Habermas on communicative action presents a universal theory of language which suggests that all language is oriented towards three fundamental validity claims: truth, rightness and sincerity. What is most compelling about this theory, however, is that all three validity claims are communicatively mediated. This viewpoint is most radically seen in respect of the truth claim, where it is proposed that such a claim results not from the content of descriptive statements, but from the Wittgenstinian approach casting them as arising in language games which are linked to culture: truth claims are socially contextual.

'Truth', can therefore be assessed by reference to communi-cation. Rightness is about norms of behaviour, which are culturally relevant, and are therefore to be determined by reference to that which is acceptable to those involved and affected in the system of concern as a cultural group. Finally, sincerity is about the speaker's internal world: his/her internal subjectivity. These ideas can now be taken forward to provide a KM approach to e-banking which is theoretically grounded, and closer to that which is experienced in action.

6

Architecture of Online Banking

INTRODUCTION

In today's world of emerging technologies, enterprises are moving towards the Internet for businesses. People are rushing towards the e-commerce applications for their day-today needs, which in turn are making the Internet very popular. Online Banking has given both an opportunity and a challenge to traditional banking.

In the fast growing world, banking is a necessity, which in turn takes a lot of time from our busy schedule. Going to a branch or ATM or paying bills by paper check and mailing them out, and balancing checkbooks are all time-consuming tasks. Banking online automates many of these processes, saving time and money. For all banks, online banking is a powerful tool to gain new customers while it helps to eliminates costly paper handling and manual teller interactions in an increasingly competitive banking environment.

Banks have spent generations gaining trust of their customers, and the goal for this project is to develop a user friendly, secure Online Banking Application. The application will be built using Java Server Pages (JSP), tomcat as the application server, and Microsoft Access/ SQL Server as a database.

The Online Banking Application is based on 3-tiered model. The Enterprise architecture for Online Banking Application is shown.

The 3-tiered architecture shown has the following major components:

1. *Client*: There will be two clients for the application. One will be a web-based user-friendly client called bank customers. The other will be for administration purposes.
2. *Application Server*: It takes care of the server script, takes care of JDBC-ODBC driver, and checks for the ODBC connectivity for mapping to the database in order to fulfill client and administrator's request.
3. *Database*: Database Servers will stores customer's and bank data.

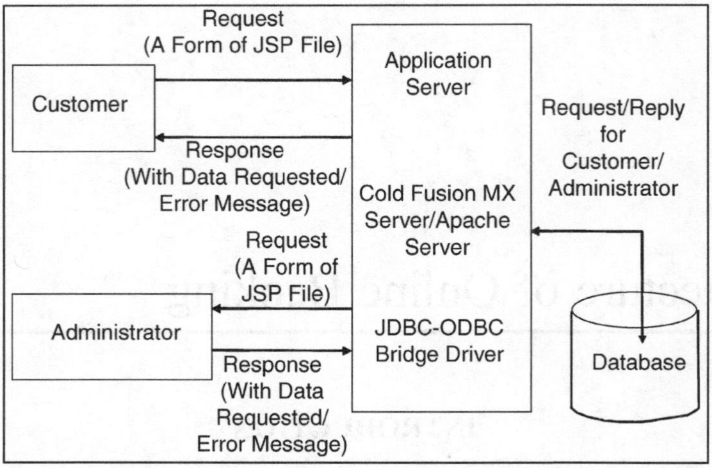

Fig. Architecture of Online Banking Application

Simply stated, the application works based on a request/response protocol. A client initiates a request to the server. The server responds by executing the business logic hosted inside the JSP programme and if required, communicates with the Database Server to fulfill a client's request.

The Online banking Application project will be divided into 4 modules namely:

1. Bank Account
2. Bank Account Administrator
3. Credit Card Customer
4. Credit Card Account Administrator

SIMILAR BANKING APPLICATIONS AVAILABLE IN THE MARKET

A considerable amount of research has been done in the past few months on this project. Many banks had migrated from paper based banking system to electronic/ online banking. Each bank had its own, user friendly interface, which helps its customers to interact with their account at their ease. A wide variety of online banking applications are available in the market, which in turn help the bank to function smoothly without reducing the quality of service. All banks which are using online banking application use the same basic principle.

National City Bank has excellent features, which allows customers to check their accounts and view their statements. The best thing about this bank's system allows us to schedule payments and do online transactions. The security feature is the best; it gains the trust of the customer and allows them to do their transitions in an efficient and secure manner. However, the interface is very complicated for novice users. The interface for credit card customer is confusing

Bank One is the fastest growing bank in United States with millions of customers, who perform their transactions online. The security issues are wonderful, and it allows the customer to view their transactions, pay bills online, ATM/branch locator and provide calculators and educators that will help customers to determine savings, mortgages and loan amounts. Educators are learning materials covering several financial topics which help the customer to learn more about the facilities that the bank has for them. The user interface is not as useful for the novice customers

TCF bank Online banking is a safe, fast and convenient way to access the accounts. It has all functionality but was lacking in user interface

COMPARISON BETWEEN JSP AND OTHER TECHNOLOGIES

- *JSP vs. Active Server Pages (ASP):* ASP is a similar technology from Microsoft. The advantages of JSP are Saturday, March 13, 2004two fold. First, the dynamic part is written in Java, not Visual Basic or other MS-specific language, so it is more powerful and easier to use. Second, it is portable to other operating systems and non-Microsoft Web servers.
- *JSP vs. Pure Servlets.* JSP doesn't give you anything that you couldn't in principle do with a servlet. But it is more convenient to write and to modify regular HTML than to have a million println statements that generate the HTML, by separating the look from the content, you can put different people on different tasks. Your Web page design experts can build the HTML, leaving places for your servlet programmers to insert the dynamic content.
- *JSP vs. JavaScript:* JavaScript can generate HTML dynamically on the client. This is a useful capability, but only handles situations where the dynamic information is based on the client's environment. With the exception of cookies, HTTP and form submission data is not available to JavaScript. And, since it runs on the client, JavaScript can't access server-side resources like databases, catalogs and pricing information, to understand the distinction between Java Script and Java Server Pages. *Java Script code is generally executed by the web client (browser)* after the web server sends the HTTP response. *Java Server Pages are executed by the web server* before the web server sends the HTTP response. In fact, JSP is what creates the HTTP response. Thus, Java Script is said to be a "Client Side" technology. Its underlying code can be viewed by the web user, while Java Server Pages are a "Server Side" technology and its underlying code is not exposed to web users. JSP is processed by the web server before result reaches the client.
- *JSP vs. Static HTML:* Regular HTML, of course, cannot contain dynamic information. JSP is so easy and convenient that it is quite feasible to augment HTML pages that only benefit marginally by the

insertion of small amounts of dynamic data. Previously, the cost of using dynamic data would prevent its use in all but the most valuable instances.

SOFTWARE DEVELOPMENT METHODOLOGY

ANALYSIS

The table below lists the functionalities to be included in the Online Banking Application, as well as certain features that will not be supported. This list is a tentative, since it may be discovered during development that additional features are required or some existing features may prove to be unworkable or impractical due to time limitations.

The application will be written Java Server Pages (JSP), as it is easier to write and maintain pages.

All the necessary hardware and software requirement for the complete application are included in this paper. Table represents the features supported by Online Banking Application.

Table: Functionalities for an Online Banking Application

Feature	Support
Support 3-tier architecture(Client, Server, Database)	yes
Creation of design for all common components	yes
Creation of design for all Server Side	yes Components
Support session tracking	yes
Easy means of navigation through pages containing proper session tracking.	yes
Support Application Servers	Tomcat
Support Secure Socket Layer (SSL)	yes
Easy means of navigation through different pages, which are secured using SSL.	yes
Support the ODBC conn}ections and	yes JDBC-ODBC as well
Database	MS-SQL Server or MS-Access
Establish database connection	yes
Generation of Use case and Data flow diagrams	yes
Programming Language support	JSP
Operating System support	Windows'2000 or higher

DESIGN

Dataflow diagrams are depictured below to give the clear understanding of Online Banking Application.

The Online banking Application project will be divided into 4 modules namely:

1. Bank Account
2. Bank Account Administrator
3. Credit Card Customer
4. Credit Card Account Administrator

Module 1

In this module the customer is allowed to logon to the website and can access his/her account by getting user name and password which will be verified with the server and the database. Once he/she gets verified then they are allowed to view their personal account and perform operations such as change of address, paying bills online, viewing transactions and transferring money into other accounts. The data will be highly secured using Secure Socket Layer (SSL) technology. Once the customer finishes the task the update information instantly gets stored into the database. The customer is then allowed to sign out from his/her account.

Module 2

In this module the administrator is allowed to log on to the website and can access his/her administrative account by using the user name and password which will then be verified with the database. Once he/she gets verified the administrative interface will be displayed, where the administrator can perform operations for both new customers and existing customers. Administrator will help a new customer in opening their account by taking complete information from them. Administrator provides services like withdrawal, deposit, transfer and deleting customer during the time of closing the account.

In this module administrator provides great customer service to the customers who want to do phone banking or teller banking. The data will be highly secured using Secure Socket Layer (SSL) technology. The interface for administrator will be both very user friendly and efficient. The data gets stored in the database instantly when the administrator hits the submit button.

Module 3

In this module, the customer is allowed to apply for the credit cards (Student, Premium and Basic) or for the loan (home, auto and education). Depending upon their selection the corresponding page will be shown when they will be asked to fill out the form. Depending on the credit rating the customer will be either accepted or rejected. Usually the credit rating will be checked with national credit bureau, which will be internally connected to INS and Social Security office database. Once the customer gets approved for the credit card or loan, their credit card will be sent to them by postal service.

Once they decided to register themselves to an online credit card banking they enroll by using the enroll form, where they will be asked to enter their credit card number, their Social Security Number and user defined password(Numbers only). To access the account, customers should visit the credit card website and get verified with the database by entering the user name and the password they have created. If the verification is successful then they will be allowed to view their credit card account which will display information about their credit limit and balance.

They are also allowed to make online bill payments using their credit card account. As this module contains allimportant data like credit card numbers, account user name and password and online bill payments, it needs to be secure, therefore Secure Socket Layer (SSL) will be used. It encrypts the data before it is sent and gets decrypted at the server and vise-versa. This will prevent the hackers to view the data, which is being transferred through any media.

Module 4

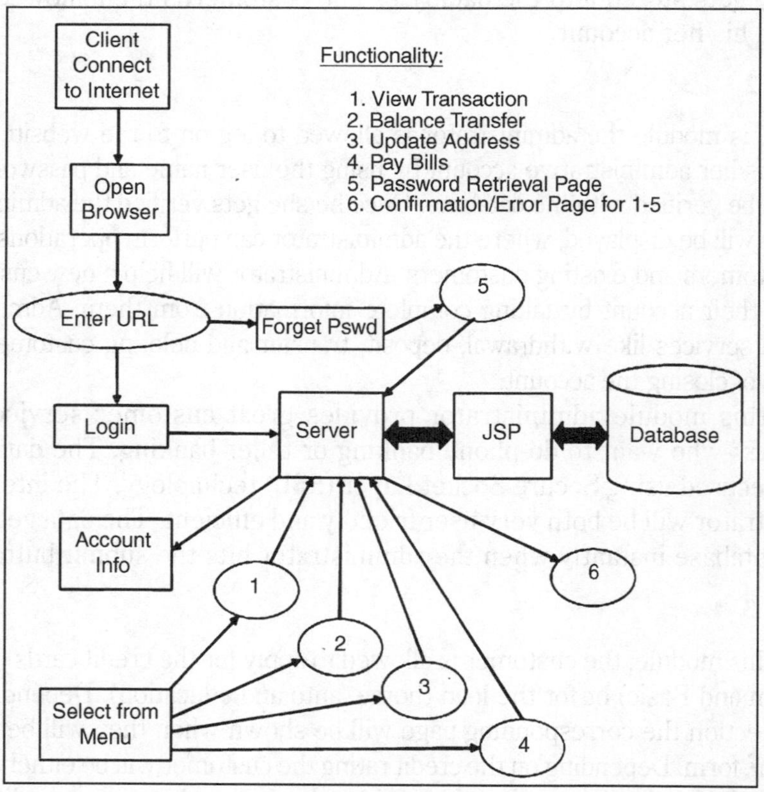

Fig. Data Diagram for Bank Account Customer

In this module the administrator is allowed to log on to the website and will be allowed to access his/her administrative account by using its user name and password which will then gets verified with the database. Depending upon their authentication, the administrative page will be displayed, where administrator is allowed to assign credit limits for the customer depending upon what kind of request the customer has made.

The administrator will be allowed to put a hold on the credit card account for security reasons, like lost/stolen credit card and this facility will protect customer information from getting misused by others.

Once the administrator selects the type of card or loan requested and the social security number from the database on a single click the credit limit will be assigned. There will be a special field in the database, which will allow the administrator to keep track of the customers who have already been issued their cards.

The application will be having other functionalities such as:

- Password retrieval for existing customer.
- Locator [in case of teller banking]
- Career at the bank.
- Enrollment for online banking.

The application will be using a backend as MS- Access database, all the front-end will be written in Java Server Pages (JSP) and Jakarta Tomcat application server will be used as a middle ware which will take care of the connection between front-end and backend.

IMPLEMENTATION

As the Online Banking Application is develop in increments, features will be coded as soon as the designs for that feature have been completed. If design changes are required due to requirements changes of flaws that are discovered, work on this phase will be suspended and the analysis and design phases will be reinitiated to make the necessary design changes. After those changes have been made, the implementation phase will continue. A new design version is created every time that a design change is required.

The following technologies are used in this project:

- Java Server Pages (JSP)
- Database (MS-SQL Server2000)
- Tomcat-apache server.
- Secure Socket Layer (SSL)
- Java Database Connectivity (JDBC)

Java Server Pages *(JSP)* is use create dynamic web content even easier, Java has introduced Java Server Pages (also called JSPs). While to write Servlets can require some pretty extensive knowledge of Java, a newbie to Java can learn how to do some pretty neat things with JSPs in a hurry.

"The JSP technology is actually built on top of Servlets; the two technologies actually work well together. It is common to use both in the same web application".

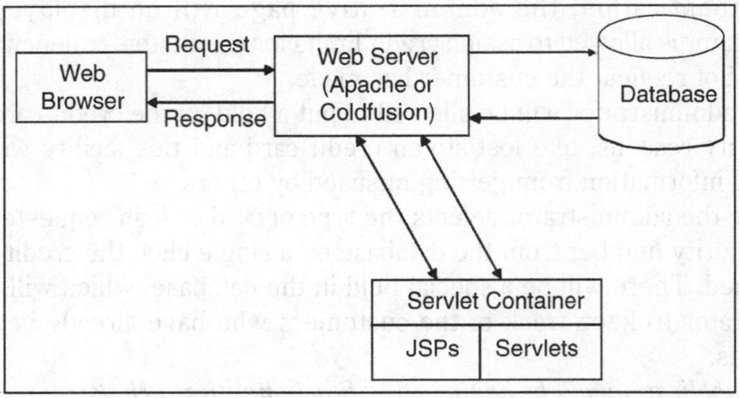

Fig. Architectures of JSP

Advantages of Java Server Pages:

- Easier to use JSP technology without needing to learn the Java language
- Easier to extend the JSP language
- Easier to write and maintain pages

Database

A collection of programmes that enables you to store, modify, and extract information from a database. Information of the users gets stored in a relational database. The application works well with MS- Access as database, it also works well with SQL Server 2000 and Oracle.

Data Manipulation Language (DML) is used to modify the data present in database:

- *Select*: Extracts data from a database table
- *Update*: Updates data in a database table
- *Delete*: Deletes data from a database table
- *Insert Into*: Inserts new data into a database table

The Data Definition Language (DDL) is used to define the data:

- *Create Table*: Creates a new database table
- *Alter Table*: Alters (changes) a database table
- *Drop Table*: Deletes a database table
- *Create Index*: Creates an index (search key)
- *Drop Index*: Deletes an index

The relationship diagram for the application is shown under Database Design. It contains 13 tables, relationship present in the table are one-to-many and one-to-one. The database design is fully normalized in third normal form 3NF to maximum extent.

Java Database Connectivity (JDBC)

JDBC technology is an API that lets us access virtually any tabular data source from the Java programming language. It provides cross-DBMS connectivity to a wide range of SQL databases, and now, with the new JDBC API, it also provides access to other tabular data sources, such as spreadsheets or flat files.

Secure Socket Layer (SSL)

SSL, or Secure Socket Layer, is a technology, which allows web browsers and web servers to communicate over a secured connection. This means that the data being sent is encrypted by one side, transmitted, and then decrypted by the other side before processing. This is a two-way process, meaning that both the server AND the browser encrypt all traffic before sending out data. Another important aspect of the SSL protocol is Authentication.

This means that during your initial attempt to communicate with a web server over a secure connection, that server will present your web browser with a set of credentials, in the form of a "Certificate", as proof that site is who and what it claims to be. In certain cases, the server may also request a Certificate from your web browser, asking for proof that *you* are who you claim to be. This is known as "Client Authentication," SSL uses public key encryption for encrypting data. The figure below will give a better understanding about public key encryption.

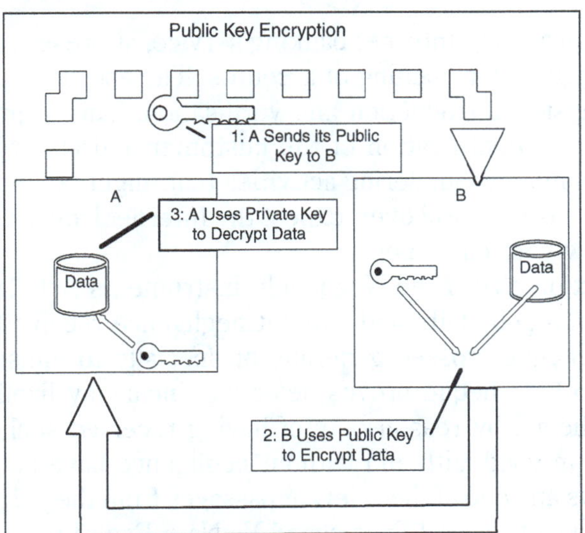

Fig. Public Key Encryption

SYSTEM REQUIREMENT

Minimum system requirements are listed below:

Table: Hardware and Software Requirements

Processor	Pentium III 550 MHz or Athlon AMD 1GHz
RAM	256 MB or more
Operating Machine enabled	Windows 2000 Server, Windows XP with Java System Virtual
Database	Oracle/MS Access/SQL Server 2000
Hard Disk space	20 MB
Web Server Apache	Cold fusion Server or Jakarta-Tomcat-
Web Browser	Internet Explorer 5.0 or higher
Software	Macromedia Dream waver MX, SSL, MS-Access,

CONCLUSION

This chapter shows, how Distributed applications like online Banking, can easily be developed using Enterprises Java Technologies and its distributed architectures. A more efficient approach would be to utilize Model View Controller 2 architecture, which makes application reusable, robust, and more object-oriented. J2EE, as distributed component architecture, is the right solution in developing web applications.

ONLINE OPENING OF ACCOUNT

The banks providing Internet banking service, at present are only willing to accept the request for opening of accounts. The accounts are opened only after proper physical introduction and verification. This is primarily for the purpose of proper identification of the customer and also to avoid benami accounts as also money laundering activities that might be undertaken by the customer. Supervisors world over, expect the Internet banks also to follow the practice of 'know your customer'.

As per Section 131 of the Negotiable Instruments Act, 1881 (the Act) a banker who has in good faith and without negligence received payment for a customer of a cheque crossed generally or specially to himself shall not, in case the title to the cheque proves defective, incur any liability to the true owner of the cheque by reason only of having received such payment. The banker's action in good faith and without negligence have been discussed in various case laws and one of the relevant passages from the judgment of Justice Chagla in the case of Bapulal Premchand Vs Nath Bank Ltd.

(AIR 1946 Bom.482) is as follows:

- "Primarily, enquiry as to negligence must be directed in order to find out whether there is negligence in collecting the cheque and not in opening the account, but if there is any antecedent or present circumstance which aroused the suspicion of the banker then it would be his duty before he collects the cheque to make the necessary enquiry and undoubtedly one of the antecedent circumstances would be the opening of the account. In certain cases failure to make enquiries as to the integrity of the proposed customer would constitute negligence".

Further the Supreme Court of India in Indian Overseas Bank Ltd. Vs. Industrial Chain Concern has stated that as a general rule, before accepting a customer, the bank must take reasonable care to satisfy himself that the person in question is in good reputation and if he fails to do so, he will run the risk of forfeiting the protection given by Section 131 of Negotiable Instruments Act, 1881 but reasonable care depends upon the facts and circumstances of the case.

Similarly, the Delhi High Court was also of the view that the modern banking practice requires that a constituent should either be known to the bank or should be properly introduced. The underlying object of the bank insisting on producing reliable references is only to find out if possible whether the new constituent is a genuine party or an imposter or a fraudulent rogue. Thus, the introduction of a new customer by a third party reference is a well-recognized practice followed by the banks before opening new accounts in order to prove the reasonable care and absence of any negligence in permitting the new customer to open the account.

Further, in order to establish the reasonable care the banks have to make enquiries about the integrity/reputation of the prospective customer. It is not a mere enquiry about the identity of the person. The Group, therefore, endorses the practice presently followed by the banks in seeking proper introduction before allowing the operations of the customers' accounts. In the context of Internet banking and after the coming into force of the Information Technology Act, 2000, it may be possible for the banks to rely on the electronic signatures of the introducer. But this may have to await till the certification machinery as specified in the Information Technology Act, 2000 comes into operation.

SECRECY OF CUSTOMER'S ACCOUNT

The existing regime imposes a legal obligation on the bankers to maintain secrecy and confidentiality about the customer's account. The law at present requires the banker to take scrupulous care not to disclose the state of his customer's account except on reasonable and proper occasions. While availing the Internet banking services the customers are allotted proper User ID, passwords and/or personal identification numbers and/or the other agreed authentication procedure to access the Internet banking service and only users with such access methodology and in accordance with the agreed procedure are authorized to access the Internet banking services.

In other words a third party would not be able to withdraw money from an account or access the account of the customer unless the customer had divulged his/her password in the first place. However, if the password or the identification number is misplaced or lost or gets into the hands of the wrong person and such person procures details about the customers account then the banker may be faced with legal proceedings on the grounds of violation of the obligation to maintain secrecy of the customer's accounts. This concern of the bankers is very high especially in the case of joint accounts where both the parties share one personal identification numbers or relationship numbers and operate the account jointly.

Further, by the very nature of Internet the account of a customer availing Internet banking services would be exposed to the risk of being accessed by hackers and inadvertent finders. The Internet banking services at present are being provided by most of the banks by systems which are only accessible through "secure zones" or SSL (Secure Sockets Layer) to secure and authenticate the user through a secure browser.

Most of the banks have adopted 128 Bit strong encryption which is widely accepted worldwide as a standard for securing financial transaction. To reduce the risk of the customers' account information being accessed by third parties, it is very important that the banks continue to be obliged to protect the customer account. However, it is equally important to note that the banks may still be exposed to the risk of liability to customers and hence they should adopt all reasonable safety controls and detection measures like establishment of firewalls, net security devices, etc. Further, banks should put in place adequate risk control measures in order to minimize possible risk arising out of breach of secrecy due to loss/ misplacement/ theft of customers' ID/PIN, etc.

REVOCATION AND AMENDMENT OF INSTRUCTIONS

The general revocation and amendment instructions to the banks are intended to correct errors, including the sending of an instruction more than once. Occasionally, a revocation or amendment may be intended to stop a fraud. Under the existing law, banks are responsible for making and stopping payment in good faith and without negligence. In an Internet banking scenario there is very limited or no stop-payment privileges since it becomes impossible for the banks to stop payment in spite of receipt of a stop payment instruction as the transactions are completed instantaneously and are incapable of being reversed. Hence the banks offering Internet banking services may clearly notify the customers the time frame and the circumstances in which any stop payment instructions could be accepted.

RIGHTS AND LIABILITIES OF THE PARTIES

Typically, the banker-customer relationship is embodied in a contract entered into by them. The banks providing the Internet banking services currently enter into agreements with their customers stipulating their respective rights and responsibilities including the disclosure requirements in the case of Internet banking transactions, contractually.

A Standard format/minimum consent requirement to be adopted by the banks offering Internet banking facility, could be designed by the Indian Banks' Association capturing, inter alia, access requirements, duties and responsibilities of the banks as well as customers and any limitations on the liabilities of the banks in case of negligence and non-adherence to the terms of agreement by customers.

INTERNET BANKING AND MONEY LAUNDERING

One of the major concerns associated with Internet Banking has been that the Internet banking transactions may become untraceable and are incredibly mobile and may easily be anonymous and may not leave a traditional audit trail by allowing instantaneous transfer of funds. It is pertinent to note that money-laundering transactions are cash transactions leaving no paper trail. Such an apprehension will be more in the case of use of electronic money or e-cash.

In the case of Internet Banking the transactions are initiated and concluded between designated accounts. Further Section 11 of the proposed Prevention of Money Laundering Bill, 1999 imposes an obligation on every Banking Company, Financial Institution and intermediary to maintain a record of all the transactions or series of transactions taking place within a month, the nature and value of which may be prescribed by the Central Government. These records are to be maintained for a period of five years from the date of cessation of the transaction between the client and the banking company or the financial institution or the intermediary. This would apply to banks offering physical or Internet banking services. This will adequately guard against any misuse of the Internet banking services for the purpose of money laundering. Further the requirement of the banking companies to preserve specified ledgers, registers and other records for a period of 5 to 8 years, as per the Banking Companies (Period of Preservation of Records) Rules, 1985 promulgated by the Central Government also adequately takes care of this concern.

MAINTENANCE OF RECORDS

Section 4 of the Bankers' Books Evidence Act, 1891, provides that a certified copy of any entry in a banker's book shall in all legal proceedings be received as a prima facie evidence of the existence of such an entry. The Banking Companies (Period of Preservation of Records) Rules, 1985 promulgated by the Central Government requires banking companies to maintain ledgers, records, books and other documents for a period of 5 to 8 years. A fear has been expressed as to whether the details of the transactions if maintained in an electronic form will also serve the above purpose. The Group is of the considered opinion that that this has been adequately taken care of by Section 7 and Third Schedule of the Information Technology Act, 2000.

INTER-BANK ELECTRONIC FUNDS TRANSFER

The Electronic Funds Transfer via the Internet, in its present form is provided only between accounts with the same bank. The transaction is effected by the originator who gives the electronic payment order to one branch of a bank offering the Internet banking facility ("the Sending Branch"). The electronic instruction is processed by the backend software of the branch to confirm the account number and the person's identification and instruction is issued by the Sending Branch to the branch having the account of the beneficiary ("Beneficiary Branch") to credit the account of the beneficiary.

The Sending Branch debits the account of the originator at its end. At present there is no clearing mechanism in place for settlement of inter-bank electronic funds transfer. The entire gamut of electronic funds transfer and the legal issues and risks involved in the same are currently being examined by a committee set up by the Reserve Bank of India. The 4th Schedule to the Information Technology Act, 2000 has amended the Reserve Bank of India Act. 1934 empowering the Reserve Bank of India to regulate electronic funds transfer between banks and banks and other financial institutions.

MISCELLANEOUS

During the course of deliberations, the Group discussed certain issues where the legal position is not clear but have a bearing on Internet banking. Certain issues have also not been addressed by the Information Technology Act, 2000. The Consumer Protection Act 1986 defines the rights of consumers in India and is applicable to banking services as well.

The issues of privacy, secrecy of consumers' accounts and the rights and liabilities of customers and banks, etc. in the context of Internet banking have been discussed in earlier paragraphs. In cases where bilateral agreements defining customers rights and liabilities are adverse to consumers than what are enjoyed by them in the traditional banking scenario, it is debatable whether such agreements are legally tenable. For example, whether a bank can claim immunity if money is transferred unauthorizedly by a hacker from a customers account, on the pretext that it had taken all reasonable and agreed network security measures.

In a traditional banking scenario, a bank has normally no protection against payment of a forged cheque. If the same logic is extended, the bank providing I-banking may not absolve itself from liability to the customers on account of unauthorized transfer through hacking. Similar position may obtain in case of denial of service. Even though, The Information Technology Act, 2000 has provided for penalty for denial of access to a computer system (Section-43) and hacking (Section – 66), the liability of banks in such situations is not clear.

The Group was of the view that the banks providing Internet banking may assess the risk and insure themselves against such risks. There was no specific enactment in India which protects privacy of customers. Bankers' secrecy obligation mostly followed from different case laws. In UK, the Data Protection Act 1984 specifically prohibits personal data from being disclosed for purposes other than for which the data is held. This prohibits use of customer data relating to their spending habits, preferences etc., for any commercial purpose.

The Office of the Comptroller of Currency have also issued directions to US banks enforcing customers' privacy. The Information Technology Act, 2000, in Section 72 has provided for penalty for breach of privacy and confidentiality. Further, Section 79 of the Act has also provided for exclusion of liability of a network service provider for data travelling through their network subject to certain conditions. Thus, the liability of banks for breach of privacy when data is travelling through network is not clear. This aspect needs detailed legal examination.

THE ENTRY OF INDIAN BANKS INTO NET BANKING

Internet banking, both as a medium of delivery of banking services and as a strategic tool for business development, has gained wide acceptance internationally and is fast catching up in India with more and more banks entering the fray. India can be said to be on the threshold of a major banking revolution with net banking having already been unveiled. A recent questionnaire to which 46 banks responded, has revealed that at present, 11 banks in India are providing Internet banking services at different levels, 22 banks propose to offer Internet banking in near future while the remaining 13 banks have no immediate plans to offer such facility.

At present, the total Internet users in the country are estimated at 9 lakh. However, this is expected to grow exponentially to 90 lakh by 2003. Only about 1% of Internet users did banking online in 1998. This increased to 16.7% in March 2000.* The growth potential is, therefore, immense. Further incentives provided by banks would dissuade customers from visiting physical branches, and thus get 'hooked' to the convenience of arm-chair banking.

The facility of accessing their accounts from anywhere in the world by using a home computer with Internet connection, is particularly fascinating to Non-Resident Indians and High Networth Individuals having multiple bank accounts.

Costs of banking service through the Internet form a fraction of costs through conventional methods. Rough estimates assume teller cost at Re.1 per transaction, ATM transaction cost at 45 paise, phone banking at 35 paise, debit cards at 20 paise and Internet banking at 10 paise per transaction. The cost-conscious banks in the country have therefore actively considered use of the Internet as a channel for providing services. Fully computerized banks, with better management of their customer base are in a stronger position to cross-sell their products through this channel.

PRODUCTS AND SERVICES OFFERED

Banks in India are at different stages of the web-enabled banking cycle. Initially, a bank, which is not having a web site, allows its customer to communicate with it through an e-mail address; communication is limited to a small number of branches and offices which have access to this e-mail account. As yet, many scheduled commercial banks in India are still in the first stage of Internet banking operations. With gradual adoption of Information Technology, the bank puts up a web-site that provides general information on the banks, its location, services available *e.g.* loan and deposits products, application forms for downloading and e-mail option for enquiries and feedback.

It is largely a marketing or advertising tool. For example, Vijaya Bank provides information on its web-site about its NRI and other services. Customers are required to fill in applications on the Net and can later receive loans or other products requested for at their local branch. A few banks provide the customer to enquire into his demat account (securities/shares) holding details, transaction details and status of instructions given by him. These web sites still do not allow online transactions for their customers. Some of the banks permit customers to interact with them and transact electronically with them.

Such services include request for opening of accounts, requisition for cheque books, stop payment of cheques, viewing and printing statements of accounts, movement of funds between accounts within the same bank, querying on status of requests, instructions for opening of Letters of Credit and Bank Guarantees etc. These services are being initiated by banks like ICICI Bank Ltd., HDFC Bank Ltd. Citibank, Global Trust Bank Ltd., UTI Bank Ltd., Bank of Madura Ltd., Federal Bank Ltd. etc. Recent entrants in Internet banking are Allahabad Bank (for its corporate customers through its 'Allnet' service) and Bank of Punjab Ltd. State Bank of India has announced that it will be providing such services soon. Certain banks like ICICI Bank Ltd., have gone a step further within the transactional stage of Internet banking by allowing transfer of funds by an account holder to any other account holder of the bank.

Some of the more aggressive players in this area such as ICICI Bank Ltd., HDFC Bank Ltd., UTI Bank Ltd., Citibank, Global Trust Bank Ltd. and Bank of Punjab Ltd. offer the facility of receipt, review and payment of bills on-line. These banks have tied up with a number of utility companies. The 'Infinity' service of ICICI Bank Ltd. Also allows online real time shopping mall payments to be made by customers. HDFC Bank Ltd. has made e-shopping online and real time with the launch of its payment gateway. It has tied up with a number of portals to offer business-to-consumer (B2C) ecommerce transactions.

The first online real time e-commerce credit card transaction in the country was carried out on the Easy3shoppe.com shopping mall, enabled by HDFC Bank Ltd. on a VISA card. Banks like ICICI Bank Ltd., HDFC Bank Ltd. etc. are thus looking to position themselves as one stop financial shops. These banks have tied up with computer training companies, computer manufacturers, Internet Services Providers and portals for expanding their Net banking services, and widening their customer base. ICICI Bank Ltd. has set up a web based joint venture for on-line distribution of its retail banking products and services on the Internet, in collaboration with Satyam Infoway, a private ISP through a portal named. Setting up of Internet kiosks and permeation through the cable television route to widen customer base are other priority areas in the agendas of the more aggressive players.

Centurion Bank Ltd. has taken up equity stake in the teauction.com portal, which aims to bring together buyers, sellers, registered brokers, suppliers and associations in the tea market and substitute their physical presence at the auctions announced. Banks providing Internet banking services have been entering into agreements with their customers setting out the terms and conditions of the services. The terms and conditions include information on the access through user-id and secret password, minimum balance and charges, authority to the bank for carrying out transactions performed through the service, liability of the user and the bank, disclosure of personal information for statistical analysis and credit scoring also, non-transferability of the facility, notices and termination, etc.

The race for market supremacy is compelling banks in India to adopt the latest technology on the Internet in a bid to capture new markets and customers. HDFC Bank Ltd. with its 'Freedom- the e-Age Saving Account' Service, Citibank with 'Suvidha' and ICICI Bank Ltd. with its 'Mobile Commerce' service have tied up with cellphone operators to offer Mobile Banking to their customers. Global Trust Bank Ltd. has also announced that it has tied up with cellular operators to launch mobile banking services. Under Mobile Banking services, customers can scan their accounts to seek balance and payments status or instruct banks to issue cheques, pay bills or deliver statements of accounts. It is estimated that by 2003, cellular phones will have become the premier Internet access device, outselling personal computers. Mobile banking will further minimise the need to visit a bank branch.

THE FUTURE SCENARIO

Compared to banks abroad, Indian banks offering online services still have a long way to go. For online banking to reach a critical mass, there has to be sufficient number of users and the sufficient infrastructure in place. The 'Infinity' product of ICICI Bank Ltd. gets only about 30,000 hits per month, with around 3,000 transactions taking place on the Net per month through this service.

Though various security options like line encryption, branch connection encryption, firewalls, digital certificates, automatic signoffs, random pop-ups and disaster recovery sites are in place or are being looked at, there is as yet no Certification Authority in India offering Public Key Infrastructure which is absolutely necessary for online banking. The customer can only be assured of a secured conduit for its online activities if an authority certifying digital signatures is in place. The communication bandwidth available today in India is also not enough to meet the needs of high priority services like online banking and trading. Banks offering online facilities need to have an effective disaster recovery plan along with comprehensive risk management measures. Banks offering online facilities also need to calculate their downtime losses, because even a few minutes of downtime in a week could mean substantial losses.

Some banks even today do not have uninterrupted power supply unit or systems to take care of prolonged power breakdown. Proper encryption of data and effective use of passwords are also matters that leave a lot to be desired. Systems and processes have to be put in place to ensure that errors do not take place. Users of Internet Banking Services are required to fill up the application forms online and send a copy of the same by mail or fax to the bank. A contractual agreement is entered into by the customer with the bank for using the Internet banking services.

In this way, personal data in the applications forms is being held by the bank providing the service. The contract details are often one-sided, with the bank having the absolute discretion to amend or supplement any of the terms at any time. For these reasons domestic customers for whom other access points such as ATMs, telebanking, personal contact, etc. are available, are often hesitant to use the Internet banking services offered by Indian banks. Internet Banking, as an additional delivery channel, may, therefore, be attractive/appealing as a value added service to domestic customers. Non-resident Indians for whom it is expensive and time consuming to access their bank accounts maintained in India find net banking very convenient and useful. The Internet is in the public domain whereby geographical boundaries are eliminated.

Cyber crimes are therefore difficult to be identified and controlled. In order to promote Internet banking services, it is necessary that the proper legal infrastructure is in place. Government has introduced the Information Technology Bill, which has already been notified in October 2000. Section 72 of the Information Technology Act, 2000 casts an obligation of confidentiality against disclosure of any electronic record, register, correspondence and information, except for certain purposes and violation of this provision is a criminal offence. Notification for appointment of Authorities to certify digital signatures, ensuring confidentiality of data, is likely to be issued in the coming months. Comprehensive enactments like the Electronic Funds Transfer Act in U.K. and data protection rules and regulations in the developed countries are in place abroad to prevent unauthorized access to data, malafide or otherwise, and to protect the individual's rights of privacy. The legal issues are, however, being debated in our country and it is expected that some headway will be made in this respect in the near future. Notwithstanding the drawbacks, certain developments taking place at present, and expected to take place in the near future, would create a conducive environment for online banking to flourish. For example, Internet usage is expected to grow with cheaper bandwidth cost. The Department of Telecommunications (DoT) is moving fast to make available additional bandwidth, with the result that Internet access will become much faster in the future.

This is expected to give a fillip to Internet banking in India. The proposed setting up of a Credit Information Bureau for collecting and sharing credit information on borrowers of lending institutions online would give a fillip to electronic banking. The deadline set by the Chief Vigilance Commissioner for computerisation of not less than 70 per cent of the bank's business by end of January 2001 has also given a greater thrust to development of banking technology.

The recommendations of the Vasudevan Committee on Technological Upgradation of Banks in India have also been circulated to banks for implementation. In this background, banks are moving in for technological upgradation on a large scale. Internet banking is expected to get a boost from such developments. Reserve Bank of India has taken the initiative for facilitating real time funds transfer through the Real Time Gross Settlement (RTGS) System.

Under the RTGS system, transmission, processing and settlements of the instructions will be done on a continuous basis. Gross settlement in a real time mode eliminates credit and liquidity risks. Any member of the system will be able to access it through only one specified gateway in order to ensure rigorous access control measures at the user level. The system will have various levels of security, *viz.*, Access security, 128 bit cryptography, firewall, certification etc. Further, Generic Architecture, both domestic and cross border, aimed at providing inter-connectivity across banks has been accepted for implementation by RBI.

Following a reference made this year, in the Monetary and Credit Policy statement of the Governor, banks have been advised to develop domestic generic model in their computerization plans to ensure seamless integration. The efforts would enable online banking to become more secure and efficient. With the process of dematerialisation of shares having gained considerable ground in recent years, banks have assumed the role of depository participants. In addition to customers' deposit accounts, they also maintain demat accounts of their clients. Online trading in equities is being allowed by SEBI.

This is another area which banks are keen to get into. HDFC Bank Ltd., has tied up with about 25 equity brokerages for enabling third party transfer of funds and securities through its business-to-business (B2B) portal, 'e-Net'. Demat account holders with the bank can receive securities directly from the brokers' accounts. The bank has extended its web interface to the software vendors of National Stock Exchange through a tie-up with NSE.IT – the infotech arm of the exchange. The bank functions as the payment bank for enabling funds transfer from its customers' account to brokers' accounts.

The bank is also setting up a net broking arm, HDFC Securities, for enabling trading in stocks through the web. The focus on capital market operations through the web is based on the bank's strategy on tapping customers interested in trading in equities through the Internet. Internet banking thus promises to become a popular delivery channel not only for retail banking products but also for online securities trading.

An upcoming payment gateway is being developed by ICICI and Global Tele System, which will enable customers to transfer funds to banks which are part of the project. Transfer of funds can be made through credit/debit/ smart cards and cheques, with the central payment switch enabling the transactions. Banks are showing interest in this new concept, which will facilitate inter-bank funds transfers and other e-commerce transactions, thus highlighting the role of banks in e-commerce as intermediaries between buyers and sellers in the whole payment process. WAP (Wireless Application Protocol) telephony is the merger of mobile telephony with the Internet.

It offers two-way connectivity, unlike Mobile Banking where the customer communicates to a mailbox answering machine. Users may surf their accounts, download items and transact a wider range of options through the cellphone screen. WAP may provide the infrastructure for P2P (person to person) or P2M (person to merchant) payments. It would be ideal for transactions that do not need any cash backup, such as online investments. Use of this cutting edge technology could well determine which bank obtains the largest market share in electronic banking. IDBI Bank Ltd. has recently launched its WAP- based mobile phone banking services (offering facilities such as banking enquiry, cheque book request, statements request, details of the bank's products etc).

At present, there are only 2.6 phone connections per 100 Indians, against the world average of 15 connections per 100. The bandwidth capacity available in the country is only 3.2 gigabits per second, which is around 60% of current demand. Demand for bandwidth is growing by 350% a year in India. With the help of the latest technology, Indian networks will be able to handle 40 gigabits of Net traffic per second (as compared to 10 gigabits per second in Malaysia). Companies like Reliance, Bharti Telecom and the Tata Group are investing billions of rupees to build fibre optic lines and telecom infrastructure for data, voice and Internet telephony.

The online population has increased from just 500,000 in 1998 to 5 million in 2000. By 2015, the online population is expected to reach 70 million. IT services is a $1.5 billion industry in India growing at a rate of 55% per annum. Keeping in view all the developments, Internet banking is likely to grow at a rapid pace and most banks will enter into this area soon. Rapid strides are already being made in banking technology in India and Internet banking is a manifestation of this. Every day sees new tie-ups, innovations and strategies being announced by banks. State Bank of India has recently announced its intention to form an IT subsidiary. A sea change in banking services is on the cards. It would, however, be essential to have in place a proper regulatory, supervisory and legal framework, particularly as regards security of transactions over the Net, for regulators and customers alike to be comfortable with this form of banking.

TOWARDS ONLINE BANKING

Banks and financial institutions in India are in the process of Web-enabling their services in order to offer Internet banking to its customers. The RBI has drafted certain Internet banking guidelines that have to be followed by banks about to venture into online banking. Here's what banking CIOs need to do. by Soutiman Das Gupta

It's the new generation of banking in India. Most private and MNC banks have already setup an elaborate Internet banking infrastructure. And this exercise has provided them numerous benefits like:

- Greater reach to customers
- Quicker time to market
- Ability to introduce new products and services quickly and successfully
- Ability to understand its customers needs
- Customers are given access to information easily across any location
- Greater customer loyalty

Multi-national and private sector banks in India have been very successful in setting up Internet banking services. This is mainly because these banks already had a robust automated banking environment on which they could build the Internet banking infrastructure. Most multi-national banks already have efficient Internet banking infrastructures running in other countries which could be emulated in India. And the private banks, which are relatively young, did not have to carry the burden of legacy systems. They merely invested in best-of-breed Internet banking solutions from the start.

In a Fix

Unfortunately nationalized banks have been unable to evolve as fast as most private sector and MNC banks. As a result, in many organizations there may be a mix of automated systems and manual systems, with both systems running parallel, and using half-baked applications created by smaller vendors which run in certain departments. This creates a chaotic scenario. Network management is a nightmare, the legacy systems may buckle any moment, new users and locations keep coming up, and there are also issues of security and consolidation.

This is a typical situation at a usual nationalized bank:

- A very large network of branches nationwide growing fast
- Lack of connectivity in remote locations
- A very large base of customers increasing fast
- 75-80 percent automation in main branches with less automation in remote cities and smaller branches
- Large amount of legacy equipment which doesn't integrate well with other systems
- Inefficient and outdated applications in some departments which are not flexible and don't integrate well with other applications
- Slow-to-change mentality of an Indian customer who is used to dealing with a human teller

Web-enabling banks with such infrastructure and number of branches nationwide at one go is a near-impossible task. However each of the challenges can be overcome with good planning, phased implementation, and lots of grit on the part of the CIOs.

The RBI Steps In

The Reserve Bank of India (RBI) has created a comprehensive document which lays down number of security-related guidelines and strategies for banks to follow in order to offer Internet banking. The guidelines broadly talk about the types of risks associated with Internet banking, the technology and security standards, legal issues involved, and regulatory and supervisory concerns. Any bank that wants to offer Internet banking must follow these guidelines and adhere to them as a legal necessity.

Vaidyanathan Iyer, National Manager, eSecurity Business, Computer Associates provides solutions to banks which can help them go online. He says, "the guidelines have been created with a lot of thought regarding the banking scenario in India. It is at par with international banking standards and is very comprehensive."

Background

The document broadly categorizes levels of Internet banking services into three types:

- The basic level service in which the banks' websites disseminate information on different products and services to customers. It may receive and reply to customers' queries through e-mail.
- Simple transactional websites which allow customers to submit their instructions, applications for different services, and queries on their

account balances. They do not permit any fund-based transactions on their accounts.
- The third level of Internet banking services offered by fully-transactional websites which allow customers to operate on their accounts for transfer of funds, payment of different bills, subscribing to other products of the bank, and to transact purchase and sale of securities.

Internet Banking

The document lays down some of the distinctive features of Internet banking. They are:

- It removes the traditional geographical barriers as it could reach out to customers of different countries/legal jurisdiction. This has raised the question of jurisdiction of law/supervisory system to which such transactions should be subjected.
- It has added a new dimension to different kinds of risks traditionally associated with banking, heightening some of them and throwing new risk control challenges.
- Security of banking transactions, validity of electronic contract, customers' privacy, etc., which have all along been concerns of both bankers and supervisors have assumed different dimensions given that Internet is a public domain, not subject to control by any single authority or group of users.
- It poses a strategic risk of loss of business to those banks who do not respond in time to this new technology, being the efficient and cost effective delivery.

Security—the Key Concern

It's evident from the document and from a general study of the business case of Internet banking, that security is perhaps the biggest concern. Connectivity issues to remote locations is also very important, but the need to be secure is far more pressing.

The document says that security issues include questions of adopting internationally accepted state-of-the-art minimum technology standards for access control, encryption/decryption (minimum key length), firewalls, verification of digital signature, and Public Key Infrastructure (PKI).

Concerns in Chapter 5 and 6

The concerns and guidelines about security are discussed in detail in Chapter 5 and Chapter 6 of the report. The key components of security concerns are

- Authentication: The assurance of identity of the person in a deal

- Authorization: A party doing a transaction is authorized to do so
- Privacy: The confidentiality of data and information relating to any deal
- Data integrity: Assurance that the data has not been altered
- Non-repudiation: A party to the deal cannot deny that it originated the communication or data

If these areas are not addressed, the bank may suffer operational risk, reputational risk, legal risk, money laundering risk, and strategic risk.

Chapter 6 of the report talks about technology and security standards for Internet banking. It talks about TCP/IP, the OSI Layers, and application architectures. There are guidelines for backup and recovery, list of the different types of attacks and the ways in which they can compromise a system, like sniffer attacks, DoS, and e-mail bombs.

Authentication techniques like tokens, biometrics, and smart cards are described. The concepts of firewalls, proxy servers, cryptography, digital signatures, certification, SSL, and PKI are explained in detail. Security tools like scanners, sniffers, and IDSs are also described.

Physical security is talked about and followed by guidelines of a security policy and a number of recommendations. The recommendations talk about access control, isolation of application servers, security logs (audit trails), penetration testing, backup and recovery practices, monitoring against threats, and education.

Comprehensiveness and Indian Banks

The RBI guidelines are very exhaustive and extremely comprehensive. But are Indian banks following the guidelines accordingly? Experts at Global E-Secure Limited, a security solutions company say that none of the Indian banks which offer Internet banking facilities have an IT security policy as stipulated by the RBI. While banks have been asked to file monthly reports to show compliance to the guidelines, most of them have sought time to satisfy the security policy criterion.

The RBI is insisting on a written document, signed by the Board of Directors to make the banks aware that IT security is not just an IT concern, but something that could affect overall business as well.

The company also says that while these banks do have security measures, there is no clear-cut program which incorporates all the aspects of a comprehensive security policy. Also, some banks do not have straight-through processing.

There is manual intervention, which poses a great security risk for the customer. In order to fill such gaps, the security policy guidelines clearly lay out the areas which should be looked into. To provide a further check, the RBI is also empowered to audit the compliance to the policy.

Rajeev Wadhwa, COO, Global E-Secure Limited says, "Following the release of its guideline, the RBI will also come out with a policy on similar lines.

Hence, it's imperative that banks immediately act upon the same. The RBI has asked I-banking and e-trading banks to perform ethical hacking of their servers and submit their reports. Since there is no proper ethical hacking policy and methodology published in the IT-Act nor by the RBI, these banking organizations have to depend on only security specialists who have the Service Level Agreement (SLA) and a procedure in place."

A Practical Approach

IDBI Bank has successfully implemented a robust Internet banking architecture for its customers. Neeraj Bhai, the CTO of the bank says, "RBI guidelines are stringent, but not very difficult to implement if one goes about in a systematic fashion. The rule which stipulates that the bank must have a client-level certificate, is somewhat difficult and expensive to implement in a retail banking scenario. The guidelines also prescribe certain functions be authorized at the Board level. This provision has potential to introduce delays in deployment."

"It is not important to look at which policy is to be applied first. One has to take a holistic view. Certain prescriptions of the RBI, like having an information security policy, are general in nature and not specific to Internet banking. If an organization is alive to such issues even before launching Internet banking, things become simpler. It should be viewed as a cross-functional project and managed in a controlled fashion. Many banks make the mistake of believing that all their customers would be interested in Internet banking and therefore start enabling the service to all their customers. In reality most of such 'enabled' customers do not access the service and the banks end up loading their systems unnecessarily and spending big sums on sending PIN mailers."

"Like any other product or service, Internet banking is not a one-time activity. The bank has to persuade its customers to use the service to achieve cost advantage. Since many customers do not use Internet banking, the bank has to enrich its services by additional payment tie-ups so that customers have more options. In this case, data security needs to be very thorough."

7

Principles for Electronic Banking

INTRODUCTION

Banking organisations have been delivering electronic services to consumers and businesses remotely for years. Electronic funds transfer, including small payments and corporate cash management systems, as well as publicly accessible automated machines for currency withdrawal and retail account management, are global fixtures. However, the increased world-wide acceptance of the Internet as a delivery channel for banking products and services provides new business opportunities for banks as well as service benefits for their customers. Continuing technological innovation and competition among existing banking organisations and new market entrants has allowed for a much wider array of electronic banking products and services for retail and wholesale banking customers.

These include traditional activities such as accessing financial information, obtaining loans and opening deposit accounts, as well as relatively new products and services such as electronic bill payment services, personalised financial "portals," account aggregation and business-to-business market places and exchanges. Notwithstanding the significant benefits of technological innovation, the rapid development of e-banking capabilities carries risks as well as benefits and it is important that these risks are recognised and managed by banking institutions in a prudent manner. These developments led the Basel Committee on Banking Supervision to conduct a preliminary study of the risk management implications of e-banking and e-money in 1998. This early study demonstrated a clear need for more work in the area of e-banking risk management and that mission was entrusted to a working group comprised of bank supervisors and central banks, the Electronic Banking Group (EBG), which was formed in November 1999.

The Basel Committee released the EBG's Report on risk management and supervisory issues arising from e-banking developments in October 2000. This Report inventoried and assessed the major risks associated with e-banking, namely strategic risk, reputational risk, operational risk (including security and legal risks), and credit, market, and liquidity risks. The EBG concluded that e-banking activities did not raise risks that were not already identified by the previous work of the Basel Committee.

However, it noted that e-banking increase and modifies some of these traditional risks, thereby influencing the overall risk profile of banking. In particular, strategic risk, operational risk, and reputational risk are certainly heightened by the rapid introduction and underlying technological complexity of ebanking activities.

RISK MANAGEMENT CHALLENGES

The EBG noted that the fundamental characteristics of e-banking (and e-commerce more generally) posed a number of risk management challenges:

- The speed of change relating to technological and customer service innovation in e- banking is unprecedented. Historically, new banking applications were implemented over relatively long periods of time and only after in-depth testing. Today, however, banks are experiencing competitive pressure to roll out new business applications in very compressed time frames – often only a few months from concept to production. This competition intensifies the management challenge to ensure that adequate strategic assessment, risk analysis and security reviews are conducted prior to implementing new e-banking applications.
- Transactional e-banking web sites and associated retail and wholesale business applications are typically integrated as much as possible with legacy computer systems to allow more straight-through processing of electronic transactions. Such straight-through automated processing reduces opportunities for human error and fraud inherent in manual processes, but it also increases dependence on sound systems design and architecture as well as system interoperability and operational scalability.
- E-banking increases banks' dependence on information technology, thereby increasing the technical complexity of many operational and security issues and furthering a trend towards more partnerships, alliances and outsourcing arrangements with third parties, many of whom are unregulated. This development has been leading to the creation of new business models involving banks and nonbank entities, such as Internet service providers, telecommunication companies and other technology firms.
- The Internet is ubiquitous and global by nature. It is an open network accessible from anywhere in the world by unknown parties, with routing of messages through unknown locations and via fast evolving wireless devices. Therefore, it significantly magnifies the importance

of security controls, customer authentication techniques, data protection, audit trail procedures, and customer privacy standards.

PRINCIPLES OF RISK MANAGEMENT IN BANKING

Based on the early work of the EBG, the Committee concluded that, while traditional banking risk management principles are applicable to e-banking activities, the complex characteristics of the Internet delivery channel dictate that the application of these principles must be tailored to fit many online banking activities and their attendant risk management challenges. To this end, the Committee believes that it is incumbent upon the Boards of Directors and banks' senior management to take steps to ensure that their institutions have reviewed and modified where necessary their existing risk management policies and processes to cover their current or planned e-banking activities. Further, as the Committee believes that banks should adopt an integrated risk management approach for all banking activities, it is critical that the risk management oversight afforded e-banking activities becomes an integral part of the banking institution's overall risk management framework.

To facilitate these developments, the Committee asked the EBG to identify the key risk management principles that would help banking institutions expand their existing risk oversight policies and processes to cover their e-banking activities and, in turn, promote the safe and sound electronic delivery of banking products and services. These *Risk Management Principles for Electronic Banking*, which are identified in this Report, are not put forth as absolute requirements or even "best practice" but rather as guidance to promote safe and sound e-banking activities. The Committee believes that setting detailed risk management requirements in the area of e-banking might be counterproductive, if only because these would be likely to become rapidly outdated by the speed of change related to technological and product innovation.

Therefore the principles included in the present Report express supervisory expectations related to the overall objective of banking supervision to ensure safety and soundness in the financial system rather than stringent regulations. The Committee is of the view that such supervisory expectations should be tailored and adapted to the e-banking distribution channel but not be fundamentally different to those applied to banking activities delivered through other distribution channels. Consequently, the principles presented below are largely derived and adapted from supervisory principles that have already been expressed by the Committee or national supervisors over a number of years.

In some areas, such as the management of outsourcing relationships, security controls and legal and reputational risk management, the characteristics and implications of the Internet distribution channel introduce a need for more detailed principles than those expressed to date. The Committee recognises that banks will need to develop risk management processes appropriate for their individual risk profile, operational structure and corporate governance culture, as well as in conformance with the specific risk management requirements and policies set forth by the bank supervisors in their particular jurisdiction(s).

Further, the numerous e-banking risk management practices identified in this Report, while representative of current industry sound practice, should not be considered to be all-inclusive or definitive, since many security controls and other risk management techniques continue to evolve rapidly to keep pace with new technologies and business applications. This Report does not attempt to dictate specific technical solutions to address particular risks or set technical standards relating to e-banking. Technical issues will need to be addressed on an on-going basis by both banking institutions and various standards-setting bodies as technology evolves.

Further, as the industry continues to address e-banking technical issues, including security challenges, a variety of innovative and cost efficient risk management solutions are likely to emerge. These solutions are also likely to address issues related to the fact that banks differ in size, complexity and risk management culture and that jurisdictions differ in their legal and regulatory frameworks. For these reasons, the Committee does not believe that a "one size fits all" approach to ebanking risk management is appropriate, and it encourages the exchange of good practices and standards to address the additional risk dimensions posed by the e-banking delivery channel.

In keeping with this supervisory philosophy, the risk management principles and sound practices identified in this Report are expected to be used as tools by national supervisors and implemented with adaptations to reflect specific national requirements where necessary, to help promote safe and secure e-banking activities and operations.

The Committee recognises that each bank's risk profile is different and requires a risk mitigation approach appropriate for the scale of the e-banking operations, the materiality of the risks present, and the willingness and ability of the institution to manage these risks. These differences imply that the risk management principles presented in this Report are intended to be flexible enough to be implemented by all relevant institutions across jurisdictions. National supervisors will assess the materiality of the risks related to e-banking activities present at a given bank and whether, and to what extent, the risk management principles for e-banking have been adequately met by the bank's risk management framework.

RISK MANAGEMENT PRINCIPLES FOR ELECTRONIC BANKING

The e-banking risk management principles identified in this Report fall into three broad, and often overlapping, categories of issues. However, these principles are not weighted by order of preference or importance. If only because such weighting might change over time, it is preferable to remain neutral and avoid such prioritisation.

Board and Management Oversight (Principles 1 to 3):

- Effective management oversight of e-banking activities.
- Establishment of a comprehensive security control process.
- Comprehensive due diligence and management oversight process for outsourcing relationships and other third-party dependencies.

Security Controls (Principles 4 to 10):

- Authentication of e-banking customers.
- Non-repudiation and accountability for e-banking transactions.
- Appropriate measures to ensure segregation of duties.
- Proper authorisation controls within e-banking systems, databases and applications.
- Data integrity of e-banking transactions, records, and information.
- Establishment of clear audit trails for e-banking transactions.
- Confidentiality of key bank information.

Legal and Reputational Risk Management (Principles 11 to 14):

- Appropriate disclosures for e-banking services.
- Privacy of customer information.
- Capacity, business continuity and contingency planning to ensure availability of ebanking systems and services.
- Incident response planning.

As they relate to e-banking and the underlying risk management principles that should be considered by banks to address these issues.

BOARD AND MANAGEMENT OVERSIGHT (PRINCIPLES 1 TO 3)

The Board of Directors and senior management are responsible for developing the banking institution's business strategy. An explicit strategic decision should be made as to whether the Board wishes the bank to provide e-banking transactional services before beginning to offer such services. Specifically, the Board should ensure that e-banking plans are clearly integrated within corporate strategic goals, a risk analysis is performed of the proposed ebanking activities, appropriate risk mitigation and monitoring processes are established for identified risks, and ongoing reviews are conducted to evaluate the results of e-banking activities against the institution's business plans and objectives.

In addition, the Board and senior management should ensure that the operational and security risk dimensions of the institution's e-banking business strategies are appropriately considered and addressed. The provision of financial services over the Internet may significantly modify and/or even increase traditional banking risks (*e.g.* strategic, reputational, operational, credit and liquidity risk). Steps should therefore be taken to ensure that the bank's existing risk management processes, security control processes, due diligence and oversight processes for outsourcing relationships are appropriately evaluated and modified to accommodate e-banking services.

Principle 1: The Board of Directors and senior management should establish effective management oversight over the risks associated with e-banking activities, including the establishment of specific accountability, policies and controls to manage these risks

Vigilant management oversight is essential for the provision of effective internal controls over e-banking activities. In addition to the specific characteristics of the Internet distribution channel discussed in the Introduction, the following aspects of e-banking may pose considerable challenge to traditional risk management processes:

- Major elements of the delivery channel (the Internet and related technologies) are outside of the bank's direct control.
- The Internet facilitates delivery of services across multiple national jurisdictions, including those not currently served by the institution through physical locations.
- The complexity of issues that are associated with e-banking and that involve highly technical language and concepts are in many cases outside the traditional experience of the Board and senior management.

In light of the unique characteristics of e-banking, new e-banking projects that may have a significant impact on the bank's risk profile and strategy should be reviewed by the Board of Directors and senior management and undergo appropriate strategic and cost/reward analysis. Without adequate up-front strategic review and ongoing performance to plan assessments, banks are at risk of underestimating the cost and/or overestimating the payback of their e-banking initiatives.

In addition, the Board and senior management should ensure that the bank does not enter into new e-banking businesses or adopt new technologies unless it has the necessary expertise to provide competent risk management oversight. Management and staff expertise should be commensurate with the technical nature and complexity of the bank's e-banking applications and underlying technologies. Adequate expertise is essential regardless of whether the bank's e-banking systems and services are managed in-house or outsourced to third parties.

Senior management oversight processes should operate on a dynamic basis in order to effectively intervene and correct any material e-banking systems problems or security breaches that may occur. The increased reputational risk associated with e-banking necessitates vigilant monitoring of systems operability and customer satisfaction as well as appropriate incident reporting to the Board and senior management. Finally, the Board and senior management should ensure that its risk management processes for its e-banking activities are integrated into the bank's overall risk management approach. The bank's existing risk management policies and processes should be evaluated to ensure that they are robust enough to cover the new risks posed by current or planned ebanking activities.

Additional risk management oversight steps that the Board and senior management should consider taking include:

- Clearly establishing the banking organisation's risk appetite in relation to e-banking.
- Establishing key delegations and reporting mechanisms, including the necessary escalation procedures for incidents that impact the bank's safety, soundness or reputation (*e.g.* networks penetration, employee security infractions and any serious misuse of computer facilities).
- Addressing any unique risk factors associated with ensuring the security, integrity and availability of e-banking products and services, and requiring that third parties to whom the banks has outsourced key systems or applications take similar measures.
- Ensuring that appropriate due diligence and risk analysis are performed before the bank conducts cross-border e-banking activities.

virtually unlimited geographic territory, including across national borders. Such cross-border e-banking activity, particularly if conducted without any existing licensed physical presence in the "host country," potentially subjects banks to increased legal, regulatory and country risk due to the substantial differences that may exist between jurisdictions with respect to bank licensing, supervision and customer protection requirements.

Because of the need to avoid inadvertent non-compliance with a foreign country's laws or regulations, as well as to manage relevant country risk factors, banks contemplating cross-border e-banking operations need to fully explore these risks before undertaking such operations and effectively manage them. Depending on the scope and complexity of e-banking activities, the scope and structure of risk management programmes will vary across banking organisations. Resources required to oversee e-banking services should be commensurate with the transactional functionality and criticality of systems, the vulnerability of networks and the sensitivity of information being transmitted.

Principle 2: The Board of Directors and senior management should review and approve the key aspects of the bank's security control process

The Board of Directors and senior management should oversee the development and continued maintenance of a security control infrastructure that properly safeguards e-banking systems and data from both internal and external threats. This should include establishing appropriate authorisation privileges, logical and physical access controls, and adequate infrastructure security to maintain appropriate boundaries and restrictions on both internal and external user activities.

Safeguarding of bank assets is one of the Board's fiduciary duties and one of senior management's fundamental responsibilities. However, it is a challenging task in a rapidly evolving e-banking environment because of the complex security risks associated with operating over the public Internet network and using innovative technology.

To ensure proper security controls for e-banking activities, the Board and senior management need to ascertain whether the bank has a comprehensive security process, including policies and procedures, that addresses potential internal and external security threats both in terms of incident prevention and response.

Key elements of an effective ebanking security process include:

- Assignment of explicit management/staff responsibility for overseeing the establishment and maintenance of corporate security policies.
- Sufficient physical controls to prevent unauthorised physical access to the computing environment.
- Sufficient logical controls and monitoring processes to prevent unauthorized internal and external access to e-banking applications and databases.
- Regular review and testing of security measures and controls, including the continuous tracking of current industry security developments and installation of appropriate software upgrades, service packs and other required measures.

Principle 3: The Board of Directors and senior management should establish a comprehensive and ongoing due diligence and oversight process for managing the bank's outsourcing relationships and other third-party dependencies supporting ebanking

Increased reliance upon partners and third party service providers to perform critical ebanking functions lessens bank management's direct control. Accordingly, a comprehensive process for managing the risks associated with outsourcing and other third-party dependencies is necessary. This process should encompass the third-party activities of partners and service providers, including the sub-contracting of outsourced activities that may have a material impact on the bank.

Historically, outsourcing was often limited to a single service provider for a given functionality. However, in recent years, banks' outsourcing relationships have increased in scale and complexity as a direct result of advances in information technology and the emergence of e-banking. Adding to the complexity is the fact that outsourced e-banking services can be sub-contracted to additional service providers and/or conducted in a foreign country. Further, as e-banking applications and services have become more technologically advanced and have grown in strategic importance, certain e-banking functional areas are dependent upon a small number of specialised third-party vendors and service providers. These developments may lead to increased risk concentrations that warrant attention both from an individual bank as well as a systemic industry standpoint. Together, these factors underscore the need for a comprehensive and ongoing evaluation of outsourcing relationships and other external dependencies, including the associated implications for the bank's risk profile and risk management oversight abilities.

Board and senior management oversight of outsourcing relationships and third-party dependencies should specifically focus on ensuring that:

- The bank fully understands the risks associated with entering into an outsourcing or partnership arrangement for its e-banking systems or applications.
- An appropriate due diligence review of the competency and financial viability of any third-party service provider or partner is conducted prior to entering into any contract for e-banking services.
- The contractual accountability of all parties to the outsourcing or partnership relationship is clearly defined. For instance, responsibilities for providing information to and receiving information from the service provider should be clearly defined.
- All outsourced e-banking systems and operations are subject to risk management, security and privacy policies that meet the bank's own standards.
- Periodic independent internal and/or external audits are conducted of outsourced operations to at least the same scope required if such operations were conducted in-house.
- Appropriate contingency plans for outsourced e-banking activities exist.

SECURITY CONTROLS (PRINCIPLES 4 TO 10)

While the Board of Directors has the responsibility for ensuring that appropriate security control processes are in place for e-banking, the substance of these processes needs special management attention because of the enhanced security challenges posed by ebanking.

The following issues are particularly pertinent:

- Authentication
- Non-repudiation
- Data and transaction integrity
- Segregation of duties
- Authorisation controls
- Maintenance of audit trails
- Confidentiality of key bank information

Principle 4: Banks should take appropriate measures to authenticate the identity and authorisation of customers with whom it conducts business over the Internet.

It is essential in banking to confirm that a particular communication, transaction, or access request is legitimate. Accordingly, banks should use reliable methods for verifying the identity and authorisation of new customers as well as authenticating the identity and authorisation of established customers seeking to initiate electronic transactions. Customer verification during account origination is important in reducing the risk of identity theft, fraudulent account applications and money laundering.

Failure on the part of the bank to adequately authenticate customers could result in unauthorised individuals gaining access to e-banking accounts and ultimately financial loss and reputational damage to the bank through fraud, disclosure of confidential information or inadvertent involvement in criminal activity. Establishing and authenticating an individual's identity and authorisation to access banking systems in a purely electronic open network environment can be a difficult task. Legitimate user authorisation can be misrepresented through a variety of techniques generally known as "spoofing." Online hackers can also take over the session of a legitimate authorised individual through use of a "sniffer" and carry out activities of a mischievous or criminal nature.

Authentication control processes can in addition be circumvented through the alteration of authentication databases. Accordingly, it is critical that banks have formal policy and procedures identifying appropriate methodology(ies) to ensure that the bank properly authenticates the identity and authorisation of an individual, agent or system by means that are unique and, as far as practical, exclude unauthorised individuals or systems. Banks can us a variety of methods to establish authentication, including PINs, passwords, smart cards, biometrics, and digital certificates.

These methods can be either single factor or multi-factor (*e.g.* using both a password and biometric technology to authenticate). Multi-factor authentication generally provides stronger assurance. The bank must determine which authentication methods to use based on management's assessment of the risk posed by the e-banking system as a whole or by the various subcomponents. This risk analysis should evaluate the transactional capabilities of the ebanking system (*e.g.* funds transfer, bill payment, loan origination, account aggregation etc.), the sensitivity and value of the stored e-banking data, and the customer's ease of using the authentication method. Robust customer identification and authentication processes are particularly important in the cross-border e-banking context given the additional difficulties that may arise from doing business electronically with customers across national borders, including the greater risk of identity impersonation and the greater difficulty in conducting effective credit checks on potential customers.

As authentication methods continue to evolve, banks are encouraged to monitor and adopt industry sound practice in this area such as ensuring that:

- Authentication databases that provide access to e-banking customer accounts or sensitive systems are protected from tampering and corruption. Any such tampering should be detectable and audit trails should be in place to document such attempts.
- Any addition, deletion or change of an individual, agent or system to an authentication database is duly authorised by an authenticated source.
- Appropriate measures are in place to control the e-banking system connection such that unknown third parties cannot displace known customers.
- Authenticated e-banking sessions remain secure throughout the full duration of the session or in the event of a security lapse the session should require reauthentication.

Principle 5: Banks should use transaction authentication methods that promote nonrepudiation and establish accountability for e-banking transactions.

Non-repudiation involves creating proof of the origin or delivery of electronic information to protect the sender against false denial by the recipient that the data has been received, or to protect the recipient against false denial by the sender that the data has been sent. Risk of transaction repudiation is already an issue with conventional transactions such as credit cards or securities transactions. However, e-banking heightens this risk because of the difficulties of positively authenticating the identities and authority of parties initiating transactions, the potential for altering or hijacking electronic transactions, and the potential for e-banking users to claim that transactions were fraudulently altered.

To address these heightened concerns, banks need to make reasonable efforts, commensurate with the materiality and type of the e-banking transaction, to ensure that:

- E-banking systems are designed to reduce the likelihood that authorised users will initiate unintended transactions and that customers fully understand the risks associated with any transactions they initiate.
- All parties to the transaction are positively authenticated and control is maintained over the authenticated channel.
- Financial transaction data are protected from alteration and any alteration is detectable.

Banking organisations have begun to employ various techniques that help establish nonrepudiation and ensure confidentiality and integrity of e-banking transactions, such as digital certificates using public key infrastructure (PKI). A bank may issue a digital certificate to a customer or counterparty to allow for their unique identification/authentication and reduce the risk of transaction repudiation. Although in some countries customers' rights to disclaim transactions is provided in specific legal provisions, legislation has been passed in certain national jurisdictions making digital signatures legally enforceable. Wider global legal acceptance of such techniques is likely as technology continues to evolve.

Principle 6: Banks should ensure that appropriate measures are in place to promote adequate segregation of duties within e-banking systems, databases and applications

Segregation of duties is a basic internal control measure designed to reduce the risk of fraud in operational processes and systems and ensure that transactions and company assets are properly authorised, recorded and safeguarded. Segregation of duties is critical to ensuring the accuracy and integrity of data and is used to prevent the perpetration of fraud by an individual. If duties are adequately separated, fraud can only be committed through collusion. E-banking services may necessitate modifying the ways in which segregation of duties are established and maintained because transactions take place over electronic systems where identities can be more readily masked or faked.

In addition, operational and transactionbased functions have in many cases become more compressed and integrated in e-banking applications. Therefore, the controls traditionally required to maintain segregation of duties need to be reviewed and adapted to ensure an appropriate level of control is maintained. Because access to poorly secured databases can be more easily gained through internal or external networks, strict authorisation and identification procedures, safe and sound architecture of the straight-through processes, and adequate audit trails should be emphasised.

Common practices used to establish and maintain segregation of duties within an e-banking environment include the following:

- Transaction processes and systems should be designed to ensure that no single employee/outsourced service provider could enter, authorise and complete a transaction.
- Segregation should be maintained between those initiating static data (including web page content) and those responsible for verifying its integrity.
- E-banking systems should be tested to ensure that segregation of duties cannot be bypassed.
- Segregation should be maintained between those developing and those administrating e-banking systems.

Principle 7: Banks should ensure that proper authorisation controls and access privileges are in place for e-banking systems, databases and applications.

In order to maintain segregation of duties, banks need to strictly control authorisation and access privileges. Failure to provide adequate authorisation control could allow individuals to alter their authority, circumvent segregation and gain access to e-banking systems, databases or applications to which they are not privileged.

In e-banking systems, the authorisations and access rights can be established in either a centralised or distributed manner within a bank and are generally stored in databases. The protection of those databases from tampering or corruption is therefore essential for effective authorisation control.

Principle 8: Banks should ensure that appropriate measures are in place to protect the data integrity of e-banking transactions, records and information.

Data integrity refers to the assurance that information that is in-transit or in storage is not altered without authorisation. Failure to maintain the data integrity of transactions, records and information can expose banks to financial losses as well as to substantial legal and reputational risk. The inherent nature of straight-through processes for e-banking may make programming errors or fraudulent activities more difficult to detect at an early stage.

Therefore, it is important that banks implement straight-through processing in a manner that ensures safety and soundness and data integrity. As e-banking is transacted over public networks, transactions are exposed to the added threat of data corruption, fraud and the tampering of records. Accordingly, banks should ensure that appropriate measures are in place to ascertain the accuracy, completeness and reliability of e-banking transactions, records and information that is either transmitted over the Internet, resident on internal bank databases, or transmitted/stored by third-party service providers on behalf of the bank.

Common practices used to maintain data integrity within an e-banking environment include the following:

- E-banking transactions should be conducted in a manner that makes them highly resistant to tampering throughout the entire process.
- E-banking records should be stored, accessed and modified in a manner that makes them highly resistant to tampering.
- E-banking transaction and record-keeping processes should be designed in a manner as to make it virtually impossible to circumvent detection of unauthorised changes.
- Adequate change control policies, including monitoring and testing procedures, should be in place to protect against any e-banking system changes that may erroneously or unintentionally compromise controls or data reliability.
- Any tampering with e-banking transactions or records should be detected by transaction processing, monitoring and record keeping functions.

Principle 9: Banks should ensure that clear audit trails exist for all e-banking transactions

Delivery of financial services over the Internet can make it more difficult for banks to apply and enforce internal controls and maintain clear audit trails if these measures are not adapted to an e-banking environment. Banks are not only challenged to ensure that effective internal control can be provided in highly automated environments, but also that the controls can be independently audited, particularly for all critical e-banking events and applications.

A bank's internal control environment may be weakened if it is unable to maintain clear audit trails for its e-banking activities. This is because much, if not all, of its records and evidence supporting e-banking transactions are in an electronic format.

In making a determination as to where clear audit trails should be maintained, the following types of e-banking transactions should be considered:

- The opening, modification or closing of a customer's account.
- Any transaction with financial consequences.
- Any authorisation granted to a customer to exceed a limit.
- Any granting, modification or revocation of systems access rights or privileges.

Principle 10: Banks should take appropriate measures to preserve the confidentiality of key e-banking information. Measures taken to preserve confidentiality should be commensurate with the sensitivity of the information being transmitted and/or stored in databases.

Confidentiality is the assurance that key information remains private to the bank and is not viewed or used by those unauthorised to do so. Misuse or unauthorised disclosure of data exposes a bank to both reputation and legal risk. The advent of e-banking presents additional security challenges for banks because it increases the exposure that information transmitted over the public network or stored in databases may be accessible by unauthorised or inappropriate parties or used in ways the customer providing the information did not intend. Additionally, increased use of service providers may expose key bank data to other parties.

To meet these challenges concerning the preservation of confidentiality of key e-banking information, banks need to ensure that:

- All confidential bank data and records are only accessible by duly authorised and authenticated individuals, agents or systems.
- All confidential bank data are maintained in a secure manner and protected from unauthorised viewing or modification during transmission over public, private or internal networks.
- The bank's standards and controls for data use and protection must be met when third parties have access to the data through outsourcing relationships.
- All access to restricted data is logged and appropriate efforts are made to ensure that access logs are resistant to tampering.

LEGAL AND REPUTATIONAL RISK MANAGEMENT (PRINCIPLES 11 TO 14)

Specific customer protection and privacy regulations and laws will vary from jurisdiction to jurisdiction. However, banks generally have a clear responsibility to provide their customers with a level of comfort regarding information disclosures, protection of customer data and business availability that approaches the level they would have if transacting business through traditional banking distribution channels.

Principle 11: Banks should ensure that adequate information is provided on their websites to allow potential customers to make an informed conclusion about the bank's identity and regulatory status of the bank prior to entering into e-banking transactions.

To minimise legal and reputational risk associated with e-banking activities conducted both domestically and cross-border, banks should ensure that adequate information is provided on their websites to allow customers to make informed conclusions about the identity and regulatory status of the bank before they enter into e-banking transactions.

Examples of such information that a bank could provide on its own website include:

- The name of the bank and the location of its head office (and local offices if applicable).
- The identity of the primary bank supervisory authority(ies) responsible for the supervision of the bank's head office.
- How customers can contact the bank's customer service centre regarding service problems, complaints, suspected misuse of accounts, etc.
- How customers can access and use applicable Ombudsman or consumer complaint schemes.
- How customers can obtain access to information on applicable national compensation or deposit insurance coverage and the level of protection that they afford (or links to websites that provide such information).
- Other information that may be appropriate or required by specific jurisdictions.

Principle 12: Banks should take appropriate measures to ensure adherence to customer privacy requirements applicable to the jurisdictions to which the bank is providing e-banking products and services.

Maintaining a customer's information privacy is a key responsibility for a bank. Misuse or unauthorised disclosure of confidential customer data exposes a bank to both legal and reputation risk.

To meet these challenges concerning the preservation of privacy of customer information, banks should make reasonable endeavours to ensure that:

- The bank's customer privacy policies and standards take account of and comply with all privacy regulations and laws applicable to the jurisdictions to which it is providing e-banking products and services.
- Customers are made aware of the bank's privacy policies and relevant privacy issues concerning use of e-banking products and services.
- Customers may decline ("opt out") from permitting the bank to share with a third party for cross-marketing purposes any information about the customer's personal needs, interests, financial position or banking activity.
- Customer data are not used for purposes beyond which they are specifically allowed or for purposes beyond which customers have authorised.
- The bank's standards for customer data use must be met when third parties have access to customer data through outsourcing relationships.

Principle 13: Banks should have effective capacity, business continuity and contingency planning processes to help ensure the availability of e-banking systems and services.

To protect banks against business, legal and reputation risk, e-banking services must be delivered on a consistent and timely basis in accordance with customer expectations. To achieve this, the bank must have the ability to deliver e-banking services to end-users from either primary (*e.g.* internal bank systems and applications) or secondary sources (*e.g.* systems and applications of service providers).

The maintenance of adequate availability is also dependent upon the ability of contingency back-up systems to mitigate denial of service attacks or other events that may potentially cause business disruption. The challenge to maintain continued availability of e-banking systems and applications can be considerable given the potential for high transaction demand, especially during peak time periods. In addition, high customer expectations regarding short transaction processing cycle times and constant availability (24 X 7) has also increased the importance of sound capacity, business continuity and contingency planning.

To provide customers with the continuity of ebanking services that they expect, banks need to ensure that:

- Current e-banking system capacity and future scalability are analysed in light of the overall market dynamics for e-commerce and the projected rate of customer acceptance of e-banking products and services.
- E-banking transaction processing capacity estimates are established, stress tested and periodically reviewed.
- Appropriate business continuity and contingency plans for critical e-banking processing and delivery systems are in place and regularly tested.

Principle 14: Banks should develop appropriate incident response plans to manage, contain and minimise problems arising from unexpected events, including internal and external attacks, that may hamper the provision of e-banking systems and services

Effective incident response mechanisms are critical to minimise operational, legal and reputational risks arising from unexpected events such as internal and external attacks that may affect the provision of e-banking systems and services. Banks should develop appropriate incident response plans, including communication strategies, that ensure business continuity, control reputation risk and limit liability associated with disruptions in their e-banking services, including those originating from outsourced systems and operations.

To ensure effective response to unforeseen incidents, banks should develop:

- Incident response plans to address recovery of e-banking systems and services under various scenarios, businesses and geographic locations. Scenario analysis should include consideration of the likelihood of the risk occurring and its impact on the bank. E-banking systems that are outsourced to third-party service providers should be an integral part of these plans
- Mechanisms to identify an incident or crisis as soon as it occurs, assess its materiality, and control the reputation risk associated with any disruption in service.
- A communication strategy to adequately address external market and media concerns that may arise in the event of security breaches, online attacks and/or failures of e-banking systems.
- A clear process for alerting the appropriate regulatory authorities in the event of material security breaches or disruptive incidents occur.
- Incident response teams with the authority to act in an emergency and sufficiently trained in analysing incident detection/response systems and interpreting the significance of related output.
- A clear chain of command, encompassing both internal as well as outsourced operations, to ensure that prompt action is taken appropriate for the significance of the incident. In addition, escalation and internal communication procedures should be developed and include notification of the Board where appropriate.
- A process to ensure all relevant external parties, including bank customers, counterparties and the media, are informed in a timely and appropriate manner of material e-banking disruptions and business resumption developments.
- A process for collecting and preserving forensic evidence to facilitate appropriate post-mortem reviews of any e-banking incidents as well as to assist in the prosecution of attackers.

SOUND SECURITY CONTROL PRACTICES FOR E-BANKING

- Security profiles should be created and maintained and specific authorisation privileges assigned to all users of e-banking systems and applications, including all customers, internal bank users and outsourced service providers. Logical access controls should also be designed to support proper segregation of duties.
- E-banking data and systems should be classified according to their sensitivity and importance and protected accordingly. Appropriate mechanisms, such as encryption, access control and data recovery plans should be used to protect all sensitive and high-risk e-banking systems, servers, databases and applications.
- Storage of sensitive or high-risk data on the organisation's desktop and laptop systems should be minimised and properly protected by encryption, access control and data recovery plans.
- Sufficient physical controls should be in place to deter unauthorised access to all critical e-banking systems, servers, databases and applications.
- Appropriate techniques should be employed to mitigate external threats to e-banking systems, including the use of:
  - Virus-scanning software at all critical entry points (*e.g.* remote access servers, e-mail proxy servers) and on each desktop system.
  - Intrusion detection software and other security assessment tools to periodically probe networks, servers and firewalls for weaknesses and/or violations of security policies and controls.
  - Penetration testing of internal and external networks.
- A rigorous security review process should be applied to all employees and service providers holding sensitive positions.

SOUND PRACTICES FOR MANAGING OUTSOURCED E-BANKING SYSTEMS AND SERVICES

- Banks should adopt appropriate processes for evaluating decisions to outsource ebanking systems or services.
  - Bank management should clearly identify the strategic purposes, benefits and costs associated with entering into outsourcing arrangements for ebanking with third parties.
  - The decision to outsource a key e-banking function or service should be consistent with the bank's business strategies, be based on a clearly defined business need, and recognise the specific risks that outsourcing entails.
  - All affected areas of the bank need to understand how the service provider(s) will support the bank's e-banking strategy and fit into its operating structure.

- Banks should conduct appropriate risk analysis and due diligence prior to selecting an e-banking service provider and at appropriate intervals thereafter.
  - Banks should consider developing processes for soliciting proposals from several e-banking service providers and criteria for choosing among the various proposals.
  - Once a potential service provider has been identified, the bank should conduct an appropriate due diligence review, including a risk analysis of the service provider's financial strength, reputation, risk management policies and controls, and ability to fulfil its obligations.
  - Thereafter, banks should regularly monitor and, as appropriate, conduct due diligence reviews of the ability of the service provider to fulfil its service and associated risk management obligations throughout the duration of the contract.
  - Banks need to ensure that adequate resources are committed to overseeing outsourcing arrangements supporting e-banking.
  - Responsibilities for overseeing e-banking outsourcing arrangements should be clearly assigned.
  - An appropriate exit strategy for the bank to manage risks should it need to terminate the outsourcing relationship.
- Banks should adopt appropriate procedures for ensuring the adequacy of contracts governing e-banking. Contracts governing outsourced e-banking activities should address, for example, the following:
  - The contractual liabilities of the respective parties as well as responsibilities for making decisions, including any sub-contracting of material services are clearly defined.
  - Responsibilities for providing information to and receiving information from the service provider are clearly defined. Information from the service provider should be timely and comprehensive enough to allow the bank to adequately assess service levels and risks. Materiality thresholds and procedures to be used to notify the bank of service disruptions, security breaches and other events that pose a material risk to the bank should be spelled out.
  - Provisions that specifically address insurance coverage, the ownership of the data stored on the service provider's servers or databases, and the right of the bank to recover its data upon expiration or termination of the contract should be clearly defined.
  - Performance expectations, under both normal and contingency circumstances, are defined.
  - Adequate means and guarantees, for instance through audit

clauses, are defined to insure that the service provider complies with the bank's policies.
   - Provisions are in place for timely and orderly intervention and rectification in the event of substandard performance by the service provider.
   - For cross-border outsourcing arrangements, determining which country laws and regulations, including those relating to privacy and other customer protections, are applicable.
   - The right of the bank to conduct independent reviews and/or audits of security, internal controls and business continuity and contingency plans is explicitly defined.
- Banks should ensure that periodic independent internal and/or external audits are conducted of outsourced operations to at least the same scope required if such operations were conducted in-house.
   - For outsourced relationships involving critical or technologically complex ebanking services/applications, banks may need to arrange for other periodic reviews to be performed by independent third parties with sufficient technical expertise.
- Banks should develop appropriate contingency plans for outsourced e-banking activities.
   - Banks need to develop and periodically test their contingency plans for all critical e-banking systems and services that have been outsourced to third parties.
   - Contingency plans should address credible worst-case scenarios for providing continuity of e-banking services in the event of a disruption affecting outsourced operations.
   - Banks should have an identified team that is responsible for managing recovery and assessing the financial impact of a disruption in outsourced ebanking services.
- Banks that provide e-banking services to third parties should ensure that their operations, responsibilities, and liabilities are sufficiently clear so that serviced institutions can adequately carry out their own effective due diligence reviews and ongoing oversight of the relationship.
   - Banks have a responsibility to provide serviced institutions with information necessary to identify, control and monitor any risks associated with the ebanking service arrangement.

SOUND AUTHORISATION PRACTICES FOR E-BANKING APPLICATIONS

- Specific authorisation and access privileges should be assigned to all individuals, agents or systems, which conduct e-banking activities.

- All e-banking systems should be constructed to ensure that they interact with a valid authorisation database.
- No individual agent or system should have the authority to change his or her own authority or access privileges in an e-banking authorisation database.
- Any addition of an individual, agent or system or changes to access privileges in an e-banking authorisation database should be duly authorised by an authenticated source empowered with the adequate authority and subject to suitable and timely oversight and audit trails.
- Appropriate measures should be in place in order to make e-banking authorisation databases reasonably resistant to tampering. Any such tampering should be detectable through ongoing monitoring processes. Sufficient audit trails should exist to document any such tampering.
- Any e-banking authorisation database that has been tampered with should not be used until replaced with a validated database.
- Controls should be in place to prevent changes to authorisation levels during ebanking transaction sessions and any attempts to alter authorisation should be logged and brought to the attention of management.

SOUND AUDIT TRAIL PRACTICES FOR E-BANKING SYSTEMS

- Sufficient logs should be maintained for all e-banking transactions to help establish a clear audit trail and assist in dispute resolution.
- E-banking systems should be designed and installed to capture and maintain forensic evidence in a manner that maintains control over the evidence, and prevents tampering and the collection of false evidence.
- In instances where processing systems and related audit trails are the responsibility of a third-party service provider:
  - The bank should ensure that it has access to relevant audit trails maintained by the service provider.
  - Audit trails maintained by the service provider meet the bank's standards.

SOUND PRACTICES TO HELP MAINTAIN THE PRIVACY OF CUSTOMER E-BANKING INFORMATION

- Banks should employ appropriate cryptographic techniques, specific protocols or other security controls to ensure the confidentiality of customer e-banking data.
- Banks should develop appropriate procedures and controls to periodically assess its customer security infrastructure and protocols for e-banking.

- Banks should ensure that its third-party service providers have confidentiality and privacy policies that are consistent with their own.
- Banks should take appropriate steps to inform e-banking customers about the confidentiality and privacy of their information. These steps may include:
  - Informing customers of the bank's privacy policy, possibly on the bank's website. Clear, concise language in such statements is essential to assure that the customer fully understands the privacy policy. Lengthy legal descriptions, while accurate, are likely to go unread by the majority of customers.
  - Instructing customers on the need to protect their passwords, personal identification numbers (PINs) and other banking and/or personal data.
  - Providing customers with information regarding the general security of their personal computer, including the benefits of using virus protection software, physical access controls and personal firewalls for static Internet connections.

SOUND CAPACITY, BUSINESS CONTINUITY AND CONTINGENCY PLANNING PRACTICES FOR E-BANKING

- All e-banking services and applications, including those provided by third-party service providers, should be identified and assessed for criticality.
- A risk assessment for each critical e-banking service and application, including the potential implications of any business disruption on the bank's credit, market, liquidity, legal, operational and reputation risk should be conducted.
- Performance criteria for each critical e-banking service and application should be established, and service levels should be monitored against such criteria. Appropriate measures should be taken to ensure that e-banking systems can handle high and low transaction volume and that systems performance and capacity is consistent with the bank's expectations for future growth in e-banking.
- Consideration should be given to developing processing alternatives for managing demand when e-banking systems appear to be reaching defined capacity checkpoints.
- E-banking business continuity plans should be formulated to address any reliance on third-party service providers and any other external dependencies required achieving recovery.
- E-banking contingency plans should set out a process for restoring or replacing ebanking processing capabilities, reconstructing supporting transaction information, and include measures to be taken

to resume availability of critical e-banking systems and applications in the event of a business disruption.

MANAGEMENT PRINCIPLES OF ELECTRONIC BANKING

Continuing technological innovation and competition among existing banking organisations and new entrants have allowed for a much wider array of banking products and services to become accessible and delivered to retail and wholesale customers through an electronic distribution channel collectively referred to as e-banking. However, the rapid development of e-banking capabilities carries risks as well as benefits.

The Basel Committee on Banking Supervision expects such risks to be recognised, addressed and managed by banking institutions in a prudent manner according to the fundamental characteristics and challenges of e-banking services. These characteristics include the unprecedented speed of change related to technological and customer service innovation, the ubiquitous and global nature of open electronic networks, the integration of e-banking applications with legacy computer systems and the increasing dependence of banks on third parties that provide the necessary information technology. While not creating inherently new risks, the Committee noted that these characteristics increased and modified some of the traditional risks associated with banking activities, in particular strategic, operational, legal and reputational risks, thereby influencing the overall risk profile of banking.

Based on these conclusions, the Committee considers that while existing risk management principles remain applicable to e-banking activities, such principles must be tailored, adapted and, in some cases, expanded to address the specific risk management challenges created by the characteristics of e-banking activities. To this end, the Committee believes that it is incumbent upon the Boards of Directors and banks' senior management to take steps to ensure that their institutions have reviewed and modified where necessary their existing risk management policies and processes to cover their current or planned e-banking activities. The Committee also believes that the integration of e-banking applications with legacy systems implies an integrated risk management approach for all banking activities of a banking institution.

To facilitate these developments, the Committee has identified fourteen *Risk Management Principles for Electronic Banking* to help banking institutions expand their existing risk oversight policies and processes to cover their e-banking activities.

These *Risk Management Principles* are not put forth as absolute requirements or even "best practice." The Committee believes that setting detailed risk management requirements in the area of e-banking might be counter-productive, if only because these would be likely to become rapidly outdated because of the speed of change related to technological and customer service innovation. The Committee has therefore preferred to express supervisory expectations and guidance in the form of *Risk Management Principles* in order to promote safety and soundness for e-banking activities, while preserving the necessary flexibility in implementation that derives in part from the speed of change in this area. Further, the Committee recognises that each bank's risk profile is different and requires a tailored risk mitigation approach appropriate for the scale of the e-banking operations, the materiality of the risks present, and the willingness and ability of the institution to manage these risks. This implies that a "one size fits all" approach to e-banking risk management issues may not be appropriate.

For a similar reason, the *Risk Management Principles* issued by the Committee do not attempt to set specific technical solutions or standards relating to e-banking. Technical solutions are to be addressed by institutions and standard setting bodies as technology evolves. However, this Report contains appendices that list some examples current and widespread risk mitigation practices in the e-banking area that are supportive of the *Risk Management Principles*.

Consequently, the *Risk Management Principles* and sound practices identified in this Report are expected to be used as tools by national supervisors and implemented with adaptations to reflect specific national requirements and individual risk profiles where necessary. In some areas, the Principles have been expressed by the Committee or by national supervisors in previous bank supervisory guidance. However, some issues, such as the management of outsourcing relationships, security controls and legal and reputational risk management, warrant more detailed principles than those expressed to date due to the unique characteristics and implications of the Internet distribution channel.

Continuing technological innovation and competition among existing banking organisations and new entrants have allowed for a much wider array of banking products and services to become accessible and delivered to retail and wholesale customers through an electronic distribution channel collectively referred to as e-banking. However, the rapid development of e-banking capabilities carries risks as well as benefits.

The Basel Committee on Banking Supervision expects such risks to be recognised, addressed and managed by banking institutions in a prudent manner according to the fundamental characteristics and challenges of e-banking services. These characteristics include the unprecedented speed of change related to technological and customer service innovation, the ubiquitous and global nature of open electronic networks, the integration of e-banking applications with legacy computer systems and the increasing dependence of banks on third parties that provide the necessary information technology. While not creating inherently new risks, the Committee noted that these characteristics increased and modified some of the traditional risks associated with banking activities, in particular strategic, operational, legal and reputational risks, thereby influencing the overall risk profile of banking.

Based on these conclusions, the Committee considers that while existing risk management principles remain applicable to e-banking activities, such principles must be tailored, adapted and, in some cases, expanded to address the specific risk management challenges created by the characteristics of e-banking activities. To this end, the Committee believes that it is incumbent upon the Boards of Directors and banks' senior management to take steps to ensure that their institutions have reviewed and modified where necessary their existing risk management policies and processes to cover their current or planned e-banking activities. The Committee also believes that the integration of e-banking applications with legacy systems implies an integrated risk management approach for all banking activities of a banking institution.

To facilitate these developments, the Committee has identified fourteen *Risk Management Principles for Electronic Banking* to help banking institutions expand their existing risk oversight policies and processes to cover their e-banking activities.

These *Risk Management Principles* are not put forth as absolute requirements or even "best practice." The Committee believes that setting detailed risk management requirements in the area of e-banking might be counter-productive, if only because these would be likely to become rapidly outdated because of the speed of change related to technological and customer service innovation. The Committee has therefore preferred to express supervisory expectations and guidance in the form of *Risk Management Principles* in order to promote safety and soundness for e-banking activities, while preserving the necessary flexibility in implementation that derives in part from the speed of change in this area. Further, the Committee recognises that each bank's risk profile is different and requires a tailored risk mitigation approach appropriate for the scale of the e-banking operations, the materiality of the risks present, and the willingness and ability of the institution to manage these risks. This implies that a "one size fits all" approach to e-banking risk management issues may not be appropriate.

For a similar reason, the *Risk Management Principles* issued by the Committee do not attempt to set specific technical solutions or standards relating to e-banking. Technical solutions are to be addressed by institutions and standard setting bodies as technology evolves. However, this Report contains appendices that list some examples current and widespread risk mitigation practices in the e-banking area that are supportive of the *Risk Management Principles*.

Consequently, the *Risk Management Principles* and sound practices identified in this Report are expected to be used as tools by national supervisors and implemented with adaptations to reflect specific national requirements and individual risk profiles where necessary. In some areas, the Principles have been expressed by the Committee or by national supervisors in previous bank supervisory guidance. However, some issues, such as the management of outsourcing relationships, security controls and legal and reputational risk management, warrant more detailed principles than those expressed to date due to the unique characteristics and implications of the Internet distribution channel.

The *Risk Management Principles* fall into three broad, and often overlapping, categories of issues that are grouped to provide clarity: *Board and Management Oversight; Security Controls; and Legal and Reputational Risk Management*.

8

Future Developments In E-business Technology

THE INTERNET

Just as the internal combustion engine (the motor car) and jet engine (aeroplane) have radically changed our lives, the Internet is beginning to do the same. In the short time of its existence the Internet has greatly affected business and society. The Internet's evolution and future development are set to continue. The TCP/IP protocol is evolving with the development of IPv6, the next generation of the Internet protocol. The improvements in IPv6 are scalability, security and support for real-time media quality. Companies such as Ciena Corporation are working on improving bandwidth. They have a product called Wave Division Multiplexing (WDM) that moves data at the speed of 100 billion bits per second (100,000,000,000 b.p.s.). This contrasts with the standard modem's 36,600 b.p.s.

THE WORLD WIDE WEB

The Web's HTTP protocol is evolving to encompass better performance and flexible interactions between clients and servers. Companies compete in complex and increasingly competitive markets. They do so by following, for example, competitive strategies of product differentiation or cost reduction. Similarly, *relationships* are becoming increasingly important in business models. Current developments in Web technology are best placed to enable companies to exploit their differences and build personal relationships with customers, suppliers or business partners. For example, the eXtensible Mark-up Language, the Semantic Web and other Internet developments are leading the way to providing tailoring capability in e-Business technology.

Extensible mark-up Language

The extensible mark-up language (XML) is gaining popularity over HTML with companies. XML offers companies the ability to define tags that uniquely describe their products, services or customer service culture. Companies can design XML tags to display price or product or service descriptions that cannot be done in HTML. In short, XML allows a company to tailor the feel and look of its Web site and order forms to its needs.

The Semantic Web

Semantic Web is the name given to developments in Web technology by the World Wide Web Consortium (W3C), headed by Tim Berners-Lee, who invented the Web. The Semantic Web enables communication of contextual data and information. Information makes sense to humans only when it is used in context. The Semantic Web enables such context to be captured in Web applications. The primary contribution of the Internet, the Web and associated technologies is to enable collaboration and sharing of information and knowledge among people. The types of collaboration are numerous, ranging from intra-organizational to inter-organizational and across the boundary of the organization with the customer. Future technology development will focus on this collaborative aspect of e-Commerce and will lead to radically different organizational structures and patterns of interaction among and between businesses and their customers.

THE WORLD OF E-RETAILING E-RETAIL

The business of *e-retail* has been defined as the sale of goods and services via Internet or other electronic channels, for personal or household use by consumers. This definition includes all e-commerce activities that result in transactions with end consumers (rather than business customers), i.e. *B2C* rather than *B2B*. Some e-marketing activities that do not directly involve transactions, such as providing (free) information or promoting brands and image, are considered to be part of B2C but are not normally considered as being within the scope of e-retail.

Despite the *dot.com crash* of 2000, e-retailing has been growing, particularly for the 'top eight' categories that account for three-quarters of all European sales. These major growth areas comprise: books, music and *DVD* movies, groceries, sex products, games and software, electronic and computer equipment, travel, and clothes.

DISADVANTAGES OF E-RETAILING FOR RETAILERS

Retailers have been slow to take up e-retailing. This is to some extent understandable in the light of many disadvantages and problems. Retailers, for example, may lack the technical know-how, the substantial investment required or the order fulfilment capabilities. Set-up costs start from around £20,000 for a small site and up to £500,000 for a large operation ($A53,000 to $A1.4 million). And set-up costs are only the start - Datamonitor estimates that high street retailers are spending more on ongoing costs than on setting up new sites. A continuous cost will be fulfilment and logistics. Successful e-retailers such as Next and Land's End have had the advantage of already operating profitable mail-order catalogues.

There can be legal problems. For example, if purchaser and supplier are in different countries, there may be conflict between the laws and taxation of the two countries. In Europe, the *VAT (Value Added Tax)* position is still unclear, but Richard Branson's Virgin group's e-retail operation is registered in Madeira, the country with the lowest VAT rate in the European Union (EU).

A further disadvantage is that e-selling is less powerful than face-to-face selling (it is easier to say 'no' to a computer). This viewpoint is linked to a concern of traditional high street retailers that e-retailing offers a diminished role for their expertise. For example, there are obvious difficulties with products sold by 'atmosphere' - touch, feel, smell - and impulse purchases. In addition, consumers have a perception of lower prices online. This puts pressure on margins for e-retailing, and can lead to shoppers expecting consistent low prices in-store. Finally, aftercare can be difficult, especially if the shopper is overseas.

DISADVANTAGES OF E-RETAILING FOR RETAILERS

- May lack know-how and technology
- Substantial set-up, investment and ongoing costs
- Complex logistics of fulfilment
- e-Selling less powerful than face-to-face - uptake slow for goods selected by taste or smell
- Fewer impulse purchases
- Legal problems
- Lesser role for traditional high street retail expertise
- Pressure on margins and prices in-store
- After-sales care difficulties

ADVANTAGES OF E-RETAILING FOR RETAILERS

On the other hand, there are a number of advantages for retailers. First, location is unimportant. According to some textbooks, adapting an old saying, the three most important elements in *retail* are 'location, location and location'. The best high street locations are therefore expensive. The e-rétailer, though, can sell equally well to anywhere in the country and even overseas. Second, size does not matter - small e-retailers can compete on equal terms to large ones, can reach a larger audience than the high street and can be open 24 hours a day. For example, the independent, northern UK-based Botham's of Whitby has been a pioneer of e-retailing.

There are many other advantages. The socio-demographic profile of e-shoppers is attractive to many retailers, with higher-than-average education, employment and disposable income levels. In theory at least, online selling saves on the wages costs of face-to-face sales people and the costs of premises. The savings may be

less than expected, though, as there are still costs in Internet customer contact, and packaging and delivery can be more expensive to provide. Perhaps a more substantial advantage is the ease with which e-retailing integrates with *customer relationship management (CRM)* and micro-marketing systems - identifying and treating the customer as an individual. This, together with the easier provision of product information, leads to greater opportunities for cross-selling and selling up. Finally, the late entrants into e-retailing are largely being driven by 'if we don't, our competitors will'.

ADVANTAGES OF E-RETAILING FOR RETAILERS

- Location is unimportant
- Size does not matter
- Saves on the wages and premises costs
- Reaches a larger audience
- Higher disposable income profile than average
- Accepts orders 24 hours a day
- More opportunities for CRM, micro-marketing, cross- and up-selling
- If we don't, our competitors will

Other retailers, though, are put off e-retailing by what they perceive as consumer resistance. According to e-research company Forrester, nearly 40 per cent of UK homes are now connected to the Internet, but estimates vary from only 12 per cent (Verdict) up to 20 percent (Forrester) of UK adults shopping online. This contrasts with the faster take-up of e-business for B2B, with 25 per cent of businesses ordering online.

THE (E-)RETAIL MIX: SALE THE 7CS

The (e-)retail mix is a shorthand term for the blend of tools and techniques that (e-)retailers use to provide value for customers. It is a development of the well-known marketing mix, more specific to retail and e-retail. As far back as the first half of the twentieth century, the job of the marketer was described as a 'mixer of ingredients'. Marketers devise strategies and tactics aimed at providing satisfaction and adding value for customers. The various elements are blended into a 'marketing mix' - a phrase first coined by Neil Borden (1964) of Harvard Business School.

The marketing mix is most widely known as E. Jerome McCarthy's (1960) '4Ps': Place, Product, Price and Promotion. 'Place' is not quite self-explanatory, but refers to the routes that organizations take to get the benefits of the product or service to the intended customers - channels of distribution. 'Product' means both tangible product and also 'service', and all the ways that an organization adds value. 'Price' means not just the price charged, but also all aspects of pricing policy, including, for example, distributor margins. 'Promotion' is not just the more specialized 'sales promotion', but also every way that a product is promoted to customers - from print advertising to websites.

In recent decades there have been numerous attempts to update and revise the marketing mix. One development is particularly descriptive of the way that marketers think about the customer. The '4Cs' imply more emphasis on customer wants and concerns than do the 4Ps. The 4Cs (in the same order as the equivalent 4Ps listed above) are: Convenience for the customer; Customer value and benefits; Cost to the customer; and Communication. Reflecting the emphasis of 'new' marketing on long-term relationships with customers, we include 'Customer relationships' within the umbrella of the 'Communication' C.

C1 Convenience for the Customer

'Place' (from the 4Ps), rather than implying management's methods of placing products where they want them to be, can be thought of as 'Convenience for the customer', recognizing customers' choices for buying in ways that are convenient to them.

For the retailer, 'Place' incorporates what can be the most critical decisions concerning 'location'. For the e-retailer, this is also important, as many customers prefer a multi-channel approach: browse on the Web, buy in-store or vice versa - or buy on the Web, return to the store for a refund! This perhaps goes some way towards explaining the success of *high street* and *multi-channel retailers* in e-retail, as compared to the 'pureplays'.

Physical location can also be important for the e-retailer as many customers prefer to buy from, or are more likely to trust, an e-retailer based at least in the same country, where carriage costs and maybe taxes are cheaper.

'Location' for the e-retailer also means virtual location and the ease of finding the website. This entails registration with search engines, location in e-malls and links from associates.

Convenience also includes key aspects of website design, such as navigation, layout and ease of purchase. For the *'bricks'* retailer, convenience decisions include shelf space allocation and layout. The equivalent in 'clicks' e-retail is site design and page layout - for example, whether layout follows the 'free-flow' or 'grid' type of layout, or indeed a combination such as 'free-grid'.

C2 Customer Value and Benefits

'Product', rather than being something that a company has to sell, can be thought of as 'Customer value and benefits' - meaning the bundle of service and satisfactions wanted by customers. People do not buy 'products' as such, but rather solutions to problems or good feelings. Retailers and e-retailers now specify (and sometimes design) products to a much greater extent than previously, reflecting closeness to the customer and appreciation of benefits that customers want.

An essential task of retail and e-retail is selecting the range of products offered for sale - assembled for target markets from diverse sources. The wide and deep range that can be offered is one of the areas where the clicks e-retailer can score relative to the bricks retailer.

When buying online, customers are far less likely to request help than they are in the store. Rather, e-shoppers who need help in understanding a product are more likely to abandon the transaction and find an alternative supplier or even buy through a different channel. Therefore, e-businesses need to be particularly careful about describing products clearly in customer value and benefits terms.

C3 Cost to the Customer

'Price' may be what companies decide to charge for their products, but 'Cost to the customer' represents the real cost that customers will pay, including, for example, in the case of bricks retail, their own transport costs. For clicks e-retail, there are also the costs of carriage and perhaps taxes to be added to the quoted prices. High carriage charges may be one reason for the high rate of carts abandoned at the checkout. Customers also need to consider the costs of Internet and telephone access.

Consumers have a perception that prices should be lower online than in-store, and this can cause problems when customers buying via other channels realise that they are paying more than online customers. For example, Screwfix, a well-known supplier of tradesperson's supplies via paper catalogue and telesales, has a number of attractive special offers available only online.

Customers who have looked up what they want online, then telephone to order, can be irritated to learn that the extra discounts are not available when ordering by phone.

C4 Communication and Customer Relationships

'Communication' is equivalent to the final 'P' in the 4Ps: 'Promotion'. Promotion suggests ways in which companies persuade people to buy, whereas communication is a two-way process also involving feedback from customers to suppliers. Reflecting an increasing control of elements of the retail mix by retailers rather than manufacturers, retailers spend more on advertising than manufacturers do (assisted by advertising allowances from manufacturers). Retailers are closer to the customer than are manufacturers and have more access to customer feedback.

Communication is not just advertising, though, but all the ways in which retailers communicate with their customers, including, for example, marketing research surveys, public relations (PR), direct mail, *e-mail*, Internet, marketing database and loyalty schemes. Successful e-retailers often use offline advertising such as magazines and 'click here' sections of newspapers integrated with online marketing communications. Online methods include banner ads and pop-ups (often incentivized); paid-for listings in search engines and directories; and affiliate programmes. In addition to solving problems, there is another reason for customers buying products - to get good feelings. This is a particularly difficult area for e-retailers. The bricks retail store and the face-to-face salesperson are often much better at identifying and satisfying customers' emotional needs and wants. The physical store uses *atmospherics* in the attempt to change mood and give shoppers a pleasant emotional experience when buying. Emotional cues may be visual (decor), olfactory (perfume), tactile (smooth and cool or soft and cuddly) and aural (music).

e-Retailers can create a 'web atmosphere' using, for example, music and visuals such as 3-D displays and downloadable video clips. Such enhancements must always be a compromise, on account of the need to avoid long download times. One way of tackling the problem is to provide a 'click here for *broadband*' 'Customer relationships' is an area that successful bricks retailers such as Tesco have used to gain a major lead over competitors. The importance of the emotional aspects of selling has already been mentioned. The sales representative selling face-to-face in the bricks retail store can use verbal and non-verbal (body language) communication to build personal relationships with customers, enhancing the emotional value of products. In trying to replicate the physical buying experience, the e-retailer is at a disadvantage.

On the other hand, with transaction data ready-digitized, the e-retailer is well placed to enhance product value using CRM techniques. For example, data mining can be used to build a picture of products most likely to be wanted by individual customers. Products tailored specifically can be offered pro-actively. Amazon, for instance, uses such a system to match new books to existing customers who are likely to be interested in them.

There has been a number of suggestions for structuring a 'retail mix', equivalent to the 4Ps or 4Cs of the marketing mix, adding other aspects that may be key to retailer success. For example, McGoldrick (2002) uses a nine-element mix. In addition to those that can be incorporated into the 4Cs framework above, McGoldrick also includes factors such as 'brand image', 'logistics' and 'information'. Most versions of the retail mix are not as 'catchy' as the 4Ps or 4Cs of the marketing mix.

Therefore we propose a simplified '7Cs' for the *e-retail mix*, adding Computing and category management issues; *Customer franchise*; and Customer care and service.

C5 Computing and Category Management Issues

The success of retailers has been founded on supplying the products that customers want, in the right sizes and quantities, at the right time and in the right place. With the growth in consumer choice has come a proliferation of products. Superstores carry 20,000-plus branded products and department stores from 100,000, and even up to one million or more. Efficient control of this degree of complexity needs effective computer and logistics systems.

Retail logistics have been changing rapidly over recent decades. First, the growth of retailer power has involved major retailers taking more control of their supply chains. The involvement of wholesalers has been reduced, tending to give way to contract logistics (under retailer control). At the same time, supply chains have become more efficient with computer network links between suppliers and retailers - many still based on *electronic data interchange (EDI)*.

Pre-dating the Web, EDI is based on privately owned third-party computer networks. Stock levels have been reduced using techniques such as *efficient customer response* (*ECR* -the retailers' equivalent of *Just in Time* or *JIT*). EDI networks are expensive to install, costing at least hundreds of thousands of pounds. There is a growing trend towards the use of the Internet, particularly for smaller businesses (suppliers and customers) and smaller order quantities. Increasingly, retailers such as Tesco are allowing Internet access to their suppliers for realtime *Electronic Point of Sale (EPoS)* data. Trusted supplier partners can thus respond more quickly to changes in customer demand.

Cooperation between suppliers and retailers has been key to improving the efficiency of satisfying customers while minimizing stocks and costs. On the larger scale, this cooperative process is known as *category management (CM)*, the retailer/ supplier process of managing categories as strategic business units.

High efficiency of the computer-controlled logistics systems is largely behind the success of 'bricks and clicks' retailers such as Tesco. Ironically, deficiencies in this area have been a major factor in the failure of a number of pureplay dot.coms that have concentrated on advertising and promotion at the expense of other areas of the e-retail mix. One exception is Amazon, which is founded on efficient logistics systems and customer care and service.

In the UK, Amazon is using its logistics expertise to carry out distribution services on contract for bricks retailers such as WHSmith and Toys R Us.

Apart from Amazon and the major bricks and clicks retailers, many of the e-retailers with the most efficient computer and logistics efficiency are established direct-selling businesses. For example, Quill and Screwfix, office supplies and tradesperson supplies respectively, operate established mail businesses via a paper catalogue. Dell have been pioneers in telemarketing and direct selling since the late 1980s, demonstrating that a complex product like a computer could be sold without face-to-face contact. Much of the success has been due to investment in computer-based *mass customization* systems, along with excellent customer care and service. The company was one of the first e-retailers and is the market leader worldwide for computer hardware.

SCREWFIX

Screwfix started out as a UK trade wholesale supplier, but also now sells extensively for DIY. Screwfix.com earned *Retail Week's* 'Retailer of the Year' award for 2002. Screwfix is an example of the successful niche e-retailer and one of few to gain favourable mentions in the *Sunday Times* (UK) survey. Screwfix is owned by Kingfisher, i.e. in the same stable as the B&Q UK DIY stores. Although the branding, ordering and fulfilment are completely separate, the supply chains are integrated, resulting in economies of scale and buying power. Screwfix has 0.5 per cent of the UK repairs, maintenance and home improvement market, but a massive 20 per cent of the *direct* market for those products. Web sales are over £20 million per year (15 per cent and growing of Screwfix's total business). The (e-)retail mix is summarized below.

Convenience for the Customer

Express shopping: if you have the catalogue, simply type in the quantities and catalogue number, or alternatively use 'search' to find what you want. A freephone telephone number is available 24 hours a day, plus fax and e-mail options, offering improved personal interaction.

Customer Value and Benefits

Products include not only screws, bolts and nails, but also fixings, adhesives, tools, hardware, lighting, plumbing and cleaning products - the claim is 'Everything for the trade and DIY - next day', and 100 per cent stock availability of 6,000 products.

Cost to the Customer

A number of special offers are always available. Most prices are significantly cheaper than in DIY retail sheds.

Communication and Customer Relationships

The homepage has many examples of good practice, for example: Recommend a Friend - get a reward when they order for the first time; Open a Business Account; Testimonials - 'I have just received my order and felt I must congratulate you on an excellent service. Your site is well designed. The products are well laid out and the order processing excellent.' ... 'Your website is brilliant, the designer needs a big pat on the back. Well laid out, and to order online is so easy.'; and Register/Login - optional registration makes ordering quicker and easier. There are regular communications by mail with catalogues, 'What's new' and special offers for registered customers.

Computing and Category Management Issues

Winner of best use of Supply Chain Management at the 2001 Internet Business Awards.

Customer Franchise

Without the need for heavy advertising, Screwfix has quickly built up a reputation for cheap prices, with quick and reliable delivery based on actual performance.

MAIN E-RETAIL PRODUCT CATEGORIES

The top categories that account for three-quarters of all European sales comprise: books, music and DVD movies, groceries, sex products, games and software, electronic and computer equipment, travel and clothes. In addition, although perhaps not a category, auctions are among the most popular UK e-retailing sites.

BOOKS

Books are by far the largest e-retailing category in the UK. Research carried out by Ernst & Young illustrates that 65 per cent of the purchases made by Web shoppers in the UK consisted of books. This is understandable in the light of books scoring highest in de Kare-Silver's (2001) ES (electronic shopping) test. In de Kare-Silver's sample table, books score a total of 38 points out of a maximum of 50, ten points ahead of the next category (hotels). Books score highly on *product characteristics*, being low-touch products that are simple to deliver by post, and *familiarity and confidence*, as customers usually know exactly what they are ordering. Finally, the higher-weighted *consumer attributes* parameter is particularly favourable to books: typical book buyers and the e-shopping early majority tend to be younger, better educated and of a higher socio-economic group than the general population.

Amazon is the outstanding leader of the books e-retail category, with a market share of over 50 per cent (and is also market leader for CDs/DVDs). When readers of the *Sunday Times* were asked for their experiences of e-shopping, Amazon 'streaked ahead' of all others as the country's favourite e-retailer. This means that Amazon is the undisputed favourite on considerations such as convenience, reliability and customer service.

Amazon has achieved worldwide success and brand recognition by attention to these considerations and heavy (offline) advertising, becoming one of only three dot.com brands in the Interbrand world league table. It is an illustration of the power of branding that Amazon is the world's top e-retailer and head-to-head with Barnes and Noble for the title of the world's biggest bookstore.

Other dot.coms such as Easy Value have attempted to exploit the Web's facility for quick and easy price comparisons, claiming that 'people know the products and price is driving them'. Indeed, a price comparison site such as Book Brain can often find prices for identical books significantly cheaper than Amazon. These cheaper prices often come from suppliers such as Swotbooks that do not have Amazon's heavy marketing costs. Nevertheless, even competitors such as Tesco, with offers like 'the top 100 books 10 per cent cheaper than Amazon' have failed to make a substantial impact on the online books market. As Brynjolfsson and Smith (2000) put it, 'the most expensive is not always the least patronised', pointing out that Amazon.com maintained a US market share of 80 per cent while charging 10 per cent more than the cheapest.

MINI CASE STUDY 2.1: BOOKBRAIN.CO.UK AND SWOTBOOKS.COM

BookBrain does not sell books, but is a shopbot that claims to provide 'the most accurate and comprehensive price search of UK online bookshops on the Web'. Fourteen sites were searched at the time of our site test.

Once you've found your ideal read, a quick search reveals prices of postage and packing, often with significant differences.... The site lets you know the availability of each title, how long it takes to be delivered, and it has smart editorial reviews too. Bravo.

For our site test we chose a book that might be useful for various disciplines, *Discovering SPSS for Windows: Advanced Techniques for Beginners* by Andy Field, published by Sage. The search took 13 seconds, returning a table of the cheapest eight suppliers, with links to the book on the suppliers' sites, details of how delivery charges are calculated (useful if you are considering buying more than one book), stock availability, base price, delivery charge and total price. The pricing information is particularly helpful, as, when going directly to many of the suppliers' sites, it is difficult to find the delivery costs until the very last stage at the checkout.

MUSIC

From the suppliers' point of view, the music industry is largely not a happy story. According to Lehman Brothers figures, music as a percentage of consumer

	Lower cost	Differentiation
Broad target	Cost leadership Swotbooks	Differentiation Amazon
Narrow target		Focus Abebooks

Fig. Exemplar Strategic Positioning of Books e-retailers

Expenditure is falling and music sales in the UK dropped by 8.1 per cent in 2002. The biggest drop was in compact disc (CD) singles, which, according to British Phonographic Industry (BPI) figures, slumped by 25 per cent.

Consumers have often complained about what are alleged to be unfairly high prices for CDs. On the other hand, the major companies tend to blame piracy and illegal Internet downloads for the slump (single tracks are obviously quicker and easier to download than albums), claiming to have lost US$1 billion in revenue worldwide in 2002. In the US, the Recording Industry Association of America (RIAA) has taken legal action against hundreds of 'major offenders' alleged to have illegally distributed an average of more than 1,000 copyrighted music files. It was widely reported that a 12-year-old girl, a university professor and an elderly man who rarely uses his computer were included in the first wave of actions, resulting in negative publicity for the RIAA. E-Retailing of music can be considered under two categories: CDs and online.

CDs :There are many different formats which are used to listen to music such as tapes, CDs, records, mini discs, etc., but since the 1980s the most popular form has been CDs. According to the BPI, music buyers spend on average over £80 per year on albums, of which 92 per cent are CDs. The BPI estimates that market penetration of CD albums is 50 per cent of UK households. Many leading retailers of music products such as HMV and Tower Records have now begun selling CDs on the Internet but are facing huge competition from pureplays such as CD WOW and CDNOW - now owned and run in conjunction with Amazon). Indeed, CDWOW has grown hugely in the competitive CD market and was recently voted by *Net* magazine readers as number two in the world's 20 best online stores, second only to Amazon. Similarly, in the UK, *Sunday Times* Doors readers voted CDWOW the country's second-favourite e-retailer, again behind only Amazon.

PRICES OF CDs

It is usually said that the Internet enables consumers to find cheaper products. This is an important consideration for CDs, as there has long been a consumer perception that CDs are overpriced in the high street.

One of the main advantages of e-shopping vs. bricks shopping for consumers was found to be 'prices favourable'. Table reports our comparison test, indicating a wide range of prices. The cheapest overall was CDNOW, e.g. for U2's album Best of 1980-1990 CDNOW's price was £8, compared to CD WOW in second place selling the same CD for £13.99.

E-RETAILING CDS - THE ES TEST

The Electronic Shopping (ES) test was developed by de Kare-Silver (2001) and is used to assess a product to evaluate the likelihood that it will be purchased online. According to de Kare-Silver, a product's potential for e-retailing can be judged by assessing three factors: 'Product characteristics', 'Familiarity and confidence' and 'Consumer attributes'. Consumer attributes are considered to carry more weight than the other two and are therefore loaded three times as highly in the model. The example of CDs follows below.

Table: Price Test Results for CDs

HMV	*Tower Records*	*CD WOW*	*CDNOW*	
U2 Best of 1980-90	£18.99	£23.65	£13.99	£8.00
Justin	£13.99	£12.78	£8.99	£8.50
Timberlake				
Big Brovaz	£10.99	£13.42	n/a	£18.70
Best of David Bowie	£15.99	£15.66	£12.99	£8.00

Product Characteristics

A CD is a product that a consumer either wants or doesn't and is down to personal preference. The consumer gets the same product whether they buy from HMV or Tower Records. A CD does not need to be tried on, smelt or touched before it is bought. The only thing that the customer may want to do is listen to it, and they will probably have heard the music already on the radio or TV.

Familiarity and Confidence

A consumer will usually be familiar and confident when choosing a CD. They will buy a CD of their own taste, whether rock, soul, hip hop, etc. Furthermore, leading brands such as HMV sell online and CDNOW uses Amazon as a channel to sell their CDs at cheaper prices. They are well-known brands so consumers are likely to feel confident buying from them.

Consumer Attributes

The typical music buyer is younger, better educated and of a higher socioeconomic group than the general population, i.e. closely fitting the profile of the typical Internet user. *Score: 22 out of 30*.

Table. Evaluation of the E-shopping Potential of CDs Using the ES Test

Product	Product characteristics (10)	Familiarity and confidence (10)	Consumer attributes (30)	Total
CDs	8	8	22	38

The total score for selling a CD online was 38 out of 50. De Kare-Silver stated that if a score is above 20 then the product has good potential of being bought by consumers online. The total score therefore indicates that CDs have a high potential to be purchased on the Internet, which justifies the reason why CDs have high sales online. This can be compared to basic clothing that de Kare-Silver scored at only 19 in the ES test. This means that clothing has a lower potential for e-retailing compared with CDs.

Online music

Industry insiders estimate that three times as much music is downloaded on the Internet (largely for free) as is being sold on CD. A Forrester research study found that 45 per cent of European broadband users download music and half of them saw no problem in not paying for it. Nevertheless, following a settlement between AOL Time Warner and Microsoft, legal, paid for online music now seems to be taking off.

ONLINE PAID CONTENT

Online paid content from the US grew by a massive 22 per cent in 2003. According to eMarketer (2003), music is the biggest category. For example, over 17 million tracks have already been downloaded from Apple's iTunes, despite competition from free file-sharing services such as Kazaa.

Paid content is not new. Financial news and pornography (now mainly downloaded videos and 'live' webcams) have been around since the early days of the Web. What is new is the fast rate of growth of many other categories.

There are two ways of receiving music online: downloading or *streaming*. In the US one of the leaders, iTunes, launched by Apple Computers, has been successful in persuading consumers to pay 99 cents per download - 6.5 million times in the first three months. The biggest sellers included The Eagles and U2 - perhaps appealing to a more mature and affluent market than the typical pop music buyer. iTunes is also popular in Europe, with each track costing around £0.60, even though it is still only available to Apple Mac users.

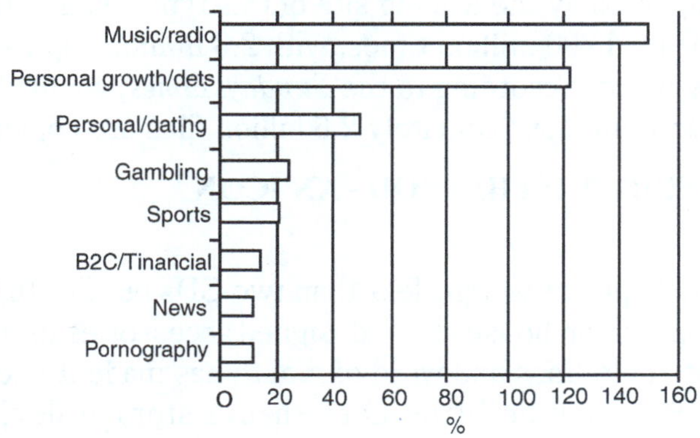

Fig. Paid Online Spending Growth Rates for the US for 2003 - percentage increases on 2002

Streaming means playing the track live through a computer, rather like broadcast radio. In fact, the most frequently used type of streaming is digital radio. Interactive services where you choose your listening are gaining ground. For ex-ample, in the UK, On Demand Distribution provides a 'music club' service for HMV and Internet service providers such as Freeserve and BT, charging a fixed monthly fee for streaming and limited downloads. But if you stop your subscription the downloads stop playing. OD2 has deals with all the big five music companies, managing the transfers to ensure that artists and record companies get paid the royalties. The company has more than 200,000 tracks by 8,500 artists. OD2's success may be partly due to the personal influence of founder Peter Gabriel (former singer with the 1970s' band Genesis). 'I have helped open doors' says Gabriel. 'We are pretty much the only player left in town'.

OD2 music is also available as downloads from MSN and from Virgin, costing from around £0.60 to £0.99 per track. One incentive that OD2 uses to lure consumers to pay is offering music up to six weeks before release on CD (i.e. less likely to be available as illegal downloads). OD2 also includes exclusive versions and extra songs not available in the CD format.

For a reasonable sound quality, a broadband Internet connection is essential. Even with broadband, though, streamed sound quality is not as good as from downloaded files. A variety of systems is available to enable near hi-fi quality from the computer, either streamed or downloaded. The paid-for downloads mainly use Windows Media Audio (WMA) format, which contains controls to ensure that copyright fees are paid. 'Free' music downloads usually utilize the useful MP3 format, which is more flexible than WMA. For example, you can transfer your CDs and downloaded tracks on to a blank CD to play in-car or in a portable MP3 player such as Apple's portable iPod.

The Napster free file-swapping site has been closed down, but there are many other websites dedicated to helping users download music for free. For example, Kazaa, probably the leading site of this type, claims that its software has been downloaded 200 million times, with 2.8 million copies of its software downloaded per week. According to the *Sunday Times*, when all *P2P* services are taken into account, approximately 2.6 billion files are copied per month.

MINI CASE STUDY 2.2: THE IPOD - AN ICON FOR THE 00S

The iPod MP3 player weighs less than two CDs but fits 10,000 songs into your pocket. Top fashion houses have designed accessories for it, TV directors have included it in plotlines and word of mouth has made it one of the coolest gadgets. The iPod may be little more than a storage device, but it has revolutionized the way we listen to music and has become a cultural icon at the same time. Small, light and easy to use, it has helped non-technical audiences to catch on to the benefits of the personalized music library that can be enjoyed on the move. Annual sales of 1.5 million iPods have made this one of Apple's most popular products. Its success comes from not just a stylish design, but also the ultra-fast FireWire connection for transferring music from the computer. It is also an alarm clock, games console and, with optional attachments, a voice recorder and radio.

MINI CASE STUDY 2.3: KAZAA

According to www.download.com, by February 2003, Kazaa had been downloaded 192, 921, 732 times! Obviously, consumers like free products. Kazaa offers searching for music, video (e.g. episodes of soaps or movies) and image files. The process is relatively simple: download the free software, agree to the terms and conditions and launch the Kazaa Media Desktop. Click 'Search', type in an artist or track title and the results are then displayed. To download, click on one of the files listed. At the time of our test, there were 4,130,879 users online sharing 810,495,758 files! Once the file has been downloaded, the user has obtained the music, initially for free, although it is the users' responsibility to pay the copyright royalties. The operators of the site state explicitly that they do not condone activities and actions that breach the rights of copyright owners: 'As a Kazaa Media Desktop user you have agreed to abide by the end user agreement and it is your responsibility to obey all laws governing copyright in each country.'

The software is free, with the costs covered through advertising revenue. Kazaa and Morpheus (a similar service) have been reported to earn US$400,000 per month from advertising. During the 20 minutes or so of download time, the user is subjected to many pop-up advertising windows. In addition, users' personal details may be used for marketing purposes (any users who have not read the terms and conditions may be unaware of this).

Apart from the advertising and the requirement to pay royalties to the copyright owner, there are other potential problems. For example, any file that is downloaded may contain a computer virus or worm. Because of the operation of the P2P system, only the owner of an infected system can delete it and stop its circulation, not Kazaa. In order to share music with other users, the software creates a shared folder where all files can be uploaded or downloaded. The setting can be changed so that no one can obtain files from your computer, but on the default the settings can be changed by another user in such a way that your entire computer's files can be shared with everyone. In a test by HP Laboratories, a dummy file called 'credit-cards.xls' was added and the computer left online for 24 hours. The file was downloaded four times. The same report drew attention to another problem that may be worrying to parents: pornography. For example, over 70 per cent of the results obtained while searching for Britney Spears' videos on Kazaa were of pornographic content.

In our survey of 765 young people carried out in 2003, 65 per cent said that they used the Internet to download music. Eighty-eight per cent of these said that they used Kazaa or similar software, but only 12 per cent said that they used 'legal' sites (artist's web page or legal distributor). The 'legal' users also tend to be infrequent users. Respondents to our survey (of a single, West London, UK, school) have downloaded an estimated 92,000 'free' files, representing 6,600 albums. By comparison, the 'legal' downloads were only 1,000 files, equivalent to 75 albums. Worryingly, 32 per cent of the respondents were unaware of the security risks of file sharing.

DVD movies and Videos

DVD movies and videos are mainly available from the same suppliers as are CDs (Amazon is market leader) and carry the same advantages for e-retailing. High street retailers have, of course, long supplied videos. Happily for e-retailers, the expansion in popularity of DVDs over the last couple of years has coincided with a period of rapid growth in consumers' willingness to e-shop.

MINI CASE STUDY 2.4: BLACKSTAR

Blackstar was founded in February 1998 and operates from Belfast in Northern Ireland. It began by selling a comprehensive library of 50,000 video titles. With widespread consumer support for the new DVD format that has built up over the past two years, Blackstar logically moved into the DVD movies market and now also sells games console titles as well. Blackstar has enjoyed newsworthy successes in its short history. It has managed to attract and retain customers through its commendable level of customer service.

Typical high street video/DVD shops typically stock up to 3,000 titles, but Blackstar offers a much wider range with many otherwise-rare titles. Blackstar also offers a video/DVD hunt facility for rare or deleted titles. This service has proved to be very popular and a key factor in the company's success. However, Blackstar, like most other British e-retailers, has yet to achieve profitability. Blackstar was awarded Retail Online Success of the Year at the BVA Awards 2000.

GROCERIES

e-Grocery shopping in the UK is only around 1 per cent of total grocery shopping, but that small percentage adds up to around a billion pounds per year. The nature of groceries as non-durable necessitates delivery quickly and in such a way that quality is not lost in the delivery process. Perishable grocery deliveries can also be difficult if the recipient is not there to receive them - unlike other goods that may be popped through the letterbox or left in a lockable delivery drop. In addition, many grocery items tend to be variable in characteristics and quality and are often selected by look, feel and smell. Compared to typical shoppers for products such as CDs, grocery shoppers tend on average to be older and less educated, and therefore less susceptible to new technology such as e-shopping. Indeed, de Kare-Silver's ES test rates groceries at 27 (out of 50), well behind Books (38) and DVD movies.

When US bookstore magnate Louis Borders founded e-grocer Webvan in 1997, he believed he could revolutionize the grocery business. The idea was deceptively simple. It was to take orders for groceries over the Internet and use highly automated centralized warehouses and computerized logistics systems controlling a local fleet of trucks to efficiently deliver groceries to a customer at a cost no greater than if the customer had gone to the supermarket themselves. The scheme was launched in San Francisco, followed by another 26 cities at an investment cost of US$35 million per city. Including marketing costs, the total investment US$1.2 billion was second only to Amazon in the history of e-retail startups. With marketing costs of 30 per cent of sales and only 50 per cent capacity utilization of the distribution centres, Webvan struggled for cash. The company folded in 2001, laying off its 2,000 employees and announcing losses of close to US$0.5 billion - the largest single e-commerce loss ever.

Tesco, the leading UK grocery supermarket, is a very different story. Tesco's online shopping service has been one of very few grocery e-retailing successes worldwide, with 1 million users, 85,000 orders per week and profit since 2001. Tesco is the world's biggest e-grocer, and is the UK's number one by a considerable margin, with a 53 per cent share of the world's biggest online grocery market. The key has been twofold. First, Tesco had first-mover advantage, rapidly increasing its operation to cover 95 per cent of the population. By contrast, the main rival, Sainsbury's, reaches 71 per cent of UK households. Second, the initial operation (still true for most food items) employed pickers to select the goods from the shelves of local stores.

This simple approach enabled Tesco to get the operation off the ground quickly and cheaply. In a warehouse, fresh food that was unsold would have to be thrown away. In addition, when e-orders are quiet, Tesco's pickers can do other work. Meanwhile, competitors have struggled. Somerfield attempted the purpose-built distribution centre approach, and retired hurt. Safeway (formerly one of the 'big three' UK supermarkets) never launched a home delivery service and has now closed down its e-retail business completely. Sainsbury's uses a combination of warehouses and in-store picking, but is still not in profit at the time of writing. Wal-Mart Asda's two dedicated warehouses have been closed. Both Sainsbury's and Wal-Mart Asda offer delivery to less than half of households across the country at the time of writing. Iceland claims 97 per cent coverage, but is reticent about its trading results.

The Tesco e-retailing model has now been introduced into the US through a deal with Safeway Inc. (not connected with the UK Safeway). Customers in Portland, Oregon, were the first to try the service, followed by San Francisco (where Webvan tried and failed). Tesco.com is also growing rapidly in the Republic of Ireland, where the service covers 70 per cent of the population, and in South Korea through a joint venture with Homeplus.

The main challenge to Tesco.com's approach in the UK may come from Ocado. Ocado operates in conjunction with Waitrose, one of the UK's top six supermarkets with stores mainly in the south of England. Ocado is 40 per cent owned by department store group John Lewis Partnership, owners of Waitrose. Ocado are committed to the warehouse model with central warehouses to the north of London and in Birmingham that can each process the same amount of groceries as 20 superstores. From a pilot in Hertfordshire, the e-retailing service has been rolled out to the London area. Ocado's managing director pointed out that the company bases marketing on a low level of substitutions (claimed to be 2 per cent vs. an 'industry standard' of 15 per cent) and one-hour rather than two-hour delivery time slots. The operation has a long way to go to catch Tesco, though, and even Waitrose's managing director estimated that it would take three to five years to reach profitability.

EIGHT WAYS TO CUSTOMER VALUE AND PROFITABILITY IN GROCERY E-RETAILING

- Customer density
- Loyalty
- Buying power
- Ordering efficiency and customer information
- Operational efficiency and customer service level
- Large range of products
- Price level
- Shopping convenience

Tanskanen *et al.* (2002) reported on 'six lessons learned' for profitable grocery e-retailing and Anckar *et al.* (2002) identified 'four sources of customer value' - see Box 2.4. As the UK's leading supermarket, Tesco has the advantage in loyalty, buying power and range of products. Economies of scale should also give the market-leader a potential advantage in good-value selling prices. In theory, therefore, the other players need to try to gain their competitive advantage from the remaining factors: shopping convenience, operational efficiency, customer service, the ordering interface and product information. These can be addressed by, for example, making the website informative, quick and easy to use, supplying exactly (or with a minimum of substitutes) what is ordered and providing accurately timed delivery slots.

CLOTHING AND FOOTWEAR

Clothing is not an obvious product for e-retailing. First, of course, clothing is normally bought by look, feel and fit, all of which are difficult for the e-shopper to evaluate on the Web. Second, clothing is bought not just for warmth and modesty, but also to express our self-image. Any purchase errors in (e.g.) style, therefore, carry a particularly high perceived risk. Indeed, de Kare-Silver's ES test rates basic clothing at 19 (out of 50), well behind books (38), DVD movies and groceries (27). (For a product to be suitable for e-retailing, de Kare-Silver recommends a minimum score of 20.) Nevertheless, clothing represents one of the major categories in UK e-retail (although worldwide it is one of the slowest-growing categories). One reason may be that clothing has historically been one of the major mail-order categories in the UK. Both shoppers and suppliers are used to home delivery channels for clothing. The clothing e-retail market leader Next has been supplying fashion clothing by mail order since 1988.

Surprisingly, lingerie and hosiery is one of the most popular product categories for e-retailing, perhaps driven by the success of the leader, Fig Leaves (www.figleaves.com), in the same way that Tesco has driven the expansion of grocery e-retailing. Fig Leaves has a winning approach both in the creative permission-based marketing and the novel online bra measuring system. In particular e-shopping for lingerie appeals to men, who may often be embarrassed to buy these products in-store. 'Look and feel' goods tend to be compared and evaluated before buying - i.e. they are high involvement purchases. For example, a survey reported in the *New Straits Times* in 2001 found that 85 per cent of respondents would not buy clothes online because they prefer to try them on before purchase. Enjoyment is often a motivation for in-store clothes shopping (and other comparison shopping). In the bricks retail store, 'atmospherics' are often used to increase enjoyment and hence sales. The effectiveness of such techniques is well known in-store, we argue that equivalent considerations are also important for the e-retailer.

Emotional aspects such as enjoyment strongly predict shoppers' attitudes towards e-shopping. According to Chicksand and Knowles (2002), equivalent features can be identified to help in overcoming the difficulties of selling 'look and feel' goods like clothing online. The equivalent stimuli for the clicks store include: sound, personalization/customization, usability of the website, visuals and text. *Web atmospherics* can help compensate for the lack of sensory experience in e-shopping. Nevertheless, the indications are that shoppers' needs for enjoyment (rather than just utilitarian) benefits are not being satisfied by e-retailers. Even clothing market leader Next makes little attempt at the use of web atmospherics on the e-retail site.

Personalization is a key element of web atmospherics, but most clothing e-retailers personalize very little. Developments aimed at helping to overcome this drawback include the Eddie Bauer (US clothing retailer) 'virtual closet' which allows shoppers to match up items with a 'Style Builder'. With Virtual Model (www.virtualmodel.com - one of the '100 best websites' from *Internet*

Magazine) you can create a 3-D virtual model of yourself online and dress yourself with clothing from top suppliers such as Lands End - claimed to increase the likelihood of a sale by 19 per cent. These e-retailers keep a database of sizes and items bought that is available on your next visit, personalizing the experience and saving purchase time. The potential for clothing includes the body scan. For example, shoppers can visit selected Levi stores for the scan, which is then held on a database. In theory, this could then be used for e-shopping, incorporating the scan data into a 3-D virtual closet such as Virtual Model. Shoppers could be confident that the clothes would fit. Unfortunately, Levi does not actually offer the body scan data for e-retailing on the Virtual Model/Kohls (www.kohls.com) site.

Customization is another key element of web atmospherics for clothing. Mass customization refers to self-designed products. Shopper involvement in the design of the products adds considerably to the personal feel of the shopping experience. Shopper satisfaction can be enhanced by more closely matching exact needs. In the case of Nike, shoppers can customise shoes, not just with colours and styles, but also, for example, with a name or message. A potential drawback of this system, though, is concern over what happens if the customer wants to return the product for any reason? Fanbuzz e-retails clothes, allowing shoppers to decide their own styles, colours, graphics and sizes. These custom items are 10-20 per cent more expensive than non-custom ones, but many customers are prepared to pay more for customized products.

Although the market for e-retailing clothes is growing only slowly, if the mass-market e-retailers such as Next and Marks & Spencer were to improve web atmospherics, e.g. more attractive, interactive site design and layout, more personalization and customization incorporating features used by specialists such as Lands End and Nike, there should be considerable scope for further growth.

CASE STUDY: AMAZON.CO.UK

This case illustrates Amazon.co.uk's retail mix and the application of the Ansoff matrix. I buy all my books at Amazon.com because I'm busy and it's convenient. They have a big selection, and they've been reliable.

Bill Gates

Amazon has established itself worldwide as an online retail success, the world's biggest e-retailer of books and head-to-head with Barnes and Noble for the title of the world's largest bookstore, even though Amazon sells only online. From a start-up in 1995, annual sales have grown to more than US$1 billion and the company has over 2.5 million customers - but reported its first profit only in 2002. The UK site, www.amazon.co.uk, was formed in 1998 by the takeover of Bookpages, and the UK is now Amazon's biggest market outside the US. Amazon is also the clear UK market leader for CDs, DVD movies and videos and offers many other product lines, including electronics, software, games, toys, travel and auctions. According to a survey by Global Online Retailing, one in eight UK Internet users have made a purchase at Amazon.co.uk. Amazon is the market leader in the UK for selling online books with a market share of over 50 per cent, and its main advantage is the ability to deliver low-cost

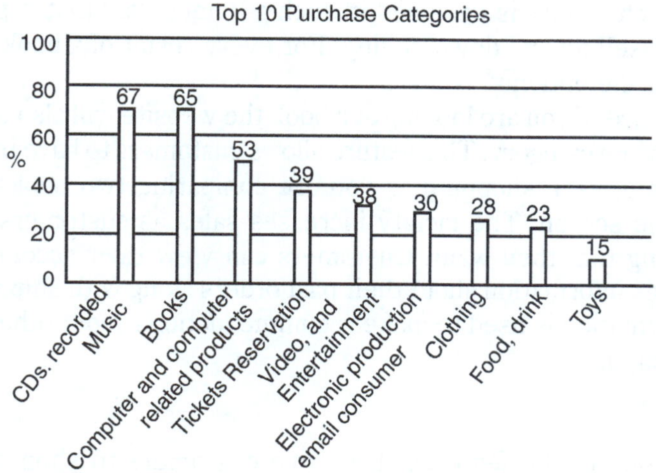

AMAZON'S E-RETAIL MIX

Convenience

Convenience plays an important role in gaining and maintaining new customers. There are several factors driving the level of customer convenience. First, the speed of downloading amazon.co.uk's website is fast, as it takes only three to five seconds although it is full of images of their products. Customers can quickly find the desired product, as the search facility is second to none. Once the result is located it provides value-added services such as book reviews and ratings, and displays its own price and a comparison price. Comparative pricing allows customers to see the value they are receiving from Amazon, i.e. how much they are saving. Amazon makes it easy to source and buy products and track the progress of delivery.

Amazon offers industry-leading state-of-the-art online shopping technology, the '1-click' system, which streamlines the customer buying process by storing personal information such as credit card number and shipping address, saving time and hassle. According to a survey carried out by Knowledge Systems & Research, consumers become frustrated after having to click more than six times to complete a purchase and as a result they move to other websites. The website offers secure socket-layer connection, which means that sensitive credit card information is transmitted in encrypted format. In some cases it even provides a guarantee that, if unauthorized transactions are made, it will reimburse the customer. All major credit and debit cards are accepted.

One of the prime factors of convenience is based on availability. If any of the titles are unavailable, Amazon will still take your order and will let you know when the title will be available. Amazon.co.uk's main aim is to maximize customers' convenience so they do not look anywhere else for their books.

The search facility is designed in such a unique way that it provides up-selling, cross-selling and down-selling. For every result of a book title search you are given the options.

For instance, if you are looking at a book the website will also display other books in the same category. This feature allows customers to have better choice. This is e-comparison shopping as you are comparing two books while only looking at one screen. The facility increases sales as customers can always find something that they want. Customers can view their account any time, which includes information about their past orders along with shipment details. Account information is used to make recommendations about other books that customers may like.

Cost

Cost is one of the features that drive customers to shop on the Web. Nevertheless, Jeff Bezos, Amazon's CEO, believed that online customers considered selection and convenience to be more important than price. This belief is probably justified as Brynjolfsson and Smith (2000) pointed out that amazon had a market share of 80 per cent while charging 10 per cent more than the cheapest. Therefore, Amazon did not seek to compete on price alone. Customers want to get the best price with excellent customer service. Most of the books at amazon are available at a discounted price, ranging from 1 per cent to 50 per cent off the recommended retail price. Consumers are always shown three prices: 'list price', 'our price' and 'how much you save'. Amazon has reasonable delivery charges. There are often seasonal promotions such as free delivery if the order is over a certain amount. Different options are available, including (as an optional extra) overnight delivery.

Following a similar arrangement in the US, amazon.co.uk has a deal with Toys R Us for in-store pick up, which allows customers to collect the books at their convenience. With this option, there is no delivery charge.

Communication

Amazon has established its brand name through customer intimacy and customer relationship management. From day one their aim has been to be a customer-centric company. It welcomes returning customers with their name, e.g. 'Welcome back Charles Dennis', with the help of a cookie file stored on the user's computer. This has been referred to as the Web equivalent of customizing a storefront to suit the taste of each person walking through the door.

Customers can opt in if they wish to receive more information, for example when a new novel comes out by their favourite author. Consumers can always opt out as well if they are not interested in receiving any more information. Amazon monitors the customer's ordering process through the Oracle database environment that feeds all the content to its website. It can track the speed and performance of each step in a transaction, including placement of an item in a cart, completion of an order and e-mail notification to the customer.

Amazon offers personalization by recommending similar books according to what other customers have bought. For example, the personalized screen will say: 'Customers who bought titles by this author also bought titles by these authors'. These features help users to make up their minds quickly and they can also read spotlight reviews by other readers. Amazon is to some extent a virtual community where users express their views about authors. Publishers and authors can also contribute. Amazon uses an integrated marketing communications strategy that encompasses advertising, public relations, promotions and online marketing. Offline advertising includes TV commercials and billboards in train stations. Online activity includes the associates programme and deals with major search engines and portal pages such as Yahoo.com and MSN. The associates programme uses other sites to promote Amazon by links that directly take users to Amazon's site. In return associates receive a small percentage commission on the total transaction value.

Computing

Amazon uses state-of-the-art technology in its back end (warehouse) and front end (website). The company has developed a customized information system and dedicated ordering system, which is linked with suppliers to automatically order books. The search engine employs XML and Oracle database technology, which bring up results in a matter of seconds. Once the book or an item is found, users sign in using the 1-click system and the purchase is complete. The company's software processes the orders via electronic interfaces or electronic data interchange with suppliers and all the stages in the supply chain are computerized.

Customer Care

According to an internal customer research survey carried out by amazon.co.uk, 70 per cent of sales are made by repeat customers of whom 97 per cent are satisfied or very satisfied with the service - which must be one of the highest satisfaction scores among pureplay dot.coms. Its FAQs section is very informative as it explains all the main issues such as ordering process, delivery charges and returns policy.

Customer Franchise

Amazon's brand relationship is like someone who knows you, understands your preferences and tells you something new every time you make contact. This builds up a strong relationship as if dealing with assistants who have come to know customers in the course of many shopping trips.

ANSOFF MATRIX

Market Penetration

Market penetration means seeking to achieve growth with existing products in their current market segments and aiming to increase their share of the market. Amazon has increased market penetration through value-added service. For example, as mentioned previously, it takes on the responsibility to order books that they do not have at present and let the users know as soon as they become available. It allows users to sell used books, and prices for used books appear alongside the selling price for a new book. The extended service and options translate into greater sales. This gives the reader a chance to read the book before actually buying it. The more services offered, the more chances there are it will lead to a sale.

Product Development

Here new product offerings are developed to market to existing customers. Amazon has added second-hand books to its product range, giving its customers the opportunity to sell their used books. Amazon also now sells e-books - readable on Personal Digital Assistants (PDAs).

Product / Market	Present	New
Present	Market Development	Product Development
New	Market Development	Diversitication

Fig. Ansoff Matrix

Market Development

Market development concerns the marketing of existing products to a new audience. Amazon has extended purchasing to users of WAP or 3G mobile phones.

In addition, Amazon has signed deals with bricks and mortar bookshops such as Waterstones and Borders to sell books online for them. Customers typing in www.waterstones.co.uk will be directed to a version of the Amazon website that carries Waterstone's name (although the appearance and co-branded name are still clearly Amazon). A percentage of the profit from any books they subsequently buy will go to Waterstones in a concept similar to the associates programme.

Diversification

Diversification refers to entering new markets with new products. Amazon has broken into new markets by offering travel services, software, electronics and toys. This is known as unrelated diversification, as Amazon had no previous market experience in these areas. Nevertheless, having built up a successful brand name with a large number of loyal customers, the company is well placed to extend the franchise.

E-SHOPPING

DISADVANTAGES

Consumers have been slow to embrace e-shopping. Back in 1996, the UK's largest e-consultancy, Cap Gemini, carried out an employee survey. The main disadvantages for shoppers, in ranked order were: 'Availability', 'Can't be in to receive delivery', 'Premium charged for delivery' and 'Can't see or feel the merchandise'. With years' more experience, many e-retailers still do not have satisfactory answers to these problems. Typical shopper comments have included: 'They left it in the garden and didn't tell me', 'It's a 24-hour shopping service but only a 6-hour delivery service' and 'Returning unwanted products is when it all goes low-tech' consumer surveys from Vincent *et al*., 2000).

Fig. Why Internet-connected Consumers do not E-shop

Another survey reported, in ranked order, reasons why Internet-connected shoppers do not e-shop: 'Prefer personal shopping, seeing goods', 'Credit card worries' and 'Don't know how'. In 2001, Verdict confirmed security fears as the number one barrier to more consumers shopping online. Our own surveys (e.g. Dennis *et al*., 2002a - discussed more fully in the following section) have indicated that sixth-form (year 12) pupils are avid e-shoppers using their parents' credit cards. This is an obvious security worry for parents, but also a nuisance for young people, restricting their e-shopping activities. Credit cards are only offered to those of 18 years of age and above, although alternative 'plastic cash' is available for children, with transactions authorized (in the example of the Solo card - www.solocard.co.uk) only up to what is in the bank account.

The disadvantage is that so far these cards are accepted by only a tiny fraction of (www.llbean.com) could claim to be the pioneer of mail order, selling goods to rural farmers since way back in the mid-1800s. Today the company has put their reputation for customer responsiveness, helpfulness, cheerfulness and reliability to use in becoming world leader in e-retailing outdoor equipment and clothing, with an efficient, award-winning site.

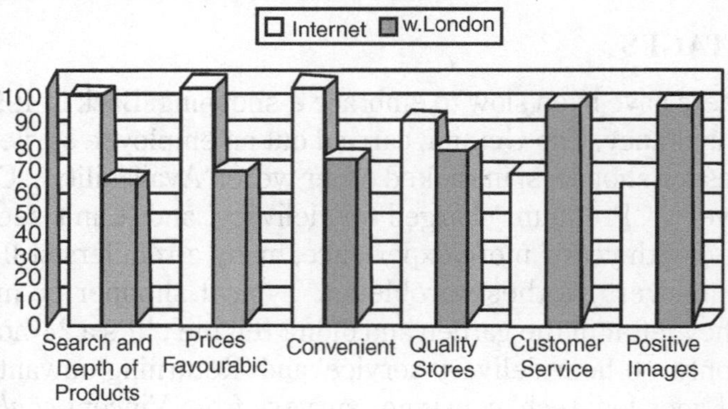

Fig. Comparing ratings - Internet vs. West London shopping centre

DISADVANTAGES OF E-SHOPPING FOR CONSUMERS

- Credit card and security worries
- Lack of personal and social interaction
- Can't see or feel the merchandise
- Don't know how
- Can't be in to receive delivery
- Premium charged for delivery
- Difficulties with returning goods for refund

ADVANTAGES

Counterbalancing the disadvantages and the slow responses of many UK e-retailers to addressing them, there is a number of advantages for shoppers.

First, in ranked order from the Cap Gemini survey: 'Convenient/easy', 'Saves time' and 'Fits in with other activities'. Other commonly cited advantages, typified by responses to our own survey, include: 'Breadth and depth of products', 'Prices favourable' and 'Convenient' . According to Verdict, 'cost effectiveness' (rather than just low prices) is the key reason for shoppers to buy online, followed by convenience and ease of purchase.

ADVANTAGES OF E-SHOPPING FOR CONSUMERS

- Cost effective
- Convenient
- Easy
- Saves time
- Fits in with other activities
- Breadth and depth of products
- Easy search of many alternatives
- Personalization of presentation and merchandise
- Prices favourable

MOTIVES FOR E-SHOPPING

- Socializing
- Enjoyment
- Usefulness
- Ease of use
- Convenience
- Navigation
- Knowledge and ability to make a purchase
- Influence of friends and family

STUDY 1

We have already referred to this first study (initial results in Dennis *et al.*, 2002a) in the sections above. The method used was a questionnaire survey that compared shoppers' opinions of Internet shopping versus bricks shopping centres. The 308 respondents were sixth-form (year 12) and university undergraduate students - the shoppers of tomorrow. One of the main themes from the qualitative part of the study was a preference for shopping in shopping centres as more enjoyable and sociable. Shoppers who both e-shopped and shopped in shopping centres commented typically: 'Internet shopping is not a personal experience. You cannot try and see what you're buying.... Shopping [should] be very sociable.'Results from the questionnaire indicated that shoppers rated e-shopping higher than shopping centres for *favourable prices* and *convenience*. On the other hand, shopping centres were preferred for *positive image* and more emphatically for *customer service*. The results for the sixth-form (year 12) students, but the results for undergraduates were similar.

One striking figure is that 57 per cent of the sample were e-shoppers - compared with the UK average for all adults of around 15 percent. The average expenditure of the Internet shoppers on e-shopping was £22 per month, compared to £86 per month on conventional shopping. Thus, over half of the student sample shopped on the Internet, spending on average over 20 per cent of their non-food shopping by Internet.

SOCIAL MOTIVES FOR E-SHOPPING

- Social experiences outside the home
- Communications with others having a similar interest
- Peer group attraction
- Status and authority - raising the standing of the shopper in the eyes of friends and colleagues
- Virtual communities

STUDY 2

Our second study concerned motivations for e-shopping. Enjoyment, usefulness, ease of use, convenience, navigation, knowledge and ability to make a purchase, and the influence of friends and family were found to be important motivations.

Our results apply to students and are not representative of the average population. Indeed, these are people who within a few years are likely to be earning and spending significantly more than the national average. Bearing in mind this income effect and the high computer literacy of graduates, these are shoppers who will account for a disproportionately high percentage of discretionary income and comparison shopping. Our results, and those of other researchers, show a consistent picture of the importance of the social and experiential aspects of e-shopping. These motivators are being satisfied to good effect by the most successful e-retailers such as, for example, eBay - one of the most successful sites in terms of sales, time spent on the site and providing enjoyment.

ENJOYMENT AND E-SHOPPING

Enjoyment Motives for e-shopping

- Involvement
- Not boring
- Fun for its own sake

Enjoyment and social Features of e-retailing sites

- Chat rooms
- Bulletin boards

- Customer written stories
- Product reviews
- Suggestion boxes
- Personalization of offers

The most Popular 'Enjoyment' e-shopping sites (in Ranked order)

- Amazon (www.amazon.com)
- CD WOW (www.cd-wow.co.uk)
- eBay (auction, www.ebay.co.uk)
- Ticketmaster (show tickets, www.ticketmaster.co.uk)
- Ryanair (www.ryanair.co.uk)
- EasyJet (www.easyjet.co.uk)
- Opodo (air tickets, www.opodo.co.uk)

DIFFERENCES BETWEEN MALE AND FEMALE SHOPPING STYLES

Differences between male and female shopping styles may go back a long way. In hunter-gatherer societies, females tend to carry babies, are based around the camp and do the gathering. Males on the other hand are more likely to protect the group and do the hunting. Humans may have evolved in such a way that those best at their respective roles have been more likely to find a mate and to survive. For females, this meant excelling in gathering: finding the best food and other materials for the family. For males, it entailed being good hunters: fast, strong and decisive. Both sexes would look for those respective qualities in a potential mate, resulting in persistent traits. These differences in mate-seeking behaviour have survived into a wide cross-section of modern cultures (Buss, 1989). In Western consumer societies, gathering may have translated into comparison shopping, hunting into earning money to support the family.

Even in the US, where gender equality in the workplace is greater than most countries, differences in shopping styles can be clearly observed. The female style involves searching, comparing, weighing the advantages and disadvantages of alternatives, finding the best value and taking a pride in the shopping activity (Underhill, 1999). This pride is justified as on average women make a 10 per cent better cost saving than men do, making women the 'better shoppers' (Denison, 2003). Women see the activity of shopping as a satisfying experience in itself - i.e. a leisure activity. On the other hand, men see shopping as a mission and tend to go straight for what they want in a purposeful way (Underhill, 1999). For men, the focus is on 'the kill' - the actual moment of purchase when their heart rate quickens.

Evolutionary psychology has been founded on research demonstrating consistency of mating behaviour across widely different cultures. Accordingly, our own study has sought empirical evidence for an evolutionary basis to shopping sex differences by comparing shopping styles across cultures (reported in more detail in Dennis, 2004). Thirteen 'mini focus groups' wrote shopping scenarios about the national culture(s) that they were most familiar with. Fourteen cultural nationalities were represented: five judge participants represented the UK national culture, eight Continental European and 23 Asian, i.e. 36 judge participants in total. In general, there were some differences in shopping styles between the national cultures, but the differences between males and females were much more striking, reflecting the hunter and gatherer roles and providing support for the evolutionary hypothesis.

The stereotypes are not 100 per cent accurate but in the UK have been found to apply to 80 per cent of women and 70 per cent of men (Denison, 2003). The styles have been found to be equally valid for e-shopping (Lindquist and Kaufman-Scarborough, 2000). As with bricks shopping, the stereotype reverses when the product purchased is technical and expensive (Dholakia and Chiang, 2003).

SHOPPERS IN CYBERSPACE: ARE THEY FROM VENUS OR MARS?

Female shopping style - the gatherer

- Ritual of seeking and comparing
- Imagining and envisioning the merchandise in use
- Tallying up the pros and cons
- Taking (justified) pride in ability as shoppers
- The total shopping process (not just buying) is a leisure activity
- Women like to spend longer shopping than men do
- Social interaction is an important part of shopping
- Women favour sites designed for women - e.g. iVillage (www.ivillage.co.uk) - with horoscopes, health, beauty and diet
- Women are more likely to browse online, then buy in-store

Male shopping styles - the hunter

- Men are incisive, decisive and determined shoppers
- Men's excitement with shopping is at the moment of 'kill' (purchase)
- Men try to complete the shopping activity in the shortest possible time
- Men's lack of patience means they often miss the best buy
- But the stereotype reverses when the product is technical and expensive. Men do take a pride in shopping for, for example, cars and computers (and women are purposeful for those products)
- Men's favourite sites tend to include games, gambling and pornography
- Male e-shoppers are heavier Internet users and are more likely to shop via mobile devices and PDAs

MALE AND FEMALE SHOPPING STEREOTYPES?

Is this cultural stereotyping? Or is there any truth in this research? BBC News (2003) ran a story on the Denison (2003) research asking readers to post their own answers to these questions. Of 64 replies posted, 19 asked further questions or made different points ('Louise [who hates shopping] - will you marry me?' *Debt-ridden husband*). Of the remainder, 22 per cent disagreed with the stereotypes and 78 per cent agreed.

Perhaps reflecting the greater attention given to the selection process, US women are 30 per cent more likely to browse online, then buy in-store (Lindquist and Kaufman-Scarborough, 2000). In the early days of the Internet, male users heavily outnumbered females, but this is now changing, with 50 per cent of US e-shoppers now female. The UK is catching up with 44 per cent in 2000 (up from 30 per cent reported by Pavitt in 1997). Countries that are less developed in terms of Internet use tend to have lower proportions of female e-shoppers. Men tend to be major users of games sites (eTypes, 2001), gambling and pornography. Male e-shoppers form the large majority of the most sophisticated eTypes life-cycle stage 'Wired 4 life' - heavy Internet users and also heavier than average in usage of mobile Internet devices and personal digital assistants (PDAs).

MINI CASE STUDY 4.1: ETYPES.INFO

An award-winning tool for understanding online consumer behaviour, eTypes features extensive information on how consumers behave and transact online, and has been constructed by combining demographic and lifestyle datasets from profiling company CACI with data from Forrester, the leading Internet research organization. The system works by classifying consumers into seven groups denoting life stage; Internet usage levels and 23 eTypes - detailing online behaviour; and five e-shopping lifestyle stages.

The system aims to tell e-retailers about the characteristics of e-shoppers and what they use the Internet for - whether it's finding holidays, buying CDs, managing their stocks and shares or just chatting, and claims that this means e-retailers can get more from their e-shopper data - and a higher return on website investment.

BOX 4.8: E-SHOPPING LIFE CYCLE STAGES

- *Stage 1 - Virtual virgins* Only 12 per cent of these Internet users have bought online - half the average. A high proportion is female. Age tends towards the youngest and oldest
- *Stage 2 - Chatters and gamers* These are avid Internet users, spending 20 per cent more time online than the average. Twenty-five per cent are e-shoppers (the national average). This group tend to be more worried about security than average

- *Stage 3 - DotCom dabblers* Forty per cent of these Internet users are e-shoppers. They are heavy users of entertainment and scientific sites
- *Stage 4 - Surfing suits* These are heavy e-shoppers, but spend less time online - only 60 per cent of the average. They tend to be professional and financially aware
- *Stage 5 - Wired 4* life The heaviest e-shoppers - 70 per cent have purchased online. Many are graduates or cosmopolitan. These users tend to be in the mid-range age groups

CONSUMER SATISFACTION: BRICKS AND CLICKS SHOPPING COMPARED

Even at modest projections, e-retail will soon take a share approaching 10 per cent of total retail sales. This may seem a small percentage, but it represents around £12 billion in sales. High street banks, other financial services and travel agents are most at risk. Some forecasters predict the eventual disappearance from the high street of any businesses that work better as e-businesses: banks, travel agents and book, music and electronics shops. 'Clothes shops will persist because the experience of shopping for clothes is too deeply ingrained, especially in women, to be abandoned'.

Also specialist, up-market retailers who require expertise and offer the consumer a specific experience will flourish. 'The high street will be freed of its ranks of the same old stores and become a more interesting place'. The winners in the high street are likely to be well-branded retailers offering service and added value. Indications so far are that most e-retail success too is going to existing, well-branded retailers - likely to have efficient supply-chain and fulfilment systems - a trend likely to continue for several years (BCSC, 2001).

According to a *Computer Weekly* survey, the three top-rated e-retailers for customer satisfaction and service are Marks & Spencer (www.marksandspencer.com), Littlewoods (www.littlewoods.co.uk) and Iceland (www.iceland.co.uk).

Researchers attempting to answer why people e-shop have tended to look to various components of the 'image' of e-retailing and specific e-retailers, in a similar way to measurements of the image of a bricks store. This may be a valid approach for two reasons. First, 'image' is a concept used to mean our overall evaluation or rating of something in such a way as to guide our actions. For example, we are more likely to buy from a store that we consider has a positive image on considerations that we may consider important, such as price or customer service. Second, this is an approach that has been demonstrated to work for bricks stores over many years and it is largely the bricks retailers with strong images that are making the running in e-retail. According to Kimber (2001), shopper loyalty in-store and online are linked.

For example, Tesco's customers using both on- and offline shopping channels spend 20 per cent more on average than customers who only use the store. Tesco is well known as having a very positive image both in-store and online, being the UK grocery market leader in both channels.

Measurements of e-retail image that have been used by commercial marketing research studies include ease of use, product selection, product information, price, on-time delivery, product representation, customer support and privacy. There is empirical support for some of these dimensions of image, for example 'product selection' and 'ease of use' (Dennis *et al.,* 2002a; Dennis and Papamatthaiou, 2003 respectively), but in general the connection between the components of image and e-shopping spending behaviour remains an under-researched area.

Perhaps the most extensive investigation to date has come from Wolfinbarger and Gilly (2003), who carried out focus groups and quantitative surveys to determine the components of e-retail quality. The qualitative analysis identified four factors:

- Fulfilment/reliability,
- Website design,
- Customer service and
- Security/ privacy.

Fulfilment/reliability includes both the description of a product and efficient delivery. *Website design* includes navigation, search and ordering. *Customer service* means reactive and helpful service, and responding to customer enquiries quickly. The quantitative surveys indicated that these three factors were all significantly related to e-shoppers' understanding of e-retail quality.*Security/ privacy* refers to credit card payments and privacy. Security worries have often been reported as one of the most important reasons for not e-shopping. It is surprising, therefore, that the survey did not find this factor to be significantly associated with e-retail quality. Other studies have shown that, as e-shoppers become more experienced, they tend to shop more and become less concerned about security. In the case of the Wolfinbarger and Gilly study, those e-shoppers who were satisfied with e-retailers' reliability, website design and service may well have been more confident e-shoppers and therefore suffered fewer security worries, resulting in security/privacy being swamped by the other factors in the analysis.

COMPONENTS OF E-RETAIL QUALITY

Fulfilment/reliability

- Accurate display and description of a product so that what customers receive is what they thought they ordered
- Delivery of the right product within the time frame promised

Website design - all elements of the consumer's experience at the website:

- Navigation
- Information search

- Order processing
- Personalization
- Product selection
- Customer service
- Reactive, helpful and willing service that responds to customer inquiries quickly

Security/privacy

- Security of credit card payments
- Privacy of shared information

There is a distinct geographical distribution of e-shopping in the UK, with a heavy concentration in London and the Southeast. According to Kimber (2001), this is being driven by affluence and high credit card ownership. Also, e-shoppers in that region are more confident about security. After London, the highest e-shopping areas are Reading, Cambridge, Bristol and Birmingham. Conversely, areas further away from London and less affluent areas tend to e-shop less and to be more concerned about security.

The balance of the evidence available is that a wide range of image and other attributes are important in consumer satisfaction and behaviour for e-shopping. Many attributes that are important for bricks shopping are also important for e-shopping. Some e-retailers have often paid less attention to elements such as the social and enjoyment aspects of e-shopping, but the best and most successful e-retailers are deliberately and successfully satisfying e-shoppers on motivators such as these. Emphasizing the importance of addressing the overall experience of e-shopping, one survey indicated that, if the worst-rated e-grocery were to improve the online experience to match the best competitor, online sales could be improved by 480 per cent. For the average e-retailer, improved user experience could result in a 33 to 54 per cent sales increase (Meekings *et al.*, 2003).

MINI CASE STUDY 4.2: CUSTOMER SERVICE FROM SCREWFIX (WWW.SCREWFIX.COM)

Screwfix's approach to customer service can be illustrated by our experience with a concrete mixer. After a few weeks' use, the electrical contactor start button failed, meaning the mixer would only run if the start button was held in by hand. We informed Screwfix, explaining that the machine had already had some use, expecting to be offered a replacement electrical contactor. With such a large item of equipment, and the length of time it had been used, we did not realistically expect a replacement mixer. Nevertheless, the Screwfix help desk could not have been more helpful and did authorize the replacement mixer - asking us just to pack up the old one in the original packaging and hand it over to the delivery driver who brought the new one. The problem was that the (very bulky!) packaging had been disposed of some time ago. No problem for Screwfix: 'we'll send you the new one. Unpack it over the next few days, then dismantle the old one and put it into the new packaging. We'll send another lorry to pick it up next week.'

MINI CASE STUDY 4.3: CUSTOMER SERVICE FROM MCWILLIES (NOT ITS REAL NAME!)

A contrasting approach to that of Mini case study 4.2 can be illustrated by our customer service experience from McWillies. We used the shopbot Kelcoo to identify the best deal for a photo printer - which turned out to be from McWillies. Not only was McWillies cheapest for the printer but also there was a special offer including a free pack of photo print paper. McWillies sent an e-mail confirmation showing the price and the two items, printer and paper. The printer arrived within a few days, but without the paper. Some weeks later, despite an (unanswered) e-mail, the paper had still not arrived, so we phoned the 'customer service' line. Here is a summarized extract from the conversation:

McWillies (M): The paper was sent with the printer.

Customer (C): But we didn't receive it.

M: You must have received it because it was sent in the same box.

C: There was only one box, the original packaging, and it was completely full with the printer.

M: Well we sent it.

C: Well we haven't received it [and so on for a few minutes], until:

C: Can I speak to a supervisor?

M: The supervisor's busy.

C: Well, can I speak to someone at head office?

M: I'll speak to head office, please hold. [Long wait.]

M: I've checked with head office and they say it's too late to do anything about it now.

C: I would still like to speak to a supervisor [audible click in mid-sentence]:

M: Supervisor speaking. We can PROVE that we sent the paper, because we weigh all the parcels, so all we have to do is to check the weight on the docket and we'll prove that we sent it.

C: That's great! What a good idea. Could you check it now, please, as it will prove that the paper wasn't in the box.

M: NO! We will not be doing that because YOU should've sent us an e-mail to let us know that the paper had not arrived.

C: As I've already explained, we did send an e-mail.

M: Well we have no record of it so the matter ends here.

C: Can you check with head office before you refuse to confirm the weight of the parcel as that will prove that we didn't receive the paper?

M: NO! We can't check the weight and I'm not going to discuss this any further. (Line went dead.)

Postscript: We still have not received the paper and have given up trying to get it.

THE COMMUNICATIONS MIX FOR THE E-RETAILER

All elements of the e-retail mix can actually form part of the communications mix. For example, *Convenience* can include the ease of finding the site, say by paid links from other sites or search engines communicating the existence of the site to the potential customer. *Customer value and benefit* can be reflected in the width and depth of product offered and ease of navigating around this large range, communicating a benefit of buying online rather than in-store. *Cost to the customer* can communicate price positioning in the case of a cost leadership strategy. Alternatively, high prices with 'round' figures can communicate quality and prestige.

Computing and category management can communicate added value from the availability of a wide range of products on short delivery times. *Customer franchise* is largely a communications and branding issue. For example, improving the information value of an e-retailing site can improve image and branding. Similarly, *Customer care and service* can communicate a positive image. Although many of the critical aspects of service are not visible until the order is fulfilled, a generous returns policy can act as a proxy in communicating an image of good service. Finally, *Communication and customer relationships* describes the communications mix proper, which can have a huge variety of elements from marketing research surveys to e-mail, and from advertising to sponsorship. Rather than try to cover everything (which would need another book).

MINI CASE STUDY 4.4: THE E-RETAIL MIX COMMUNICATES WITH THE CUSTOMER

Compass 24 boat chandlery and Accessories (www.Compass24.com)

Compass 24 is Europe's largest direct sales boating equipment company. A brief illustration of how the Compass 24 e-retail mix is utilized to communicate positively with customers follows below.

Convenience

Entering 'boating equipment uk' in the Google search engine (www.google.co.uk) brings up Boatz.co.uk (www.boatz.co.uk) close to the top of the non-sponsored links. This is because many boating information sites are linked to the Boatz site. Many boat equipment sites are linked by paid links from Boatz.co.uk precisely because it is near the top of the Google (unpaid link) search results. There is a link to Compass 24 (www.compass24.co.uk) in the 'Chandlers' section. Links from Boatz and other popular sites related to the product category represent added convenience for the customer and greatly increase exposure to surfers interested in the specific product types.

Customer Value and Benefit

The huge range of 8,000 products is clearly available and easy to find. Navigation is by a close approach to 'free grid'. This is a combination of a grid hierarchical tree structure with a free-flow navigation capability. Shoppers can either move through the e-store in a logical progression through departments or obtain direct access to end-products using a search engine. Product categories are displayed in a 'left-frame'. The ease of finding products and the huge amount of boating equipment that can be supplied communicate the site's ability to satisfy wide-ranging customer requirements.

Cost to the Customer

The Compass online shop page does not offer 'bargain' positioning but, rather, promises 'good value'. With a separate search facility for 'brands', there is an emphasis on differentiation rather than price leadership. The pricing therefore communicates value, for example 'Magellan [a top brand] GPS 320 top value offer'. Nevertheless, the value pricing is strongly emphasized by using 'psychological pricing'. For example the GPS 320 is priced at £139.95, i.e. psychologically below the price point of £140 - emphasizing the communication of good value. There are often premium-based rather than price-based special offers, for example 'spend £20.00 or more and we'll give you a free vacuum flask'. Promotions such as this communicate extra value for the customer without risking damage to the customer's perceptions of quality and the price goods are worth, as can be the case with price-based promotions like '£10 off'.

Computing and Category Management

Compass is based on established and efficient supply-chain arrangements with suppliers. Thus, there is a huge range of products available either from stock or drop-shipped directly from suppliers on short delivery times. Compass delivers 'Just in Time': tell Compass when you want the goods (for example when you expect to return from your boating cruise), and for a small extra fee it will deliver that exact day. Supply-chain efficiency is used to communicate the site's ability and desire to satisfy customers' particular needs.

Customer Franchise

The Compass site communicates established branding and image by links to bodies such as the Royal Yachting Association, weather forecasts from the Met. Office and tides data from Yachting and Boating World (www.ybw.com, Europe's top marine website). When the site was launched in the UK (it is

German-based), added credibility in the form of endorsement from Sir Robin Knox-Johnston, the famous record-breaking ocean rower and yachtsman, communicated an established brand.

Customer care and Service

Compass offers a 14-day 'no questions asked' return policy. Deliveries are fast and reliable. Fast and easy e-mail help is available, with the e-mail pages also showing telephone numbers. The telephone helpline is courteous, knowledgeable and helpful. Some months after we got our 'free' vacuum flask (the offer mentioned above), the top started to leak. We contacted Compass 24 to ask if we could buy a replacement top but it was unable to supply one as it was no longer selling that flask. Compass 24 quickly sent a replacement, better quality, flask - free. Such surprisingly good service communicates a commitment to putting the customer's interests first, despite the costs to the company.

Communication and Customer Relationships

In addition to the communication tools mentioned above, Compass 24 uses a wide range of communication mix elements, including:

Advertising - in specialist paper-based yachting magazines in addition to websites such as Boatz.

Direct mail - catalogues, mini catalogues and special offers.

Word of mouth - e.g. recommend Compass 24 to a friend and get a free tool set.

Customer relationships - customers can opt in to the e-mail newsletter for tip-offs on special offers and other news.

Web atmospherics - good illustrations and snappy animation that does not take too long to load.

Marketing Research Surveys

When we bought a new digital camera from Samsung, we had to register the software online. The registration process entailed uploading basic information on the use of the product that the supplier can use, for example to inform us of updates or new products that may be of interest. Other suppliers use a huge lifestyle questionnaire that gives the impression of being the guarantee registration. The lifestyle data can be used for profiling, but also may be rented for a highly selectable mailing list by other companies. To comply with data protection legislation, there is an 'opt out' box that can be checked, but the 'if you don't want this service, please tick' message is sometimes in very small print almost hidden among many pages of conditions. Most e-shoppers just click 'accept' and never even know.

Offline Advertising

The scope of offline advertising is too wide to cover in detail here. Suffice it to say that an e-retailer should naturally include the Web address not only in

TV, radio and press ads, but also on all brochures, stationery, plus the label and packaging of the product (whether sold on or offline). Advertisements in specialist targeted publications are often more cost-effective than the mass media, especially for smaller niche markets.

For example, for boat insurance, craftinsure (www.craftinsure.com) advertises in publications like *All at Sea*, a monthly newspaper distributed partly by subscription but mainly distributed free at boating shops and marinas. For a product of general interest to most people, like the department (e-)store John Lewis (www.johnlewis.com) e-retailers can advertise in Internet magazines such as *.Net* (www.netmag.co.uk), the biggest selling UK Internet magazine, whose readers are likely to e-shop. Another tip for the e-retailer is to advertise in the 'click here' sections of the general press (e.g. *Sunday Times*, *Daily Mail*), which are a lot cheaper and likely to be more cost-effective than large colour advertisements.

Public Relations (PR), Sponsorship and Publicity

PR and publicity aim to communicate positive messages without paying directly for the media space as advertising. An example of publicity came from the conjurer David Blaine hanging in a box under Tower Bridge for weeks without food - with the www.channel4.com logo visible. Most news reports at the time mentioned Channel 4's sponsorship. PR activity also includes press releases and press conferences, which can contribute towards positive press coverage. Publicity and PR opportunities are not limited to the official sponsors of such stunts. Searching for 'david blaine' on Google (www.google. co.uk) produced many sponsored links, including ten from 'Search the Web' (www.searchtheweb .com). These included 'Magic tricks by David Blaine' - magic tricks, books, DVDs and videos for both professional and amateur magicians from Merchant of Magic (www.mercha ntofmagic. co.uk); David Blaine's new book and 'many items from his TV specials' from Magic Tricks (www.magictricks.co.uk); and a David Blaine video from Amazon (www.amazon.com). These were all in addition to David Blaine's official website (www.david blaine. com).

The car e-retailer Edmunds (www.edmunds.com) illustrates PR in action. The website has a dedicated media area providing easy contact with the PR department, press releases (such as forecasts of changes in the levels of car prices) and 'Edmunds in the News'. For example: 'One of the leading online automotive resources continues to upgrade its services' - *Entrepreneur* magazine.

Direct mail

Many of the most successful e-retailers communicate regularly with customers by post. Tesco (www.tesco.com) is a well-known example, mailing news, vouchers and special offers every three months. Tesco have found that expenditure on direct and database marketing can be far more cost-effective than traditional above-the-line advertising. This cost-effectiveness also leads niche marketers in particular to use direct mail. For example, Screwfix posts regular catalogues, mini catalogues and special offers.

e-Mail Permission Marketing

Permission marketing via e-mail is increasing. The response rates to *opt-in* e-mail campaigns are significantly higher than to other online ads; the cost per acquisition is lower; turnaround time is faster; and results can be accurately tracked. More companies are moving greater proportions of budget from postal direct mailings and conventional advertising to e-mail. Unfortunately, spam has also increased dramatically. More aggressive spam filters have been developed but, even so, most e-mail users are experiencing unacceptably high levels of unwanted e-mail -100- messages. Responsible marketers use opt-in or even *double-opt-in* permission marketing and also make it easy for customers who have opted in to opt out again. For example, *Web Promote* (www.webpromote.com), one of the largest Internet marketing newsletters, has over 170,000 double-opt-in subscribers.

THE PRINCIPLES OF AN E-MAIL MARKETING CAMPAIGN

- Acquire e-mail addresses (e.g. of people who have registered to receive information)
- Obtain permission to use the e-mail address for marketing. This is best done at the time of collection, e.g. registration or free samples may only be possible if the respondent checks the 'yes' box
- Select the addresses to target for the particular message
- Execute the campaign (possibly in conjunction with other communications channels)
- Respond to customer replies
- Correct and clean the e-mail list
- Track and measure the campaign performance.

Short Message Systems (SMSs) and Multimedia Messaging Services (MMSs)

While mobile phones and other mobile devices can be useful for 'distress' purchases such as paying a congestion charge (to drive into a city), the growth of m-commerce has been slow, even since the introduction of 3G. Nevertheless, even though it represents a small proportion of marketing budgets, advertising via *short message systems (SMSs)* and *multimedia messaging services (MMSs)* achieves high response rates. Because of this, spending on mobile advertising has been predicted to rocket to £6 billion over the next year or two. Mobile advertising is growing in popularity not just because of the high response, but also because mobile Web users represent an attractive demographic, with the majority being males aged 20-39 with incomes over £30,000. They are well segmented as a target for games, gambling and travel services - currently the biggest mobile advertising categories. For example, in the US, the marketing agency Mobliss has launched Snow Report (www.mysnowreport.com). Customers who have registered their interests can receive text messages detailing snow conditions at winter sports resorts. Recipients of the message can follow a link for a travel package to the resort. As with e-mail, the key to success is opt-in, with customers giving permission for these marketing activities when they register for the information service.

Viral Marketing

Viral marketing is growing as more companies use it to promote and brand their products and services. For example, the low-budget horror movie *The Blair Witch Project* owed worldwide success to a vast volume of 'word of mouse' recommendations passed around Internet chat rooms. These campaigns are becoming more sophisticated with tracking of open, click-through and success rates.

A potential problem with viral marketing campaigns is that the company is reliant on each individual in the chain to have permission to send such messages to each recipient. In many cases this is not done: viral marketing spreads much spam. The responsible marketer will be using tracking systems that can be used for follow-up of sample recipients to ensure that they do not object to such communications.

As an example of *opt-out* viral marketing, consider the hypothetical way that this book could be promoted. Prospects may initially receive an information-only message, for example an invitation to a marketing conference, ending with something along the lines of: Please forward this message to anyone else who may be interested. In the future we may want to inform you of other services and products (for example books) in which we think you may be interested. If you do not wish to receive such messages, please contact the sender to be removed from the list.

Banners, pop-ups and Interstitials *

Online advertising expenditure on media such as banners and pop-ups is growing and has reached well over £150 million per year (£30 million more than cinema advertising, for example). The interstitial - a pop-up that interrupts browsing to show an ad - is a much more active form of advertising than banners. Some people using the Web for a specific purpose find these irritating, though. Online advertising company RealMedia (www.uk.realmedia.com) is using a less-intrusive system called adPointer. This generates an ad when the cursor has not moved for a specific time. Schemes that incentivize users to look at advertisements have been around for some years, but in the UK

Bananalotto.com (www.bananalotto.com) has raised the stakes by offering the chance to win one million pounds as you click the banner ad. KPE, the media and entertainment consultancy, has developed around ten games for their clients. Managing Director Paul Zwillberg says:

* This section is summarized and adapted from Marketing Business e-business supplement So much of the Internet has been characterised by repurposing things that worked well in print or TV. 'Advergaming' is ... a new combination that's made for the medium.... You take one of the most popular uses of interactive content and marry it with tried and tested advertising models like brand association, trial or data capture and you get something really wonderful.

Customer Relationships

The direct mail and e-mail activities described above are part of the management of customer relationships. Building on these basic communication tools, the most successful e-retailers such as Amazon (www.amazon.com) and Tesco (www.tesco.com) use various techniques of data mining, personalization and customization. For example, Amazon customizes the web page, making offers for new books, music or movies that are likely to be of interest based on past purchase patterns. Tesco likewise personalizes its communications and special offers almost down to the level of the individual. These e-retailers are thus able to satisfy customers more specifically and therefore are better using the customer relationship and data mining tools.

Web Atmospherics

Web atmospherics is too important and complex a topic for this single section, in greater depth. Briefly, atmospherics includes *visual* (e.g. text, design, colour management, video clips, 3-D), *aural* (e.g. music or sound effects) and *olfactory* (e.g. perfume and samples) stimuli. The Edmunds (www.edmunds.com) car sales site is a good example of the use of exciting downloads of video and sound effects to illustrate cars in action. With effects like this, there is a need to avoid long download times (e.g. by having a separate 'click here for broadband' version for the larger memory effects).

Perfume is available by e-retail, although most suppliers rely on description and well-known brands, rather than offering samples, for example Perfumania (www.mydesign erperfume.com): 'Contains citron, rose, jasmine and is accented with honeysuckle, vanilla and oakmoss making Allure by Chanel perfect for romantic use'. Atmospherics, even when fairly low-tech, have much to offer in communications mix design.

Link Popularity

Search engines use 'link popularity' in locating and ranking sites. Improving link popularity by persuading other sites to link to yours raises a site in search-engine rankings and is therefore a critical aspect of the communications mix.

Case Study: EBAY.CO.UK

The eBay site was founded in the US in 1995, originally under the name Auctionweb. The UK site was launched in 1999, growing after a slow start to become the UK's top e-commerce site measured by monthly audience numbers, with 6.8 million people (compared with Amazon's 6.1 million and Tesco's 2.7 million). In the year to March 2003, eBay's audience increased by 160 per cent, compared to Amazon's 28 per cent. Internet growth overall was only 7 per cent.

The figures are 'a significant sign of the potential of [the most profitable and successful Internet players] to sell to consumers', according to Nielsen/NetRatings (www.nielsen-netratings.com), who supplied the figures. Cheap though most individual products may be, eBay still sells over £1 billion of them per year. If eBay were considered to be an e-retailer, this would make them number one in UK market share. While many dot.coms are mainly hype, eBay is profitable, making a quarter of a billion dollars on worldwide operations in 2001. It survived the dot.com crash relatively unscathed and the share price rose from US$18 in 1998 to US$110 by 2003.Visitors to eBay spend an average of 1 hour and 11 minutes per month on the site - one of the longest of any UK site.

Visitors return to the site to check the status of items they are bidding for or selling and ebay.co.uk is one of very few e-retailers to achieve over a billion pages views per month.Many UK users are earning a healthy living as 'power sellers', taking advantage of the worldwide market to offer everything from sports utility vehicles (SUVs) to comics, records and oddments like garden gnomes, T-shirts and kettles. In the same way as the major bricks retailers are suffering increasing competition from charity shops and car-boot sales, so the established e-retailers face growing competition from online auctions.Most sellers are private individuals.

For example, Pat Austin makes £30,000 per year selling an assortment of bric-a-brac that she finds in charity shops, car-boot sales and physical auctions. She sells 1,000+ items per year and 99.9 per cent of her transactions have been positive. It is a full-time job, though, with correspondence and despatch taking up the mornings and sourcing goods the afternoons. Rosie English has a turnover of £100,000+ selling high-class women's fashion for prices of £100 to £1,000+.

She reads the fashion press to identify what editors recommend and what celebrities are wearing, then buys from sample and factory sales or direct from designers. However, eBay is not all one-person businesses, as the 'big boys' are seeing the opportunities and joining in with companies like Dell, Dixons and Sears using eBay to shift excess stock.It's a case of 'buyer beware', as auction sites do not take responsibility for deals that go wrong and offer only low insurance cover for losses. The way for buyers to identify the most reliable sellers is from feedback ratings - many regular sellers have hundreds of positive ratings.

HOW EBAY WORKS

- Signing up is free
- Buyers bid online and the highest wins
- Sellers and buyers rate each other
- Listing fees vary in the approximate range £0.15 to £2
- The site also charges a percentage of the sale price, between approximately 1.75 per cent and 5.25 per cent - the more valuable the item, the lower the percentage

BOX 4.12: AUCTIONS

Tips for auction sellers

- *Provide a detailed description* Include a photograph if possible. Be honest about any faults in order to avoid negative feedback
- *Choose a suitable category* The categories help bidders to find goods quickly. Fees are higher in some categories than others
- *Sell internationally* This is how to reach a bigger audience - but always get the payment cleared before sending the goods
- *Provide a 'little extra' customer service* Rosie English gift wraps everything. She has 500 positive feedback messages and 100 per cent feedback rating

Tips for auction buyers

- *Read the description carefully* Make sure that you know what you are getting. For example, one buyer bid for a rug, then found out that it was from a doll's house!
- *If in doubt, contact the seller* The relationship may be important if things go wrong
- *Think whether it is too good to be true* In-demand items like home theatre, plasma screens and digital cameras can attract the dodgy deal at very low prices
- *Check for spelling mistakes* For example, the 'Stradivarious' violin offered at a fraction of the price you would expect
- *Bid high, then stop* Research shows that the final price can be up to 30 per cent higher when bids arrive fast (Haubl and Popkowski Leszeczyc, 2003). Limit spending from the outset in order to avoid bidding frenzy

Bibliography

Alak Ghosh: *Emerging Money Market in India*, Deep & Deep Publication, Delhi, 2001.

Amitabh Shukla: *International Money Market and Indian Economic Reforms*, Kanishka Publication, Delhi, 2000.

B.N. Dash: *Commercial Banking : Risk and Credit Management*, Arise Publication, Delhi, 2011.

B.R. Nanda: *Indian Banking : Its Fraud and Crime*, Surendra Publication, Delhi, 2011.

B.S. Sharma: *Analysis of Commercial Banking*, Vista International Publication House, Delhi, 2011.

Benton E. Gup and James W. Kolari: *Commercial Banking: The Management Of Risk*, Wiley, 2001.

Bijay Kumar Sinha: *Indian Banking and Economic Reforms : Problems and Prospects*, Classical Publication, Delhi, 2007.

Deepak Tandon, Neelam Tandon and Kanhaiya Ahuja: *Indian Banking : Technology Innovations and Key Concerns*, Kunal Books, Delhi, 2011.

G P Kapoor: *Commercial Banking*, APH Publication, Delhi, 2004.

Harbans Lal Sharma: *Commercial Banking Development : A Study*, Rajat Publication, Delhi, 2003.

K.R. Gupta: *Economics : For UGC-NET/SLET and Other Competitive Examinations*, Atlantic Publication, Delhi, 2011.

Keshava, S R.: *Economics*, New Age International, Delhi, 2009.

M.S. Gopalan: *Indian Money Market : Structure, Operation and Developments*, Deep & Deep Publication, Delhi, 2000.

N.K. Sharma: *Economics : Theory and Practice*, DND Publications, Delhi, 2015.

PAUL: *No Money Marketing*, Tata McGraw-Hill, 2009.

R K Uppal and Rimpi Kaur: *Indian Banking : Transformation Through Information Technology*, Mahamaya Publishing House, Delhi, 2008.

R K Uppal: *Indian Banking Industry and Information Technology*, New Century Publication, Delhi, 2006.

R.K. Uppal: *Indian Banking : A New Vision*, Mahamaya Publication, Delhi, 2009.

R.K. Uppal: *Indian Banking : Scaling New Heights*, Kunal Books, Delhi, 2009.

R.K. Uppal: *Indian Banking and Contemporary Issues*, Kunal Books, Delhi, 2011.

R.K. Uppal: *Indian Banking in New Global Order*, Sarup Publication, Delhi, 2012.

R.K. Uppal: *Indian Banking in the Globalised World*, New Century Publications, Delhi, 2008.

R.K. Uppal: *Indian Banking Industry : Issues Challenges and Opportunities*, Sarup Publication, Delhi, 2013.

Rajesh Pal: *Indian Banking and Globalization*, Adhyayan Publication, Delhi, 2009.

Ravishankar Kumar Singh: *Indian Banking and Financial Sector Reforms : Realising Global Aspirations (2 Vols-Set)*, Abhijeet Publication, Delhi, 2006.

Richard Lipsey and Alec Chrystal: *Economics*, Oxford University Press, Delhi, 2007.

Index